PLEASURE

After reading music at St Hilda's College, Oxford, Margaret Leroy became a social worker and social work researcher involved in counselling couples, in sex therapy programmes, and in work with abused children and teenagers. Since taking her MA at Leicester University she has published a number of articles and a book, *Miscarriage*, and has spoken on women's issues at several conferences. She is married with two daughters.

MARGARET LEROY

Pleasure

The Truth about Female Sexuality

HarperCollins*Publishers*

HarperCollins*Publishers*
77–85 Fulham Palace Road,
Hammersmith, London W6 8JB

This paperback edition 1994
1 3 5 7 9 8 6 4 2

First published in Great Britain by
HarperCollins*Publishers* 1993

ISBN 0 00 638100 6

Set in Linotron Ehrhardt by
Rowland Phototypesetting Ltd
Bury St Edmunds, Suffolk

Printed in Great Britain by
HarperCollinsManufacturing Glasgow

Contents

Part One

♀

CHAPTER ONE

The Problem:
Forgetting, Faking and Giving Up

Above the bed that used to be my mother's hangs a sepia portrait of my grandmother. It was a picture that my mother could never look at without sadness, for my grandmother had died of Spanish flu in 1919 at the age of thirty-two, weakened, according to the family story, by child-bearing. She had borne six children in nearly as many years, and three of them had died at or shortly after birth. Her image represented something very significant for the women in my family. She was at one and the same time a benign female principle watching over us, and a poignant reminder of the terrible fragility at the heart of things.

We are still so near to that time before widespread contraception was available, and before modern obstetric methods reduced infant and maternal mortality – a time when sex was a very serious business for women. In my grandmother's time, not only was sex outside marriage associated with guilt and public disgrace for women, but even the most socially approved sexual act was contaminated with the fear of death – the frequent deaths of both mothers and babies.

Today we hear a different story about sex. Sex manuals tell us that sex is simply 'a delicious part of the human condition',[1] and that if we dare to try lots of different positions and techniques we'll have wonderful sex lives. Sex education videos assert that 'with practice and imagination you'll find that your instincts will take you into realms of pleasure you never dreamed of.'[2] Sex therapy books tell how couples who didn't enjoy sex went to a sex therapist, and learned to communicate and came into their birthright of joyous sexual expression. Articles in women's magazines quote from women's sexual fantasies, with commentary from a 'psychosexual analyst' who explains that it's healthy to have such fantasies, and that it doesn't mean you really want to be raped. The news stories favoured by the tabloid press tell how even the powerful and

successful and morally exemplary are just as much into sex as
the rest of us: even the Director of Public Prosecutions is seen
approaching 'seedy girls of the night'. And our public fictions –
our stories, films and songs – reiterate the theme that sex is fun
and sexual pleasure is everyone's birthright.

There are of course some dissenting voices. Many feminist
writers have been uneasy about heterosexual sex, taking their cue
from Simone de Beauvoir, who saw penetration as trespass and
invasion. For some feminists, only lesbian sex has been ideologically
sound: 'Feminism is the theory, lesbianism is the practice' ran the
slogan. We have also heard many stories over the past decade about
the dark side of desire – the rape of children. But the dissenting
voices have had little impact on mainstream culture, and sexual
abuse has remained something apart, with little attempt to make
the experiences of offenders and survivors part of a broader understanding of sexuality. Turn back a page from the newspaper story
expressing outrage at the sexual abuse of children, and you may
find a photograph of a topless teenage model. The picture and the
news report inhabit different worlds.

Today we not only believe that sex is for fun, we even believe
that sex is good for you. The idea that sexual activity brings health
benefits goes back to Wilhelm Reich, who maintained that orgasm
was essential to health.[3] His belief had certain bizarre ramifications
– such as his invention of an 'orgone box' to conserve 'orgone
energy'. But his baroque excesses are now forgotten, and the belief
in the health benefits of sex persists in spite of certain inconvenient
facts, such as the well established longevity of nuns.

Sexual pleasure then is taken to be a fundamental aspect of
human fulfilment: sex should be enjoyable for everyone. And the
writers on sex assure us that women can and should be part of the
sexual good life. Masters and Johnson established that women have
an orgasmic capacity that is greater than men's.[4] Alex Comfort in
The Joy of Sex refers to 'the antique idea of the woman as passive
and the man as performer'.[5] Nancy Friday asserts that women have
sexual fantasies every bit as explicit and arousing as men's.[6] Women
are not only permitted but actually expected to enjoy sex too. But
just how enjoyable is sex for women today?

When we look at the research there is overwhelming evidence
that women have yet to enter the sexual promised land. A study
carried out for London Weekend Television in conjunction with
the *Mail on Sunday* found that half the women in their random

sample of a thousand were dissatisfied with their sex lives, compared to one-fifth of the men, and that almost a third of the women never or rarely achieved orgasm during sex.[7] Shere Hite found that 99 per cent of men would not want to change or redefine sex[8] – but according to sex therapist John Bancroft, one in three women are unhappy with their sex lives.[9] Sex surveys carried out by *Woman* magazine suggested that four out of five women have problems getting aroused, and that one in two wish they enjoyed sex more.[10] Men may consult sex therapists about physical problems like impotence, but most women who consult sex therapists are concerned about their low interest or lack of enjoyment.[11] And of course the problem is not confined to the UK. A study of women in Denmark – a country with a reputation for sexual progressiveness – found that one in three reported current sexual problems;[12] and the most comprehensive recent research on female sexuality – Shere Hite's research carried out in the US – found massive evidence of sexual unhappiness among American women.[13]

Listening to one another's stories, we may hear something very different from the cheery public refrain that sex is fun, sex is good for you, and even women enjoy sex too today.

SEX TALK

In order to explore women's experiences of sex, I talked to fifty women about their sex lives.

I talked to women at all stages of the life cycle, with a roughly even spread over the different decades. I make no claim to have achieved a representative sample, though the proportions of black women and women who had come out as lesbians did correspond to the proportions in the general population, and I also found that where I asked about experiences that had been researched in much bigger studies – child sex abuse, for instance – the numbers of women in my sample who recalled such experiences were in line with the results of the more comprehensive research.

I used a structured interview schedule, so that certain key topics were covered with every woman. All the conversations were taped, except for three interviews where the women preferred me to take notes. All the conversations were on a one-to-one basis, except for four women whom I talked with in a group at their request, and the 14- to 16-year-olds, whom I also talked with in a group, and with whom I covered different topics appropriate to their stage of the life cycle.

I reached women partly through organizations such as Age Concern and the Youth and Community Service, but mainly through networks: women I talked to introduced me to other women – their mothers, daughters, sisters, friends – who were willing to be interviewed. Using networks introduces one kind of bias, in that some of the women knew each other – and friends or relatives might share opinions about sex. But it also removes another kind of bias that is present in much writing about sex – the bias towards women whose sense of their sexuality is such that they would have the confidence to respond to an advertisement or survey in a newspaper or magazine. None of the women I talked with said they would ever respond to an advertisement from someone who was writing a book about sex. Quite a number demurred at first, because they felt their very 'ordinariness' disqualified them: 'Yes, I'll talk to you ... but do you really want to talk to *me*? I'm sure you could find somebody better.' There was sometimes a kind of assumption that it was the other women, the sexy ones, that I really ought to be talking to ...

As we drank our coffee or wine and started to talk, the themes that emerged were often quite different from those of the upbeat public sexual stories. There were certainly plenty of stories of pleasure and delight – but there were also more downbeat themes, those themes of faking, forgetting and giving up that pervade so much of women's sexual experience.

FAKING, FORGETTING AND GIVING UP

Bernadette said, 'I was always under the impression, right into my early twenties, that there was something wrong with me because I didn't have an orgasm during sex. I faked all through my marriage to Faisal. I think I had the idea that most women did this. With Faisal, it was just about bonking, loads and loads of bonking, and I just never had an orgasm and I could never talk to him about it. I've heard friends say quite a few times, you know, you're having sex and when they go to the toilet you start to really enjoy yourself then. I used to think, he'll go to the toilet in a minute and I'll be able to have an orgasm.'

Shere Hite found that 'an enormous number of women' fake orgasms.[14] Faking used actually to be advocated by the sex manuals

– and a recent article in *She* magazine continued the tradition, advising 'If you can't make it, fake it!' on the grounds of 'plain, old-fashioned politeness'.[15] The faking of orgasms is the most striking version of a theme that recurs in female sexuality.

Faking is a huge element in women's self-presentation. Women have often resorted to clever subterfuges to mould their bodies into the shapes currently deemed to be desirable. The Victorians used tightly laced corsets and full skirts to create the illusion of willowy waists and ample hips. Today the female body that is seen as most desirable – very slim but with prominent breasts – rarely occurs naturally: most women can only achieve it with the aid of cosmetic surgery.

In societies where virginity is prized, fakery has also often been necessary to ensure that women's bodies fit with the patriarchal requirements. In Japan, hymen rebirth clinics recreate virginity for a woman's wedding night. In other cultures brides have concealed blood-soaked sponges in their vaginas to ensure that they bled.[16]

There is a lot of faking too in the world of public female sexuality. Many female sexual icons have been abused women who seem to have derived little pleasure from sex – like Marilyn Monroe, the ultimate sex symbol, who was sexually abused as a child, or Linda Lovelace, star of pornographic films like *Deep Throat*, who was brutalized by her manager husband.[17] And sometimes there's also been a touch of fakery about the women who articulate the female sexual experience for others. Anaïs Nin wrote her erotic stories as a lucrative joke: when her anonymous male patron, 'the Collector', demanded more sex in her stories, she says she 'began to write tongue-in-cheek, to become outlandish, inventive, and so exaggerated that I thought he would realize I was caricaturing sexuality.'[18] Marie Stopes wrote the lyrical descriptions of sexual ecstasy in *Married Bliss*, her best-selling and highly influential sex manual, when she was still a virgin in a marriage that remained unconsummated for seven years.[19]

We fake. We also forget. In her book, *The Mirror Within*, psychologist Anne Dickson tells how it was only after ten years of active and unsatisfactory sexual life that she discovered she had a clitoris.[20] It is a story that many women could tell, yet most of the women who tell it masturbated in childhood. As mature women we so often forget about our bodies, unlearning the knowledge we had as little girls. Emily said, 'When I was married, and really not feeling anything much at all when we had sex, I used to think back to when

I was a child, and all the pleasure I'd got from masturbating then. One day I tried to do it, but I'd forgotten how. I gave up because I didn't feel anything.'

There are other things too that we forget from childhood – the sexual curiosity that most little girls have is lost as we grow up, and with sexual maturity we so often forget how to take sexual initiatives and to be bold. And Nancy Friday describes how she found that women 'forgot' that they had sexual fantasies, and it was only when she gave them permission by showing them copies of other women's fantasies that they recalled their own.[21]

We fake. We forget. We also give up. Many women simply give up on sex, abandoning any aspirations they once had towards sexual pleasure. I've not got much of a sex drive, they say. Many women decide that sexual pleasure is not for them, not something they own for themselves: sexual pleasure is for other people. Gwen said, 'It wasn't anything I particularly liked – I think I could have done without it. I lay back and thought of England. You think, Where did I go wrong? Perhaps I wasn't doing something I ought to have done. He said he'd read about it before we got married, he knew I shouldn't be like that. I wondered afterwards if that was a lot of talk on his part. He said I was cold and a bit – what's the word? – frigid. Well, maybe I was so – I was unhappy in a way, deep down. When I was forty-eight, I had a hysterectomy and we settled into a way of life without it.'

Giving up sex, of course, doesn't have to be a second-best alternative. For many women in the past – the priestesses who wielded great power in Babylon in the third millennium BC, or the medieval abbesses like Hildegard of Bingen who were renowned for their learning[22] – the celibate life has been a path to power. And today, as ever, celibacy can be a life-affirming choice, whether for the religious initiate who chooses a monastic life, or for the person who simply decides at some point in the life cycle that sex is not important to him or her. But the woman who gives up on sex because she has never realized her own potential for physical pleasure is in a very different situation. There is much sadness in Gwen's account.

SEX DIFFERENCES

How does society make sense of the sexual dissatisfactions that women like Bernadette and Emily and Gwen describe?

The usual explanations are based on beliefs about sex differences. According to these theories, women have different sexual needs to men and sex has a different place in their lives. For instance, it is said that women can enjoy sex without orgasm, whereas this would cause men physical distress. In the Kinsey Report on female sexuality, published in 1953, Kinsey wrote, 'It must always be understood that we are well aware that [orgasm] is not the only significant part of a truly satisfactory sexual relationship. This is much more true for the female than it would be for the male. It is inconceivable that males who were not reaching orgasm would continue their marital coitus for any length of time . . .'[23] The idea that orgasm matters less to women is echoed in Andrew Stanway's sex education video, The Lovers' Guide: 'Surveys show that many [women] greatly enjoy sex even if they only have an orgasm from time to time.'[24]

Another common explanation for women's sexual difficulties suggests that women are slower to be aroused than men. In the 1930s, Magnus Hirschfield, founder of the World League for Sexual Reform, produced graphs showing the different pace of arousal in men and women; he commented: 'The man has passed the peak point of sexual excitement while the woman is still getting there.'[25] This theory is echoed in contemporary sex manuals. In The Joy of Sex, Alex Comfort wrote, 'Male sexual response is far brisker and more automatic: it is triggered easily by things, like putting a quarter in a vending machine.'[26]

Connected to the notion that male response 'is far brisker and more automatic' is the belief that women aren't turned on by looking. This again is an idea that we find in the Kinsey Report, and it is echoed in current sex advice that women should do all they can to turn men on visually. A recent article in Cosmopolitan magazine that promises the 'best sex tips ever' urges women to remember that men are 'erotic visualists': we are encouraged to make love 'in positions that emphasize your best body parts', to wear 'sexy lingerie', to 'learn the art of erotic undressing', and to keep a 'favourite X-rated cassette' in the video at the ready.[27]

Then there is the common belief that the relationship part of sex, the sense of emotional connection, is more important to women. Alex Comfort wrote, 'The releasers for the male are garments which emphasize breasts and buttocks or, like tight panties, simplify the outline of the female. Women are not so dependent on this sort of concrete signalling – having the right man is their chief releaser, a social and emotional one.'[28] The idea that female turn-ons are largely 'social and emotional' is linked to the belief that women are less sexual and more loving than men; according to this very prevalent perception of the difference between the sexes, men want power and orgasm, while women go for intimacy and tender loving care. The belief that women's sexuality is much 'nicer' than men's has been given a considerable boost by revelations about child sex abuse, which is mostly perpetrated by men.

In Lucy Goodison's book, *Moving Heaven and Earth*, I found a quote from Hélène Cixous, who writes about the power relations between a 'fantasized obligatory virility meant to invade, to colonize, and the resulting phantasm of woman as a "dark continent".'[29] Female sexuality as a 'dark continent': it's a marvellous image for the conceptualization of female sexuality that underlies all these common assumptions about the differences between the sexes – female sexuality as mysterious, elusive, shadowy, hard to understand, an undiscovered country.

Many of the beliefs that are rooted in the 'dark continent' theory of female sexuality have been disproved by research. Masters and Johnson found women to be just as quickly aroused as men, Shere Hite found that most women who were orgasmic could masturbate to orgasm in four minutes, and Schmidt and Sigusch established that women too are turned on by looking.[30] Others scarcely stand up to a moment's consideration. Do orgasms matter less to women? Shere Hite found that 'only two women didn't *seem* to mind not having orgasms'[31] – and it's been established since the Kinsey Report that after prolonged sexual excitement without orgasm women experience just the same pelvic congestion that leads to the 'blue balls' syndrome so many of us have dreaded giving our boyfriends. Is relationship more important to women than men? If we look at the relative psychological health of women and of men compelled to live independently after divorce,[32] or the way many men can only confide in their sex partners, we might very well conclude that men are far more dependent on the relationship part of sex than women. Is female sexuality mysterious and elusive? Deliciously simple interventions can make a huge difference to female sexual pleasure. Helen Kaplan describes doing sex therapy with pre-orgasmic Spanish-speaking women in Harlem. She simply sent the women home with a large diagram of the female genitals with the clitoris prominently marked, and instructions to point out the sensitive areas to their husbands. The therapy was very successful.[33]

Why do the old ideas persist in the face of all the evidence? I think they persist because they make both men and women feel more comfortable about the problem of female sexuality, for the most prevalent beliefs are those that seem to account for women's sexual dissatisfactions. Many women aren't having orgasms during sex – but they don't need them, not like men need them. Many women aren't enjoying sex all that much as a physical experience – but what women really want is touching and closeness and intimacy. Few heterosexual men are visually gratifying – but it doesn't matter because looking doesn't play a big part in female sexuality . . . Yet by their very persistence these beliefs may actually add to the problem.

To say that these common assumptions about sex differences are fallacious is not to say that there are no differences between the sexes in patterns of arousal and pleasure. There are certain clear sex differences for which there is sound physiological evidence – for instance, the cyclicity of desire in women, especially once they have had children; the very different pattern of sexual ageing in men and in women; the fact that for the majority of women sexual intercourse affords only mild sexual stimulation; and the fact that female arousal is heightened rather than ended by orgasm, giving women the potential for multiple orgasms. Yet these genuine sex differences, far from being acknowledged, are actually obscured by the way we organize sexual relationships.

SEXIST THINKING ABOUT SEX

Why are the real sex differences obscured, and the dubious or downright fallacious assumptions widely believed? And if the common but fallacious assumptions about sex differences do little to explain women's sexual unhappiness, how then may it be explained? The answers to both questions can be found in the same place. Like all patriarchal societies, we have made male sexual pleasure paramount, and suppressed female sexual pleasure. Women have problems with sex because female sexual pleasure is made subordinate to male, and the widespread acceptance of fallacious assumptions about sex differences serves to perpetuate that subordination.

Earlier this century, Maxine Davis wrote that sexual desire was not natural in a woman since 'she was not born with it as her husband was', and Marie Bonaparte stated that it was the masculine part of a woman which allowed her to have an interest in sex,[34] and Freud reflected, 'Indeed, if we were able to give a more definite connotation to the concepts of "masculine" and "feminine", it would even be possible to maintain that libido is invariably and necessarily of a masculine nature, whether it occurs in men or in women and irrespectively of whether the object is a man or a woman.'[35] In these writings libido and arousal and sexual interest are explicitly given a gender. And today, just as in Freud's time, sexual pleasure still has a gender, and that gender is still male. Many gains have been made over the past three decades – yet female sexuality is still suppressed.

The very words we use reflect this. The word vagina comes from the Latin for sheath or scabbard: the vagina is a 'sheath' for the penis, and when the woman is aroused she produces 'lubrication' – for the penis. The hormone that governs sexual desire in both male and female – testosterone – is called the male sex hormone; and the expression 'her sexuality' is frequently used to mean, not a woman's own sexual experiences and feelings, but her attractiveness to men.

Then there is the fact that our usual model of sexual functioning is a male model. The way we envisage sex originates with Reich, who defined orgasm as 'the capacity for complete discharge of all damned-up excitation through involuntary pleasurable contractions of the body.'[36] But the discharge model simply doesn't work for women, whose 'involuntary pleasurable contractions' may end in a state of heightened arousal.

The construction of sexual pleasure as something predominantly owned by, sought by and felt by males is evident too in research on sexuality. The science of sexology, which came into being around the turn of the century, has been largely preoccupied with categorizing aberrant sexual behaviours – the perversions. But the perversions are almost exclusively male behaviours: the impulses that give rise to deviant sexual behaviours seem to be differently expressed in women. Except for masochism, which has one female to twenty males, less than one per cent of cases cited as sexual perversions are females. So the study of sex has been focused almost exclusively on male sexuality. There is also a male bias in studies of sexual dysfunction; research on the effects of diabetes, drugs, spinal injuries or alcohol on sexual functioning is almost exclusively concerned with men, and research that has direct relevance to women's sexuality – for instance, research on the effect of the contraceptive pill on libido, or on the efficacy of the spermicide Nonoxynol-9 in destroying HIV – is notably lacking. Even the discussion about sex in the most obviously feminist enclaves is rooted in exclusively male experience: much of the discussion about sexuality that appears on women's studies courses in Britain and the United States is based on the theories of Michel Foucault, a gay male.[37]

SELF-KNOWLEDGE AND SELF-ASSERTION

It is clear that there is still a strong male bias in our thinking and talking about sex. Yet it is also indisputable that today we do have a climate in which women are encouraged to enjoy sex. But permission is not enough. I would argue that if women are to have equality of access to sexual pleasure, there are certain basic conditions that must be fulfilled. Self-knowledge and the capacity for self-assertion are both essential. To enjoy sex, you have to understand how your body works, and you have to believe that you have a right to a degree of sexual pleasure.

This is where men start from. It is unthinkable for a man not to understand the basic mechanisms of arousal and orgasm, not to know what he must do to achieve sexual pleasure. But it is not unthinkable for a woman: there are plenty of sexually active women who do not have that kind of knowledge about their own bodies. And it is unthinkable for a man not to believe that he has some kind of right or entitlement to sexual pleasure, not to believe that he has the right to help himself to this kind of human fulfilment – whether with brutal ruthlessness or with tender care. It is not like that for most women. Masters and Johnson comment that for many a woman 'her "permission" to function as a sexual being . . . has been impaired.'[38] Women often conceptualize sex as a gift or a chore, something that is done for someone else. In sexual activity, the woman gives and the man takes.

Self-assertion and self-knowledge then are fundamental to female sexual fulfilment – and the story of the suppression of female sexuality that I shall tell in this book is the story of how women are discouraged from asserting themselves and denied knowledge of their own bodies. In Part I of the book I shall consider the different stages of the female life cycle, and ask what happens at each stage to obscure our knowledge of our bodies and to make sexual self-assertion so difficult. Throughout the life cycle, sexuality is shaped by the imagination. In Part II, I shall look at the role of the imagination in female sexuality, exploring the contradiction between public and private female sexual fantasies, and the ways the public fantasies also serve to restrict women's chances of sexual pleasure.

It is customary for sex manuals to start with a disclaimer to the effect that this book isn't only about sex, it's about relationships too. 'Sex is not just mechanics or genital geography,' say the authors of *Sex Life*.[39] 'This book is about love as well as sex,' writes Alex Comfort in *The Joy of Sex*.[40] But my conversations with women were not about love, they were about sexual pleasure – How do we find out about it? How do we forget about it? Why does it elude us so much of the time? – and in this book I have endeavoured to keep the focus on sex rather than on relationships. There are many women for whom such a focus is not just appropriate but necessary. The young woman who derives tremendous excitement from other kinds of sexual activity but who finds intercourse disappointing. The woman whose sex life was happy until she had children, and who still loves her husband but now finds sex a chore. The woman – be she seventeen or sixty-seven – who finds herself in bed with someone she loves and lusts after, and finds sexual fulfilment eluding her. And the woman in her seventies or eighties, who looks back over a long life of sexually unhappy marriage to a man she loved deeply, and reflects, 'What a difference if I'd known more . . .' and who hopes things will be better for her granddaughters.

All these women are already experts on love and relationships: all of them have done a lot of loving. But sexual pleasure may be quite a different matter.

To ask what is wrong with things as they are now, is also to ask how things could be. To suggest that female sexuality is suppressed, is also to ask what it would be like if it were given freer expression. And despite all the continuing frustrations of women's sex lives, we are today beginning to get some sense of what female sexuality might be like in more propitious conditions. The shape of a new female sexuality is just beginning to be seen – as when women working together on some vast quilt or patchwork put their individual efforts together, and a pattern starts to emerge.

The new female sexuality that is now emerging has its origins in the women's movement, but the line of descent is not quite direct. Explicitly feminist writing has had a lot to say about the sexual division of labour, the acquisition of sex roles, reproductive rights, and sexual violence to women, but it has had very little to say about sexual pleasure as such – beyond suggesting that heterosexuality is fundamentally unsound. The proposition that only lesbian relationships can be truly feminist is a philosophy of despair that has alienated many women who love men and hindered them from fully embracing and identifying with feminist ideas. Because feminist writing has focused so strongly on lesbianism, there has been little recognition of the changes that women who love men have started to make in their sexual relationships. But many of us have made changes – or know what changes we would like to make, if only we could find the courage. Things are starting to shift – not fast, not everywhere – but there are hints of movement, something in the air. Something is starting to emerge that my grandmother wouldn't recognize, but would surely welcome.

CHAPTER TWO

Childhood:
How Little Girls Forget

'We'd go upstairs,' said Melissa, 'put the lights down, pull jumpers up and play Doctors and Nurses. We didn't know what we were doing, it's just that we got a good feeling from it. It was in the dark, you got that thrill in your stomach, it was like playing ghosts under the table with torches . . .' To ask women about childhood sexual activity is to mine a rich vein of memories like Melissa's.

Yet for the last four hundred years, our ideas about how best to bring up children have been shaped by a deep-rooted belief in childhood sexual innocence. Historian Philippe Ariès has traced this belief back to the pedagogues and moralists of the fifteenth and sixteenth centuries.[1] It was during this period that teachers first thought of providing expurgated versions of the classics for the use of children, and that the clergy first warned that the ancient custom of sleeping several to a bed could lead to moral depravity. Around this time too, the innocence of children was held up as a shining example to all. In edifying tales children were often compared to angels.

For the Romantic writers of the nineteenth century, the innocence of childhood took on a special value. Dickens raged against the cruel treatment meted out to innocent children. For Blake, the naked child who lay sleeping 'among tygers wild' symbolized all that was free and creative about the human being.[2] For Wordsworth, the child came 'trailing clouds of glory . . . From God, who is our home'.[3] But something was lost as the child grew up. The glory faded as the child left the innocence of childhood behind and grew into sexual knowledge.

In our own century, the pendulum has swung away from childhood innocence and then back again. First there was Freud, with his theory of childhood sexuality based on the stories women told him about childhood sexual experiences with adult males, stories which Freud interpreted as childhood fantasies. Then came the more recent revelations about child sex abuse. We know now that Freud got it wrong: far from being evidence of the vividness of children's sexual imaginations, those stories he heard told of the rape of innocent children. So now the pendulum has swung back, and any overt sexual activity in a child can be taken as a warning sign. The child who masturbates or engages in sex play with other children may have the wary teacher or playgroup worker on the phone to Social Services, worrying lest the child has been abused.

Yet all the time, whatever the vagaries of public beliefs about childhood sexual development, children continue with their secret sexual lives. In the early 1950s, Kinsey found that 13 per cent of women recalled masturbating before the age of ten, and one in three remembered childhood sexual games.[4] Kinsey's studies were based on people's memories in an era when there wasn't much sex talk. Predictably, more recent studies have found still higher percentages of children taking part in sexual games.[5]

When I talked to women about childhood sexual activity, I heard many stories of the sort that the Kinsey researchers collected. Not every little girl masturbates; not every little girl plays sexual games with her friends. But among the women I talked to, the only women who had no memories of childhood sexual activity were those who'd had unusually troubled childhoods, or women who said they had virtually no childhood memories of any kind. Memories are always tricky things, and our memories of childhood have to be approached with particular caution. Adult awareness imposes its own shape on what happened, a shape that may be a distortion. Yet these stories do at the very least lift the curtain a little, giving us fascinating glimpses into the secret sexual world of little girls. And, as we shall see, it's a world in which little girls take initiatives, display abundant sexual curiosity, and explore their bodies with at least as much relish as do little boys.

In a sense those Romantic poets were right. For women at least, something is indeed lost as we grow up – but it is not our innocence.

LOOKING

Sally said, 'There was a game I used to play with my sister and a friend. One of us would go out of the room, and the other two would dance round the room in the nude, and the idea was that before the person who was outside opened the door and walked in, pretending to be an adult, we had to be covered up. We used to play this for hours. The funny thing about the game being mainly around nudity was that my family all belonged to a nudist club that wasn't at all sexual, as they're not. But there was always that feeling of the forbidden, even though I know that if my Mum had walked in and seen us nude she wouldn't have thought anything, because we were quite that sort of family anyway.'

Fran said, 'I had an older girlfriend, and I remember I was once playing outside on the street and she called me into her house and I felt really honoured because she was so much older. And she showed me how the dog would lick her, and I was amazed and mesmerized; I watched that and then went out again. It's quite amazing.'

Sophie said, 'My brother and I were both artistically inclined, and we used to play at artists' models, on Saturday mornings, when our parents didn't get up particularly early, and I would pose in the nude for him. He used to arrange me in all sorts of poses, and it was very interesting, you know. And in the first class of junior school I started doing pornographic drawings of people, men on top of women, and passing them round the class for people's entertainment. I used to think it was quite good fun. Once it caused disturbance in the class, and the teacher said what was all the fuss, and there was no way I could say what all the fuss was about, and because I wouldn't tell her she caned me.'

The most familiar sex games of childhood are those in which children look or are looked at: 'I'll show you mine if you'll show me yours.' The excitement of looking lies in that feeling of the forbidden that Sally describes. Sally and her sister have been brought up to feel that nakedness is comfortable and ordinary. In their game, they actively seek to rediscover the illicitness of nakedness in the company of their friend. Here, there is none of the Edenic innocence of Blake's vision. Sally and her sister clearly knew that they were naked – that was the fun of it.

In these games, little girls experience different kinds of sexual power, sometimes looking, sometimes being looked at. In Sally's game, the girls take turns to play the role of the adult, the one who makes it exciting by looking and disapproving. Fran is essentially a voyeur, invited to witness an act of sexual bravado: gratifyingly for her friend, she is tremendously impressed. Sophie remembers playing both active and passive sexual roles in childhood, showing off her body to her brother on those secret Saturday mornings, and doing drawings that shock or amuse her classmates.

Fran feels 'honoured'; for Sophie it's all 'fun' and 'interesting'. Children's sexual activities are not essentially kind or caring, any more than any other childhood activity, but I found that women usually remembered these exhibitionistic and voyeuristic games with pleasure. As long as the activities are reciprocal, there is no sense of abuse, and reciprocity – 'taking turns' – does seem to be one of the rules.

If the rules were broken, the memory may be less pleasant. Melissa said, 'It was always Tom, he was always the manipulator in the group, the one who got other people to jump over ponds or blow up tadpoles. Once we were all in the bedroom upstairs and he got Brenda to undress. He was fourteen then, she must have been four or five. It was just: "Look at her!" I felt angry that they were making her do it. I said, "Let's look at one of the boys." It was "Ooh, we're not going to show what we've got – huh!"' Tom, at fourteen, is on the brink of sexual maturity, and here there is an intrusion of adult sexual values. He abuses his power as leader of the group, and the game is played by the adult rule – that men look, and women and girls are looked at. By demanding that the boys show themselves too, Melissa attempts to re-establish the rules of the childhood sexual order.

TOUCHING

For many girls, the earliest remembered sexual sensation comes from 'hands on' sexual experiences. These are also the earliest sexual experiments we observe in our own children.

The word 'masturbation' makes many of us cringe, which is scarcely surprising, given the draconian approach to childhood masturbation that prevailed in our culture even in living memory. Surgical instrument catalogues dating from as late as the 1930s advertised 'chastity belts' to prevent masturbation in children,[6] and the word was until recently defined in the *Oxford Dictionary* as 'self-abuse'. But however unpleasant the connotations of the word, women's early memories of solitary self-pleasuring are often rather delightful. We may recall how we used a toy or one of the cuddly comfort objects of childhood in a special secret way – sitting astride a woolly donkey at a particular angle, pushing a hot water bottle right up between our legs on cold nights, rolling around on pillows and rubbing against them. Sylvia said, 'I can remember having a very small doll – this will sound very strange – but actually putting it in my knickers so it rubbed against me. I just remember walking up a path – and I presume I must have found it pleasurable.' For older girls, horse-riding is a potential source of sexual pleasure, leading sometimes to a first orgasm either on horseback or during sleep after a hard day's riding.

Fantasy may be part of the memory, as it was for Eve: 'I can remember getting quite aroused when I was four. I'd been to the ballet with my aunt, and I was in bed and I wanted to take all my clothes off and feel my tummy, and I was like wriggling round in bed feeling incredibly aroused, and I wanted to tie something round my waist, and it all felt very exciting, but I didn't know what on earth the feeling was about.' For Bernadette at ten or eleven, the fantasy was becoming more focused: 'I used to get my pillows and lay them down in a line and cuddle up to them and lie on top of them, and dream about William Foster and David Jilkes, who were boys in my class.'

Given the great variety of ways in which women touch themselves or like to be touched, there is an element of luck in finding a method that works. If a little girl does happen upon a good method, she may tell all her classmates about it, or even demonstrate it to her best friend. There is a hidden culture of little girls talking together with delectable candour about the best methods of masturbation, discovering them together, demonstrating them to one another, or trying them out together. In the late 1940s, thirty years before Betty Dodson in California carried sex therapy to baroque extremes by having participants in her groups all use vibrators together,[7] thirty years before UK sex therapist Anne Hooper's sex workshops were liberating women into feeling almost comfortable about masturbation, Sophie's classmates in a Devon village school were talking together about the best ways of doing it: 'At junior school I remember having big conversations with my girlfriends about the best ways to masturbate, and I was amazed at some of them. Oh yes, that was marvellous. One girl had discovered this wonderful technique. She had a bed with knobs at the bottom end, and she said, "If you get a sock and wrap the knob up and then straddle it and rub yourself on it, it is Absolutely Amazing," and we all thought, Wow! It was great, swapping stories.'

Where these discoveries are put into practice together, the experience is usually parallel rather than reciprocal. These little girls are not enacting a sexual relationship, but rather exploring side by side to find out what the body can do. Though the experience may be sexually thrilling, the relationship between the girls is about friendship rather than sex, and the activity is a shared experiment, like seeing who can jump farthest, or a demonstration given in a spirit of generosity, bravado or pride. Marianne said, 'I can remember when I used to go and stay the night with another girl. I must have been quite young – about six. One of the things we used to do was to get blankets and roll them up into bits: she showed me – it was her idea, it wasn't mine! – and she said if you put them between your legs and rolled about in the bed with them between your legs it was very exciting, so we used to do this endlessly.' Jacqueline said, 'I remember discovering masturbation – climbing ropes. I was about ten, it was with my friend. We both discovered this wonderful thing and we were at it all the time and we made our legs terribly sore. What had happened, we built a tree house made with string – country children, we used the farmer's baling string – and we'd made this intricate sort of web with the string, and a rope-ladder up to it, and that's how we discovered it, climbing up this rope-ladder, this new experience: we were at it every day all day through the summer holidays. And we didn't know what it was of course, we just had no idea what this fantastic sensation was. We only had this sort of vague feeling that nobody should know about it. We tried to give it a name: on one occasion we saw the postman going down the lane when we were doing it, so we tried calling it "postman", but it didn't actually stick, it didn't work. We were quite baffled, but somehow we knew it wasn't on to ask anyone about it. We tried to initiate this little boy who we knew, the farmer's little boy, into our wonderful new game, and of course he couldn't do it – and we couldn't understand why he couldn't do it, and he wasn't at all impressed at our newfound game.'

For Marianne during those secret evenings with her friend, or for Jacqueline all through that richly self-indulgent summer, there was so much uncomplicated pleasure at such little cost. But for both women, something was lost or forgotten as they grew older. Physical pleasure in adult love affairs proved much more elusive: neither Marianne nor Jacqueline had orgasms during marriages or love affairs in their early and mid twenties, and both remember thinking, 'There must be something wrong with me.' Their appetites for those easy pleasures were shamelessly indulged in childhood, but adult sexuality proved much more problematic.

SHARED SEX-PLAY

Monica said, 'I mean I never actually had intercourse with my brother – but I did pretend to, really experimenting and seeing what it was all about. It was me who started it. My brothers were younger – in fact it was the brother who was four years younger than me that I remember these kinds of things with. We have since always felt rather shame-faced about this.' Olive said, 'I had two sisters and we had to share a bed, and on one occasion, I made my younger sister put her finger on my clitoris – not knowing what I was doing, but it just felt good – I've often wondered if she remembers that.'

Monica thinks back fifty years, and Olive nearly seventy, to the kinds of sex games, more reciprocal than parallel self-pleasuring, in which children touch or kiss one another. Sometimes such games are devoid of sexual feeling, akin to other childhood role-plays like being hairdressers or bus drivers, but sometimes they will induce that 'thrill in the stomach' that Melissa described.

In this kind of play, little girls start things off and control what happens. In the games they remember, Monica and Olive called the tune: Monica is even a little embarrassed when she recalls her brazen behaviour. But little girls also see with devastating clarity that in the 'real' world that the grown-ups inhabit, the taking of sexual initiatives is something reserved for men: men do, women are done-to. Sally said, 'We used to take each other's clothes off, mainly the top half, and pretend to be men and women, and we'd sort of play the roles, one of you was a male – and it would be always the man or the boy who would be the one that was doing the touching.'

This sexual play involves many gradations of feeling. It may be tender and loving, it may be rude 'bottom play', it may even be sado-masochistic. Marianne said, 'When I was six, I used to go into the bushes with little boys, and we used to hit each other with twigs and sticks, and there was a lot of looking. No penetration though, we wouldn't have thought of that. Our mother used to beat us, I've wondered if that was why.' Psychoanalyst Alice Miller has suggested that sado-masochism in adult sexuality derives from the eroticization of the disciplinary, authoritarian aspects of the parent/child relationship,[8] especially where the discipline includes physical punishment; it's a theory that occurs to Marianne as she tries to make sense of her memories. Whatever its origins, the eroticization of violence is clearly yet another sexual potential that is present in some children's sexual play. But there is a marked contrast here with the monotonous distribution of roles in many adult relationships and much of our adult imagery. Little girls play many parts: in these childhood scenarios, it isn't always the female who is hit and the male who does the hitting.

Ambiguity hovers over women's accounts of this kind of sex play. Sometimes the games move from role-play towards relationship. In some memories, the focus of the girl's sexual interest was not the part the other child was playing, but the child him or herself. When is a game not a game?

Bernadette said, 'There was a family called the Jacksons who used to live up the road – they lived in a caravan so they were like the ruffians of the area, and Mum used to look after them. I can't remember the lad's name, but I know we used to go into bed and go under the covers, and I just remember feeling incredibly turned on by the whole thing. I don't think we actually touched or anything, we probably tried to kiss. I must have been under ten, I can remember the feeling now – just incredibly excited.' Sophie said, 'I always remember there was an evacuee in our village. He was about eleven to my seven, and he came from London, and he seemed to be a real sort of informed person, and I remember this wonderful day in this field when he showed me what leg massage was all about, and some awful little girl rushed home and told my mother, who took it terribly seriously and said, "We have to talk about this, Sophie . . ." Now of course from a parent's point of view I can see what it was all about, but it was great fun then and I felt completely in control of the situation and it felt terrific.'

In these games, the identity of the other player matters. The beguiling roughness of the local tearaway, the sexual sophistication of the worldly-wise evacuee: these are essential elements in the excitement. Nobody else, one feels, would quite do.

As puberty approaches, sex games will have a closer relationship to the 'real' sexual activities that will follow when girls are sexually mature, and play may be redefined, as 'practice' for the real world, or as a demonstration of adult skills: 'I'll show you what they do.' Fran said, 'I had a friend at school, and she was a very wild character, we got on really well. I'd had a boyfriend prior to this, we'd kissed, and that was all, and at one point Diane and I practised kissing so that we could improve . . . Well, I don't know what she was thinking, obviously, but that's what she said she was doing . . .

and I in my heart of hearts really felt it was just practice.' Hilary
said, 'At eleven I can remember lying on a bed with another girl
who was slightly older than me, and her saying, "This is what they
do," and touching me – which wasn't very much of me at eleven
– and saying "This is how they kiss," which wasn't a peck on the
cheek, it was like kissing. I think I just found it really interesting.
I wasn't repulsed, it was just part of growing up.'

The idea of sexual practice is highly subversive. These accounts
raise the same questions as 'practice' sex with a surrogate at Dr
Martin Cole's clinics. Is there any difference between real and practice sex? Fran and her 'very wild' friend are 'practising' for the
socially sanctioned world of adult heterosexuality: it's an acceptable
cover for a very different agenda. As heterosexual stereotypes start
to impinge on these girls at the brink of adolescence, lesbian kissing
feels forbidden. The notion of practice keeps the illicit sexual kissing
safe.

This kind of sexual intimacy with a girlfriend during puberty
was quite commonly remembered by the women I talked to. Most
of the women with these memories had relationships with men in
adult life, though they remained perhaps more curious about lesbian relationships than other women. But some became lesbians,
like Fran above, or Eve, who remembered a sexual game that moves
still further towards relationship.

'I didn't play sex games or anything like that till I was about
twelve, when I had an experience with another girl. It was my best
friend and she was leaving the area, and her parents came round
to say goodbye to my parents, and we'd gone upstairs to play in
my bedroom, and we ended up taking our clothes off and playing
with each other's breasts – nothing genital, just enjoying each
other's bodies. We kissed as well.'

For Eve, the sexual touching is a way of saying goodbye to her
friend. Goodbyes are often intimate affairs, because you don't have
to live with the consequences of what you do. For Eve, the physical
intimacy is also a way of expressing her sadness at the loss of her
friend, and it involves a tender expression of feeling which seems
to transcend playing.

FANTASY

Some women recall sexual fantasies from childhood. Of all memories, remembered fantasies will be most vulnerable to misinter-

pretation, viewed as they are through the distorting lens of adult desires and adult meanings. Yet perhaps these memories can serve as signposts that point to the rich hidden world of childhood sexual imaginings.

Josephine said, 'Between eight and eleven, I can remember having some really disgusting fantasies. It's a blur, a sort of blurry fantasy which was repeated of bodily fluids oozing, kind of milk and things. It was probably all to do with breasts developing and periods and doing a wee. That's all I can remember, lying in bed and fantasizing about all those sorts of fluids.'

Josephine's memories – part image, part physical sensation – have the fragmentary inchoate quality of most remembered childhood sexual fantasy. Only a few women have such memories, and usually only snatches and fragments linger in the mind. Often the fantasy is recalled from the time between sleep and waking, from those moments when we lay and stared into the dark, seeing fearful shapes in the shadows on the ceiling, or beguiling colours in the darkness behind the door. A woman may not be certain whether her fantasy started as a conscious imagining or a dream.

Some of these remembered fragments are sado-masochistic in content. Marianne said, 'I had a fantasy about being raped with a milk bottle. You know, the crates of them they had, the little tiny bottles. The context is my infant school, so I must have been under six.' Jacqueline also remembers a fantasy from when she was six: 'I think it started off as a dream, and it was based in my infant school in Scarborough and it was about the cloakroom, which was upstairs, and it was quite horrifying really, I find it awkward knowing what I know now. It was very masochistic, and I was tied up – something to do with the coat-hooks – and the boys were doing something to me, I don't know what it was, but the theme of it was very sadistic. It used to recur – but whether it was a fantasy or whether it was still a recurring dream I don't know.'

Like much adult sexual fantasy or pornography, these fantasies integrate inner urgings with the banal impedimenta of everyday life. Here little girls read disconcertingly sado-masochistic meanings into half-pint milk bottles or coat-hooks in the school cloakroom. These fantasies, like Josephine's 'disgusting' ones, are not remembered with pleasure. 'Knowing what I know now' gives these fantasies a context: the abuse of women in pornography. As adult women we may be troubled by the arousing potential of fantasies in which women are degraded; how much more troubling if we recall, like Jacqueline, that such things excited us even in early childhood.

But some of these remembered fragments of sexual fantasy have a very different quality, more Mills and Boon than Marquis de Sade. Sally said, 'I had fantasies about men, male teachers and things like that. It wasn't a direct sexual thing, but semi-romantic and semi-exciting – I wasn't quite sure what I was going to do with this man.' Penny said, 'I used to fantasize about older men, very much older than me – it wasn't really sexual, it was him taking care of me. If I hurt myself I would have fantasized about a nice-looking doctor looking after me and being nice. It was attention, really, from men.'

Here there are glimmerings of what adult female sexuality has often been meant to be for women: the object of sexual interest is the strong but affectionate adult male figure, the perfect father. These fantasies are about that pleasure in being protected and cared for that adult women under patriarchy have so often had to accept as a substitute for physical pleasure. Both women here make a distinction between the romantic and the sexual, and both feel that their childhood fantasies of the Mills and Boon hero were only a limited source of sexual excitement.

Sophie at ten makes no such distinction. In her remembered fantasy she integrates sexual excitement with acceptable adult het-erosexuality. 'I persuaded myself for a long time that you got babies without sex when you were really in love, and I used to have a big thing about James Mason, it was a very pure love affair we had, and we didn't actually do it, you know, and I persuaded myself up to ten-ish that it could be like that, and then sort of pre-pubescence I got very interested in fantasizing what it was like to actually have a penis between your legs. I remember one day in particular sitting on a sunny park bench, and my brother was sitting down talking to me, and I remember sitting with my legs apart, and all the time I was fantasizing the James Mason character actually sliding his penis into me, and I was really excited by that.'

In her fantasy, Sophie successfully reconciles the romantic and the sexual: the memory is highly erotically charged, but the imagery is also acceptably romantic. Here there are no musings on the messy mysteries of the body, no arousal from thoughts of rape or bondage. Sophie's sexual excitement is all centred in the image that society presents to us as the perfect object of desire, the male film star, and in the moment that patriarchy tells us is the epitome of female pleasure, the moment of penetration.

Freud had a prescription for how to become a proper woman. He asserted that a woman attained sexual maturity by giving up the 'polymorphous perversity' of earlier childhood and learning to focus her desires on genital sexuality with a man, and especially on the magic penis which would make her whole.[9] When Sophie describes how she came to focus her erotic energies on the dream of penetrative sex with James Mason, she seems to be following Freud's prescription to the letter. Perplexingly for the orthodox psychoanalyst, however, she gets there at ten, an age at which Freud considered children to be devoid of sexual interests.

For Jill, the male was the focus of her sexual interest at an even earlier stage in her development, at age three or four, and her early fantasies about little boys were a source of exceptional physical pleasure for her. I feel that her story makes a fitting end to this account of the sexual world of little girls, because though it starts in the sexuality of the pre-school years, it moves us on, into adolescence. And look what happens then.

'Sex was something I was always fascinated by, from being a very little girl. I can remember masturbating in my cot. I can remember my uncle coming into the room while I was doing that. I was so embarrassed at being caught out. He didn't say anything, but I never wanted to be found out. I suppose my mother must have already told me off for it. This was in Antigua where we grew up. We had maids then and one of them caught me, they went, "Ha ha, you're waxing," that's what they called it, "Who taught you waxing, Jill?" I felt so embarrassed.

'My fantasies were all about kissing a little boy. There would be me and the little boy, and it would build up and up till I kissed the little boy, and that would be it. It had to strike me as being very rude, and kissing a little boy when I was small seemed very rude. I knew that something happened, that you got this lovely warm feeling and didn't have to go on any more. Then when I found out about orgasms and started to read about them, I thought I wasn't having them. That was when I was thirteen – when you start to think, what's wrong, what's wrong with me . . .'

FORGETTING

Jill's story of easy and delightful childhood sexuality ends on a troubled note. For Jill at thirteen, issues of right and wrong now enter her sense of her sexuality. This is nothing to do with morality.

Jill was always aware of sexual morality, as all children are: like virtually every child over two, she wanted to keep her sexual activity secret from grown-ups. What troubles Jill at thirteen is rather the idea that there is a right and a wrong sexual response, a right and a wrong way to be sexual. The body that responded so magically at the age of three or four is subjected to sceptical teenage scrutiny and found wanting. Here, as so often, the story of the girl's arrival at sexual maturity is a story of loss.

Jill loses trust in the easy magic of the body. But there are many other possible losses for women in this transition from child to adult sexuality. At adolescence, as gender stereotypes impinge on us and we learn what is expected of us as adult females, we may also lose the capacity to be active sexually. As adult women, we no longer know how to be sexually curious, to explore another person's body, to take sexual initiatives. As children, we may have the shameless curiosity of Alice in Wonderland, and the careless sexuality of those wonderful little girls in some of Paula Rego's paintings, who raise their skirts at passing dogs. But once mature, we become the sexual equivalent of Beth in *Little Women*: sweet, passive, yielding. We lose that capacity to play a great variety of roles which we had as little girls. Sophie at eight drew sexy pictures as well as playing at artists' models with her brother. As grown women, we know all about how to be a good artist's model, how to pose and look pretty, how to keep still and be looked at. Somewhere along the way, we forgot that it was also in our power to do pornographic drawings and distribute them round the class.

In Freud's account, the change from the active sexuality of childhood to the passive sexuality of female adulthood was about the change from the clitoris to the vagina as the focus of sexual feeling, with orgasms to match. The notion that some orgasms are more mature than others now strikes us as nonsensical, but there is perhaps an underlying truth here, though not the one that Freud intended. For the most startling loss or forgetting in the transition from child to adult sexuality is the loss of the clitoris itself. For one woman, the capacity to have orgasms at all is lost. So Jacqueline, who simply happened upon this capacity of her body while shinning up ropes of baling string, forgets as an adult how to do it at all: making an orgasm is a skill that is lost. Another woman who as a little girl enjoyed masturbation though not to orgasm may lose this source of pleasure entirely: adult women troubled by their lack of sexual response who follow the advice in sex manuals and try to masturbate, may find that their genitals seem anaesthetized. Or we may forget altogether about the existence of the clitoris, the source of our childhood pleasure: sex therapists find that many pre-orgasmic women who come to them for help either don't know about the clitoris, or don't know how to find it.[10] And the woman who knows of the existence of the clitoris but doesn't know how to find it may even decide that what's wrong with her is that she was born without one, a belief that is quite commonly held by pre-orgasmic women. Any of these losses or forgettings can make us ask, like Jill at thirteen, 'What's wrong, what's wrong with me?'

WHY DO LITTLE GIRLS FORGET?

One answer to the question 'Why do little girls forget?' might be 'Because of guilt'. This is the answer we would probably find in most books about sex, and in the agony columns of women's magazines.

The idea that all our sexual ills are caused by guilt is a cornerstone of our contemporary understanding of sexuality. Today we believe with Wilhelm Reich that if only we could bring our children up to be free of sexual guilt, everything in the garden would be lovely. Guilt has become something of an all-purpose explanation, a kind of theoretical Polyfilla to smooth over the cracks in our understanding of sexual development.

Children's sexual games are certainly not free of guilt. But those childhood sexual guilts are by no means entirely negative. They may be protective or even pleasure-enhancing. One effect of guilt is to make children keep these games secret from grown-ups. As Sara said, 'You didn't tell your parents, just like you didn't tell them if you'd nicked sixpence from the purse.' This guilt-driven inhibition against letting grown-ups know may actually serve to protect children from the abuse that might well follow from an adult intrusion into this childhood sexual world. For the potential abuser, hearing about or witnessing children's sex play can have a disinhibiting effect. An abuse survivor interviewed by pornography researcher Andrea Dworkin on a BBC 'Omnibus' programme in November 1991 told how her father had first raped her when he found her engaged in sex play in the bath with her brother. A little guilt may also increase the child's excitement. Guilt was part of the 'feeling of the forbidden', the sense of doing something wickedly adult, that so added to the fun for Sally and her sister as they played their naked dancing game.

But there are some kinds of guilt that it seems very likely will indeed have a destructive effect on childhood sexuality – those guilts that follow from forceful parental prohibitions or punishments. Not so long ago, the conscientious parent was expected to prevent children from masturbating and to punish any child caught in the act, in order to protect the child from the debilitating effects that were believed inevitably to ensue. Though the advice of the childcare experts has now changed completely, the old attitudes linger on.

Some of the women I talked to had been stopped from masturbating, or punished for sexual games. Linda was told always to keep her hands on top of the sheets when she went to bed. Fran was smacked by her father after being observed in an incident with an older girl that bordered on abuse. Stella, who had been playing a looking game with a little boy in the mud at the bottom of the garden, was given a painful enema: the justification was that she might have caught worms because she had her knickers off, but Stella experienced the procedure as a covert punishment.

Sheila cried as she told me what had happened to her at twelve, over forty years ago: 'It was just me and this boy, and we went behind some bushes, and he pulled his trousers down, and I lifted my skirt up, and pulled my knickers down – and a man poked his head over the fence and saw us, and that frightened me, and I knew by the look on his face that he was going round to my house to tell my parents – so I ran, and I ran and ran until my little legs nearly dropped off, and I was terrified to go home and I went and hid in some bushes until it was dark, when I knew I'd have to go home. And I knew the moment I walked into the house that this man had been and told my parents, and the questioning went on for hours and hours, and needless to say I denied everything, until eventually I got thrashed. It was the only time that my father ever thrashed me, and he took a rubber belt off his trousers and stripped me naked across his bed and thrashed me with this belt, and when he'd finished, he said, "That was for lying to me, not for what you did," and that's also what my mother said. I will never ever forgive either of them for that. My father's dead, he died three years ago, and I didn't feel in the least sorry.'

It is a shocking story, and we might expect that such experiences would have a very damaging effect on a child's sexuality. If what you did warrants such punishment, it must be a very wicked thing; if what you did warrants such punishment, it's certainly not worth the risk of doing it again. Disabling guilt and an avoidance of sexual activity could be seen as the almost inevitable consequences of such parental cruelty.

Yet boys too may be told that masturbation is wrong, and punished for sexual activity, so how do we explain the apparently greater impact of sexual guilt on little girls? The explanation favoured by many feminist writers is put succinctly by Jane Cousins-Mills in her book for teenagers, *Make It Happy, Make It Safe*: 'Many boys, even in this day and age, are discouraged from masturbating, but parents can't tell their sons not to touch their penis or they wouldn't be able to pee. But parents often firmly discourage their daughters from playing with their sex organs . . . This means that girls, even more than boys, grow up thinking that to feel themselves is somehow "naughty" or "wrong" or in some way dangerous.'[11] The difference here seems to be one of quantity. Both boys and girls feel guilt, but girls feel *more*. Boys may be told off, but without conviction, whereas parents are genuinely shocked when they find their daughters doing the same sort of thing.

There is some evidence that masturbation is indeed still seen as unnatural in little girls. A child psychologist told me, 'We've always had girls referred to us for masturbation – never boys. Before we knew about child sex abuse, the worry was that the girl's masturbation was a sign of disturbance, that something was wrong. Now with girls the assumption is that they've been sexually abused if they masturbate.'

The message that sexual activity is unnatural for girls may also be conveyed in a more subtle way. In *My Mother My Self*, Nancy Friday suggests that even where girls aren't told off for masturbating, and the mother does try to talk positively about sex with her daughter, the girl will learn from her mother's unease, conveyed in her tone of voice and non-verbal communication, that sex is a problematic part of women's lives.[12]

The guilt theory can take us some way towards understanding the losses and forgettings of female sexual maturity. If a little girl learns that masturbation is unnatural in girls, that sex is a male sphere, that good girls don't, that sex is not quite nice for women, then her sexuality will clearly be shaped by these powerful messages. But I would argue that the guilt theory is at best only a partial explanation. In our concern with what is subtle – the non-verbal messages, the hidden agendas, the covert teachings – it is important not to overlook what is obvious. It isn't only guilt that makes little girls forget.

NAMING

Childhood is a time for naming. First words delight both parent and child: the toddler is praised and applauded as she triumphantly names a cup or a caterpillar. Some of the earliest words she learns will be parts of the body, named first on a doll and then on herself. As the little girl grows, there are more words, more naming – seven different kinds of spider, the longest rivers in the world – and, in biology classes at school, the words for the structure and functions of the body in all their intriguing complexity. It is through naming that we make the world real: what is not named sooner or later ceases to exist.

But girls cannot name their genitals. A study of three- to six-year-old children, for instance, found that only 14 per cent of the girls could offer any word for the female genitals, while over 50 per cent of the boys could give a name for their genitals. More girls had a name for penis than for their own genitals.[13] And among those few girls who do have a word for their genitals, it is always the vagina that is named: virtually none have a word for clitoris.

There is nothing subtle about this omission. It is simply that no one has told the little girl what to say. A recent survey of eighty parents found that while they all named their sons' genitals for them, where their daughters were concerned 27 per cent used vagina or a derivative of it, 29 per cent used bottom or front bottom, and 39 per cent used no particular word at all.[14]

Why this huge disparity between the information given to boys and to girls? And in particular, why the total silence about the main site of female sexual pleasure?

One obvious issue is that the girl's genitals are much less conspicuous than the boy's. The penis cannot be ignored, but the clitoris is tucked away. This doesn't stop the little girl from finding the clitoris: you only have to watch little girls, once freed from the constraints of nappies and starting to explore, to know just how accessible those hidden genitals are. But because the clitoris is tucked away and cannot be clearly seen, the little girl may not ask about it: she may think of it as a sensation rather than a bodily organ. She is dependent on being told, and she does not get told.

Among the women I talked to, only three had named the clitoris for their daughters. Even those of us who've read Shere Hite and *The Women's Room*, who've bravely answered our daughters' questions about reproduction on crowded traffic islands or in the queue at Sainsbury's, who've taken our partners to childbirth classes or taught those classes ourselves, who believe passionately in doing all we can to give our daughters a better start to their sex lives than we had: even women like these all shy away from giving their daughters this crucial piece of information.

What makes it so difficult to talk about? For a start, those of us who are now mothers of young girls mostly grew up without any words to name our genitals. 'Bottom' was usually the only word we had, or, in the most bashful households, 'BTM' or 'down there'. 'Actual genitals,' reflected Marianne, who had been enjoying hers since pre-school days, 'were a complete surprise.' Information about the function of the clitoris in particular is quite new, and has only been widely available since Masters and Johnson: many of us have only learnt the word ourselves over the past ten or fifteen years. In our own lives, the information about the clitoris was tagged on later to what we knew about sex. It still doesn't feel quite natural: it's not part of our sense of what real sex is all about. 'Then the daddy puts his penis in the mummy's vagina': this for us was the statement at the heart of sex education. For our daughters, we think, the bit about the clitoris can be added on later, when they're ready for it, when they're bigger, when they want to know.

Because the word is so new to us, it is still awkward to say. As June remembered, 'For a long time I saw this word written down and was worried silly because I didn't know how to pronounce it. So I used to avoid saying it in case I made an idiot of myself.' It would be so much easier if there were comfortable slang substitutes, as there are for the penis. But there are no easy affectionate words for female genitals – with the exception of 'fanny' – and there are none at all for the clitoris. Whatever line their parents may take on baby talk, children tend to favour diminutives, and in fact, of the three daughters who had had the clitoris named for them and who therefore had words of their own for clitoris, two said 'willy'. The penis and clitoris are analogous organs, and these little girls have intuited the similarity. But the use of the male word, though much better than nothing, still grates. How badly we need a user-friendly word to offer our daughters.

The clitoris is the only organ in the human body whose sole function is the transmission of pleasure. The penis has a reproductive function, but the clitoris has an exclusively sexual function; the boy has to handle his penis to pee, but the clitoris is only touched for pleasure. Here is a further reason for discomfort in talking to our children. To name the clitoris for a child probably means to be asked why it is there and what it is for, and answering those questions means talking, however lightly, about sexual pleasure – perhaps explaining that this is the bit that feels good when the mummy and daddy are having that special cuddle that makes a baby. It isn't easy: it feels much safer to talk about sex as purely reproductive.

With so many reasons for discomfort, it is hardly surprising that parents often fall back on our received wisdom about sex education – the belief that too much sexual knowledge might worry, confuse or damage the child. When they told me what they'd said to their daughters about sex, a lot of women commented, 'I don't want to tell her more than she wants to know.' Yet this is not an approach we would take to a child's questions about where butter comes from or why the sky is blue. Does it have its roots in that theory of the sixteenth century Jesuit pedagogues, the theory that children could be corrupted by being given too much sexual knowledge too soon? Do we sometimes use the notion of childhood innocence as a way of dealing with our own discomfort?

There may indeed be times when we can tell from a child's reaction that we have given more information than can be coped with. Lesley recalled, 'When Alan had his affair, Hannah would have been seven, and she kept asking in more detail why he had – "But *why*? I didn't hear you arguing." And I tried to explain it to her, and she absolutely switched off, as if to say, "I'm not listening to that, that's not my world." I was quite struck by that, because everything else she'd absorbed, she'd wanted to know more and more, but the idea of sexual intercourse with someone else outside marriage was either too much or irrelevant, she closed off to it; so I thought then, Well, she's not ready for that.' There may be childhood memories too of being given information we didn't want. Sophie said, 'When I was about twelve, my mother used to talk a lot to me about her sexual problems, and I used to hate it. I used to think, I wish she wouldn't tell me these things, I don't want to know.'

These two accounts have a clear common denominator. They

show that there is one kind of sexual information that children would much rather not be given – and that is information about their parents' own sexuality. Children don't want to think about their parents making love.

Freud laid much stress on the potentially traumatizing effect of witnessing the 'primal scene' – the child's mother and father having sex. It is one possible explanation for children's unease about being burdened with information about their parents' sex lives. The incest taboo is another and perhaps more plausible explanation: any conversation which leads the child to focus too directly on her parents' own sexual experience will invoke the incest taboo and its concomitant discomfort. But words for genitals and information about sexual functioning presented objectively will be accepted by the child like any other information about what things are called or where they come from, and as with everything else the child learns, she will half remember and half forget, and the facts will co-exist in her head with incompatible fantasies about how things are, as she struggles to put a picture together of how the world works. If precise information about how her body is made is never offered, that picture will be devastatingly incomplete.

Perhaps we know this, but we just can't do it: our sense of embarrassment may be too great to be overcome. There is then an obvious solution – to give the child a book. Unfortunately, though, if we want to give our daughters basic information about their sexual organs, we will get little help from most of the books currently available. For instance, consider Claire Rayner's *The Body Book*, one of the most popular sources of sexual information for the under-tens. This book contains very explicit drawings – a sketch of an erect penis, and of a couple having sex. But it is very much less than explicit about female sexuality. The sense of her own body that the little girl is given is entirely reproductive, rather than sexual. The female body parts are described as the woman's 'big, round, soft breasts', her 'storehouse of tiny baby-making cells', and 'a place inside her where a baby can grow'. Making love, according to *The Body Book*, involves just one female part – the 'baby-making hole'.[15]

These evasions, though so damaging to girls, are only to be expected in the present climate, for the writer who does dare to tell the little girl how she is really made risks public condemnation. Joani Blank and Marcia Quackenbush's *Playbook for Kids About Sex* tells children, 'Every boy has a penis and every girl has a clitoris.

Those are the most good-feeling places but they are not the only sex parts that people have. Boys also have testicles and girls also have vaginas.'[16] Not only is the clitoris actually named, but the placing of the 'also' gives primacy to the sexual rather than reproductive view of the girl's body. For statements like these, and for its recognition of what every mother knows – that children masturbate – this book was considered so dangerous that Education Secretary Kenneth Baker decided even teachers shouldn't see it, and banned it from the ILEA library of teachers' research materials. The Conservative Party publicity managers were so confident that the *Playbook* would inspire universal repugnance that they used a picture of it in the 1987 election campaign, with the slogan 'Labour's Education Policy'.

'THERE MUST BE SOMETHING WRONG WITH ME'

The little girl who can name her brother's penis but not her own clitoris, and who knows that babies are made when 'the daddy puts his penis in the baby-making hole', has been given some very powerful lessons about sex which will be hard to undo. To name the boy's genitals but not the girl's is to tell both boy and girl that male genitals are more important than female ones, and that male sexual pleasure matters more than female. And to describe intercourse just in terms of penises and vaginas is to give the boy the information he needs to get pleasure from sex; not so for the girl – or at least not so for those girls, the majority, who will grow up into women who never have orgasms from intercourse alone.

Hopefully nowadays the girl will find out later about female sexual pleasure. Alex, now in her early twenties, had felt 'there must be something wrong with me' because she didn't have orgasms, but she also vaguely knew there was something else you had to do, and went off to read books and find out what it was. This is a great improvement on how things used to be, though even for women like Alex, who had every possible advantage – an enlightened upbringing, a university education – there may still be unnecessary years of ignorance and frustration. But when this information is rediscovered, when it has not been part of early lessons about the body, there is a risk that it will remain something 'tagged on', not integral to our sense of what sex is about. It is a supplement to our sexual knowledge, part of the revised edition. In adult life, struggling to reach orgasm from clitoral stimulation, we think, I really must hurry up – he must be getting fed up – if only I could come, then we could get on with the real thing . . . Attention to the clitoris feels like an extra: it's selfish or demanding to expect too much of it. And if daughters aren't told about the clitoris, it seems even less likely that sons will be. The boy who is told how babies are made learns how to feel sexual pleasure himself, but not how to give it. So for the man too, even the enlightened man, the good lover, this is information that's tagged on, added later, not real sex; and when he is touching her there, he may say, like one of Julia's lovers, 'Oh do hurry up, Julia, I can't go on with this all night . . .'

Not naming the clitoris means that the vagina becomes the main female sexual organ. What does it mean to little girls, who have mostly already experimented with sexual sensations, to learn that grown-up sex is really about the 'baby-making hole', an organ of which she may be virtually unaware and from which she has derived very little sensation, or none at all? Not only does this terminology fail to connect with her own inner map of her body, it is also powerfully symbolic. To be told the main female sexual organ is the 'baby-making hole' is to be told that you are passive, a container, a receptacle. This is sex for the Sleeping Beauty, very different from the sexual experiences of little girls, climbing ropes, twisting blankets between their legs – so different that there may be a dramatic rift between the experiences. It is the fact that the clitoris isn't named that breaks the continuity between child and adult sexual experience. This is why in some women's sexual histories there are startling feats of forgetting.

When Jacqueline learnt to have orgasms climbing ropes at ten, she didn't know what part of her body was producing the feeling. In such a situation, it will be the objects involved – in Jacqueline's case, the rope-ladders – which are believed to make this lovely thing happen and which get imbued with magic properties, rather than the girl's own body. The experience may then become impossible to reproduce, in the absence of long summer days and ropes of baling string. When, after years of sexually unhappy marriage, Jacqueline finally had an orgasm during sex, she was amazed to find that it was *that* feeling.

For Emily, too, there had been a complete disjunction between childhood and adult sexuality. 'I used to masturbate a lot when I was four or five. I remember lying in the dark feeling really excited . . . Sex was awful when I was married. My marriage broke up because of that really, and I thought it was bound to be better with someone else. But it wasn't, not much. I felt I was a fraud because I could never have an orgasm. Then I started to look for books about sex, and I found out about the clitoris. But I couldn't find mine, and I distinctly remember standing there in the bathroom thinking: The answer must be, I haven't got one. Then I read a bit more, and quite quickly I was having wonderful orgasms. I just find it extraordinary now – that there's this crucial bit of your body, and I didn't know it was there. I mean, I wasn't a child, I was in my twenties. How the hell are you meant to enjoy sex when you don't even know about the sexual bits of your body?'

Emily 'wasn't a child'. As a child, she knew how to get pleasure from her body. It is only later, when the rest of the world is named but not her clitoris, that the knowledge is lost.

Many words have been written about Freud's theory of the male castration complex, and its female equivalent – what Louise Kaplan calls the 'just-so story' of female penis envy.[17] According to the theory, the little boy worries that his penis will be stolen from him, but the little girl worries that she once had one, and it has been stolen already. For psychoanalyst Karen Horney, penis envy was a metaphor for the girl's envy of the boy's social advantages: she argued that the girl doesn't *really* want a penis, she just wants the kind of power that men can wield in the world. This view has been largely accepted by later feminist writers. Yet the story of castration anxiety in its specific genital sense describes very accurately what actually happens to girls as they grow up, when the unnamed source of their childhood sexual pleasure ceases to exist for them.

Emily is angry, and she has good reason to be angry. For there is a kernel of truth in the Freudian fantasy. Something has indeed been stolen from her.

CHAPTER THREE

Child Sex Abuse:
Sex Education for Girls

There is a version of Cinderella that is an incest story. Variously called Sapsorrow, Donkeyskin, or Many-Furs, it tells of a girl who is forced to flee from her incestuous father. Recently I've kept coming across this Cinderella variant. Jim Henson used it in his series 'The Storyteller', and Angela Carter tells it in her fairy-tale collection for children.[1] This is the Cinderella story for our times.

The story of the sexual abuse of the girl by her father was a story that Freud heard time and again when he tried out his 'talking cure' in Vienna in the 1890s. When he started to explore with them the origins of their adult neuroses, he found that the respectable middle-class women he was attempting to treat would often recall incidents of sex abuse from childhood. At first he believed them; later he came to doubt the truth of their accounts. To explain away their stories, he constructed the complex theoretical apparatus of the Oedipus complex, proposing that all young children have fantasies about sexual intercourse with the parent of the opposite sex. The shadow of Freud's theory still falls across our understanding of child sex abuse: this is why people still think that children fantasize about these things and are not to be believed. It is a terrible paradox that it was Freud, the first person to learn that sex abuse was something that frequently happened to ordinary girls in ordinary families, who also, by the way he chose to theorize about it, effectively locked this knowledge up again and threw away the key.[2]

In the period between Freud's time and our own, researchers have occasionally stumbled upon clues to the prevalence of child sex abuse. For instance, the Kinsey researchers inevitably turned up data on child sex abuse because they asked people direct questions about their sexual histories. They found that almost one in four of all adult women reported that they had had some sort of childhood sexual encounter with an adult male. Most of these

women said they'd been upset; Kinsey said they shouldn't have
been: 'It is difficult to understand why a child, except for cultural
conditioning, should be disturbed at having its genitalia touched,
or disturbed at seeing the genitals of other persons, or disturbed
at even more specific sexual contacts . . .'[3] Kinsey's potentially dramatic discovery remained hidden in the research data, its significance unexplored. As recently as the mid 1970s, a widely used
American psychiatric textbook estimated the frequency of all forms
of incest at one case per million.[4]

It is only over the past ten or twelve years, since about 1980,
that the secret has come to be told and heard again. The timing
is no coincidence, for it is over this period that the ideas promul-
gated in the second wave of feminism that started in the late 1960s
have won wide acceptance. It is feminism as both theory and practice that has placed child sex abuse firmly on the public agenda.
The knowledge has been made public through feminist practice,
in particular through the experience of workers in Rape Crisis
Centres, who found that more of the women who came to them
for help had been raped or sexually abused in childhood than in
adult life. And the knowledge has been made comprehensible
through feminist theory. Freud stopped believing that child sex
abuse actually happened because it didn't fit into his world view.
How could those splendid men, the fathers of families, the pillars
of society, commit this terrible crime? But feminist theory about
how patriarchy works has made child sex abuse comprehensible,
for feminist theoreticians established that patriarchy is at root about
the possession of women and children by men. Under patriarchy,
which psychiatrist Judith Herman in her study of child sex abuse
calls 'the rule of the father'[5], many men feel entitled to certain
services, including sexual ones, from those in their possession.

As a social worker, I've come across several cases which would
seem particularly puzzling without some understanding of patriarchy, and the primitive rights of men over their children that 'the
rule of the father' bestows. The stories go like this. The girl, who
has not previously been abused by her father, is abused by a man
outside the family. Her father hears of this, and his anger with the
other man knows no bounds. He then proceeds brutally to reassert
his prior sexual rights over his child by raping her himself.

Now that the secret is out, the public imagination is preoccupied
with child sex abuse. Every month brings new revelations. We
hear of child sex abuse in strict religious communities, in exclusive

boarding schools. We learn that child sex abuse is rife in many of the children's homes to which children may be removed following disclosures of abuse in their own families. Revisionist versions of the lives of the famous – Lawrence Durrell, Anne Sexton, Marilyn Monroe – include accounts of the child sex abuse they suffered or perpetrated.

In the ways these stories are presented we see the interplay of denial and belief, as society struggles with the meaning of this huge phenomenon. The public analysis remains almost entirely at a very primitive level, at the level perhaps of detective fiction – 'Did he or didn't he?' – or, in the case of the Satanic abuse controversy, at the level of the child's question – 'Do you or don't you believe in witches?' – rather than at a more adult level, which might include, for instance, a serious examination of the evidence for organized child prostitution that underlies the stories of Satanic abuse. There is still a massive amount of denial. Newspaper editors, television reporters and government spokespersons by and large take the side of the abusing adult: they assure us that they don't believe he did it, and they certainly don't believe in witches. But still the stories get told.

Many researchers have set out to establish the prevalence of child sex abuse in the general population. The highest estimates suggest that between one in four and one in three women have been sexually abused in childhood.[6] Not all victims of child sex abuse are girls: boys are also abused, but, as far as we know at present, in considerably smaller numbers. And not all abusers are men. For instance, in 1990 in the UK, there were a number of cases of people posing as social workers, who knocked on doors and asked to examine children and tried to undress and touch them: these bogus social workers were mostly women. But such incidents are rare. Female abusers are at present reckoned to account for only 2 to 3 per cent of incidents of child sex abuse. A large majority of incidents of child sex abuse then involve the abuse of a girl child by a sexually mature male.

In order to work out how many of the women I talked to had been abused in childhood, I've defined abuse in the narrowest possible way, counting only those incidents where the girl was raped, or had her genitals or breasts touched, or was made to touch the man's genitals, and excluding a number of incidents with much older children where the age gap implies a potential abuse of power but where the girl did not experience the activity as abusive. Using these narrow criteria, my numbers match the highest results of the larger-scale studies. Just over one in three of the women I talked to – fifteen out of forty-four* – had been sexually abused in childhood.

One in three is a lot of women. Yet it is likely that even this is an underestimate, because of the way we so often forget traumatic incidents from childhood, the process that psychoanalysts call repression. Bernadette said, 'My grandad sexually abused my sister and me when we were very young and I never remembered that as a child, I lost that memory from eight to twenty. When we stayed with our grandparents, my sister and me, we used to get in bed on either side of my grandad while my grandmother made the tea. It was supposed to be cuddles and things, but he used to try and make us wank him off. I remember the feeling and pulling away. In later years it was in a regular sexual relationship that I suddenly thought, Ugh, this is what he must have tried to make us do.'

Women who have experienced and forgotten abuse may be startled when some trigger brings the memory back into consciousness: like Bernadette, we may be amazed that we could have forgotten something so significant. Because child sex abuse is remembered with the body, the trigger will often be physical. For Bernadette, it was the experience of touching her lover's penis: for Joy, whose story follows, it was a rough gynaecological examination that brought the memory back. But how many memories are simply never recovered?

If we accept an incidence rate of roughly one in three, we can say that more women in our society have been sexually abused in childhood than have blonde hair, or go to church, or have had some form of higher education. The proportion of women who have been sexually abused in childhood is much the same as the proportion of men who have ever visited a prostitute,[7] or of married men who have ever had extramarital sex[8] – both behaviours that are frequently believed to tell us a lot about typical male sexuality.

The effects of this very common experience on women's sexual pleasure can be devastating. In a study at the University of Manitoba, sex researcher Derek Jehu worked with fifty women who had been sexually abused in childhood. He found that forty of them reported some sort of sexual dysfunction. The sexual problems included vaginismus, impaired orgasm (having the orgasm but not

---

* I didn't raise this issue with the six adolescent girls whom I talked to in a group.

enjoying it), impaired sexual motivation, and arousal that was impaired by stress reactions such as vomiting.[9]

If one in three women experience sex abuse in childhood and run the risk of suffering such potentially devastating effects on their sexuality, then this experience has to be brought right into the centre of our understanding of women's sexual development. 'Joy and woe,' wrote Blake, 'are woven fine': in so many women's sexual development, the threads that are woven fine are pleasure and abuse. What do women themselves say about the effect of sexual abuse in childhood on their adult capacity for sexual pleasure?

KATE AND JOY: NEVER REALLY DECIDING

Kate said, 'I was one of five children and we were all sexually abused by my stepfather. I've clear memories of being in hospital on my eleventh birthday having my tonsils out, and coming out on the 5th of August and it starting to happen that night. That was the reason I eventually left home at sixteen. It was three or four times a week throughout that time.

'The effects on my sexuality were dreadful, absolutely dreadful. I think I allowed myself to be manipulated by men for years. I don't think I ever as a young woman decided, clearly decided, whether I wanted sexual relationships or not. And I faked all the time. I could orgasm perfectly well manually, but that wouldn't be enough for a man, who'd have to prove that there was this other way which has never been particularly good for me. Maybe it's to do with my early history; it's a particularly, a significantly male organ – and maybe I reject it because of that. But it's never been something I've particularly enjoyed – even before it was fashionable to reject penetrative sex.

'I think the most devastating thing was that I really didn't – and still don't to a large extent – trust men, either sexually or in other ways, and that extended to Mark, my husband. There were all sorts of things that I wouldn't or couldn't tell him – I told him what had happened to me but I never went into detail. We separated in 1978 and divorced, and we've actually remarried each other. That was an absolute turning-point for me. We started to see each other while we were still separated, I'd set the divorce in motion and for the first time I wasn't sure whether I really wanted to leave a huge chunk of my past behind. That had been my history – I'd go into a relationship and in various ways couldn't cope with it, and then

I'd move on, move away, and I wasn't sure I wanted to do that any more. So I contacted Mark, and I was absolutely aware that if it was going to be different it had to be honest, and I made him listen that night to what had happened – and having trusted him with that information, it became possible not to allow things to fester in the way that they had before.

'We've deliberately brought our daughter up to be aware of herself and in control. She doesn't like being interfered with physically, she likes to choose if she's going to give kisses and hugs or not. When she first went to school there was a boy in the playground who chased them all and kissed them, and she was clearly unhappy about it. We said, "You just say to him, 'I choose who I kiss,' and if he insists, push him away."'

Joy said, 'I was abused by my father. I think my earliest memory is from about four years old. I forgot a lot about it until I was pregnant for the first time. A ham-fisted obstetrician gave me an internal without any warning, he just threw on a pair of plastic gloves and did it. I find it quite upsetting to think about even now. His attitude was basically "Women don't have any say in what happens in childbirth", and I think that's what triggered the memory, this power thing.

'I was very secretive about it because I blamed myself. But my sister knew, and on one occasion my sister told my mother and my mother flatly denied it, she just shouted me down; she said it was me, and I had a disgusting mind and I shouldn't be making these things up, which of course fed into my guilt, and I just felt more and more guilty.

'For a long time it affected the relationships I had with women more than the relationships I had with men. I found I could talk to men, and men's attitude tended to be "What a brute, I could never be like that", so in a way that would affirm me and take away any guilt from me. My mother had tended to talk about how girls should be virgins when they got married, and I think that put a lot of guilt on me and affected the way I saw other women. Other women were virtuous and better than me and not so guilty of these terrible things.

'In sexual relationships for a long time I found it very difficult to say no. I think it's to do with this idea that you should have said no when you were a child, only at that time you're not capable of making that sort of judgement, you don't really know what you're dealing with. Then as an adult it's almost like you think, If I let it happen with my father, how can I say no to this man, when this is legitimate?

'I think till recently I used to feel very guilty about enjoying sex. It's still not gone completely, there still is an element of that.

'When I had the flashback during that vaginal examination, I tried to tell my mother about it and she couldn't cope with it either. She immediately started pouring out all sorts of other problems for me to deal with, so that she didn't have to acknowledge this. It was like taking the lid off a Pandora's box and having it promptly shut again, which was quite damaging. But then I went on a "Human Growth" course, and I found that a lot of memories flooded back suddenly because I accepted them. Following that I was able to talk to my mother, and since then we've kind of healed our relationship, and become closer again, as we were when I was younger.

'Once I was at a meeting for women who were planning Home Births, and they were talking about how people who were abused become abusers, and I got quite angry because I feel this is such a labelling prophecy anyway. If people are told that because you were abused you're likely to abuse your children, I think it's almost like when you do get that angry with your children, there's a voice in your head, "Well, they said you'd hit them . . ." So I said, "You know, I don't abuse my children, and I was abused myself," and there was this real shock-horror in the group, that I had the effrontery to say this. And within about thirty seconds, one woman was saying, "Well, I suppose as a child you were quite coquettish, and maybe you do tend to flirt with people."'

It is frequently argued that home is the best place for sex education. Joy and Kate receive sex education of the most graphic and cruel kind in the home. What do they learn?

For both girls, one of the earliest lessons is that sex is about power. Sex is something that men do to women and girls, and what the woman or girl thinks is of no account. It follows that there is no point in sexual self-assertion. Kate has had seven years of learning that sex is something in which she has no say. After all those sexual experiences that were never chosen, how do you learn that now you are an adult you can decide for yourself? For Kate the most basic act of self-assertion – choosing when or with whom you will have sex – remains problematic for years. Joy, recognizing a similar issue in her own adult sexual life, traces out a slightly different connection. She feels that she couldn't say no because she'd already said yes – to any sex, even the sex which more than any other she didn't want. How, she thinks, can I justify saying no now – for the mere reason that I don't particularly fancy him, or don't feel like it tonight – when I didn't say no to my father, when it was a sin and a taboo act, when it really mattered?

Joy learns too that there are good girls and bad girls. A girl who has sex is bad, and the fact that the sex is forced on her is irrelevant to that judgement. When her sister tries to tell the secret, the result only serves to reinforce Joy's perception of herself as 'dirty': her mother blames Joy for making the whole thing up, and the story is taken as evidence of Joy's 'dirty mind'. Because a girl who has sex is a bad girl, guilt becomes part of sex for her. The association between guilt and sex is so strong that it still hasn't been fully exorcized twenty years later.

Kate identifies a different problem about having sex with men. Through her experiences of abuse, Kate has learned to identify intercourse with male aggression. She rarely enjoys intercourse because for her the penis is 'a particularly, a significantly male organ' which reminds her of her abusive experiences.

In our sexual culture, it is the aggressive meanings of intercourse that are paramount. Intercourse is 'penetration', and the penis is a weapon: '. . . as he began to enter her,' writes Harold Robbins in a typical passage, '. . . it was as if a giant of white-hot steel were penetrating her vitals.'[10] There could of course be other meanings to intercourse. The vagina is constructed of powerful muscle: intercourse could also be about containment, enclosure and embrace. When therapists work with sex abuse survivors who dislike intercourse, these are the very meanings which they will encourage the women to substitute for the familiar aggressive meanings. Sex therapist Keith Hawton describes an exercise used with sex abuse survivors which is called 'vaginal containment'. The woman goes on top, takes the penis inside her, and learns to squeeze it with her vaginal muscles, and if she chooses experiments with various movements while her partner remains passive. Rediscovering pleasure in intercourse is about removing its aggressive meanings, and about becoming assertive and being in control, containing and holding rather than 'being penetrated'.[11] At least for the child sex abuse survivor, there is nothing to be enjoyed in those meanings of intercourse that are celebrated everywhere, from male pornography to Mills and Boon romance.

Both Joy and Kate also learn not to trust. The kind of abuse that they experience is a betrayal of the most basic trust in society, the trust on which families are built – the child's dependence on her parents. The man who is meant to be the child's guardian is her secret abuser, and the woman who is meant to be her nurturer fails to protect her. The whole social fabric is built on a lie. Afterwards all relationships may become suspect. For Joy it is relationships with women that are suspect, for Kate it is relationships with men.

Psychologist Dorothy Rowe has written about the 'propositions that enclose',[12] those unexamined statements we make to ourselves about the world, that we regard as axiomatic, and that limit our chances of happiness. These propositions, like tinted glasses, will colour how we see the world, but they may also shape what actually happens to us. 'Men cannot be trusted' is one such proposition. The belief that men cannot be trusted may affect sexual relationships in all sorts of ways. A woman who can't trust men may put up with a poor relationship, since she doesn't expect very much. She may fail to seek out partners who are loving and dependable, since 'all men are the same', and so she may have her beliefs confirmed when her partner's behaviour proves she was right not to trust him. And she will almost certainly have problems with sexual self-assertion, for how can you risk saying what you want if you do not feel safe?

Kate marries, but still does not trust. Eventually the marriage breaks down, at least in part, she feels, because of the secrets that festered because she couldn't trust her husband. But after the marriage breakdown, she does something rare: she makes herself an opportunity to go back and relive a part of her life, and this time get it right. Tired of 'moving on, moving away', she puts her proposition – 'Men cannot be trusted' – to the test. She makes Mark sit down and listen. Mark proves trustworthy, and Kate's inner world shifts a little. The relationship can be rebuilt on a firmer foundation.

There is a moment like this in Joy's story, too. For Joy, the proposition that encloses is 'Women cannot be trusted'. Women who were sexually abused as children often feel rage towards the mothers who failed to protect them. For Joy too, there is the sense that the 'holier than thou' attitudes which make her feel so guilty are usually expressed by women. It was her mother who told her that girls should be virgins when they married, and that she had a disgusting mind to imagine the abuse, and, years later, it was a group of women who greeted her disclosure by suggesting that the abuse was probably her own fault for flirting.

When, as the result of deliberately recalling and reclaiming her past, Joy talks to her mother about what happened, she confronts the secret for both of them. Such an action will not be appropriate for every woman who has been abused: another woman might cope best by breaking all ties with her mother, as Kate did. But for Joy, talking to her mother leads to a 'kind of healing'.

Joy and Kate are both survivors, and in adult life they eventually learn the essential elements of sexual self-assertion – to choose and to trust. The fruits of what they have learnt are apparent in their relationships with their daughters. These women, who have experienced the sexual oppression of women at its most stark, are still able to give their daughters very clear messages about their own sexual value. Joy's six-year-old daughter has names for her genitals and a rare sense of pride in her body. Kate's daughter at eight has already learnt the most basic lesson of sexual self-assertion: 'I choose whom I kiss.'

The kind of abuse that Joy and Kate describe – frequently-repeated rape by a close care-giver – is one of the categories of abuse that is most likely to lead to psychological problems for the woman in later life. The stories that Joy and Kate tell show some of the implications of such abuse for a woman's sexuality. We learn from them that the woman who has experienced this kind of abuse may feel deeply guilty about her sexual arousal, she may find no pleasure in intercourse because of its associations with abuse, she may not be able to trust, and she may have enormous difficulty with sexual self-assertion.

Lise and Tina in contrast both describe a one-off incident of abuse in the context of an otherwise happy childhood. The lessons for Lise and Tina are different from the lessons for Joy and Kate, but once again, sexual self-assertion is a central issue.

LISE AND TINA: I JUST CAN'T BREATHE ANY MORE

Lise said, 'I was raped at eleven. I knew the lads that did it, it was two kids I was at school with. I didn't talk about it, I just went home and that was it. I think I convinced myself that because I hadn't started my periods I was alright, nothing had been taken from me, it wasn't real rape. Having said that, now I can't stand . . . you know when you're messing about with your partner, I can't stand it when he starts to get too aggressive, like if he pins my arms down. There's a point where I just can't breathe any more, and he recognizes that and he'll stop. I always have to be the dominant one when we're having sex, which he loves.

'I told him about the rape quite early on in our relationship, and he just dismissed it, which made me really angry. I had a punch-up with him and everything, and we realized then how much it meant to me. I made him realize, "Don't you *dare* dismiss it like that" – even though I had probably shrugged it off – "Don't you *dare*!"

'I wonder if it did affect me in as much as I was all out to have sex and be naughty and really shock a man, which I always have done. Maybe I didn't hide it that well, or didn't really dismiss it.

'I didn't want to tell anybody, I didn't even want to tell Mum. I didn't tell her because it would have upset her so much. Once I did say to her, "Mum, why is it so important to be a virgin when you get married?"'

A girl of eleven, who has been told that she should stay a virgin till marriage, is raped by two boys. How can she hold on to a sense of herself as good, and in particular how can she hold on to a positive sexual self-image? Lise decides that because she wasn't sexually mature, 'it wasn't real rape'.

Lise's story, like Joy's, reminds us that virginity is still very much an issue for women. Plenty of women that I spoke to who had been brought up in the 'sexually liberated' sixties and seventies had been told that they ought to stay virgins until they got married. In all, one in eleven of the women I talked to had lost their virginity as a result of rape in childhood or adolescence. Several of these women described how guilty they felt about being told how precious their virginity was when they had 'lost' it already.

We may rage at the injustice that makes a girl who has been raped feel the guilt of a wrongdoer. Yet the guilt is made inevitable by patriarchy's two-faced attitude to virginity. In cultures where virginity is important, as it was until quite recently in our own, a set of moral values is attached to it. To be a virgin is to be pure, innocent and untainted, and these moral qualities are clearly not lost in a sexual act which is forced on you. But these moral values are only ever a superficial aspect of the cult of virginity, which is primarily concerned with preserving the male line of inheritance. Before World War II, unmarried women who had become pregnant as a result of rape were frequently thrown out by their families.[13] The injustice of this appals us now, yet from the patriarchal perspective such acts have their own cruel logic. Under patriarchy it is the fact not the feelings that matter. A forced 'loss of virginity' is still a loss of virginity and incurs opprobrium because it is a threat to the male line of inheritance.

Over the past twenty years, patriarchy in its formal sense has been losing its grip on our society. Yet there is still enough of a hangover of patriarchal attitudes for the girl who is raped in childhood to feel guilty about her lost virginity. Lise manages to find a way of thinking about the experience which serves to limit the rage and sense of deprivation she might feel. She decides that because she wasn't sexually mature 'nothing had been taken' from her.

Later in life, Lise continues to cope by shrugging off the experience and saying it didn't matter too much. It is only when her lover takes her definition of what happened at face-value and shrugs it off too that they both recognize the other meanings of the experience, the meanings that she has kept buried in the recesses of consciousness where we hide those things that are too painful to live with day by day.

And the effects are indeed lasting. Twenty years on, her attackers are still a potential presence in Lise's bed. If a loved sexual partner makes a gesture that reminds her of the rape, she can't breathe any more. For another woman, this would make sex impossible. Lise fights back by being in control. She is the dominant one, and she turns her need to stay in control to her own advantage by deriving sexual excitement from it, and by enjoying a sado-masochistic scenario in which she dominates her partner, a solution to the sexual problem posed by the rape that works well for both herself and her partner.

Tina said, 'I had an experience when I was about fifteen. Looking back on it, I actually think this guy was impotent. My memory of it is quite blurred, but I don't think you would have said we had full sex. To my mind when I got married I was a virgin – whether that was physically the case I don't know.

'He'd taught me piano for years, he was part of a couple that were friends of the family. This particular evening he was on his own in the house. It was the first time I actually encountered somebody doing something to me that was totally uninvited, I wasn't aware of people taking advantage, I didn't fight particularly because I think I was just so stunned, but I did get up and run away, and I ran home and didn't tell anybody. I could never understand why my parents didn't know, I felt they should have known even though I didn't tell them. I stopped the piano lessons straight away. I thought, They're bound to want to know why. But I must have given them a reason, and they accepted it.

'I was one of three girls growing up together and with friends of the family we would flirt incorrigibly. I suppose I'd been protected in that we had lots of family friends and they were uncle figures and I hadn't been brought up with this idea that men are only there to have one thing. I think that afterwards I thought, Maybe I asked for it, maybe that's what happens to girls who behave like that. I think I made sense of it by thinking I'd egged him on.

'Up to then I probably felt that I was in control. It made me more aware of sex as a power thing. I suppose I'd got this naive view of the world that men were gentlemen and that you have control of your own body, and if you decide something you don't have to actually force somebody to give you your space.

'I think it's made me more resistant if I don't feel sexy and Simon does. I find that harder to handle than perhaps I would have done, I'm more likely to freeze up than be persuaded, I think. I need to decide for myself. Sometimes I feel guilty about that. There's some Christian literature on marriage that says that the wife should never refuse her husband – you know, the woman should be spending her entire day preparing for the man to come home, hang your red nightie off the lampshade and put your best perfume on when he comes home, and there's an element of guilt that's provoked by that, I think, for people who perhaps want to be on equal terms or at least on terms that they can handle.'

The atmosphere in Tina's childhood home is secure, open about sexuality, and loving. Then at fifteen she is confronted with a first sexual experience which is terrifying, furtive, and totally disregarding of her feelings. As a child she had learned certain lessons about sex and relationships – that sex is an enjoyable expression of love between husband and wife, that men are basically benign, and that if you don't want sex you only have to say. Onto these lessons another set are now superimposed – that sex is about power, that men are only after one thing, and that you may have to struggle to keep safe.

Perhaps because this is an isolated incident in the context of a loving upbringing, Tina arrives at a compromise between these two lessons that works for her. Sex *can* be an enjoyable expression of love between two people, but only under certain conditions: she has to know she has chosen it. Sexual self-assertion has become crucial, not just to her enjoyment of sex, but to her ability to handle it without panic.

Tina, like Lise, found ways of thinking about the rape that enabled her to make sense of it. Like so many girls struggling with a similar psychological problem, she had decided that it was her fault for flirting. It is safer to feel that she is bad and it was her fault, than to face up to the chaos implicit in a world in which a family friend, known and trusted for years, suddenly turns into a rapist. And Tina, like Lise, decides it wasn't really rape. For both girls this is a way of holding on to something that matters to them, a sexual self-image as a virgin. This self-image has a special importance for Tina, who had wanted to be a virgin on her wedding night in line with the teachings of her church.

Tina and Lise's themes are different from Joy and Kate's themes. Tina and Lise need to assert themselves to enjoy sex without panic: Joy and Kate learn that sexual self-assertion is pointless. Bring these two themes together, and you have a truly vicious circle. Successful sexual self-assertion may be essential to arousal and pleasure for the child sex abuse survivor, but the very experience that made self-assertion so crucial to her pleasure also taught her that self-assertion is useless, because in sex men have all the power.

The lesson that sexual self-assertion may be useless and men's wills must not be thwarted is one that Penny also learns, in the account that follows.

PENNY: THE WILD LOOK IN THEIR EYES

Penny said, 'You'd call it abuse these days, I didn't at the time. It was all kept very secret, and I knew it was wrong. It started when I was about ten, and he was about seventeen. He was a cousin of mine, and it went on for about three or four years on and off, because he was away from home in the Merchant Navy, but he would stay in our house when he did come home. I remember really enjoying it. It was the attention I enjoyed though, rather than the actual touching. There was no actual intercourse but there was a lot of heavy petting, he'd really get me to do quite a lot for him, and I remember feeling slightly revolted, especially when he came, sort of all over my hand. But I still enjoyed the attention. He wasn't horrible to me at all, he was very loving, very nice. It only ever happened when he was drunk, and I used to hope he would come home drunk so that this would happen. I do remember getting some pleasure from the things he did to me sometimes, but I didn't particularly like doing anything to him, but I liked it in a way because he liked it and he'd give me more attention. But he never ever forced me to do anything I didn't want really ... I remember once he asked me to spend the night with him, and I knew I didn't want actually to have sexual intercourse with him, I wasn't prepared to go that far. I knew it was going to hurt, I was only ten, it was bound to ...

'After I left school I went abroad for a while. And once I met a chap on the beach, and to save money we booked a room together in a hotel, hoping for twin beds but in fact it was a double bed, and that led to all sorts of problems, because I mean I just didn't want it. He was perfectly OK but I just didn't like him, I didn't fancy him, but he did sort of force himself on me. I didn't struggle too much, because I thought, He's not revolting, he's not horrible or anything. I told him I didn't want it and I made that quite clear, but he was quite insistent, so in the end I just let him get on with it. I thought that he could turn violent if I kept on saying no, because he had the wild look in his eyes like they do, you know. He was very apologetic afterwards. I didn't share with him again, I just moved on. I knew already what men could be like, so I wasn't shocked. I knew that when men want it, a lot of men will do what they can to get it, and I just accepted it really. It's the wild look in their eyes, you know what they want, I think it's their nature really.

'If I had a teenage daughter, I'd be very worried that she'd be wanting sex with the wrong sort of person, I'd so want it to be a nice man that she was having sex with, I would be very protective, and I wouldn't really want her to have sex very young at all ... I know it's unrealistic these days, but I'd much rather she waited till she was twenty or twenty-one. I don't suppose if I have a daughter she will. I'd rather that though.'

*

In Penny's feelings about her sexual experiences with the cousin, there is deep ambivalence. There are aspects of what happens that she finds revolting, and aspects that she likes. There are some enjoyable sexual feelings for her, but the main pay-off is the attention – being loved, being made to feel special.

In her autobiography, *I Know Why The Caged Bird Sings*, Maya Angelou describes her childhood experience of abuse by her mother's lover, Mr Freeman. Some of the feelings she remembers are similar to Penny's. She actively sought out physical contact: 'I began to feel lonely for Mr Freeman and the encasement in his big arms,' she writes, and she loved to feel special to him: 'I buried my face in his shirt and listened to his heart, it was beating just for me.'[14] But when the longed-for encounter became sexual, Maya was so traumatized that she remained mute for years.

Where girls crave the comfort of physical contact with adults but then feel revulsion because the encounter becomes sexual, they learn very young about the bargain on which heterosexual relationships are based when male sexual pleasure is made paramount. The sexual bargain is based on stereotypical notions of the emotional and sexual differences between men and women, and also serves to reinforce those differences. For women the bargain is sex-for-love: for men it is love-for-sex. According to the terms of the bargain, women trade sexual intercourse, which they don't like, for other things they need – attention, affection, intimacy – while men trade intimacy, promises of commitment and vows of love for sex, which of course they want all the time ... Penny knows all about the sexual bargain. She is 'slightly revolted' when the cousin comes all over her hand. But though she is repelled, she gets something in exchange: because it gives him pleasure, he makes her feel loved and special.

There is another lesson, too, which Penny states baldly: 'When men want it, a lot of men will do what they can to get it.' In adult life, she has sex with the man in the hotel room because she is afraid. She knows how men can be if they want sex and are denied it. She sees 'the wild look in his eyes'.

Some studies suggest that women who have been sexually abused in childhood are more likely than others to be raped in adult life.[15] Penny's story hints that if abuse survivors are in fact raped more often than other women there may be a very simple explanation. Faced with a situation of sexual threat, the abuse survivor is once again the powerless little girl. Compared with a woman who has not been abused, she may be more helpless, more afraid.

Penny has learned that male sexuality is inexorable and cannot be controlled. You simply have to put up with it, like the tides or bad weather. 'When men want it,' she says, 'a lot of men will do what they can to get it.' This is perhaps the most fundamental lesson of abusive experiences. To see this as something that Penny has learned specifically from the abusive relationship with her cousin is not to suggest that it is essentially a distortion and to deny the truth of it, for that truth is clearly apparent from the sexual crime statistics. Yet it is only one of many possible truths about men, and to believe it will be to limit your capacity for self-assertion. Choosing and being in control will seem inappropriate, dangerous, or simply pointless if you believe that men will stop at nothing. If learnt too well, this lesson is yet another 'proposition that encloses'.

Eve: Pretending to be Asleep

Eve said, 'I was abused by my father. There's only one time I can actually remember, but I was always quite alarmed at the idea of physical contact with him. When he'd say, "Come and sit on Daddy's lap," it used to make my hackles rise, so I wouldn't be surprised if there were other experiences I've actually blocked out. But I remember one time lying in bed, I was elevenish, and he came in and thought I was asleep, and touched my breasts, and I pretended to be asleep.

'I never liked men. My father was a very difficult sort of person, emotionally very unstable. He used to have the whole house in absolute fear of him, and I never liked him being at home. If I was round my friends' houses at five or six o'clock when the father came home, I always started to get uncomfortable. I loved the mothers.'

Eve's father, like the fathers who abused Joy and Kate, was authoritarian, dominant and domineering. Judith Herman describes such men as 'perfect patriarchs', the typical abusers whose authority within the family is absolute, and who often assert it by force. For Eve, the incident or incidents of abuse are part of an emotional distancing from men which she feels may have played a part in her move towards lesbian relationships in her thirties: fathers are frightening, she loves the mothers. For some women, lesbianism represents an excellent solution to the psychological and sexual problems posed by abuse.

Eve copes with the abuse by pretending to be asleep. By acting asleep she doesn't have to confront him, she doesn't have to react, and she can almost pretend it isn't happening. To pretend to be asleep is one of a number of strategies for coping with abuse which involve distancing yourself from the situation, keeping safe by not really being there, or making yourself an observer rather than a participant. Psychologists call such strategies 'depersonalization' or 'de-realization'. Some children develop hypnotic rituals that help them withdraw in this way. Sex researcher Derek Jehu describes the case of Eileen, who during the abuse would repetitively recite the names of the colours in the lino on her bedroom floor. In adult life, when she was stressed, she would do the same – red, yellow, black, white, green . . .[16] The most extreme form of this absenting of the self, where the child switches off and does not feel any more, has been called 'concentration camp syndrome' because of its similarity to the reactions of adults in situations of unremitting physical danger.

The term 'defence' is used in psychoanalysis to mean a way of coping which may outlast its usefulness and in fact become a way of not coping. Keeping safe by not being there is a good example of such a defence. The child may be protected by distancing herself, but the implications for adult sexual pleasure will be devastating if sexual activity willingly entered into brings the old defences into play. What of the woman in bed with a man she loves and desires, who finds herself distanced and detached, an observer on the outside looking in?

CHILD MOLESTERS: KEEPING OURSELVES SAFE

The stereotype of child sex abuse is stranger abuse – the child molester in the park or playground, the dirty old man who offers sweets and tries to entice the child into his car. This is the kind of abuse that current child-rearing methods are intended to protect children from. The modern custom of not letting children 'play out' and keeping them under constant adult supervision largely arises from parents' fears about child molesters. Ironically, this caution could be seen as counter-productive. On a purely statistical basis, children are safer from sexual abuse out of the home than in it. The term 'family' is still often used as though it is the symbol of decency and the antithesis of sexual violence – for instance Don Wildmon's pressure group which campaigns against sexual explicitness in public imagery is called the 'American Family Association'. But it is in the family that many of the worst sexual crimes, the rapes of daughters and sons, are committed. Far more men abuse children in their own family, or well known to them, than abuse children they don't know.

But the chances of a child encountering a paedophile who is a stranger are still quite high, because men who abuse children not known to them usually abuse vast numbers. In prison, such men routinely admit to hundreds of crimes.[17] One in seven of the women I talked to had experienced this kind of abuse in childhood, and many more had come across such men but managed to get away. From these incidents girls learn further lessons about adult sexuality, a supplement to the orthodoxies of sex education.

Sylvia said, 'I was out with some friends, and a man said he'd lost a dog, could we help him look for it, and we said, "Yes," and he said, "It's probably best if you split up and look in different directions," and so everybody went in different directions, and he said, "Will you come and help me look in these sheds over here?" So I went, and he was trying to fondle my vulva, just generally around the outside, and I didn't think anything of it except that it was a bit strange and what about this poor dog? And then when it came out in conversation in the evening with my parents, nobody said, "This is wrong, this is naughty," it was dealt with very lightly, but I'm still aware, when I think of it now, I think, Golly, I was lucky that things didn't go further.'

Sandy said, 'I was with a friend and we went round to his uncle's house, and his uncle decided that we would take his dog for a walk, and I remember walking through cornfields, and we were sat down in the grass, my friend was off running round the field with his dog, and the uncle unzipped his flies, got it out and put my hand on it. It only lasted a few seconds, and I immediately forgot about it. Maybe because I just trusted the adult and that was it.'

Heather said, 'Once in the park an oldish chap cornered my friend and me while we were having an illicit smoke, and so we were feeling pretty guilty about that anyway. It was just being touched. I was frightened about the whole thing, and so guilty about being caught doing something that we shouldn't have been doing anyway.

But it seemed such a one-off thing, just something very strange, and I thought so long as one looked after oneself and was in a safe place, one would be OK.'

Monica said, 'I went to visit my grandma and went out into the fields with friends whom I met occasionally there, and we were picking buttercups, and another boy, who must have been in his mid-teens, came along with us, and at some point he settled down and it was obviously a recognized activity for him to display himself and have the younger children stimulate him, and I found that quite off-putting. I was encouraged to take part in it and didn't want to, and was regarded as stuffy, and I said I was going home and wasn't having anything more to do with it.'

Indu said, 'This was back in India, twenty years ago. We used to play outside, I was twelve or thirteen, and there was a man walking round there, he used to come and touch his penis to the girls. He touched me here, on the arm, and I still remember. I couldn't discuss it with my parents, because those things were never explained, and I thought, If I discuss it with them, they will stop me going out. These things are horrible, horrible, because you are so young, you are thinking there is no one to listen to you, to understand what you are thinking.'

Winifred said, 'I've not told this to anyone, it makes me feel so ashamed. We were about eight, my girlfriend and me, and there was an old man who lived in a shack across the field. He was friendly to start with, he talked to us, and then he asked us into his room, he stood us up on the table and he put his hand into us, you know, between our legs and gave us a penny. That happened twice. I hate it now, the thought of it.'

These girls, out playing with their friends in the normal way, suddenly find themselves in situations where the normal childhood values no longer apply. They have been brought up to trust grown-ups, to do what grown-ups say, to worry about lost pets, to believe they must be in the wrong if someone catches them smoking – and suddenly these rules have no relevance. They learn that there are other values governing some relationships between adult men and children, and that sometimes they have to switch from one way of seeing the world to another, because men may take advantage of their good nature and childhood sense of right and wrong to get what they want. Paedophiles base their power over children on the childhood moral code – never tell a secret, never break a promise, trust grown-ups. Frank Beck, the Leicester social worker who recently received five life sentences for child sex abuse, told the children he abused, 'You can trust me'.

All six girls cope in their individual ways with situations that they describe as frightening or threatening. Sylvia is able to tell her parents, and her parents handle the situation with textbook skill. Sandy dismisses the incident from her mind, and decides that because it was all over so quickly it was of no significance. Heather decides that this was something exceptional: not all men are like this, the incident doesn't have to be integrated with the rest of life, with those other lessons she has learned about relationships, which this incident appears to contradict. Monica, perhaps because the abuser is not much older than her and she is not alone with him, is able to assert herself and walk off. Indu, brought up in a culture in which 'those things were never explained', is unable to confide in anyone at the time, but in adult life she finds it a great relief to tell her husband. Predictably, the woman who has suffered most is the one who has never told. For Winifred, who was seventy-six when she talked to me, and who had never disclosed the incident before, the memory is still imbued with a sense of shame.

In Winifred and Indu's accounts, too, there is a strong sense of disgust. For Indu, the incident was 'horrible, horrible'. The words we use to describe child molesters – the 'dirty old man', the 'sex beast' – convey our sense of revulsion. The uncouth stranger with the unbuttoned flies embodies the animal aspect of sexuality, the aspect that is not redeemed by human values like love and caring, or even aesthetic appreciation. For some children, an encounter with such a man will be their first experience of genital touching. What a powerful association between sexuality and disgust.

Heather feels the experience didn't affect her – yet the message she learns is a powerful one: 'It was just something very strange . . . and I thought so long as one looked after oneself and was in a safe place, one would be OK.' Women learn very young that we have to look after ourselves and be constantly vigilant to keep our-selves safe from sexual danger, that we have to plan and organize our lives in order to protect ourselves, and that the only answer may indeed be to stay in a 'safe place': many women won't go out alone after dark. Indu knew that if she told her parents they would keep her in – their only way of protecting her would have been to restrict her freedom.

Girls are taught in so many ways about the sexual dangers of the world outside the home. The television news details the murders of children, and even fairy stories tell what happens to girls who put themselves at risk, like Little Red Riding Hood who like Monica was out in the countryside near Grandma's home. An encounter with a child molester proves the darkest warnings to have been justified. What effect does this have on our sexuality and sexual self-assertions, to learn that sex and sexual relationships are potentially full of danger, and that to keep ourselves safe we have to be constantly on our guard?

JENNIFER: IMAGINE WHAT HAPPENED THEN

Jennifer said, 'This idea of a part of a man's body thrusting into you, into a very vulnerable part of you, I don't like it in a lot of ways, the idea of it, and I don't know why. I wonder if I've always had that feeling, really. I look back and think, that would be a reasonable idea for someone to hold who'd been violated as a child, but I wasn't. But interestingly enough, my mother was, as a child, and only told me a few years ago. Where I grew up, working-class children get loads of Easter eggs and when we were talking about that she told me about one time when she was a child, about four or five. She'd seen a lot of Easter eggs in a window of the house on the corner of their street, and the man who lived in that house said, "There are so-and-so's Easter eggs, would you like to come up and look at them?" and so she went up to see them, and she said to me, "And you can imagine what happened then," and this man – I don't know what he did, I assume he raped her, I could never ask her and she presumably could never say. Quite strange. I don't know if that put her off sex. But somehow it's put me off.'

Kate linked her feelings about the penis, 'that significantly male organ', and her tendency to reject it, with her experience of abuse. Jennifer speculatively connects her similar feelings about the penis with her *mother's* experience of abuse. Jennifer traces out the connections between our parents' life-stories and the way we see the world. Significant moments in our parents' lives become part of the 'family myths', the beliefs about what life is like that are handed down from one generation to the next. The mother's reality becomes the daughter's fantasy, and that fantasy in turn shapes the daughter's reality. As Eve suggested to me, as we mused together on the power of our mothers' beliefs to shape our lives: 'It's like archaeology – you peel off one layer and it's your mother, another layer and it's your grandmother.' So for Jennifer, penetration is about violence in fantasy, as it was for her mother in reality.

Jennifer knows that she wasn't abused, yet in some sense she still feels as though she was. How many women share that feeling? How many women have no conscious memories, yet sense that there is something just round the corner they can't quite recall? As Josephine said, 'I can't remember that I was abused, and yet I wonder, because when all the stuff on sexual abuse came out, I really empathized with those women, I know how it feels . . .'

We know how it feels. For the girl growing up in our society, a society in which the sexual abuse of children is endemic, that story of the vulnerable little girl and the dirty old man is one of the earliest stories about sex that she hears. This was just as true, of course, before the revelations about child sex abuse in the early eighties. At some level people knew, though the knowledge was hidden, stored away, as it were, in the 'unconscious' of society. This is the dark side of the image of men as eternally sexually rapacious. 'And you can imagine what he did then . . .' – for this is what all men will do given half a chance.

According to all the researchers, child sex abuse can have devastating effects on women's sexual functioning. Sexual dysfunctions are not an inevitable result of sex abuse, but abusive experiences in childhood do increase the risk that women's sex lives in adulthood will be beset with problems. This is clear too from the women's stories in this chapter. Joy, for instance, talked about the association of sex with guilt, Indu about feelings of disgust, and Kate about the rejection of intercourse as a source of pleasure. But there is one thread that links all the accounts, and that is the issue of sexual self-assertion. Child sex abuse is an abuse of power: the experience of child sex abuse teaches women that men have all the power in sex: the legacy of child sex abuse is that sexual self-assertion becomes highly problematic. Joy and Kate felt they couldn't say no, or couldn't decide whether or not they wanted sex. Lise and Tina both had to feel in control to enjoy sex, and might be reduced to panic if they felt that their partner was being too dominant. Penny came to see male sexual demands as inexorable, something that one simply has to put up with. Eve defended herself from abuse by switching off, pretending to be asleep. And women like Heather who were abused by strangers in isolated incidents in childhood may learn that sex is tied up with danger, and that actively to seek out pleasure is simply too risky.

I've suggested that sexual self-knowledge – knowing how your body works – and the capacity for sexual self-assertion are the two crucial components that give us the potential for sexual happiness. Without this knowledge and this capacity for assertiveness, we do not pass Go. In the previous chapter we saw how basic knowledge about her body is hard to come by for the girl growing up. Now we can add another piece of the puzzle.

Child sex abuse has to be central to our understanding of female sexuality because one in three women have experienced it directly. But the experience of abuse survivors is also the key to understanding many troubling aspects of sexuality for those of us who were not abused, for there is a continuity between what the abuse survivors say and the experiences of the two out of three women who were not abused. The abuse survivors experience these problems with far greater intensity, but they are there for the rest of us too. Many of us who were not abused can see in our own feelings about sexuality a reflection of the experience of the abuse survivors: if we are fortunate, the reflection is blurry and indistinct, but it is the same image, the same shape. If we were not abused ourselves, our mothers or sisters or schoolfriends were, and we learned from their attitudes to sex. If we were not abused by genital touching or rape, we still experienced other less traumatic kinds of abuse – flashing, unwanted touches, unwanted kisses, a sense of sexual threat – and learned some of the same lessons from them: that sex is something men do to children and women, that sex is about power, that men cannot be trusted, that the male sexual urge is overwhelming and must be given in to. For all girls, sexual danger is part of the air we breathe, part of the atmosphere in which we grow up. Child sex abuse is not a peripheral issue: sexual abuse is a persistent subtext to the sexual education of girls.

CHAPTER FOUR

Menarche:
Hating Our Bodies

In *The Life and Loves of a She Devil*, a novel with enormous appeal to women, Fay Weldon tells the story of two women – Ruth the wife, and Mary Fisher the mistress. Mary Fisher is 'small and pretty and delicately formed': but Ruth is six foot two inches tall, and has 'one of those jutting jaws that tall dark women often have,' and 'four moles on her chin and from three of them hairs grow . . .'[1]

I suspect that when we read the novel we all identify with Ruth rather than Mary Fisher. Even women who know they are beautiful hate some aspect of their bodies. Deep down we are all Ruth. And this belief that our unretouched bodies simply won't do is a tremendous spur to activity in women. Most of us devote huge resources of time, energy and money to beauty work, hiding the female body and faking the acceptable female appearance.

We can perhaps distinguish between two different kinds of beauty work. Some beauty activities have elements of sensuousness and art – smoothing on body lotion, spraying ourselves with scent, painting our eyes. Even where the driving force behind such activities is a sense of our incompleteness, the decoration of the body can be a genuine source of delight. But there are other activities which are driven by a horror of the way our bodies really are. And the aspects of ourselves that more than any others arouse that sense of repulsion are our secondary sex characteristics – body hair and fat.

Body hair and fat are signs of sexual maturity; they are about being a woman rather than a girl. The appearance of little golden hairs on a girl's legs may be the first sign of the hormonal changes that will culminate in sexual maturity, and an increased ratio of body fat to muscle is the physiological trigger for menarche. Both hair and fat revolt us. Female body hair is considered to be so repellent that it cannot be publicly shown. As Wendy Chapkis

points out in her book *Beauty Secrets*, there are no public images
of women's legs in their natural state, no Before and After pictures
in commercials for waxing kits or depilatories, yet it is commonplace
in films to show a man shaving, and this in no way detracts from
his glamour. Conventions about female body hair pose a real problem for the woman whose hair growth is too strong to be controlled
by the methods available. Wendy Chapkis describes how insults
were thrown at her by passing men because of her facial hair.[2] But
the beauty preoccupation that undoubtedly causes the most distress, the one that above all causes women to look at their bodies
and be repelled, is female fat.

I asked women, 'How do you feel about your body?' Every woman
answered by talking about her weight, and unless she was very thin,
she was too fat. As they explained how overweight they were,
women used the language of duty and moral obligation – 'I really
ought . . .', 'I know I shouldn't . . .' – and they looked guilty and
ill at ease, as though they had committed a sin – the sin of not
dieting as strictly as they 'should'. Yet many had in fact dieted with
considerable rigour. Of women under forty I talked to, nearly one
in four had had an eating disorder – anorexia, bulimia, or compulsive eating – for which medical treatment had been given, and half
of the women who had had eating disorders had dieted to the point
at which their periods stopped.

The feelings about female fat expressed by the women I talked
to are now universal in the developed world. Not to eat to appetite
is now the norm: 25 per cent of women are at any one time on a
diet, and another 50 per cent have just finished or broken one, or
resolved to start one.[3] Most women in Western Europe and North
America have a distorted sense of their shape: a survey by *Glamour*
magazine of 33,000 US women found that three-quarters of
women aged eighteen to thirty-five reported feeling too fat, while
only one-quarter of them could be so described, and 45 per cent
of the *underweight* women felt they were too fat.[4] Not to be fat has
become a key life goal for countless women: the *Glamour* survey
also found that nearly half the women, rather than achieving a
career ambition or meeting the love of their life, would choose to
lose ten pounds.

The human cost of our revulsion against female fat is staggering.
As the shape that women strive for becomes more inhuman – and
fashion models are getting thinner all the time – so the incidence
of anorexia steadily rises. In the United States, 5 to 10 per cent of

adolescent girls and young women are estimated to be anorexic, and on some US college campuses as many as 50 per cent of women are reckoned to suffer from anorexia or bulimia.[5] In the UK, the figures are lower but rising rapidly: at present we are estimated to have three and a half million anorexics or bulimics.[6] Many of these women are very young: a survey of 1,000 fourth and fifth form girls in London schools found nearly a third of the girls were dieting, and 3 per cent had developed either a full-blown eating disorder or partial symptoms. Most alarming of all, more and more pre-pubertal girls are showing up at clinics with eating disorders: Dr Bryan Lask, director of the Eating Disorders Clinic at Great Ormond Street Hospital, says he deals with twenty severe cases a year in the eight to twelve age group, double the rate in the early 1980s, and a survey from Leeds found that a quarter of nine-year-old girls expressed a serious interest in losing weight.[7]

Dieting is unpleasant and debilitating, and anorexia can be a fatal disease. Why do so many of us go hungry year after year, and run the risk of developing dangerous eating disorders? The answer surely is that we do it because we feel we must, because the rewards promised by slimness are rewards we feel we cannot do without. We do it because you cannot be beautiful unless you are slim, and unless you are beautiful you will not be loved. But note that the equation of slimness with beauty only applies to women who are seen as potentially sexually active. The Queen Mother is 'radiant' and 'beautiful' though by no means 'slim', but the media saw nothing beautiful in the Duchess of York in her more voluptuous days. The beauty that we seek to achieve through dieting is the beauty of being sexually desirable. We do it because we believe to the bottom of our hearts that slim is sexy.

SLIM IS SEXY: ORIGINS

Archaeologists have from time to time unearthed prehistoric female statuettes dating from the palaeolithic period. These statuettes are usually called Venus figurines, and are judged to have been sex symbols or fertility symbols. In these earliest representations of women, the female sexual features – the breasts and mons pubis – are ample and prominent, and the stomach and buttocks are bulging and exaggerated. Writing about one of these figures, anthropologist Richard Lewinsohn remarked, 'Sex life in the palaeolithic must have been quite unerotic, for this Venus was no more than a lump of fat.'[8]

It's a telling remark. Fat as voluptuous has become unimaginable. Yet the Venus figurine is a reminder that once fat was sexy. We still see this in other cultures; the sexual appeal of the belly-dancer depends on her fat. And even within our own culture, the tyranny of slim-is-sexy is extremely recent. Photographs of the sex workers – the artists' models and prostitutes – that Toulouse-Lautrec painted in Paris at the turn of the century, show women who by our standards are fat. Go back another three hundred years and look at the women Rubens painted. They are rounded like fruit: the painter luxuriates in the play of light and shade on their curves. Their stomachs curve outwards, as women's do: they have fat on their thighs, as women do.

Older women, I found, do not necessarily think that slim is sexy. Ruth at seventy-six recalled, 'Through adolescence I got steadily plumper. At seventeen I started to mind. I even used to say to my boyfriends, "Oh no, you can't say that, I'm *fat*!" "No you aren't," they'd say, "you're all cuddly and lovely!" I never wanted to be skinny, I had enough men around to know they liked curves. I just didn't want to be fat.'

Ruth didn't want to lose weight in order to be sexually desirable: she knew her curves didn't detract from her sexual appeal. Now everyone, it seems, thinks otherwise. No one today would relish being 'cuddly and lovely'. The belief that slim is sexy has, like Japanese knotweed, taken firm hold in a very short time. Where does it come from?

One explanation can be found in the connection between fat and fertility. The fattest woman is the one who is heavily pregnant: the largest breasts are the breasts that are feeding a baby. Fat women's bodies remind us of these female potentials. But in our over-populated world, fertility has become less desirable, and where once a woman's fertility was integral to her sex appeal in the eyes of a man who might marry her, now fertility is divorced from and even opposed to sexuality. 'Wanted children can limit the sex play of adults by being around,' writes Alex Comfort in *The Joy of Sex*. 'Unwanted children are the one moral and ecological offence which nothing today can excuse.'[9] Because fertility is no longer sexy, the pubescent pre-fertile girl, rather than the full-breasted round-hipped sexually mature woman, has become the archetype of physical attractiveness. We all aspire to be teenagers.

Then there is the issue of affluence. In a time of deprivation and hunger, when only the rich can eat meat or white bread, it is fat that suggests high status. Rubens painted those voluptuous women during lean years, at a time when poor people suffered severe material hardship. But in the fat years when food is abundantly available for everyone, slimness becomes desirable – because it is exceptional and catches the eye, and also because it is hard to attain, an expression of discipline and control. And maybe today, in the global village, there is an even more direct connection between our affluence and the urge to control our appetites. We know that about 630 million people do not have enough to eat. Is our guilt that so many people go hungry being acted out on women's bodies in the affluent world? This might account for the moral tone of diet talk, and the disgust at their lust for food that so many women express. Are we doing penance for all the developed world's sins of greed when we fast on crispbread and thin soup? Is this why we feel we have sinned in our hearts when we salivate as we pass the dessert counter?

The last few years have seen the rise of the fitness cult, which is fuelled by the widespread belief that slim is not only sexy but healthy too. This belief is in fact fallacious. Ironically, over the decade in which slimness has come to be so closely identified with health, a number of comprehensive research studies have established that, contrary to popular belief, the longest lived people in the population are those who are slightly overweight according to current ideals. According to these studies, the very thin die soonest – even when smokers and those with cancer have been excluded – and people who gain about ten pounds with every decade actually improve their life expectancy.[10] But these discoveries have yet to percolate through to the man or woman at the multi-gym. Older and now largely disproved ideas about the correlation between slimness and health are still widely believed, and provide a powerful underpinning to the belief that slim is sexy.

Feminist writers on anorexia have a different focus, looking at the symbolic meanings of fat, hunger and food. They suggest that being fat means taking up too much space, in a society that is struggling to keep women in their place. Naomi Wolf attributes the power of 'slim is sexy' very directly to anxiety in society about women's liberation. Slimness became obligatory, she says, when women got the vote, and it gets worse with each new freedom: Twiggy arrived at the same time as the pill. In all cultures, how you are fed shows how you are valued. In poorer societies this is starkly obvious. 'You feed each person as is appropriate,' says Rahima, a Bangladeshi woman interviewed by *New Internationalist*. 'Obviously my father-in-law gets most, then my husband, and then my daughter because she is the youngest. It doesn't matter if there is none left for me.'[11] In societies where there is enough food to go round, women also go hungry, and their self-denial perhaps has something in common with Rahima's loving self-abnegation. Those whom society values most, it feeds best.

Finally, a number of writers have attributed 'slim is sexy' to the rise of photography and film. Photography, according to art historian Ann Hollander, expands shapes and flattens people: slim looks better, and the moving image in particular has to be slim to look good.[12]

Concern about overpopulation, guilt about affluence, the fitness cult, the backlash against feminism, the central place of the visual image: here are some of the big themes of our times. The underweight woman embodies some of the most weighty preoccupations of our culture. And there is big money to be made out of keeping women worried about their weight. Heinz, manufacturers of numerous slimming and calorie-controlled products, also owns WeightWatchers. No wonder the belief that 'slim is sexy' has such power.

THE RIGHT TO SEX

Mostly we learn that slim is sexy from the publicly shared part of our lives. We learn it from pictures, from the lavish masquerade of exquisitely thin women in every film, every commercial, every fashion magazine. Many of the women in the pictures have eating disorders. Many fashion models are anorexic, and Jane Fonda, doyenne of the perfect body, has confessed that she stayed in such perfect shape by making herself vomit several times a day for twenty-three years.[13] But we have learned to see these disordered bodies as beautiful, and this is how we want to be.

Sometimes we learn that slim is sexy in our private lives as well. Not all men would tell us that slim is sexy: there are plenty who prefer fatter women to love. But where individual males repeat the powerful public message, these remarks can have great impact on women's lives.

Paula said, 'I was anorexic in my teens. It took me a long time to stabilize. It was the classic situation – exams, Mum and Dad having a tricky time ... Actually, I've just remembered exactly when it started. I moved from an all girls' school to a mixed comprehensive, I had a helluva lot of teasing about being fat from the boys. Up till then I'd never thought about it.'

Sophie said, 'My lover started saying, "God, you're fat!" "I'm not fat." "Oh you are, you're fat." And there he is with this great beer-gut! But I suddenly thought: I'm fat. And it's demoralized me completely. I've had a situation recently with a gorgeous young man, ever so lean and wonderful, but there's no way I could leap into bed with him. It's when you've finally got your clothes off that it shows, he would just think, Oh my God, what was I doing, telling her things like that?'

Paula had felt her anorexia was caused by stresses in her home life: it was only as she talked that she remembered the insults from the boys at school. For Sophie, it is her lover's comments that cause her to redefine herself as fat. Both Paula and Sophie show what happens when a male in the woman's private life joins his voice to the public chorus.

Sophie's remarks also illustrate a particularly devastating consequence of 'slim is sexy' for women. Women feel they have no right to sex if they're fat. It is only acceptable to express our desires, or even to feel them, if we're desirably slim. We only have a right to pleasure if we're beautiful.

The phrase 'her sexuality' is frequently used in the sense of 'her sexual appeal to men'. Sexuality is equated with the beautiful body because sex for women is about being desired, not desiring; so if we don't conform to the stereotype we are no longer sexual. This definition of our sexuality acts as a powerful curb on the erotic impulses of the woman who feels she is overweight. Sophie dare not act on her desires: if she did get into bed with her lean and wonderful friend, shame, she is sure, would follow. For another woman, it's not acceptable even to feel desire if she believes that by society's standards she is not sexy, not desirable, not slim. If he knew that I fancied him desperately, old and fat as I am – muses a woman – how ghastly, how embarrassing: somehow even to acknowledge the lust is to feel shame. And for a third woman, there are other hidden expressions of her libido that feel forbidden. Janet said, 'I'm really overweight since having Rosie. I always used to wear nice suspenders and stockings when I was slimmer. I wouldn't dream of putting those on now, I just couldn't do them justice, so I just wear miserable white cotton bras.' To wear sexy clothes publicly is always risky because it invites sexual evaluation, but for the fat woman it is especially hazardous: the fat woman dressed in shiny satin or tight trousers is a 'fat slag', a figure of cruel fun. Janet used to enjoy choosing and wearing glamorous underwear just for herself. But now that she believes herself to be overweight, even those private pleasures seem out of bounds.

The promise of being thin, then, is the promise of sexual pleasure: the risk of being fat is that sexual pleasure will be denied us – denied because no one will have us, and denied because we deny it to ourselves.

SLIMMING AND SEXUAL PLEASURE

What happens if you follow the instructions to the letter? What if you embark on the quest for this ultimately desirable, perfectly sexy, exquisitely thin body? It's a quest that is fraught with danger, for to diet strenuously is to run the risk that you will develop anorexia, a disease which can be fatal.

Food is so rich in meaning that psychological theories about what it means to reject it proliferate like flies in summer. Over the past few years we have been told that anorexia is about: mother/daughter dependency, the religious search for the pure body, a response to child sex abuse, a rejection of adult sexuality, and the daughter's rage at the loss of the nourishing breast of infancy . . . According to the principle of parsimony or Occam's razor, when observing any phenomenon we should always seek out the most economical explanation. And the most economical explanation for anorexia is this: anorexia is caused by dieting.

Near the end of World War II, physiologist Ancel Keys conducted an experiment in semi-starvation to find out what the needs of the populations of Europe would be after liberation. For six months, a group of normal active young male volunteers lived on a diet of 1,700 calories a day – higher than many modern slimming diets – and consisting of lots of fresh vegetables, complex carbohydrates and very little meat – much like the diet advocated today. The young men changed dramatically: they became withdrawn, lethargic and depressed, and obsessed with food to the exclusion of all else even in their dreams. After the experiment was over they ate ravenously until their pre-diet fat-to-lean ratios had been restored.[14]

Keys' volunteers showed all the classic symptoms of anorexia –

obsession with food, social isolation, fear of food, depression and anger. So all the psychological symptoms which psychiatrists have observed in anorexics and suggested are causes of the disease are not causes but effects – normal human responses to semi-starvation. As the body struggles to recover from the effects of deprivation, the vicious circle is established – the preoccupation with food and lowered metabolic rate that lead to more weight gain, then increasingly punitive dieting to lose that weight.

Women diet to be beautiful and desirable. To be fat, as we have seen, is to feel you have no right to sex. The quest which leads to anorexia is the quest for the beautiful body that will give you the right to sexual pleasure. But what happens to the anorexic's sex life?

Linda said, 'I used to have a thing about my weight when I was at college. I was quite heavily overweight, and I went on a drastic diet. My periods stopped for eighteen months, and I was doing a lot of laxatives, I was eating virtually nothing. It was so bad that I was constantly cold, and I couldn't sit down on my bottom because it was so bony and it was too painful, I'd have to sit on my side. My sexual feelings went completely, and at the time I was living with somebody, and there was just no sex at all because of this.'

Penny said, 'It started quite late for anorexia: I was about twenty-one, I think. I'd got no money, so I had to go easy on food anyway, and then I found I was losing weight, and I thought, Mmm, that's good – I felt better to begin with, and then it just got out of hand. I had it for a couple of years and it took me a couple of years after that to get over it completely. I think I was about seven stone, which isn't that low, but I looked desperate, really desperate, and my life just revolved around food. I didn't have periods for four or five years, and really for four or five years I had no sexual feelings whatsoever. Then there came a time when I wanted to have sexual feelings but still couldn't, so that was a bit of a going forward I suppose, because I actually wanted them but couldn't get them, and then eventually they came back when my weight went up.'

The woman who follows society's prescription for how to be sexy to the letter loses all sexual feeling. She also loses certain sexual functions such as menstruation and ovulation. This fact has led some theorists to propound the back-to-front idea that anorexia represents a rejection of mature female sexuality. But the loss of sexual feeling is not the cause but the result of the anorexia, because semi-starvation leads to hormone disturbance.

But, we may protest, I'm not anorexic – or at least not anymore. This is all very terrible, but it has nothing to do with me. I just want to be nice and slim. So we come to what is for our purposes the most interesting question about dieting. If anorexia kills sexual feeling, can more moderate dieting cripple it?

There are some clues to the answer in Keys' semi-starvation experiment. Though the behaviour of his male volunteers was characteristic of anorexia, they were eating a lot more than the average anorexic, but at 1,700 calories a day – more than you'd eat on most reducing diets – these men stopped having sexual fantasies and ceased masturbating. The Director of Loyola University sexual dysfunction clinic has made certain observations which also appear to have relevance to women who are not clinically anorexic, given that they are based on her experience with sexual problems. She has stated that weight-loss disorders have a more severe effect on sexual functions than weight-gaining disorders. 'The obese women were more eager to date, more eager to mate . . .' while those with weight-loss disorders 'were so concerned with their bodies that they had fewer sexual fantasies, fewer dates and less desire for sex.' And the results of a study carried out in Chicago are particularly intriguing. Two researchers at Michael Reese hospital attempted to demonstrate that thinner women are more interested in sex. To their consternation, they found the opposite to be true. 'They matched and compared pairs of fat and thin married women and found that . . . the fatter women wanted to have sex more than the thin, and that on scales of erotic readiness and general sexual excitability, fat women outscored thin ones by a factor of almost two to one.'[15]

When we try to understand research results like these, we must remember all the obvious curbs on the fat woman's sexual pleasure. Overweight women may feel they have no right to sex or to sexy clothes; given that men are constantly reminded to see thin women as sexy, it may be easier for thin women to find sexual partners; all women say they are more easily aroused if they feel attractive, and society tells us fat is not attractive. The fatter woman has all this to contend with, but she is still sexier than her thinner sister: she has more fantasies, more erotic readiness, more sexual excitability, more desire. These studies tell us what we risk when we pick up that diet sheet, join that diet club, or choose those calorie-controlled products. As we triumphantly lose the pounds, we may be shedding our sexual feelings along with the hated fat.

The new orthodoxy about how women should look puts us in a double bind. We diet because of the promise of sex. If we become beautifully thin, we believe that we will be desired by a wonderful lover and have a wonderful sex life. But when we diet excessively we stop enjoying sex anyway.

The belief that 'slim is sexy' is a terrible deception. It is also historically anomalous. Six hundred years ago, the Goodman of Paris told his child-bride, 'The sin of lechery is born of gluttony'[16] – the links between eating lustily and loving lustily are part of human experience. It is one aspect of the suppression of female sexuality in the late twentieth century that this self-evident truth has been forgotten.

FAT AND FERTILITY

Ever since palaeolithic artists carved those voluptuous Venus figurines, fertility symbols have been fat. This is appropriate, because female fertility is grounded in female fat. It is an increase in female fat – specifically, the achievement of a critical weight which means the girl has stored enough calories to sustain a foetus – that is the physiological trigger for menarche. And female fat plays a crucial role both in conception and in sustaining a healthy pregnancy.

Problems around fertility are common in thin women. If you are too thin, you may not be menstruating, you may be menstruating but not ovulating, you may be menstruating and ovulating but will have difficulty conceiving, or you may manage to conceive but will have difficulty carrying a pregnancy to term. Yet when underweight women go to their doctors with fertility problems they are rarely advised to put on weight. Doctors as well as lay people believe that slimness is healthy and sexy. Thin women with fertility problems are given drugs, not dietary advice.

Recently a leading endocrinologist, Professor Howard Jacobs of University College and Middlesex School of Medicine, spoke out against the practice of prescribing ovulation-inducing drugs to underweight women, which he described as 'reprehensible'. He is quoted as saying, 'Underweight women have five times the risk of producing an underweight baby. Amenorrhoea is clearly nature's way of protecting babies against subnormal nutrition.'[17]

Infertility causes heartbreak for many women. How much of it is simply caused by being a little too thin? Naomi Wolf talks of the 'One Stone Solution' – the belief that everything would be OK if only you could lose a stone . . .[18] How often is there a 'One Stone Solution' to infertility – *gain* a stone and get pregnant?

What of once the woman has conceived? When I was researching my book on miscarriage, published in 1987, I knew about the links between low maternal weight and low birthweight, but I could find no investigation anywhere of what I had come to suspect – that very thin women had more problems of all kinds in pregnancy. Subsequently, I came across a study carried out for the London Institute of Child Health that looked at the relationship between mother's weight and the risk of 'pregnancy wastage' – miscarriage, stillbirth and neo-natal death. The research was done in Bangladesh, Cameroon and Sierra Leone – yet it has relevance for the many undernourished women in our affluent society. It was found that 'underweight women were much more likely to lose their babies: of the women who weighed over 42 kg. [93 lb.], only 7 per cent reported pregnancy wastage, whereas 43 per cent of women under this weight had experienced it.'[19] A woman can increase her chances of having a healthy baby *sixfold* by not being underweight.

Poor nutrition and poor weight gain in pregnancy may be associated with other problems too. American gynaecologist Tom Brewer has argued that toxaemia, the most dangerous condition of pregnancy, is largely caused by malnutrition in the mother. He advocates a high protein diet in pregnancy, including two pints of milk and two eggs a day.[20] There are also many studies which suggest that various handicaps, including spina bifida, are associated with poor nutrition before conception and at the start of pregnancy.[21]

If you eat a nourishing diet and are not underweight before conception, you give your pregnancy the best possible start. Yet women who are planning to get pregnant are never advised to put on weight and to eat especially well. Once you are pregnant, it is essential to the health of both mother and baby that you maintain a good weight gain. Yet many pregnant women are still told by their doctors that they have put on 'too much' weight. In his widely read advice manual *Pregnancy*, Gordon Bourne insists that 'the importance of control of weight gain in pregnancy cannot be too forcefully repeated' because 'the welfare of both the mother and her child are directly related to it.'[22] This advice is rooted in now out-dated research from the 1930s, which suggested that excessive weight gain in pregnancy might cause toxaemia. Yet many GPs regularly repeat these out-dated assertions, presumably because they fit so neatly with prejudices about the virtues of being slim.

Not all women, just most, diet to be sexually attractive. But if we are told in pregnancy that we are gaining too much weight, all women will pay heed, believing it's for the good of the baby. Here we see the horror of female fat carried to extraordinary and damaging lengths, when women are given the impossible injunction that even when they're pregnant, they must stay slim.

NEVER TOO THIN

When I've talked to women about the deception that underlies 'slim is sexy', I've invariably encountered a lot of resistance. 'Oh, but for me it really is a problem . . .' Why are women so resistant to the idea that we could see plumpness the way the Victorians saw it, as our appealing 'silken layer'? Is it because staying slim involves such an effort of will? If you let your guard slip for a moment, and let yourself feel that you could like your fat, you might put on three pounds before you had time to draw breath . . .

We cannot stop seeing fat as ugly by an act of will. We will only learn to like our fat once we have visual confirmation that fat can be beautiful. We have learnt that slim is sexy through watching that endless procession of exquisite anorexics in the media, and that's the only way we will learn a different truth: by looking.

Over the past few years, we have at least been given one or two new ways of seeing fatness. In the film *Bagdad Cafe*, Marianne Sägebrecht starred as a woman who was both fat and sexually appealing. Etam and the BBC 'Clothes Show' in 1991 sponsored a model competition for big women. Most significantly, there are now a few shops in the UK, such as Dawn French and Helen Teague's venture '1647', which stock beautiful clothes for big women, clothes in the slinky fabrics and brilliant colours that fat women are always cautioned not to wear.[23] The opening of such shops is a particularly valuable development. To date, the complete absence of glamorous clothes for big women has underlined the message that fat is not sexy. Sophie said, 'I went to Joseph in London this weekend, and I found one garment in the shop in size 14. I said to this very smart saleswoman, "Do you stock size 16?" and she just looked at me and said, "No, never," and walked away.'

Beautiful big women on our TV screens and beautiful big clothes in our shops. Not an impossible prescription, but one that seems some way off at present. Yet maybe the change in sensibility will come quite soon, and for the worst of reasons. In Africa, 'Slim' means AIDS. When we see what happens to the loveliest young flesh in the terminal phase of AIDS, we know that the Duchess of Windsor's celebrated aphorism, 'You can never be too rich or too thin . . .' no longer stands. AIDS challenges our belief that slim is healthy and sexy, substituting new meanings: 'slim' as the sign of disease and the price of sexual pleasure.

THE MENSTRUAL TABOO

The reducing diet is our late twentieth century version of white lead powder or tight-lacing or foot-binding. The story of 'slim is sexy' is one more chapter in the saga of how women have damaged themselves in order to please. And the belief that the malnourished look is sexually desirable connects very directly with the suppression of female sexuality, whether we define sexuality as genital pleasure, or broaden the definition to include reproduction. To be too thin is to feel less desire: to be thin is to lower your chances of having a successful pregnancy.

The facts about the effects of being too thin on libido and reproduction are not widely known. If a woman's appearance pleases, no one asks what price she is paying to look like that. But even if the risks of dieting were more widely recognized, it seems likely that many women would still go down this path. The lure of physical perfection is for many women a more powerful motivator than the fear of damage. Given a choice between beauty with pain and ugliness with comfort, many women will choose beauty with pain. Why do we make this choice? When we are told that to be beautiful we must do something that will hurt us, why do we pay such careful attention?

It was psychoanalyst Melanie Klein who first made a connection that many feminist writers have taken as axiomatic – the connection between these feelings about our bodies and the fact that we menstruate.[24] Later writers such as Nancy Friday[25] have suggested that the desire to create the perfect body is so strong because deep down, deep inside, 'down there', we feel so imperfect. We want to change how we look, to reconstruct, make-up, even cut up the body, because the body as it is gives us such a sense of shame. And it gives us such a sense of shame because of the menstrual taboo.

Linda said, 'I was sitting on the toilet and doing a drawing with red chalk, and when I got up and wiped myself, I noticed all this red, and I thought it was from the chalk, and I remember being really puzzled how it had got on the toilet paper. I called my mother and she looked into the toilet, and, I'll never forget, she said, "We've got two women in the house now." That was it. I didn't know what it was, why it was there, nothing at all. It was a good while later – I mean, I'm talking about years – before a friend told me the facts of life. So I was menstruating and not knowing for years.'

The menstrual taboo is one of the oldest and most widespread taboos: in fact the very word taboo is said to originate from the Polynesian word for menstruation – 'tupua'. In many societies, the behaviour of menstruating women has been controlled by strict rules: they may not be allowed to cook or to touch cooking pots, they may have to spend the days when they are menstruating away from their village in menstrual huts, and in some cultures they have been punished with death for failing to keep out of the men's way when menstruating. Under the taboo, menstrual blood is feared because it is believed to have powerful contaminating properties. Roman philosopher Pliny in his *Natural History* tells us that menstrual blood 'turns new wine sour, crops touched by it become barren, grafts die, seed in gardens are dried up, the fruit of trees falls off, the edge of steel and the gleam of ivory are dulled, hives of bees die.'[26] Similar beliefs have been around quite recently in our own culture. In 1878, the *British Medical Journal* ran a six-month correspondence on whether the touch of a menstruating woman could turn hams rancid.

There are many theories about the origins of the taboo. Anthropologist Margaret Mead attributed it to the human fear of blood. Freud saw it as a response to man's fear of castration. Other writers have attributed it to male envy of women's creativity in giving birth, or to the meanings of bleeding for men, who only bleed when injured, never spontaneously.

These are all guesses. No one knows its origins. But what is clear from stories like Linda's is that the menstrual taboo is still very much in place, and still shapes women's perceptions of themselves and colours the inner map of the body. We see from Linda's story some of the effects of the taboo. The taboo means ignorance: the essence of being a woman is something secret and furtive. It means shame and disgust: so Linda learns that menstruation has to do with toilets and excretion, and is something so nasty it cannot be talked about. And it means too that there is a sense of mystery about becoming a woman: the persistent notion that women's sexuality is mysterious has its roots in the menstrual taboo. At the centre of our sexual functioning is something that has to stay hidden.

Linda was not unusual in simply not knowing what was happening to her body. If we take our society's public sexual effusions at face value and assume the wide availability of certain kinds of sexual image to mean genuine sexual openness, we will be startled by girls' persisting ignorance about menstruation. *Ms* magazine agony aunt, Tricia Kreitman, recently offered delegates at a Brooke Advisory Centres conference on teenage pregnancies some samples from her mailbag: they included a letter from a fourteen-year-old who enquired whether her bleeding meant she was the devil's child.[27] Among the women I talked to, many of those who came to sexual maturity during or after the 'liberated' sixties didn't know what was happening when they started to menstruate. In fact, I wonder how much things have changed. Plenty of women now in their seventies had been prepared for menstruation: plenty of women in their twenties and thirties had not. Of these younger women, one recalls crying in the bathroom: others feared terrible illness or injury. 'I thought my stomach had been cut open.' 'I thought bits of my liver were coming out.'

Cheryl (now thirty-one), said, 'My parents never said anything to me. I felt terrible when I started developing breasts and getting hair under my arms – I just didn't know those things were going to happen. At ten I'd seen programmes at school on making babies, but at twelve I didn't know what a period was, and when it happened I was terrified. I felt dirty and guilty and I didn't know what to do and I didn't tell anybody, I just had to wait until my mother found out. I had to rely on my mother to buy the towels and I wouldn't tell her that I'd run out, so I'd have to make two or three towels last for six days, and I'd be told off for making my pants dirty, and I'd be so screwed up, I just couldn't ask her to buy some more towels, I was too embarrassed. It made me feel very inept. You just end up thinking that life's against you – being a woman means you're going to be in discomfort and embarrassment.'

Cheryl movingly describes the price that is paid by girls who reach menarche in ignorance. When she starts to menstruate, she feels not only terrified, but guilty. Under the menstrual taboo, the stain of menstrual blood has come to represent women's sexual guilt. The 'scarlet woman' is the one who does not obey the menstrual taboo.[28]

Where girls do get told a little, the taboo and its concomitant shame will be part of the message. Women's memories of being told are full of discomfort. Our mothers were living out the taboo even more completely than we are. There was no Sanpro advertising on television when they were young, no discussion of PMT in magazines. It's hard for a mother to talk openly about something which every month she has put so much energy into concealing. So women recall the booklet left under their pillow without comment, the action powerfully conveying the mother's embarrassment. Or the mother does try to talk, but in such a way that the daughter hears not the 'facts of life' but only the covert message – 'This is too shameful to talk about'.

Melissa said, 'We were in the bathroom, and she turned to me and said, "You'll start having . . . you'll start having . . . Well, dogs do it, they bleed as well." And that was it, that was my sex talk from my mother. One day at school I got a really heavy nosebleed, and I asked my friend if that was my period starting, because I thought I was getting a period through my nose.' Christine said, 'My mother at some stage made a comment about my breasts growing, followed by, "I suppose you might start your period soon. D'you know about that?" and I said no, and she said, "Well, don't worry if you find some blood on your pants, just tell me," that was all, and I remember thinking: Oh I couldn't tell her, it'll be awful, she'll be so embarrassed and I'll be so embarrassed . . . So I made what I thought would be a sanitary towel out of cotton wool and paper and stuff, and had it all prepared in case this ever happened to me.'

Melissa doesn't hear the facts: the physical reality of menstruation remains mysterious and incomprehensible. What she does hear from her mother is devastating – this unimaginable event is to do with the way in which women are like dogs. For Christine the whole thing is so embarrassing that with touching enterprise she undertakes to protect herself from ever having to talk about it again – she makes her own sanitary towel.

Now that we can talk more openly, many of us have stories to tell, rueful memories of menstrual ignorance, our own and other people's, like the tale of the convent girl with a headache who was sent to the medical room and given a paracetamol and a sanitary towel, and who came back to class with the sanitary towel pressed to her aching forehead. Sara recalled, 'My mother told me about periods, and when my first period came I bled for a month. My parents made up a bed in the front room and I lay on this bed, with this period, and I made the most of it. I lay there menstruating for a month, and then it went, and my mother thought I'd handled it really well. When it started again the next month I was hysterical . . .'

Even when we were told, we didn't really understand: even when we were told, we didn't get the whole story. But though we didn't understand the facts, how very, very fully we understood about the taboo.

It is hardly surprising if this embarrassing and puzzling event leads to loss of self-esteem. Bernadette said, 'When I had my first period I tried to hide it from my Mum but I put the knickers in the bath so of course she found them – perhaps I was trying to tell her – and she said, "Have you started your period?" And the sense of embarrassment and disgust and anger – I couldn't talk to her about it – and we went down to my great-auntie at the farm and she said, "I hear you're a little woman now," and I was just completely freaked out. I actually had the day off school to sort myself out, I did things like run all over the farm to prove I was still the same. I remember running down the orchard in wellies and thinking: I'll show them I've not bloody changed.' Bernadette fears that menarche means loss. Her reaction is to run, striding out through the mud with the easy confident physical activity which she fears will soon be denied her, asserting the fact that she is still the person she always was.

Bernadette's intuition that something is taken from her is not a depressive fantasy. It is backed up by studies of what happens to girls' school work in adolescence. Around the time of menarche there is a loss of confidence. Up to this point, girls have the edge over boys in most fields of intellectual endeavour: now they lose their lead. For the boy, too, adolescence may be difficult, but it cannot be conceptualized as a loss, and the effect on his self-esteem will be very different. The boy may be amazed and embarrassed by his first wet dream, and this is a secret too, like menarche, but it is an exciting secret, full of the promise of adult sexual pleasures, not a loss but a gain.

There is only one kind of good feeling associated with menarche – the sense of relief a girl feels when she was worried that she should already have started. Girls are still invariably ignorant of the simple biological mechanism that triggers menarche – the 'critical weight': slim girls start later. But starting late has other connotations. The girl who is 'immature' will fear that her lack of sexual development says something about her sexuality and femaleness in a deep sense, that she is somehow less than female. If she hasn't started, she feels inadequate: but if she has started, so often she feels shame. Becoming a woman is a Catch 22 – damned if she does, and damned if she doesn't.

Feminist writing has opened up new vistas in what menarche could mean. The physical significance of the event is after all awesome: it's the sign that your beautiful, complex body is working to perfection and that soon you will be able to produce new life. One of the attractive fantasies put forward by some feminist writers is that we might mark menarche with a family celebration, perhaps a meal in a restaurant or a special trip.

Gemma and Gita are fifteen now. I talked to them in a group of girls who had recently experienced menarche. It seems unlikely that they would have welcomed such an ostentatious display.

Gemma said, 'It's embarrassing, 'cos you tell your Mum, don't you, and then your Mum tells your Dad – you go in the street and you feel everyone must know, you go bright red when somebody walks past you.' Gita said, 'My period started on a Tuesday, and on Wednesday I told my friend because I was like excited and frightened at the same time, didn't know what I was feeling. I got all mixed up, told my friend, she was supposed to be really trustful and not to tell anybody, and it was right round our class in two minutes. I felt like slapping her. I said, "I thought you were my friend!" I remember saying that to her, it ain't fair!' There is nothing here of the attractive feminist vision, the new women's meanings, the celebration. There is still so much shame.

TOTAL CONFIDENCE?

Girls at school now, and women remembering, also point to the sheer practical difficulties of managing periods at school. The menstrual taboo tells the girl to hide her period, but that may be difficult. Christine said, 'All our lessons were in our class group and so it wasn't easy to go to the loo between lessons and there was always this great embarrassment because it was obvious why you had to go to the loo because you had to take this carrier bag with you. I just hated it.' Women also recall, as did Cheryl above, being sent to school with an inadequate supply of sanitary towels. The menstrual taboo that makes it so hard for mothers and daughters to talk may make it impossible for solutions to be found to these problems.

The first Kotex towel appeared on the market in 1921, though they were not widely used until twenty or thirty years later. For women in the pre-disposable days, the practical problems were indisputably more overwhelming. Stella said, 'My mother gave me a whole lot of horrible napkins and you had to go to school all day and secretly try and change this thing and secretly hide it, it was a ghastly feeling.' But today of course we have tampons – and with them the possibility of perfect concealment.

Because successful menstruation is concealed menstruation, tampon-use has become an arena for feelings of triumph and feelings of defeat. 'I remember when I first tried to use a tampon, I wanted to cry. And when I got it in, I can remember jumping round the kitchen going, "Ooh mum, I'm wearing a tampon and I feel fine!"' 'I couldn't cope with them at all – it was a terrible effort, and I was very irritated by the fact that they were available but they didn't seem to be very available to me. I remember abandoning the struggle with relief, but at the same time feeling I'd missed out when successful friends went off swimming and I didn't.'

Marianne had a memory from boarding school: 'There were Tampax demonstrations in the school toilets. I never joined in, but I always went along to watch.' This is a rare example of a menstruation-associated activity which has elements of bravado, fun and sexual display. And it's a reminder that there are positive things about tampons. Putting in a tampon means touching your body, knowing your body, being in control. But even though tampon-use may undermine the taboo on touching your genitals, tampons actually reinforce the menstrual taboo – because the whole point of using tampons is that menstruation is completely hidden. In TV commercials for Sanpro, the sales pitch is always the promise of total concealment: a beautiful woman walks into view, her clingy silk dress draped softly around her by the Mediterranean breeze – and nobody would know she's on the rag. As Ann Treneman points out in her essay, 'Cashing in on the Curse',[29] the freedom that tampons promise is specious: it is not freedom from the taboo, but freedom from the fear that someone might observe that you are menstruating.

For girls today that fear is still there. In some ways it may have got worse. Gemma and Gita and their friends told me about a problem that Stella with her horrible napkins didn't have to face.

Robyn: I think lads can be immature about it. Sometimes if they see some tampons in your bag they're just like really stupid.

Leanne: Jim Matthews got my tampons out the other day – he was walking round with it, 'Ooh – what's this?'

Gemma: There was one time at the disco when a girl had her Tampax and she was dancing and it fell out of her pocket and everybody was lobbing it around.

Gita: They did that at our school, they pinched a sanitary towel and they stuck it on themselves. They coloured it in as well, they coloured it red.

Paradoxically, the new semi-frankness, which means that boys know about menstruation, but which leaves the menstrual taboo and its concomitant shame largely in place, makes girls vulnerable to a new kind of harassment.

THE EFFECTS OF THE TABOO

Indu was brought up in Rajasthan. 'Back home you were never allowed to use a kitchen utensil, even while you are three days in period, and some people, not in my house, they never used to let their daughter to come out of her room for three days, and on the fourth day you have a bath and you get clean. It didn't irritate me because I thought, It is our tradition, but now I think it shouldn't be because this is something natural. But I think health-wise, these old methods of doing things are good, because you're losing your blood, so it's good for your health, and after having a rest you feel so fresh, but nowadays life is so fast and you don't have a rest because even when you are on a period and you are in pain, you are still working.'

Today in the UK we are not expected to avoid touching cooking utensils, like Indu was, nor to stay behind closed doors for three days, like the women Indu knew. For us, the menstrual taboo operates in a much more subtle way. Nowadays, armed with our tampons, we carry on as if nothing is happening. Yet, as Indu sees so clearly, there are costs for women in doing it our way.

Carrying on as if nothing is happening may be fine for the minority of women who have no PMT, only a light flow, and relatively painless periods. But in conversations with women I was forcibly reminded just how much trouble periods cause. Period pain can be incapacitating, and PMT can make women's lives a misery.

If it weren't for the taboo, life could be organized in ways that were less unfair to women. It would be possible to say, for instance, 'I'd rather not schedule the meeting for then – it's the first day of my period.' The organization of examinations is often particularly hard on women. Gerry McCrum, a lecturer in engineering science at Oxford University, recently suggested that the Oxford tradition of cramming examinations into just a few days of 'Finals' might be one reason why women in his department were not getting as many first-class degrees as men. He suggested that if exams were spread out over a greater number of days this would be fairer to women, as it would lessen the effect of menstruation.[30] And Andrew Dickson, a science teacher, wrote to the *Times Educational Supplement* making the same point about the scheduling of GCSE exams.[31]

It is interesting that these two people who recently spoke about the disadvantaging effects of menstruation are both men. Women may recoil from pointing out how periods disadvantage us, because we fear that such statements could be taken down and used in evidence against us as more proof of women's weakness. Yet while it remains hidden, menstruation is a handicap for many women. But if it were no longer taboo, we could find ways of organizing life and work which would accommodate women's rhythms.

RHYTHMS OF DESIRE

The taboo makes for problems in our lives and work, and prevents us from organizing our lives as efficiently as we might. But it is of course in the area of sexuality and sexual self-esteem that the most drastic effects of the taboo can be seen.

The taboo underlies much of the ignorance about women's bodies and the belief in the mysteriousness of female sexuality that cause such problems in our sexual development. In order to keep going, the taboo needs to inculcate shame; the shame makes us feel ugly, and feeling ugly inhibits arousal: we cannot really believe that he would want to look at us there, kiss us there. It is this conviction of our own ugliness too that drives us to hide and fake, to rearrange our bodies, to diet and depilate and submit to cosmetic surgery. Some of these activities are bad for our health, some, as we have seen, have deleterious effects on our sexuality, and all take up energy that we could be putting into other things.

But it could be different. If we could magically eradicate the taboo, menstruation might have very different implications for our sexuality.

It is cyclicity which is the distinguishing experience of menstruation, a cyclicity that has no parallel in any other physical experience, or in any male experience of the body. There is something rather magical about this inner physical rhythm that puts us in tune with nature, matching the rhythm of the moon and the tides, and it has a particularly fascinating manifestation in the phenomenon of menstrual synchrony, whereby the cycles of women or girls who live together gradually coincide.

The emotional cyclicity too may be valued, provided the lows are not too profound. Eve said, 'I like that cycle feel, the ebb and flow of good feelings and bad feelings. I like the way it's all flushed away, literally as well as metaphorically – that kind of cleansing feeling every month.'

This is a physical and emotional cycle, which, especially after childbirth, may become the rhythm of desire as well. There are two main patterns. In one pattern, intensity of desire, arousal and orgasm peak around ovulation: in the other, the sexiest time is just before and around the woman's period.[32] Among the women I talked to, only one woman who hadn't had children had noticed either of these patterns, but after childbirth most women had become forcibly aware of one or other pattern in their interest in and pleasure in sex. June said, 'I had very little variation before having children – I was able to be turned on at any stage in my cycle, but now it's very distinct. Round ovulation it's very intense, and then just before my period if Martin even tries to cuddle or touch me I can get . . . "Oh, let go of me, don't touch me!" I feel quite sad about it sometimes.'

You enjoy sex more if you have it when you feel like it. If male sexual pleasure is to be maximized, whatever the cost to women, then men must choose when sex will happen. So under patriarchy it is men who pursue, men who seduce, men who take initiatives. Even within established heterosexual relationships, it is usually the man who initiates sex. Yet it is women, not men, who feel great variations in desire through the month.

Here we have a sex difference which is totally ignored in the way we organize sexual relationships. Female sexual cyclicity is an inconvenience for patriarchy. Logically, if women's desire and capacity for sexual arousal varies widely through the month, while men's sexual interest stays relatively constant, it is women and not men who should decide when sex will happen. The lack of recognition accorded to women's rhythms of desire is a clear instance of the suppression of female sexuality, and the ways in which the genuine sex differences between women and men are ignored where they have no relevance to male sexual pleasure.

For many women, one sexual initiative they might want to take would be to have sex during their period. Abstention during menstruation was a pillar of the menstrual taboo because of the fear of the dire effects of menstrual blood on men's genitals. Yet for many women, especially those who have the second rhythm of desire described above, menstruation is the time when they feel sexiest. And a great bonus of sex during menstruation is that orgasm gives effective temporary relief from menstrual pain.

In her celebrated essay, 'If Men Could Menstruate', a piece of writing that rings with women's secret laughter at men, Gloria Steinem asks what society would be like if menstruation were not tabooed but valued – because it was something that happened to men.

Men would brag about how long and how much.

Young boys would talk about it as the envied beginning of manhood. Gifts, religious ceremonies, family dinners, and stag parties would mark the day . . .

Sanitary supplies would be federally funded and free. Of course, some men would still pay for the prestige of such commercial brands as Paul Newman Tampons, Muhammed Ali's Rope-a-Dope Pads, John Wayne Maxi pads, and Joe Namath Jock Shields – 'For Those Light Bachelor Days'.

Statistical surveys would show that men did better in sports and won more Olympic medals during their periods . . .

Medical schools would limit women's entry ('they might faint at the sight of blood') . . .

She ends her essay with an invitation: 'I leave further improvisations up to you . . .'[33] So we might ask: if men could menstruate, how might sexual relationships be different? What if men only felt like sex at certain times of the month? Might the rhythm of desire be taken as incontrovertible evidence of men's God-given right to take all the sexual initiatives? And what if men had experience of the role of orgasm in relieving menstrual pain? Might we hear the occasional lecture from our husbands and lovers about the absolutely crucial importance to their health and well-being of sexual satisfaction at those times of the month?

It is now nearly twenty years since Betty Friedan's *The Feminine Mystique* sparked off the second wave of feminism. Over that time, women have made genuine gains, yet we love our bodies as little as ever we did. In some ways things have got worse. The diets have become more punitive, and the exercise regimes more harrowing: the cosmetic surgeon's knife figures in too many women's fantasies of how their bodies could be.

Body hatred inevitably corrodes women's sexual self-esteem. If we believe our bodies to be incomplete, imperfect, even repellent, we will feel less free in sexual relationships and less worthy of love. And beauty activity can affect our chances of sexual pleasure still more directly when the things we do to our bodies are done without regard for their implications for our sexual functioning: in particular, the belief that 'slim is sexy' can have dire effects on our capacity for sexual pleasure.

What of the menstrual taboo, which many writers have claimed to be the origin of women's hatred of their bodies? I was saddened by what girls told me about menarche now. There is still so much shame. The silence about menstruation has of course been broken a little. Boys know about menstruation too now, and are no longer inhibited from talking about it – or even from lobbing a girl's sanitary towel around the classroom, to her intense mortification. Some progress. It's a long way yet to that female sexual Nirvana in which women would accept and love their menstruating bodies, and both women and men appreciate and act on women's rhythms of desire.

CHAPTER FIVE

Teenage Girls:
Not Knowing What You Want

In an article called 'The New Super Beauties', *Cosmopolitan* magazine introduces us to Niki Taylor who has 'at sweet 16 . . . become a megamodel in just over a year.' A model agency spokesman explains, 'It's her innocence and her inner beauty that come through in her pictures . . .'[1] But Niki of course has not only the 'innocence' of sweet sixteen, but also the slimness and wonderfully smooth skin that so often go with the age, and that have become the most admired female attributes. In our society, girls like Niki are the archetypes of female physical perfection. All our fashion models, soft porn models and beauty queens are very young: many are under twenty, and some like Niki have only just reached the age of consent. The teenage girl is now the perfect sex object, and because in our society a woman's body is her sexuality, the woman who is regarded as the most sexually attractive is also considered to be the most sexual.

'Young is sexy,' say all the media images. But what are teenage girls' sexual experiences actually like?

TRUE LOVE

Gita said, 'Today I was collecting money for this Comic Relief netball match, and there's this boy – I've got a really bad crush on him – and I went to say to him, "5p please," and I couldn't get it out, I just couldn't, and then his 5p went in my hand, and he touched my hand, and I just about fainted . . . It was really bad.'

No one surely could doubt the intensity of those feelings of first love that Gita describes. When girls of Gita's age – about fifteen – told me what being in love is like, they talked about the physical attributes of fear: your heart pounds, your knees give way, your mouth goes dry. They made me think of those lines of love poetry that Sappho wrote in the sixth century BC:

If I meet
you suddenly, I can't
speak – my tongue is broken;
a thin flame runs under
my skin[2]

This is when love is closest to fear. This is when you avoid the person you're in love with in case he notices how you feel, when you're rude to him or snub him because you can't bear the vulnerability of talking to him, and when love is expressed in flights of fancy or romantic gestures which, remembered half an hour later, make you cringe. 'I think I was very romantic,' said Amanda. 'I went to stay with my boyfriend in London and he went to work and I had to leave by myself, and I left little notes all over his room saying, "Look under the pot" and "Look under there", and the last one was, "I love you". I was about fifteen. And I was so embarrassed, sitting on the train thinking: I wish I hadn't written it. I wanted to get off and tear it up.'

This is also the age when rejection by a lover is most likely to lead to suicide attempts by girls. Almost all the adolescents who take overdoses are girls, and most of these suicide attempts follow the end of a relationship. The casualty staff who pump the girl's stomach will probably shrug: 'This one's just boyfriend trouble'. The dismissive treatment belies the intensity of the pain involved in these early rejections.

Romantic love – the 'being in love' that Gita and her friends described to me – was not in its origins about consummated sex. Historians have traced our idea of romantic love back to the 'pure love' of the medieval Arab love song.[3] The Provençal troubadours of the twelfth and thirteenth centuries developed this notion of love into an elaborate code of feeling and behaviour – the game of courtly love. For the troubadours, romantic love didn't always mean sex, for the lady who was the focus of the troubadour's erotic yearning was often too aristocratic, pure or proud to deign to look his way, whereas today we expect romantic love to culminate in sexual expression. But there are still striking consistencies between the courtly love of the troubadours and the 'true love' that is fêted nowadays in teenage magazines and songs. Today, as in medieval Provence, romantic love is about a love object that is irreplaceable, and involves a feeling that can't be controlled and that transcends ordinary principles of conduct. 'Madly in love' is a phrase frequently repeated in magazines like *Jackie* and *Just Seventeen*. It's half tongue-in-cheek perhaps, just as the girls to whom I talked were worldly-wise enough to know that romance was in some ways suspect, and that there is another truth about sexual relationships. But the scepticism generated by feminist ideas, enlightened youth club leaders, and tired and perhaps cynical mothers, only goes so far. Romantic love is still alive and kicking, and has enormous power as an organizing principle in the sexual lives of teenage girls.

Most strikingly, researchers like Sharon Thompson,[4] Celia Cowrie and Sue Lees,[5] who have talked extensively to teenage girls, have found that 'being in love' is used by girls to justify having sex. There is a direct line of descent here from the game of courtly love. For Guilhem, poet and duke of Aquitaine in the twelfth century, and for the ladies he sought to seduce, romantic love was an ennobling emotion, an emotion that justified breaking the normal rules of moral conduct and committing adultery. It serves a very similar purpose for the girl of fifteen today.

Where being 'in love' is the justification for sex, a girl may be unable to decide, or may never even consider, what she really wants. The question she asks herself is 'Am I in love?' not 'Do I want sex?' The very question 'Do I want sex?' may seem illicit because it goes against all our stereotypes of femininity by putting the dictates of the body above the dictates of the heart. If you ask yourself the wrong question, you may well come up with the wrong answer. Romantic love here is an obstacle to the most basic act of sexual self-assertion – knowing clearly whether or not you want to have sex, and saying so. Teenage girls have sex for the most romantic and least sexual of reasons – because I'm in love, to show him I care, because I want to keep him. These reasons are rooted in the discourse of romantic love; they have more to do with the irreplaceability of the love object and the romantic gesture that transcends everyday principles of conduct, than with the prospect of physical pleasure.

The 'in love' justification for sex can cloud a girl's judgement. She may have sex when she doesn't want it – for if sex is what you do when you're 'in love', and you are and he wants it, sex becomes an offer you can't refuse. And if a girl has to be 'in love' to have sex, conversely she may have to persuade herself she is in love if she wants to try sex – that this boy is 'the one', and that this relationship is deep and meaningful and will last. She may commit herself to a relationship that brings her little joy.

STATUS

Social status is always part of sex. Issues that properly belong in the public domain constantly intrude into our most private choices; we want someone because everyone else wants them, or we adopt a sexual position not because it feels pleasurable but because it feels daring. For the prince in the folk tale, whose enchanted lover switches from beautiful woman to hideous hag and back again, it is not easy to choose whether he will have her ugly by day and beautiful in his bed at night, where only he can see – or the other way round. But it is during the teenage years that this most private of acts relates most closely to the public domain. Social prestige is more of an issue in our sexuality during the teenage years than at any other time in the life cycle. Of all the categorizations that teenage girls use to evaluate one another, sexual experience is one of the most fundamental.

There may be a class points system: 'How far did you go – from one to ten?' The girl who's not interested in sex may be consigned to an out-group – the V-group, virgins at fifteen. Or the sexual evaluations and judgements may include the public display of trophies or the public announcement of sexual conquest. Bernadette remembers her convent school of ten years ago: 'I was the person with most experience at school, I used to wank boys off. Oh God, it was a laugh! I used to have this rust-coloured pair of peg-legged trousers, and I used to knock about with this boy called Gary. You're talking about sixteen, seventeen, late on, but of course none of my friends were doing anything really at school, they used to firmly believe you should be a virgin when you got married, and I remember wanking Gary off and it making a mark on my trousers, and I took the trousers in to school and showed everybody and they were passed around and it was like this trophy, it was unbelievable – "Oh God, is this what it does?" "Is that the kind of mark it makes?" "Blimey, what was it like?"' Marianne recalls, 'Sexual experiences were very bad really, it was just snogging at parties, endless snogging at parties, and I never liked the kissing bit anyway. It was horrible, but there was prestige about doing it, so you did it. And when your parents came to pick you up, stepping over the bodies, that was prestigious and generally desirable, so you used to do that. My first boyfriend – well, everyone wanted him too, so it was wonderful when I got him, Jane Banks running down the stairs at her own party shouting, "She's got him, she's got him, it's not

fair!" It was more about that kind of thing – more about social
triumph actually.'

Where sex is about status or bravado, and where sexual sophistication is everything, the arena for approval or disapproval, triumph
or shame, is not the relationship itself but how that relationship is
viewed by your girlfriends, and the greatest sexual embarrassment
is ignorance revealed in front of your classmates. Sophie said,
'When I was about fifteen, the school went to the Lake District
for a holiday, and there was a French boy staying there, utterly
handsome, dark, sultry and wonderful. I really fancied him, and
he arranged to meet me on the bridge over this little beck one
evening, and all my chums knew I was going, and he kissed me,
and he put his hands inside my bra, my little bra that I was wearing
– and I was absolutely staggered at this, and I went back, and they
all said, "How was he, what was it like?" you see, and I said, "He
put his hand into my bra . . . !" and they all fell about laughing,
because every one of them knew all about this – and that's awful.
I thought: Why did I say that?'

It is the pressures to have sex that come from other teenagers –
'peer group pressure' – that parents particularly dread. Yet parents
may themselves be responsible for similar pressures. Parents obviously don't encourage their daughters to have intercourse, but they
may give very clear messages about the status associated with sexual
activity. Mary, now in her seventies, remembers how her father
conveyed very clearly to her the relative places of academic success
and sexual attractiveness in society's valuation of women. 'My
father once said to me, when I brought home prizes from school
for good work, "Oh, Mary'll bring home the prizes, but Clara –"
that was my sister – "Clara'll get the boys." That absolutely stung
me, and I've never forgotten it. I was determined to show him that
I could bring home the boys too – it didn't matter if I didn't
particularly like them, but I'd got to show that I'd got a boyfriend.
Boys were just something to take home as a mark of the success
of your attractiveness really.'

With the exception of Sophie's story – for Sophie did at least
fancy her wonderful sultry boyfriend – pleasure scarcely figures in
these accounts. The reasons for choosing these activities or these
relationships are social, not sexual. The choices that Bernadette
and Marianne and Mary make have nothing to do with the anticipation of pleasure and everything to do with status and prestige and
social triumph. Given the problem that was posed for the prince

in the folk tale, it's pretty clear what kind of a bargain these girls would strike: a desirable lover to walk out with during the day – and ugliness in the bed at night.

WILL HE STOP WHEN I SAY?

Sex is for love, sex is for status; and in the complex sexual landscape that teenagers inhabit, sex is also fraught with danger. The double standard operates in a particularly blatant way in the sex lives of adolescent girls.

The Victorian feminists who campaigned to raise the age of consent sought to protect young girls from sexual abuse. But one grim by-product of the new law that they never intended was the creation of a new class of sexual delinquents. Soon more girls were being sent to reformatories for sex delinquency than for any other kind of misconduct.[6]

Unfortunately these cruel incarcerations cannot be located confidently in the past. In our own time, girls have been locked up for being promiscuous. Under the Children and Young Persons Act (1969), which was the main piece of legislation affecting children until the Children Act became law in October 1991, a child could be taken into care for being in 'moral danger' – and, according to the sexual values that hold sway at the social work case conference, 'moral danger' usually meant sleeping around, and was only ever applied to girls. So the girl who constantly ran away from local authority care and slept around might well be locked up in 'secure accommodation' in a children's home – though she had committed no crime. I had a girl to whom this had happened on my own case-load in the late 1980s. It is unthinkable that the same treatment would have been meted out to a heterosexual boy who ran away and slept around but committed no crime.

A less dramatic instance of the double standard is the use of the label 'slag'. The process by which girls are categorized and categorize each other in terms of sexual 'looseness' was first identified by Sue Lees and Celia Cowrie in their conversations with adolescents in the 1980s.[7] 'Slag' is a complex and infinitely flexible category. A girl may be a slag because she sleeps with lots of boys, or sleeps with her boyfriend, or talks to lots of boys, or keeps changing boyfriends. Elaborate dress codes play a part in these sexual definitions; to be a slag may simply mean you've left too many buttons undone. I remember how I felt about those girls at my school in

the sixties who stopped the runs in their stockings with nail varnish
that was pink, rather than the innocuous colourless stuff the rest
of us used. There was something not quite nice about the pink
nail varnish girls – but there was also a kind of glamour and bravado
that I envied. And this is the other side of being a 'slag'. In our
attitudes to the sexuality of teenage girls, contradictory frames of
reference exist side by side. The girl who is a slag might also be
perceived as sophisticated, sexually knowing, sexually generous; the
concept of the slag coexists with the concept of 'frigidity'. Sally
said, 'When I was a teenager – thirteen-plus – I had a lot of friends
who were I suppose boy mad, and went to parties and they were
kissing, and I found the whole experience absolutely revolting, I
wasn't interested at all. I was always teased about being frigid –
you know, "You're fri-gid" – and although it was partly a joke it
was partly serious, and that was very young, when they weren't
having intercourse, but it was the whole not wanting to be involved
in that. I did have a few revolting sloppy experiences, and it just
actually made me want to be sick.'

'Slag' as a category widely used by teenagers is relatively new;
women over thirty didn't recall it. There is then a sense in which
the greater frankness about sex and the wider variety of sexual
activities now open to the girl have actually increased the variety
of ways in which she can get it wrong, though the changed climate
has also, thank goodness, dramatically reduced the penalties for
sexual transgressions, for teenage pregnancies, though still con-
demned, are no longer cruelly punished as they once were. But
the girl's task now is in essence the same as it was for women who
were teenagers twenty or thirty years ago. She has to decide where
along the continuum from nice girl to slag, from frigidity to generosity, from purity to licence, she wants to place herself, and to fine-
tune her sexual activities so that they match that self-definition.
Her role is to be in control, to decide how far she will go. She has
to control both herself and him. Her sexual self-definition as slag
or frigid or something in between is entirely her own responsibility.
There is nothing mutual about it; the rules are that he will go
as far as he can – and she will decide how far is too far and stop
him.

Traditionally, this task has been spelled out by the girl's mother.
Few mothers of women I talked to had failed to warn their daughters that they must not let things go too far. Eve and Josephine
both had mothers who couched their admonitions in terms at once

lugubrious and evasive. Josephine said, 'Once I went to a party with my boyfriend, and she said, "Don't let him put his long thing in you."' Eve said, 'It had been drummed into me, "As soon as a boy ever touches you, keep your legs together, otherwise anything could happen ...", and when I did a bit of heavy petting at a party it felt as though the anything was about to happen so I think I was terribly tense and frightened of what might happen next.'

How do girls control things? Ruth, looking back sixty years to when she was sixteen, remembers that she had her own unique method of keeping in control: 'I always remember Michael Davis, he was terribly attractive – killed in the war. He was my brother's friend, three years older than me, and terribly sweet and gentle; he wrote to me a few times at school, and I always remember that my idea of heaven was going to call on Michael in my jodhpurs – and there were two reasons, one that I felt more attractive in those than anything else, and secondly I was safe because – I can remember it vaguely on the sofa, there'd be terribly risky things like hands creeping up – but I was in my jodhpurs so I was safe.'

For Ruth the method was successful without being preoccupying and the memory is a happy one. But Jennifer was in a constant state of anxiety with her first boyfriend because she didn't feel in control. 'It was a slight panic of, "Will he stop when I say?" Looking back, that was stupid, because I was more in control than I thought – I could just have walked away, couldn't I? I could have just not seen him. But at the time I felt he was in charge and I had to do what he wanted.' Jennifer highlights the dilemma for many girls. She is meant to stay in control – but she fears that if she exercises her right of veto, she will lose him.

The experience of having to control these early sexual experiences has a major impact on women's sexual histories. For the effects of this task on sexual arousal can be devastating. Amanda said, 'I remember after a party once there was this guy and I got off with him. There were lots of people in the same room and my best friend was getting off with someone else at the same time. I think he'd got to my breasts, and I just knew I didn't want him to get any further, I stopped him. But then the next time it happened with someone else I thought: I've got to sometime – and I didn't really want to. I felt very much I'd be laughed at if I didn't do things; there was a lot of peer pressure, a lot of the thought of them thinking I was a square. All the pressure probably inhibited quite a lot of my sexual feelings. You can never let yourself go, never just lie back and enjoy yourself.'

There are certain situations in which men seek to inhibit their arousal. Premature ejaculation is one such situation. Men may seek to control arousal and postpone ejaculation by doing mental arithmetic or reciting railway timetables: thinking about something else is a very effective inhibitor of sexual arousal, especially if the thinking includes complicated calculations. For teenage girls involved in sexual activity there may be similarly complex calculations going on in their heads: If he touches me *there*, what will happen next? If he touches me *there*, must I stop him? If I don't let him touch me *there*, will he leave me? A kiss or caress is tolerated or rejected for reasons that have little to do with how it feels. Every impulse to let go has to be controlled, every move analysed for its implications. A by-product of all this complex calculating is that, just as for the man reciting railway timetables, arousal is controlled, to a devastating extent.

There is another situation too in which the inhibition of male sexual arousal and sexual activity is the aim – in work with sex offenders. In his pioneering work with sex offenders at Grace-well Clinic, former probation officer Ray Wyre makes use of the concept of the 'aversive fantasy'. The offender learns to bring an aversive fantasy to bear on the forbidden dangerous fantasy. For instance, every time he thinks of having sex with children, he might also make himself think of the police coming in and arresting him.

The use of aversive fantasies has been found to be an effective therapeutic tool that discourages men from acting out their sexual fantasies. And teenage girls have very powerful aversive fantasies. For the girl who has been told she has to be in control – and that means every girl – the aversive fantasy is ever present, the fear that 'the anything is about to happen.'

In her relationships with boys, the average heterosexual adolescent girl may be using the most effective known methods of inhibiting sexual arousal.

LOSS OF VIRGINITY

What is being controlled, of course, is the loss of virginity. The aversive fantasy is about the possible dire consequences of inter-course – being called a slag, or staking everything and then losing

her boyfriend, or, at worst, the image of herself in a rented room
with a crying baby and life going on elsewhere.

One in eleven of the women I talked to lost their virginity through
an act of rape. What about the others, the ones who more or less
chose? What is loss of virginity like for women?

Bernadette (1981): 'I was going out with this guy, it was quite a
long-term relationship, the oral sex was very good, and it just happened. We used to fiddle about, it just kind of slipped in, and I
completely freaked out, I started screaming hysterically, it was over
in seconds and then I said things like, "You bastard, what have
you done to me?" I remember being really shocked, it was just all
too much, I'd spent all this time fighting blokes off and saying,
"No, no, we can do this but we can't do that." I don't know what
I was waiting for, I certainly didn't have the idea that you should
be a virgin when you got married, but I just didn't want to do it.
I kind of set myself apart from a lot of the other girls that I used
to hang around with, who used to sleep with different people at
parties, I had this inner pride that I wasn't like that and that people
wouldn't be talking about me because I would be the person that
you could only go a certain way with. And of course when it first
happened, I went into school and they made me go to Confession
and I did, I confessed it. I had to do ten Hail Mary's and promise
not to do it again – but of course we did!'

Fran (1969): 'My boyfriend went to university and he asked me to
the May Ball, and I suddenly realized I would have to stay there
overnight, and I didn't want to go. Then I heard he was going out
with someone else. I really regretted it then, I thought that I was
holding my virginity over him and that was a real power thing to
do and that wasn't right. So I went to the pub with my friend and
I picked up a quiet-looking boy, and I took him home, and we
tried to have sex. We had the telly on, and it was the first time in
my life I've found "Match of the Day" interesting. I don't think
he actually managed it, but I knew so little about it that I honestly
don't know. Then I met the man who became my husband, and I
thought he looked like Jesus, and he looked wonderful. And he
asked me out for a drink, and I said "Yes," and he took me to this
country pub, and asked what I wanted to drink, and I said, "Orange
juice" because I didn't drink, and he said, "Are you a virgin?" and
I was really pleased to be able to say "No".'

Jennifer (1971): 'The summer before, when I'd been working in a café, that was the first time I'd really gone out with a boy, and he'd been groping me all over and saying, "I'd really like to . . ." and I said, "No" categorically to that, so presumably by the next summer it seemed quite normal that I would, whoever I was with, almost. I don't really remember anything about it – but I do remember I was stunned by his penis getting bigger. When he said, "Put your hand down here," I didn't know what it was. I'll never forget that, just the amazement of that. Then I stayed with him all the time I was at college. There was this feeling – now I've screwed with him, it had better be something serious. I mean, we were engaged. Stupid, looking back – this idea that just because something like that had happened it therefore had to be a serious relationship.'

Anne (1967): 'We were both absolutely shattered after this incredibly long white wedding and all the family rows that had preceded it. We got inside that flat, we shut the front door and it was, "Right, come on, let's do it! We're married now, let's do it!" and poor John couldn't get it up – thank God I had the sense to say to him, "It's just because you're tired, don't worry about it." We went to sleep, and the next morning he didn't have any trouble at all. But it was very much something that had to be got through. I wasn't aroused, I must have been really dry. I don't remember it particularly hurting but it was certainly not a wonderful experience by any means. It was a bit like having a vaginal examination at the doctor's: you get into the most comfortable position – "Are you sure you're alright? Right, I'm going to do it now. OK, here I come!"'

Amanda (1985): 'I remember lying in the bath when I was about twelve and feeling that kind of sexual warmth for the first time, when you feel really turned on. I was thinking: Is this what it's going to be like? When I first had sex with a boy, I found it wasn't!
   'I was eighteen. I really wanted to lose my virginity, because I'd had this thing about my virginity, and I thought, When I'm eighteen I can. Then when I was eighteen I was in France and I was going out with this Danish guy and we weren't actually having sex and we were both shy and couldn't go out and buy a condom. And a friend of mine, as a joke, sent me a condom because she'd been to the family planning clinic – she thought I'd lost my virginity years ago – and I said to Erik, "Look what I've got in the post!" and he said, "So what?" and I said, "Ooh maybe we'll use it

sometime," and we spoke in French to each other and I remember standing in the corridor saying, "Je veux. Oui, oui. Tu comprends?" and him saying, "What're you talking about?" Eventually we did have sex, and I didn't tell him I was a virgin because I thought he'd think I was really immature. I thought it was awful, actually, the first time, I think I was quite frightened. It wasn't painful, just like nothing particularly. I think it would have been better if I'd told him, it was stupid keeping up the pretence of being so sophisticated. Because a year later he said to me, "Were you a virgin?" And I didn't lie, I just said, "Well, what do you think?" Shit!'

Virginity is of course a patriarchal concept, a way of assessing a woman's worth in a society based on the laws of patrilineal inheritance. Virginity also has certain subsidiary meanings – being pure, immaculate, innocent, inviolable. Virginity confers a kind of power. As Angela Carter wrote of her virginal Red Riding Hood in *A Company of Wolves*: 'She is an unbroken egg; she is a sealed vessel; she has inside her a magic space the entrance to which is shut with a plug of membrane; she is a closed system; she does not know how to shiver.'[8]

In general, as patriarchy as a formal system disintegrates, these older meanings of virginity are withering away, though not nearly as quickly as might be presumed from media messages about sexuality. When Lady Diana married Prince Charles, for instance, her virginal status was publicly affirmed by her uncle. The subsidiary meaning of virginity – virginity as purity or sinlessness – is also still accorded significance in some religious contexts, and plenty of women still prefer to be virgins when they get married for religious reasons. And of course the very existence of the concept 'slag' depends on the persistence of the idea of female purity. If there were no good girls, there could be no slags.

But since the sixties, virginity has also acquired certain new meanings that derive essentially from 'sexual liberation' ideas. According to these new meanings, sexual experience equals sophistication. From the sexual liberation perspective, the 'loss' of virginity is actually a gain, wanting to stay a virgin is about 'inhibitions', and to be a virgin in your twenties is to lay yourself open to charges of 'frigidity'.

Anne, who married young and is now in her mid-forties, lost her virginity under the old dispensation: nice girls don't, wait till marriage. But in the other stories I've quoted, the stories of younger

women, the old and new meanings of virginity and its loss clash
with and contradict one another. It is because of the old meanings
that a girl will set herself rules about when and how she will lose
her virginity – I've got to be in love, I'll wait till I'm eighteen, it's
got to be the right person, it's got to be someone special. Or she
stands the 'in love' justification for sex on its head, and thinks, like
Jennifer, 'Now I've done it, it's got to be a serious relationship,'
and stays with her first sexual partner even though she doesn't like
him anymore. And it is because of the old meanings too that she
may make moral judgements about what she's done. She thinks
afterwards, 'Was that a nice thing to do?' or she feels, like Fran,
that she's lost the ability to say to other people, 'I'm better than
you'. Sometimes the moral judgements may be loaded onto her by
someone else – the boyfriend who made Marianne feel she was a
whore because she'd had sex once with a previous boyfriend, or
the priest who – in 1981 – made Bernadette do penance for having
sex.

Then there are the new meanings – sexual experience as sophistication, and loss of virginity as a sign of maturity. A woman may
decide that she must lose her virginity before she takes a further
step into the adult world: I mustn't be a virgin when I get to
university / start my nurse-training / move to London. This is
virginity as a source of embarrassment, an encumbrance more
suited to an earlier life-stage, like taking a teddy bear to junior
school. In a fascinating reversal of how things used to be, and still
are in many cultures, a woman may now hide the fact of her virginity. In Japan, a woman who has had sex before marriage can go to
a 'hymen rebirth' clinic to fake virginity and make her body fit with
the patriarchal requirements,[9] but what Amanda faked was *loss* of
virginity, even though to admit to her lack of experience might have
made for a more enjoyable time for her. Another part of the new
definition of virginity is the sense that sex is expected. It's what
you have to do eventually if you have a boyfriend, it's part of a
progression. Once you're on the roller-coaster of a relationship,
it's very hard to get off – I went this far last summer, this summer
I'll have to do it. The new meanings may also enable a woman to
feel good about her loss of virginity, and to feel that her self-image
has been enhanced, and that she has a new sophistication – I may
drink orange juice, but I'm not a virgin.

What is most striking about these accounts is the complete
absence of any reference to pleasure – pleasure hoped for, experi-

enced or fondly remembered. I found women highly sardonic about their first experiences of intercourse. Over the last twenty years, enough has been shared about female sexual experiences for us to know that our remembered feelings of disappointment are normal, and that we were not uniquely unlucky. Women are sardonic now in anticipation as well as in memory. I found girls of fourteen or fifteen quite sceptical about the anticipated pleasures of first sex – 'It'll hurt'. This refreshing scepticism has been fostered by the increasing availability of realistic representations of first sex alongside the romantic magazine images. For instance, Judy Blume's teen novel, *Forever*, has a detailed and very real account of a first sexual experience: the book is incidentally highly recommended by mothers of adolescent girls for its incentive effect on previously reluctant readers.[10]

What women recall, then, is not pleasure, but the convolutions of 'Should I or shouldn't I?' There are moral complexities here worthy of medieval theologians. In an essay on teenage sexual experience, Sharon Thompson suggests that the process of sexual maturation and sexual experience for the adolescent boy is a kind of quest.[11] But for the girl it is perhaps more a Pilgrim's Progress, a passage between conflicting moral and social imperatives, as she treads the narrow path between the Vale of Frigidity and the Abyss of the Slags in the hope of eventually coming to the City of Sexual Sophistication. This is not a great adventure but a perilous journey towards an acceptable sexual self-definition.

Occasionally the most difficult aspect of loss of virginity is not the mental debate but the physical act itself. Josephine's story is a reminder that loss of virginity can be a physical ordeal. 'I met a man and he was really nice. Neither of us had slept with anyone else, and he sort of attempted to deflower me and I was very tight and nervous and frightened, and I couldn't do it. He kept trying and he kept sort of hitting a brick wall, nothing happened. I went sloping off to the local hospital, and I saw a chap in the gynaecology department there, he must have thought I was a nut, I said, "I hope this doesn't sound silly but he's sort of bigger than me," and he said, "Yeah, yeah, that's how it is," but I didn't know, I couldn't understand how a great big penis could get into such a tiny opening. He sent me away with a glass penis used for these purposes, which I was supposed to experiment with in a hot bath. So I had a go at this glass penis, and I didn't do well, and Robert was an absolute endless paragon of sensitivity and patience, he kept doing a little

more each time until I could accept it, and then I got into the swing
of it with him. We lived together for three years, and we had a
normal neither good nor bad sex life. I was aware that by then
everybody else was having sex lives, so I was glad to be in the swing
of it. But the sex with Robert never really spoke to me in any real
way. Not as much as losing a stone . . .'

For Josephine, loss of virginity is totally about the new meanings;
just to be able to do it is a relief. This is sexual intercourse as a
passport to adult life – sex is all about being grown-up, joining the
human race, being like everyone else. This is what people do.
There is no pleasure here, because the experience is so painful
and physically difficult.

Sara's story could not be more different. But even here, when
the experience is at its most delightful, it is still not about physical
pleasure. Sara said, 'It was in Poland. I had a cousin in Poland
that was older than me, that I'd never met before – so it wasn't
brotherly. A good-looking guy! We spent a month together with
other cousins, and then at the end of the month we both went
down to my auntie's house in the mountains. There was another
cousin there too, a girl, and I'd seen the bedroom we'd all be
sleeping in: there was a double bed and a single bed, and I'd
thought the bloke would go in the single bed and me and the girl
in the double bed, and she went off earlier than we did, and when
we went into the room she was in the single bed . . . We'd spent
a month together petting and not doing anything, and yet it just all
seemed right, it just happened really, and it was nice because I
thought he was wonderful and we'd had this wonderful romantic
month together and it was all just wonderful . . . See, I remember
it being emotionally wonderful, but I don't remember having an
orgasm . . .'

This is loss of virginity as many of us would like it to be for our
daughters. There is something a little apart and special about the
setting, in the house in the mountains, and the emotional backdrop
is perfect too, as sexual intimacy grows spontaneously out of a
romantic but relaxed relationship. But even for Sara in her moun-
tain idyll, loss of virginity is not about orgasm: that's something
else.

FIRST ORGASM

The romantic notion of loss of virginity includes the promise of orgasm. For the girl or woman whose sexual explorations with her partner have not included penetration, and who has only derived limited pleasure from those explorations, it is easy to assume that all that is needed to make things right is intercourse. As Melissa remarked, 'I used to think that when you had penile penetration, that was it: you orgasmed. I didn't realize it went beyond that, that that was a very minor thing.'

The belief in the uniquely arousing power of intercourse for the woman is one of our most prevalent sexual myths. In male mythology, this belief takes the form of reverence for the magic phallus that will magically 'fix' the woman – 'All she needs is a good fuck.' In women's romantic fiction, there is the assumption that a woman's sexuality can be unlocked by the right man: the Mills and Boon heroine has her first shattering orgasm when she finally loses her virginity to the steel-eyed, mean-jawed hero. Yet first intercourse and first orgasm are of course quite separate. They only 'come together' in pornographic or romantic fictions.

When she lost her virginity in the house in the mountains, Sara had already experienced plenty of orgasmic pleasure from masturbation. 'But I really did think,' she said, 'that orgasms were my little secret and that only I had them.' First orgasm is the other initiation – and many women remember it more vividly than first intercourse.

Bernadette said, 'I started masturbating at about twelve or thirteen. It kind of just happened – you think: God, what was that? It was very good but what was it? And I associated it with this nail-varnish remover that I'd been using that night, and there was a strong smell of it in my bedroom, and I thought it had to do with the fact that I'd inhaled all this nail-varnish remover, and so I used to sniff it first before I did it after that, till I realized you didn't have to sniff nail-varnish remover in order to do it. It has funny associations for my friend as well, 'cos she'd actually lent it to me, and I ended up using it all for this purpose, and she was really cross 'cos I'd used her whole bottle of nail-varnish remover, and I couldn't tell her why.'

Michelle said, 'I was about fifteen, I can't remember how I heard the word "masturbation", but my parents had a medical dictionary, and I looked it up in the dictionary, and found out what it was, and tried it out, and until then I'd got absolutely no idea. This sounds ridiculous, but it must have been just before Christmas, and I was still at the stage when I used to get terribly excited about Christmas, and I remember, having masturbated, feeling sleepy and tired and wanting to go straight to sleep, and I can remember thinking: On Christmas Eve if I do this I'll be able to go straight to sleep!'

Eve said, 'I thought I was having them for years. With my husband, I thought the crescendo of excitement was an orgasm. When I joined women's groups I started hearing other women talking about their orgasms, and I started thinking that something didn't sound quite right about mine. Then when I was about twenty-eight, I was on my own, and I was reading some sort of pornography, and that went on about clitorises, and really that was the first time I'd ever thought I might have such a thing. So I started to explore, and bang.'

Emily said, 'I never got anywhere near coming with my first husband and when I left him I decided to try and do something about it. I tried to masturbate, but I didn't feel anything. Then I read something about vibrators – so I got out my Pifco massager I'd bought years before for my bad back, and I tried it, and I knew I was on the edge of one in about ten seconds, and it alarmed me rather, so I stopped. Next night I poured a large Martini, put on my favourite music, and did it. I was totally thrilled, amazed.'

Having an orgasm, like any other physical experience that involves control of primarily involuntary processes, is a skill that has several stages: having the experience, knowing what made it happen and how to make it happen again, trying out different kinds of stimulation to find out what works best, and learning to regulate and postpone it to intensify the feeling. For most of us, a lot of learning goes on between the first surprising involuntary experience and the point at which orgasm can be integrated into sex with a partner.

Bernadette, Michelle, Eve and Emily show us the first step on the way. Bernadette has the experience, but can't name it, and doesn't understand what caused it. For the other three women, the process is more conscious; it is knowledge they need, and the orgasm follows quickly from the knowledge. Eve merely needs to know she has a clitoris. For Michelle the initial impulse is intellectual curiosity. With admirable enterprise, she gets hold of the information she needs and puts it to good use. According to Kinsey, this is quite a common process. Kinsey found that women who began masturbating as teenagers often started simply because they'd heard that it was possible, and for teenage girls the most common source of information was something that they had read, whereas boys were more likely to hear about masturbation from friends.[12] For Emily it is more difficult; where women start to masturbate in adolescence or continue to masturbate in adolescence, orgasms come easily, but for the woman who has never masturbated – or who gave up at age five – orgasms may be harder to achieve.

But what I find most significant about these accounts is the ages of the women. Bernadette and Michelle were teenagers, but Eve and Emily were both in their late twenties. Among the women I talked to who were orgasmic, first orgasm had happened at virtually any age. The lowest age at first orgasm was four, the highest was fifty-two. There was only a slight cluster in adolescence. Kinsey also remarks on this: 'There is a slight but no marked upsurge in the incidence and frequency of arousal and orgasm during adolescence.'[13] This is in marked contrast to the male pattern, with virtually all men masturbating to orgasm for the first time in adolescence. For women, first sex and first orgasm are not just discrete events; in some women's lives they are decades apart.

DOES YOUNG EQUAL SEXY FOR WOMEN?

One woman I talked to remembered with pleasure how she'd had an orgasm during her first experience of intercourse. This woman is now in her late fifties, and she lost her virginity on her wedding night when she was twenty-four.

There are good reasons for her very unusual experience. She was a knowledgeable woman who had always felt that 'knowing about sex was part of being a complete human being', and, prior to the marriage, she and her partner had enjoyed sexual activity to orgasm, though without penetration. But I would suggest that the age at which she lost her virginity may also be a factor that contributed to her happy experience. Age at first intercourse is an important variable in pleasure. Women who had their first experience of intercourse in their mid-twenties were much more likely to say they enjoyed it than women who had been much younger – a fact that is particularly intriguing given that women who hadn't lost their virginity till their mid-twenties had invariably grown up in an age of greater sexual ignorance.

Age is not only a factor in whether women recall first intercourse with pleasure: the degree of general sexual interest that women recall from all early sexual activity also seems to vary with age. Some women said they derived no pleasure at all from teenage sexual activity and would simply rather not have done it, and several women told me they had had virtually no genital sexual feelings at all till their mid-twenties. Some of those who thoroughly enjoyed 'heavy petting' in their teenage years said they would have been happier keeping it at that, rather than moving on to intercourse.

Women's hopes and fears for their daughters also tell us something about the relationship between age and pleasure. When I asked women what advice they might give to a teenage daughter, real or imagined, women said almost without exception that they would want her not to start having sex too soon.

Much of this advice may be rooted in maternal protectiveness, for when we think about our daughters starting their sexual lives, the physical dangers of sex will be in the forefront of our minds. First there are worries about AIDS: postponing intercourse also postpones these worries a little. Then there are physical risks that are specific to the girl. There is, for instance, the research which suggests that there is a higher risk of developing cervical cancer for girls who have intercourse before the cervix is fully mature.[14] There is also of course the pregnancy issue. Putting on one side for a moment the social issues around teenage pregnancy, there are physical concerns too when very young women get pregnant. Adolescent pregnancy is associated with anaemia, retarded foetal growth, premature labour, underweight babies and complicated births. In Japan, teenage mothers are twice as likely to die in labour as their older sisters, and in developing countries like Bangladesh, babies born to teenage mothers are around 50 per cent more likely to die in their first year of life.[15] The risks for the very young woman and her baby are considerably greater than the risks for the 'geriatric primagravida' about which we hear so much.

There is no doubt that such concerns go some way to account for women's hopes that their daughters won't start having sex 'too soon'. But there is surely another factor too. Women want their daughters to have a better sex life than they had themselves. They don't want their daughters to repeat their own mistakes – and for many women who grew up since the sixties, one sexual mistake they felt they made was to start having sex 'too young'. I found that it was those women who started having sex earliest themselves

who most hoped their daughters would wait a little longer, women
like Hilary, who started having sex at fourteen: 'I thought, You're
not grown-up if you don't do it, and he'll just go away, and I hate
it now, I hate to think of it. It was awful really, it was nothing.'
Behind women's injunctions to their daughters lies the reality of
their own experience – that intercourse at too young an age is not
a source of pleasure.

The idea that men reach their sexual peak at around seventeen
and women at around forty was first suggested by Kinsey's data,[16]
and has been confirmed by various studies since. It's a theory that
goes some way to explain why so many girls derive so little pleasure
from teenage sex. And it also accounts for the prevalence of adolescent sexual activity despite many girls' limited pleasure in it, for
male sexual concerns, as usual, shape sexual conduct, and the
driving force behind teenage sex is the sexual preoccupation of the
teenage boy, for whom sex is typically a more urgent concern than
at any other stage in the life cycle.

The concept of the sexual peak inevitably raises the question –
is it cultural or biological? Or, to put it another way, what would
a woman's sexual life cycle be like in a society in which female
sexuality was less suppressed than our own? If sexual knowledge
were more available to teenage girls, and sexual pleasure were a
more acceptable goal for girls, would women still not be reaching
their sexual peak till forty?

It may be helpful to make a distinction between orgasmic capacity
and sexual interest. What does seem likely is that the availability
of greater sexual knowledge and the potential for more successful
self-assertions by girls would make orgasmic pleasure in sexual
activity much more available to young women. If girls knew how
to have an orgasm, and could really decide for themselves whether
they wanted sex, girls' early experiences would surely be much more
enjoyable, and those events which are now sometimes separated by
decades – first intercourse and first orgasm – might coincide more
closely. In a society where those conditions were met, we might
find more teenage girls experiencing pleasure during sex. But if
there is any biological basis in the notion of the sexual peak, we
might also find more teenage girls in such a society deciding they're
simply not interested, and channelling their libidinous energies
into learning the saxophone, playing football or studying nuclear
physics.

Such a choice is very hard to make today, amid all the media messages which assert that because Young is Beautiful and Beautiful is Sexy, then Young must inevitably be Sexy. The situation is riddled with paradox for girls. Our sexual culture with one hand holds out the promise of sexual fulfilment to the teenage girl – 'Have sex now, these are your golden days, you will never be as beautiful, as sexual, again' – and with the other hand snatches the possibility of sexual fulfilment away, by denying girls the necessary conditions to make the most basic act of sexual self-assertion – to ask 'What do I really want?' It's a situation that spells sexual disaster for teenage girls.

CHAPTER SIX

Young Women Without Children:
Cosmopolitan Woman

Cosmopolitan magazine was founded in the United States in 1972. Especially under the editorship of Helen Gurley Brown, author of *Sex and the Single Girl*, *Cosmopolitan* came to epitomize an ideal of liberated and assertive female sexuality. I've suggested that self-knowledge and the capacity for self-assertion are essential if women are to enjoy their sex lives. These are attributes that Cosmopolitan Woman is assumed to have in abundance.

The sexuality of Cosmopolitan Woman continues to be a matter of great public interest. In fact the public view of female sexuality is focused almost exclusively on her: the young childless sexually active woman is the subject of virtually everything that is written about female sexuality. And there are plenty of reasons why she might be expected to embody that ideal of liberated sexuality. She is the most obvious beneficiary of the changes in sexual customs that have followed from the widespread availability of contraception and the decline of patriarchy in its pure form. She controls her fertility, and few will condemn her for having a succession of partners. Though not yet at her sexual peak, she is physically more mature and probably more self-confident than the teen-ager, and since she has no children, her sexual relationships will probably be the most important intimate relationships in her life, and she may be prepared to invest a lot of energy and time in them.

The *Cosmopolitan* fantasy has become the benchmark by which all women judge their sex lives. Cosmopolitan Woman is assumed to be having what she wants when she wants it – lots of orgasms, sex at times of her own choosing, and patterns of love-making that meet her needs. How far does women's experience fit with these high hopes, at the time of their lives when women seem to have most going for them?

STILL FAKING AFTER ALL THESE YEARS

Melissa said, 'I've never had an orgasm. I'm thirty-one now and I
think I've got to the age where I don't think it matters. I'd love to
have a Mercedes SEL, but if I don't have one, I don't mind – I'd
love to have one, but I suppose I never will. The thing is, at the
beginning we did everything bar sex, we would be masturbating
each other, he'd come and everything, and I'd sort of go, "Phew,
wow," and he'd think I'd come. He still doesn't know about me
not having orgasms. Women are good at faking. We haven't had
sex for three months now. Perhaps this is why, because I don't
want to go through it any more, because I'm not getting that much
pleasure. I've got to do something about it or else our sex life is
over. But I don't know where to go or what to do. The poor
man . . .

   'I'm good in bed. It's almost like a challenge – you accept you're
not going to orgasm – so you think, Well, how good can I get then?
Oh I used to go on all night, literally all night. And I've learned
that men like this, they like that, and at the end of the day he goes
"Wow, that was fucking great!" you know. It's a power thing, you
get pleasure in a different way. You get pleasure because you've
got that power that you can make them do whatever you want.'

In the great orgasm debate there is a voice that jars. Even among
pro-woman writers there is often an air of weariness, as though
women were forever harping on about not having orgasms. Here,
for instance, is Erica Jong: 'Some day every woman will have
orgasms – like every family has color TV – and we can all get on
with the real business of life.'[1]
   Yet there are in fact a great many women for whom the subject
is closed. As Shere Hite found, 'an enormous number of women'
fake orgasms.[2] There were few women I talked to who had never
faked, and much of this faking goes on during *Cosmopolitan
Woman*'s decade. Among the women I interviewed, it was the *norm*
to fake some or all of the time at twenty-five: those who hadn't
faked at least some of the time in their mid-twenties were in the
minority.
   Looking back to her early twenties when she had always faked,
Bernadette said, 'I thought that was what women did.' As little
girls, we may share our sexual discoveries with our friends, telling
them about the wonderful feelings we can get from climbing ropes

or rolling around with blankets between our legs. As adult women, we share another kind of secret knowledge – the knowledge that women fake. This is the private counterpoint to the public sexual theme that all young women are having a wonderful time in bed.

Women who never fake can be rather moralistic about women who do. And women who do fake tend to feel bad about it. Christine said, 'It's a difficult feeling to put into words, I wanted to shut that feeling out, didn't want to think about it even. It was just something that I didn't want to face. Something that it was easier just not to deal with.' Yet, viewed as a sociological phenomenon, faking warrants congratulation rather than censure. Faking orgasm is part of a long tradition of clever female sexual subterfuge, today's equivalent of the blood-soaked sponge that a woman in other times might have concealed in her vagina on her wedding night. In both cases, women have used a degree of base cunning to cope with an impossible male demand – the demand that we bleed on first intercourse, even though the hymen may tear in the course of daily life, or the demand that we have orgasms without adequate stimulation.

Faking orgasm can also be seen as one end of a continuum of sexual pretending. There may be elements of acting and pretending in even the happiest sexual relationships. Sex is a social performance as well as a physical experience, and there may be a fine dividing line between playing and really meaning it – as there was for some of the pubescent girls in Chapter 2 who practised kissing with their girl friends. Amanda mused on this: 'If I try and put myself in a good mood at the beginning of the day, I'll often end up in a better mood, even if I fake it at the beginning, and I think sometimes with sex if I ... not exactly fake it, but *make* myself, even though I'm really tired – if I push myself into the feeling of it – I nearly always enjoy it. It's awful, but I hardly ever actually feel like it, I'd always rather read a book and lie in bed with a hot-water bottle, and Greg is the same, and yet when we've had sex, we lie there afterwards saying, "Why don't we have sex more often?"' But though Amanda pushes herself into the feeling at the start of sex, in the end for her the pleasure is real. Acting as though you're in the mood at the start of sex is one thing: acting all the way through, because you don't have an orgasm, is quite another. It is surely deeply sad that so many women feel they have to fake, because they are missing out on the most intense of physical pleasures.

Some women, however, may protest at the idea that not having

an orgasm is necessarily missing out: they will explain that you can
still enjoy sex without orgasms. Melissa did at one time, though
what she enjoyed most was her skill in making love to her partner
and giving him pleasure, a source of enjoyment that has always
been permitted to women. But there is a sound physiological basis
for enjoying sex without orgasm. Sex therapist Helen Kaplan has
refined Masters and Johnson's model of sexual response, which
suggested there was a continuous process of arousal leading to a
plateau of excitement leading to orgasm.[3] Helen Kaplan suggests
that there are actually two relatively separate systems involved in
sexual response.[4] For women these two systems are lubrication/
swelling and orgasm: for men, erection and ejaculation. So you
can have an orgasm without being very aroused – without much
lubrication and swelling – and you can have the pleasures of very
intense sexual arousal accompanied by lubrication and swelling
without an orgasm.

But even when women have enjoyed sex without orgasm, they
find orgasmic sex quite different. Jennifer said, 'When I started
having orgasms, I would actually initiate sex more – I would cycle
back to his flat in order to screw at lunchtime – or I would get up
in the morning and then ten minutes before I was due to go out
we'd both get back into bed. And I suspect that was because I felt
there was something for me out of it for the first time.' Penny said,
'I didn't have orgasms, but I still enjoyed sex a lot. When I got to
be twenty-seven or twenty-eight it started to bother me a bit, but
not particularly because I still enjoyed the sex. I didn't realize that
I could enjoy it that much more through having them.'

When sex includes orgasm, women enjoy sex more, are more
likely to initiate it, feel 'there's something for me out of it'. And
once women get used to having them, sex without orgasm is no
longer good enough. June said, 'If I don't have an orgasm, it's
terrible, I can't stand it, I have to get rid of that tension. Like
building up to a sneeze and then the sneeze doesn't come out: very
very frustrating. I'm terribly on tenterhooks inside myself until I
can have an orgasm.' Women are often warned of the dire consequences for men of sexual arousal without ejaculation, the so-called
'blue balls' syndrome. This is assumed to be one of the sexual
differences between men and women, and one of the reasons why
ejaculation is so important to men, whereas women can cope without orgasm. But when women are sexually aroused without orgasm,
there is a vasocongestive reaction that can be equally painful.

Kinsey found that a quarter of women who had had any petting experience 'reported pains in the groin which were similar to those which males frequently experience when they are erotically aroused and fail to reach orgasm.'[5] There is no name for this phenomenon, and unlike its male equivalent it is never used as a dreadful warning to partners whose sexual techniques leave something to be desired.

Even where women don't suffer from back or groin pain after sex without orgasm, or, like June, from a terrible feeling of tension, convincing yourself that it doesn't matter is difficult. Even where a woman can masturbate to orgasm on her own, to accept that you're usually or always inorgasmic during sex with a loved partner means making a difficult adjustment to your sexual aspirations. And it can only ever be a temporary adjustment. Sooner or later it starts to matter: sooner or later the faking has to stop.

Melissa arrived at this point after having a baby. With the loss of interest in sex that is so common after childbirth (see Chapter 7), her customary sexual performance came to seem pointless. Five years later, when she talked to me, her interest in sex with her partner had still not returned. She felt she had got to the point where she had to 'do something' or her marriage would be over.

Fifteen years ago, Emily had also felt she had to 'do something' about not having orgasms. She said, 'I bought a book called *Understanding the Female Orgasm*. What it said was that if you didn't have orgasms it was all to do with your relationship to your father. Well, I'd had a really good relationship with my father. The book depressed me, because it made me feel there was no solution to my problem.' Seymour Fisher, the sex researcher who wrote *Understanding the Female Orgasm*, suggested that women who didn't have orgasms were unable to let themselves go because they couldn't trust the person they loved.[6] His theory is yet another manifestation of the 'dark continent' idea of female sexuality – the idea that female sexuality is intrinsically mysterious, and emotional rather than physical in its essential nature. Seymour Fisher's ideas are no longer accepted by sex therapists, but theories like his still influence our thinking about female sexuality, especially our thinking about orgasms. Melissa's friends, for instance, tended to attribute her lack of orgasms to 'hang-ups'. The psychological theories – whether they have the sophistication of Seymour Fisher's, or the hand-me-down wisdom of the 'hang-up' theory – all locate the problem in the woman's mind and emotions, rather than in her behaviour. A pre-orgasmic woman who is aware of such theories will think, not 'What are we doing wrong?' but 'There must be something wrong with me.'

Yet the most obvious difference between women who are easily orgasmic in their twenties and women who aren't has nothing to do with 'inhibitions', trust in men, or any other psychological attribute. It is rather the presence or absence in their sexual histories of a particular piece of behaviour – adolescent masturbation. This is clear from the Kinsey report, which actually predates Seymour Fisher by twenty years: Kinsey found that masturbation before marriage meant more orgasms during marriage.[7] Women mostly learn to have orgasms as men do, by masturbating. And though the lessons of childhood masturbation are often forgotten, as we saw in Chapter 2, and the experience remains separate from adult sexuality, women who masturbate in adolescence are able to carry that knowledge through into adult life and adult sexual relationships.

If Melissa went to a sex therapist now, she would be taught to masturbate, probably by using a vibrator, and she would also be encouraged to fantasize. She might be given certain exercises – Kegel exercises – to strengthen the muscles of her pelvic floor: many women are unaware of the crucial importance of good muscle tone in the pelvic floor for orgasm. She might be encouraged to experiment with deliberately tensing her muscles as she gets aroused: the common notion that women need to 'relax' to achieve orgasm is of course rooted in the 'Sleeping Beauty' notion of female sexual passivity and is self-evidently counterproductive. She would also be helped to cope with the embarrassment she might feel about doing some of these things; as Annie said, 'Those books that tell you to pour yourself a stiff gin and have a good fumble make me curl up inside . . .'

The research suggests that the most effective element in this treatment programme is the vibrator. Studies on the effectiveness of sex therapy at Guy's and the Maudsley hospitals found that it was the vibrator that made the difference: most of the women who didn't experiment with a vibrator failed to become orgasmic.[8] Where a woman has forgotten how to masturbate, she may need a more powerful reminder than fingers can provide, and the pathway to sexual pleasure may have to be traced out on her body quite forcefully for a while. It is an intriguing reflection of the dominance of male sexuality that, even here, in the design of sex aids intended solely for women, male sexual values intrude. In an article about sex toys in *Marie Claire*, David Delvin writes, 'The realistic vibrator is designed to look like a man's penis and therefore fits the woman's vagina rather better than the standard vibrator ... The Grafenbourg Rouser has a bend in it, the idea being that the tip could touch the famous G-spot.'[9] The assumption behind the design of these vibrators, an assumption that David Delvin never questions, is that women use vibrators for penetration. Yet inserting something into the vagina is a masturbation method used by only 1.5 per cent of women.[10] Vibrating imitation penises are not particularly useful for stimulating the clitoris, and women are likely to find a massager sold to soothe sore muscles, or the back of an electric toothbrush, more sexually satisfying than the purpose-built model.

If a woman like Melissa tries out these techniques, either under the guidance of a sex therapist or by following a self-help programme,[11] she can very quickly change. Sex therapists report that a woman who has never had orgasms is one of the easiest clients to help.[12] Two of the women whom I talked to had suddenly learned to have orgasms in their late twenties – one during pregnancy, often a time of heightened interest, and one by using a vibrator: both had moved quickly from having no orgasms to having reliable multiple orgasms. 'I'd love to have a Mercedes SEL,' says Melissa wistfully; both the car and the orgasm seem like impossible dreams. But the sexual dream may be much more easily realized than she imagines.

For Melissa, as for many women, it is the faking that was once the answer to the problem that now stands in the way of finding a more satisfactory solution. If a woman who has faked decides that she wants to change, she may find herself with little room for manoeuvre. Before she can change, she has to tell her partner about the faking – in effect, to present him with a completely revised version of their whole sexual life together. Perhaps she faked to avoid the self-assertion of saying, 'This isn't working for me,' but it takes a much more difficult act of assertion to admit she has faked, in order to try and find out what will work. Two women I talked to had done this, and their relationships had survived and been strengthened. It is cheering to know that at least in some sexual relationships, such honesty is possible.

When a relationship is falling apart, the secret may be told with a different intent. Bernadette said, 'I faked right through our marriage. When we were splitting up I did the most awful thing and told Faisal that's what I'd always done, and I think now I must have gutted him. You can imagine. But I was into gutting him then.' What a hostage to fortune this is – that at any time she can tell him the whole thing was a fake.

How do we get ourselves into the faking trap in the first place? Very easily, it seems. When Melissa and her partner were first making love, she would express her pleasure in sighs or moans, he would think she had come, and she didn't disillusion him. Women smiled wryly as they told me that men never seemed to realize that they'd faked, or even seemed to encourage them to do it. Sophie said, 'I'm not very good at faking orgasms. I think I've probably tried, yes, and I think it's very easy to fool a man and make them think they're doing alright. If I feel it's really going to hurt them if I don't come – I'll go along with it a bit and pretend, and I'm always amazed that they think, It's working!' Liz said, 'I was never into faking. The first time I slept with Neville, he said, "Did you come last night?" And I said, "No, I never do," and he said, "Oh I thought you'd come, I thought we came together," and I said, "No, I didn't," and he said "Oh ... Are you *sure* you didn't come?"'

What happens if you don't come and don't fake? Alex said, 'God, he was a bastard, this bloke, he knew nothing and he put it all on me and said, "Oh, you're obviously frigid – you never have an orgasm, so you're obviously pretty young and you aren't mature enough to have one." And he told me that he'd actually said to his Mum and his sister, "Oh Alex can't come," and I was like – "*What*!" and he said, "Oh well, my sister said 'I come all the while, my boyfriend just has to touch me and I'm there,"' and I was like ... "*God*!"'

Women who are pre-orgasmic are often even more troubled by what their partners say about them than by the knowledge that they are missing out on the most intense of physical pleasures: like Alex, they may be unfavourably compared to others, or labelled 'frigid'. The woman feels she has to come – not for herself, but to please her partner, or to avoid his censure.

Somewhere along the way since 'sexual liberation', women's orgasms have been appropriated by men. This is one of the most startling developments in the suppression of female sexuality over the last twenty years. Women today may have marginally more orgasms than women who were young thirty years ago, but so often orgasmic pleasure still isn't for ourselves. Since the 1960s, the female sex partner has taken on certain new sexual duties. It's not enough to make love with him willingly, she also has a duty to show she enjoys it, and above all she has to come – for *him*.

Look at the reasons why women fake.

'If I'd nearly got there, nearly nearly got there, and it just didn't happen, well, how long can you go on for? So then I'd fake it to get it over with and not to damage his ego.'

'I do it so as to avoid the inquisition: "Why didn't you come?" "Well, I just didn't." "Why not?" "It doesn't matter." It's irritating, very much so.'

'I fake so as not to offend! A way of saying, "Thanks very much, you can stop now!"'

'I felt I ought to be having an orgasm because I was in some way insulting him by not having one – the pressure of what you read makes you feel that you ought to be experiencing it and giving it to the man.'

'I fake to make life easier for myself, I suppose, rather than being questioned about it afterwards – "Oh what did I do wrong?" and all this sort of thing. I suppose you tend to make it look as though you've enjoyed it, don't you?'

Between the sheets, it seems, Cosmopolitan Woman still plays the traditional role of the wife. Her orgasm is to avert the inquisition, to ensure he doesn't feel insulted or offended, to make life easier for her, or to stop him from being, like Alex's partner, thoroughly unpleasant. Having or pretending to have an orgasm has become part of female lore about how to handle men – today's equivalent of not asking for more housekeeping money before he's had his dinner. And the woman's orgasm is also a way of nurturing him. She 'gives' him her orgasm – whether real or fake – so as not to damage his ego or hurt him or make him feel inadequate. It's part of looking after him, like making him a pie or ironing his shirts.

Acts of nurturance are the lifeblood of loving relationships – but only if they are reciprocated. And where are the men who lavish comparable care on women's sexual self-esteem? Where are the men who say, 'It's fine if you really don't want an orgasm: if you do want one, show me how to do it . . . never mind if it doesn't work this time, it'll be fun trying . . .'? Such men do figure in women's sexual stories, but they're still very thin on the ground.

If she has to come for him, is this progress? Or is it just more of the same, a new variation on a very familiar old theme?

THE RIGHT TO CHOOSE

The second item on Cosmopolitan Woman's sexual agenda was
sex when she wanted it. In the popular imagination, Cosmopolitan
Woman is in control of her sex life, takes initiatives and makes
decisions for herself. The sexual assertiveness that I have suggested
is crucial for women's sexual happiness is peculiarly hers. Yet how
much control do young women today have over their sexual
encounters?

All women fear rape. We fear rape constantly because we're
reminded of it constantly, by news stories about sexual violence to
women, by television dramas in which women are shown to be
terribly at risk, and by the aggressively sexual remarks of men as
we walk down the street. And the rape of which we are most afraid
is the knife in the dark alley – the rape of an adult woman by a
stranger.

In her study of rape, *Against Our Will*, Susan Brownmiller suggests that the fear of rape serves patriarchy by controlling women.[13]
There is plenty of evidence to support her theory. Fear of stranger
rape is a very effective way of keeping women literally in their place.
Most women fear going out alone after dark, and many avoid it
altogether, and the reason they cite is the fear of sexual violence.
We are so afraid that to avoid sexual violence we may put ourselves
in great physical danger. Since the murder of Marie Wilkes on the
M50, women driving alone who break down on the motorway have
tended to stay in their cars on the hard shoulder while waiting for
help – yet one out of eight motorway accidents happen on the hard
shoulder.*

It is significant that the advice given to women on avoiding sexual
violence is always couched in terms of keeping away from trouble
– staying at home – rather than fighting back. Yet many women have
fought back effectively, for instance by biting the rapist's tongue.
Self-defence won't always help, but sometimes it can make the
difference between life and death. A course in self-defence should
be as crucial a part of the adolescent girl's preparation for sexual

---

* The AA advise that if you can't coast to the nearest exit you should switch on the
hazard warning lights, leave the vehicle by the nearside door and lock all doors except
the front passenger door, so you can get back in the car quickly, and wait on the
embankment, preferably where not immediately visible to approaching traffic.[14]

life as her rubella injection. The fact that this is never suggested underlines the very useful function that women's fear serves for the patriarchal status quo.

The idea that women's fear is actively encouraged under patriarchy is also supported by the way popular ideas about rape distort the facts. For the kind of rape we fear most is a relatively rare event. Women I talked to gave a number of accounts of rape or sexual assault by strangers – one rape (Penny's story in Chapter 3), two attempted rapes, and one sexual assault. But there were far fewer such incidents in women's adult lives than in their memories of childhood. Among the women I talked to, the risk of rape or sexual assault had been at its greatest when the girl was between eight and twelve. And in adult life it is not the stranger in the dark alley from whom a woman has most to fear: fear of the stranger rapist may make her stay in at night, but she is far more likely to be raped by the husband or boyfriend she is staying in with.

In March 1991 *Cosmopolitan* magazine ran an article on the newly identified phenomenon of date rape.[15] There was a massive response to the article from readers who said they had been raped by their boyfriends. Studies since then have suggested that date rape is a very frequent event. For instance, a nationwide survey of women students carried out for an ITV 'Public Eye' programme on date rape in February 1992 found that one in nine had been raped, and in five out of six cases the rapist was someone they knew.

Two of the women I talked to had been raped by boyfriends. Danielle said, 'It happened last year, and I haven't had a relationship since. I just thought, That's it – I'm going to be a celibate woman for the rest of my life. It was a really bitter experience. After that, I feel I just can't trust men.' Pippa said, 'I'm wary now. I do find myself shying away sometimes, just thinking, you know, "I can live without it." I find I sometimes get frightened. If I'm in a physical situation with someone, I sometimes just say, "No, I can't cope with this." Maybe I'm just proving to myself I can stop it. I want to know that I can say, "No," and they'll go away.' For both women the rape has had a devastating effect on their interest in sex and trust in men. Danger in sexual relationships now outweighs pleasure: the powerful 'aversive fantasy' inhibits their interest in sex.

But the kind of rape that must surely have the most devastating effect of all on women's sex lives is the kind that is repeated year on year – rape in marriage. Violent rape within marriage has always

been part of the texture of women's lives. Reay Tannahill comments
that many of the skeletons of Ancient Egyptian women have arm
fractures of the type that results from guarding the head against a
blow, suggesting that violence was a regular feature of domestic
life under the Pharaohs.[16] A recent study of married women in
Boston, USA, found that one in ten women had been raped by
their husbands: the definition the researchers applied was that the
men had 'used physical force or threat to try to have sex with their
wives.'[17] Until very recently, such behaviour was a husband's right
in the UK. When, in October 1991, the UK Law Lords ruled that
rape in marriage was a crime, it was a wonderful moment for
women. The ruling establishes that the wife is not her husband's
sexual property, and now that legislation is being proposed to confirm this principle, we can be confident that we are witnessing the
death throes of patriarchy in its formal sense.

Kathleen had mused on the concept of rape in marriage. She
said, 'Sometimes I do say no, but it doesn't always work. All this
recent debate about rape within marriage leaves me a bit uncertain.
I'm quite sure there are situations where people should be exposed,
but there are others where it's something that has to be part of the
give and take within a relationship. But there have been times when
I have been very angry indeed about such things.'

Here there is no violence or threat of violence, but Kathleen still
feels she has no choice. This is the grey area, where a woman
doesn't know how to define what happens. It may be helpful to
think of a continuum of experiences. Kathleen's experience clearly
differs in many ways from the rape at knife-point that led to the
rape in marriage ruling, and a woman in Kathleen's situation would
probably never think of going to the police. But her anger suggests
that there is a powerful element of coercion in the experiences she
describes. If this is 'give and take', the giving seems to be all on
one side, and the taking on the other.

Moving further along the continuum, we come to those situations
where there is less coercion, and where the woman can say no –
but only at a cost. Christine said, 'I think sometimes I'd have sex
to avoid an argument – that maybe it was easier to have the sex
that I didn't want than the confrontation I didn't want.' Where a
woman repeatedly has sex to avert her partner's anger or accusa-
tions, her libido is bound to suffer – both because sex when you
really don't want it is unlikely to be pleasurable, and because sex
comes to be associated with interactional patterns which are the

antithesis of eroticism – arguments, rage, resentment.

But there is, of course, another more gentle kind of 'not wanting'. As Doris said, 'I think most people with a husband have occasionally said to themselves, "Oh well," you know, rather than: "How lovely" or "Just what I wanted this evening . . ."' When I asked women who'd had any relationships lasting more than a few months if they'd ever had sex they didn't want, they all said, 'Oh yes,' with a shrug and a characteristic intonation, at once sardonic and resigned.

Sexual partners are never going to feel like sex at exactly the same time. There will always have to be some compromise. Sophie said, 'If you share a bed with someone, you've got to be fair. It would have seemed mean and unloving not to – it's part of the warmth of life.' Women often go along with sex for loving, caring reasons. Mary said, 'I think I have had sex when I was tired or bored or didn't want it, just to please him – but never against my will. I think I probably thought, Oh bless him, it's not asking very much.' June said, 'On those occasions, in a sense I do want it because I don't want to deprive him, so at some level I do want it to happen. I'm giving my permission, if you like – even though it may be irritating me.' These feelings are different from the anger that Kathleen felt because her will had been overridden: this is unwanted sex as part of the warmth of life, 'just to please him – but never against my will.' There's nothing wrong with that – as long as it also works the other way round.

What happens when the woman wants more sex than the man? Megan said, 'At the moment my husband is under terrific pressure at work, and is actually too knackered to even think about it. It's a bit of a rebuff sometimes. Whereas I might make more effort and say, "OK, let's have a go," a few times he will have made an effort, I will have started getting excited and he just isn't getting anywhere, and that's much worse probably – being let down.' June said, 'My first husband wasn't a very sexually active man, and I used to get very hung up about myself, because he'd have all these sexy magazines around, and I'd think, Why does he read all these magazines all the time, when he could come and actually do it with me? I used to be very grateful when he wanted to do it.'

There is little sign that men are doing for women what women do for men – that men are also participating in unwanted sexual activity because it's part of the warmth of life, because they don't want to deprive their partners, because, bless her, it's not asking

very much. Yet, given that few women would insist on penetration
for sexual satisfaction, there seems no obvious physical reason why
in such a situation the man shouldn't give his partner an orgasm
without essentially being very aroused himself – just as she might
at times go along with sex without expecting to climax. In women's
stories there is little indication that this ever happens.

What of the woman who wants sex and isn't afraid to ask for it?
This is Cosmopolitan Woman as she exists in the popular imagination. What happens to the rare woman who does take sexual
initiatives?

June said, 'The sex mags are full of this idea about men liking
women who are very sexy and take the initiative. I don't think that's
true, I don't think they do. When I went to university I jumped
into bed with whoever I wanted to, I had no morals! I remember
one man rushing off in a panic when I was desperately trying to
get him upstairs . . .' Here June comes up against the double standard that still operates, though in a subtle way, among 'liberated'
heterosexual women and their sex partners. The sexually enterpris-
ing woman of the porn magazines may appeal to men in fantasy;
the reality is different. Women may find their autonomy and sexual
freedom considerably constrained if they wish to retain their attractiveness to potential male partners. Men may not mind about a
woman's previous lovers – as long as there weren't too many: men
may be pleased by women taking the initiative sexually – as long
as it doesn't happen too often. For many men, the perfect liberated
woman is perhaps April O'Neill in the television cartoon series
'Teenage Mutant Hero Turtles': April is sexy, intrepid and independent, but every week she needs rescuing from some horror or
other by her trusty turtle friends.

Women like June who take sexual initiatives for their own pleasure and delight are still quite rare. For instance, during my study
I only met one woman who asked men out. But there is one situation
in which the shyest or most unsure woman will make sexual
advances – if she wants a baby. Having babies is part of our acceptable feminine role: it's much easier to ask for sex because we want
to conceive than because we want sex.

Geraldine had difficulty conceiving, and she remembers this as
a sad and troubling time. 'My husband could not understand my
desire – *overwhelming* desire – to have a baby, and therefore he
didn't want to comply with having sex at a certain time of the month,
so he went off sex virtually completely, which just compounded the

awful feelings I had.' I suspect that Geraldine's experience is quite common. The devastating effect on their sexual spontaneity of having to make love when the woman is ovulating is one of the most common complaints that men will make about their sex lives in casual conversation. Sexual spontaneity is of course a rather tricky ideal: one man's spontaneity may be his partner's rape. Men clearly find that sex at a time of the woman's choosing is much less pleasurable: Geraldine's partner went off sex altogether. But for most women in most sexual partnerships, the situation that men complain about – sex at times of the other partner's choosing – is the *norm*. And given that the man's sexual interest is likely to be more constant than the woman's because he has no cycle of desire, the deleterious effect on sexual enjoyment will be more marked for her.

Men have their own version of the biological argument. While a woman may ask for sex because she wants a baby, a man may appeal to the primacy of male sexual urges to bolster his case. Josephine said, 'Sam expects to have sex with his partner every night, and sometimes I agreed and sometimes I didn't. If we hadn't had sex the night before, he used to say to me that we must have it that night. He more or less said – and I'm paraphrasing him – "It's not that I'm attracted to you, it's not that I'm in love with you, it's just that I have all this testosterone, and I need to get it out." And that's what it felt like, I felt like a rather sore, boring, painful receptacle for testosterone. It wasn't good. It wasn't always that bad. But that was the kind of feel of it.' Here again we see how ideas about sexual difference are used to serve men's purposes and how they deny or obscure women's own sexual needs.

Having sex when you want it – at least some of the time – and not having it when you most definitely don't: these are essential preconditions for sexual happiness. But the old patterns still predominate. Women still seem to be having a great deal of sex that they don't want – and when women do want sex and take sexual initiatives, they may find that the fantasy of sexually assertive Cosmopolitan Woman is one that has very little appeal to men in reality. The fact that men take the sexual initiative makes no physiological sense, as women's sexual interest may vary widely through the month – but it does serve to maximize men's sexual enjoyment at the expense of women's.

There are still plenty of women today who would wish to be virgins when they get married for religious reasons, and the

experiences of these women exemplify just how hard it is for us to
stay in control of our sex lives. Of the three women under forty in
my sample who had wanted to be virgins on their wedding night,
two hadn't achieved their aim. Tina was raped at fifteen, and
Frances in a sense had also had her will overridden. 'We made
love when we were going out, which we shouldn't have done, strictly
by our book, as it were, but we did. I didn't feel very good about
that, but once you've started, you can't go backwards. Colin wasn't
bothered, he could justify it in that we were intending to get married
anyway. I didn't feel OK about it, but I didn't really say so, and
so I never really dealt with that I suppose.' Both Tina and Frances
had a very clear sexual aim. But in both cases the woman's will
was subordinated to male desires – in Tina's case by brutal force,
and in Frances' case by persuasion on his part and silence and
collusion on hers, and a shared assumption that his moral values
were more important than hers.

It's a gloomy picture. Yet perhaps our patterns are starting to
change just a little in women's favour. In a recent study, two advertising executives looked at the lifestyles of couples where both
husband and wife worked. They found that once the woman was
earning at least 60 per cent as much as the man, she usually started
to wield much more power in the relationship. He was then more
likely to do the housework – and she was more likely to take the
initiative in bed. They found that these couples weren't very
efficient domestically – they tended to muddle through – but that
their relationships were marked by 'great mutual respect and emotional openness.'[18]

TEACHING A MAN HOW NOT TO BE A STRANGER

There is a scene in Michèle Roberts' novel *The Visitation* in which
a woman tries to show her lover how to give her the sort of stimulation she needs: 'She guides Robert's fingers, teaching them to
dance, teaching them new rhythms, subtle and complex. But she
feels awkward, a little resentful and absent, and her ears catch the
sound of someone walking along the pavement outside, a woman
hurrying through the summer night, the soft tap and click and
shuffle of her high-heeled shoes. Most passionately, that's where
she wants to be – outside, alone in the night, roaming the streets.
Not here in this intimate bed having to teach a man how not to be
a stranger.'[19]

Teaching your lover how not to be a stranger is an essential act of sexual self-assertion for most women. We need to be able to say or to show because, except for the minority of women who have orgasms from penetration, we all need different kinds of stimulation to bring us to orgasm. Masters and Johnson found that no two of the women they studied masturbated in precisely the same way.[20]

Plenty of women don't ask for the stimulation they need because of a very justified fear of the consequences – male indifference, refusal to listen, discourtesy, or violence. But even in the most favourable circumstances, with a loving partner, asking is difficult. Behind the belief that women should be sexually passive there is a tremendous weight of tradition that presses down on the woman who dares to assert herself. If she tries to ask, she may find herself, like the woman in *The Visitation*, longing to be outside, alone in the night, anywhere but here.

In his study, *Sex and Personality*, psychologist Hans Eysenck found that women had done things they disliked in bed almost four times as often as men.[21] But most women told me that they found it quite possible to say 'No' if they were asked to do something they disliked. There is a framework for saying 'No': most women have been attempting to control male sexual activity since adolescence. Women told me that asking for something they wanted was much harder. How many times more likely than men are we to have kept silent rather than ask for something we wanted?

Jacqueline said, 'I'm awful at saying what I want in bed. I get very embarrassed. And there isn't any language to use. "I want you to touch my clitoris," just is not a turn-on, so you end up sounding like you're out of *Penthouse*, which is horrid. I find men have fixed ideas about what they think you're supposed to like, and they're very, very reluctant to let go of that. It always seems to be the grope session, ending up feeling around the woman's vagina, and then the finger on the clitoris which is always much too fast and much too hard. I don't know where they get this notion from that it's got to be very fast, unless perhaps from the way they wank themselves, but they're very very resistant to changing that. And sometimes I actually find it excruciating, I get so sensitive I can't bear it, and if I'm over-sensitive I can't come.'

Bernadette said, 'I find it hard to relax when somebody's trying to stimulate me clitorally – I always take ages, and I actually stop enjoying it. You get to the point where you think you're going to have an orgasm and you think, Ooh, he must be really tired, and

it goes away again. Last year I had a really wonderful sexual
relationship, and masturbating in front of each other was a big part
of that. This new relationship I'm in, I've not been able to talk to
him about what I like yet, and I saw him yesterday and I'd planned
that I was going to sit down and say, "Look," because we've been
sleeping together for the past two weeks but I haven't actually had
an orgasm because I haven't told him the special things that I like
to do, and that's partly about the fact that he's older than me. I
think, Maybe he'd be shocked, and I don't know how to handle
that. Maybe he'd be turned off by it.'

Both these women know what they want: it's just so hard to ask.
It's embarrassing. There are no words to use. Maybe he'd be
shocked.

Asking has other connotations too. Doris, now in her early sixties,
reflected, 'It hasn't come particularly naturally to say, "Do it this
way." It's felt like an indulgence – even so far as a sin, I think.'
Asking won't be thought of as a sin by a younger woman – but
perhaps there are echoes of the old ideas when Linda says, 'Oh
I'm very good at saying what I want. I've been told that I'm very
selfish, that I just want what I want. I don't mind because I know
it's true.' She assures me the word 'selfish' is used jokingly – but
it still hints at one meaning of sexual self-assertion for women.
Kate, on the other hand, feels she has to justify herself for not
asserting herself in bed. 'I'm very lazy in bed, I'm quite happy to
just lie there and not do very much. I think I do most things in this
house, and the people in this house depend on me tremendously in
all sorts of ways, and maybe I've decided, "Right – this is one place
where I'm not going to work too hard."'

Here again we see that familiar push-pull for women, as the
ideology of sexual liberation clashes with the continuing need to
be a nice girl: Patient Griselda versus Alexis Carrington. Under
the old dispensation, sexual assertion was a sin: under the new, it
is a duty.

Alex is one Cosmopolitan Woman who has arrived at a delightful
compromise between these contradictory expectations. 'A lot of
men still think the Big O's a vaginal thing – so I think, well, I'll
show them what to do, and maybe they'll remember it, and some
other girl won't have to put them in the right place, as it were. And
I also think, P'raps they'll do it one day with a woman who's never
had an orgasm, and it'll open a new thing in her life, and it'll be
from me!' Like the governess who initiates the young man of the

house, Alex is a sexual teacher, one sexually active female role that has always been acceptable within patriarchal sexual mythology because it still gives primacy to male sexual pleasure. But Alex gives this role a twist of her own, and her 'If I can help somebody' justification for sexual self-assertion becomes a very feminine reason for having a good time in bed.

But when women of all ages describe their attempts to tell their lovers what they want, there is often such a sense of effort. Frances said, 'I used to be quite good at asking for what I want in bed – I tell myself that when the children are bigger and I've got more energy it's something I shall try and do again.' Sexual self-assertion is hard work: it takes a lot of energy. Sometimes a kind of paralysis seems to seize us in these intimate moments. So we make a bargain with ourselves. We placate the sexually rapacious woman inside us – the woman who says 'I want, I want' – with a promise. We tell ourselves we're only postponing the moment. We'll do it one day, next week, next year, when we're more sure of him, or – as we move on to the next stage of the life cycle – when the children are bigger, when we're not so tired. There's always time . . .

Anne said, 'I was absolutely useless with John. We would murmur endearments to each other, say, "I love you", and "That's wonderful", and "Oh yes, do that, do that again", but I could never ask for what I really wanted. And I felt a great regret when he died because there was always that prospect that the children would grow up and leave home and then we would really reinvent our sex life, and it never happened. I feel real regret, a real sadness that we could never get to that point.'

Here I've concentrated on the difficulties of sexual self-assertion in relationships like Anne's marriage – with a loving partner who wants to be helpful. The difficulties are, of course, compounded in less favourable conditions. Women's stories of their attempts to assert themselves are a reminder of the persistence of those male sexual attitudes that are so destructive to women's sexual pleasure. Anne went on, 'I made a resolution that in any future partnership I had I would try to be more open, and I really tried it with the first man. He was completely put off by this, he was really repelled. Once I told him a fantasy and he said, "If you want to wank, do that at home when you're on your own."'

SMART GIRLS CARRY CONDOMS

In many relationships, women's fears about the risk of self-assertion
may be entirely justified. So why not give up? Why not just put up
with unsatisfactory sex, turn over and go to sleep?

Women obviously do decide in huge numbers that such a strategy
is preferable to the risk of being treated as Anne was by her lover.
But this won't do any longer. With the advent of AIDS, not to
assert yourself has itself become a high-risk strategy. Successful
sexual assertion has become a matter of life and death for women.

In Europe, one in six of the people diagnosed with AIDS in the
year ending April 1990 were women. AIDS is now the leading
cause of death for women between twenty and forty in major cities
in the United States.[22] And women are considerably more at risk
than men of catching HIV from heterosexual intercourse. A
research study recently reported in the *British Medical Journal* found
that: 'Male to female transmission seemed to be twice as effective
as female to male transmission.'[23]

'Smart Girls Carry Condoms' announced the cover of *Cosmopoli-*
tan magazine in January 1987. There is very little evidence, however, that Cosmopolitan Woman actually uses them. All the surveys
suggest that heterosexual people have scarcely changed their
behaviour at all in response to the AIDS pandemic. Ceri Hutton,
a worker in the AIDS field, wrote in *New Statesman* about a seminar
on safer sex she had attended: 'It was women only, and a lot of
the discussion was about how to get what we want, how to get men
to wear condoms. We talked about the language we should use,
and vigorously upheld a woman's right to say "No". It all made
me feel very uneasy. At the end of the session, a woman who'd
been working in HIV and AIDS for several years drew me on one
side, "Oh God," she said, "all I know is, when the AIDS
coordinator and I bonked not so long ago, we didn't use a
condom."[24]

Two women I talked to who had chosen a celibate lifestyle for
now felt that their fear of AIDS was an element in that choice.
Otherwise I saw little sign that AIDS had changed anyone's sexual
habits, though it had certainly raised women's anxieties. Sometimes
I found myself thinking – If this woman, intelligent, informed, and
surely more sexually assertive than most, isn't protecting herself,
who is?

Sophie is now in her fifties. 'It does worry me,' she says, 'because with my present partner, we don't use a condom. I'd have found it very hard to suggest that we do. It's got something to do with implying that both of us might carry AIDS, I suppose, and we've both had very varied sexual lives over the past few years, and it's something to do with trusting each other, and yet afterwards I think, You fool, why do you do this? I think it's one of those things that sound so logical in a workshop on safe sex, but it's incredibly difficult to talk about when you're with someone. With this fellow, we don't make love an awful lot, so sex itself is always taking me by surprise, and when it happens I wouldn't want to stop by saying, "Hang on, we haven't got anything."'

Alex is twenty. 'All the blokes I've been with, they're very sort of responsible – in the sense that if the condoms are there, they'll use them, but if they're not there, they don't adamantly say, "No, we can't do it," they will say, "Don't worry, don't worry, I'll get it out in time"* – but I wish they would say no, because I get very passionate and heated, I lose a bit of self-control. I wish that just one time a bloke would say, "No, no," – but they never do.'

In the homosexual community safer sex is now widely practised, and as a result there has been a big reduction in all sexually-transmitted diseases. Clearly the main factor at work here is that gay men know that the bad news is not just rumour and hyperbole: their friends and their lovers have died. Those in the straight community whose lives have not yet been touched by AIDS don't quite believe in it. But it seems likely that the dynamics of heterosexual relationships are also a factor in the failure of straight men and women to practise safer sex. Safer sex is not something separate. In women's accounts of why they don't insist on condoms, there are certain familiar themes.

In Alex's account, sex is something that he initiates and she controls – a division of sexual labour, incidentally, that Alex valiantly opposes. This is identical to the dynamic around contraception that leads to so many unwanted pregnancies. In this interaction, the woman is the cautious one, the one who keeps in mind the dangers of sex – pregnancy, cystitis, gonorrhoea, AIDS: she is also

---

* Coitus interruptus – penetration followed by ejaculation outside the woman's body – is of course not a safer sex method. If you practise coitus interruptus, you can still catch HIV and you can still get pregnant, as some seminal fluid is released before the man ejaculates.

the one who is swept away by the tides of passion and gives in whatever the risk. She says, Oh no, I mustn't, I might get pregnant, I might get AIDS. He says, Go on, just this once, I want you so much, I'll look after you . . .

In Sophie's account, not insisting on a condom is an aspect of sexual nurturing; she must care for him, nurture his erection, and not interrupt, not spoil his pleasure. This too sounds familiar. These are the same concerns that lead women to pretend in sex, even to the point of faking orgasm. Also implicit in Sophie's account is the assumption that condoms detract more from the man's pleasure than from the woman's. If she suggests they use a condom, then, she is asking him to make a greater sacrifice than she is making herself. I wonder whether this belief is justified, or is it just a reflection of men's tendency to give greater weight than women to their own sexual pleasure regardless of the risks?

There is also another very familiar theme that runs through all women's accounts of why they don't use condoms – women's difficulties with sexual self-assertion. Some women don't produce a condom because if they did they would be hit. But even for women who are not so cruelly constrained, like the women in this book, there are still those apparently insurmountable problems about asking for what you want. She would like to insist, but it's such an effort, not this time, she'll do it one day, when she's not so much in love or so afraid of losing him . . . If so often we won't assert ourselves for pleasure – the most intense physical pleasure we can know, and which could be ours here and now – we are unlikely to assert ourselves because of the risk of contracting a disease, a risk which, though terrible, remains at present remote. If she can't ask him to give her an orgasm, is she going to be able to ask him to use a condom?

The female condom that has recently appeared on the market might seem to offer a solution to this problem. But first reactions aren't promising. Because the female condom is highly visible in use, it will probably only be used by those women who are already very sexually assertive.

This is a huge issue for women. The woman who cannot assert herself – and that means most of us – finds herself in a highly vulnerable position, totally dependent on the man's good sense and goodwill. Never a very safe place for a woman to be.

SEXUAL PATTERNS: WHAT DO WOMEN WANT?

Intercourse with a condom is only ever 'safer', it is never 'safe'. Condoms can break. Only non-penetrative sex is 'safe'. What would it mean to women to have sex without penetration?

Feminist writers have frequently questioned the equation of sex with intercourse. More than twenty years ago, Anne Koedt in her essay 'The Myth of the Vaginal Orgasm' suggested that men had suppressed the truth about clitoral orgasm because 'they fear that they will become sexually expendable if the clitoris is substituted for the vagina as a centre of pleasure for women.'[25] By implication, intercourse might become a secondary or deviant sexual practice if women had more power to decide what sex should be.

The feelings about intercourse that women expressed to me were very much in line with the feminist critique. Women talked about penetration in lukewarm terms. They told me that they did like it – but mostly for formal, emotional or reproductive reasons. They saw that intercourse was very important for their relationship because their partner enjoyed it so much, and they liked the emotional closeness of it. They had it because it's part of the deal, or because this is what sex is: 'If you have intercourse you feel you're really fucking.' They liked intercourse because of the form or pattern of love-making: intercourse was a 'logical conclusion', a 'good end'. And some women said that they enjoyed intercourse particularly when they were trying to get pregnant, because the fantasy of the wonderful baby that might be conceived enhanced their excitement. Women rarely gave physical pleasure as a reason for liking intercourse. They were more likely to comment that it involves a reduction in sexual sensation: 'Sometimes it gets in the way of the way I was feeling before.'

Where women do talk about intercourse appreciatively, they use very active language: 'I love it when men are reaching orgasm and they're really moving, it just feels wonderful.' 'I love this whole feeling of taking someone in, it's the maternal in me I suppose.' One is reminded of the sex therapy technique used with child sex abuse survivors who had rejected intercourse, in which women learnt to experience intercourse as an active taking-in (see Chapter 3). Women who enjoy intercourse often say they prefer the woman-on-top position, which gives the woman far more freedom and control: Masters and Johnson advocated this intercourse position for all their clients with sexual problems. Where intercourse is particularly disliked, it is experienced as an intrusion rather than a taking-in. Sheila, who came out as a lesbian after many years of marriage, had enjoyed some parts of love-making with her husband, but had never liked intercourse: 'I wouldn't stick anything inside myself,' she said, 'so why should I let anybody else stick anything inside me?'

Given the lukewarm terms in which women by and large talk about penetration, it is likely that many women might actually prefer genuinely safe – non-penetrative – sex practices. Men, however, will remain reluctant to consider alternatives to intercourse. The vagina offers perfect stimulation for the penis, and intercourse gives the man total control over the stimulation he receives. While male sexual pleasure remains paramount, our definition of 'real sex' will remain unchallenged.

Given that for now sex means intercourse, can sexual activity be made more woman-friendly? Are there changes in our patterns of love-making that would suit women better?

Janet said, 'I like to have a nice evening where you have a glass of wine and you're talking and you could perhaps have a cuddle, the whole setting, not any sex to begin with, but just to feel close to one another and . . . the loving part of things. Whereas he'll sit there watching the television and then he'll expect to get to bed and that I'll feel suddenly in the mood, but it doesn't work like that with me.' Jennifer said, 'I would love a partner who would lounge around in bed with me afterwards, just to drowse together, and he will always get up and have his bath straight away, or get up and do some work, which I hate.' Anne said, 'Afterwards I want to go on talking, touching, fantasizing. Leo came round this morning, he said, "I've only got an hour and then I've got to go to Sheffield." Then later, it's "Right, goodbye!" I think, Jesus, I want to stay with you, I want to be with you. He can't understand it. A man can have sex and then it's over, he can go back to his work or whatever he was doing. I've never been attracted to a woman at all, but I was thinking, if you want to take a long time over making love, talking, touching, fantasizing, keep the flow going – it makes sense to make love to another woman.'

More time before, more time after: a familiar litany. Whenever women are given a chance to say what they would like to change about patterns of love-making, from surveys in women's magazines to Shere Hite's research, this is what they say.

Conventional explanations for these apparent gender differences draw on the 'dark continent' theory of female sexuality. According to this theory, women need more time before and more time after because of our greater need for tenderness and intimacy, our preference for cuddles over genital contact, our more 'diffuse' sexuality, and the greater subtlety and elusiveness of female sexual arousal. We need a long build-up because our arousal is less automatic than men's; we need to cuddle afterwards because emotional closeness is more important to us than it is to men.

There may be elements of truth in these explanations. Many women may indeed be slower than men to get aroused, given that heterosexual men are constantly surrounded in our culture by sexual stimulation, while the woman has to get all her psychological stimulation from the relationship, or from inside her own head. And women do value emotional closeness – or, to put it another way, it does seem that some men have problems around tenderness and intimacy. But whenever an apparent sex difference is attributed to the mysteriousness of female sexuality, we should be on our guard. And in fact there are other simpler explanations for these apparent differences, explanations that are grounded in the differing physiological patterns of sexual arousal and response in men and women. A woman likes the time 'before', the 'foreplay', because that for her is the main event; for most women, if she has an orgasm, it will be during foreplay. She wants more time after because she is still aroused, probably more aroused than when they started. So Jennifer and Anne want that sense of sexual connection to persist – to drowse with their partner or to go on touching and fantasizing – because they are still turned on.

Because of the woman's continuing arousal she could if she wished have more orgasms. Penny said, 'I've gone from having none to having five or six all one after the other, which is exhausting but lovely. I get two or three mini ones and then a massive one and then one or two mini ones after that, then you know you've had enough, you know you can't have any more.' The pattern is the woman's own, but the capacity to have multiple orgasms is one that all women have, though a woman who finds that her clitoris is too sensitive after one orgasm for continuing stimulation may prefer not to explore this potential. In her research on female sexuality, Shere Hite found that few women knew that they could have more orgasms if the stimulation was continued, and still fewer had actually tried.[26]

There is a particular tone of voice in which women talk about multiple orgasms, the tone of voice we use to describe things that are delicious but rather disgusting, like chocolate cake with lots of whipped cream. If it is greedy for women to want as much sexual gratification as men, how much more greedy for us to want *more*. When women talk about multiple orgasms and why they don't have them there are a lot of disclaimers: 'They're too tiring,' 'I prefer to have one good one,' or 'Multiple orgasms? I'm happy if I have one.' Fran didn't like the persistence of sexual arousal afterwards: 'Ginny likes me to have two – but the more I have the more I want. When I've had one, that's really satisfying, but if I've had a few, there's no natural end to it, and also I'm very aware of myself sexually afterwards, which I probably don't want, like if I have to go to work or something.' Fran knows that more is not essentially better. Just because we can doesn't mean we should. But many women who have explored this potential relish multiple orgasms, and find like Penny that the first in the series is not necessarily the best.

Women may want time before and time after intercourse: what they generally don't want is a lot of time during. To talk about this with women is to mine a rich vein of contempt in women's sexual attitudes. If the relationship is falling part, it is the length of time that intercourse takes that she finds particularly irritating: 'I used to lie back and grit my teeth and think: Just get the hell out of here!'

Josephine remembered a wonderful lover and contrasted him with her later experiences. 'When I was married to Sam I often remembered that relationship with David, and wondered would I ever meet anyone again who was that kind of lover. He was completely different, it was all sliding and smooth with him, and *quick*. Sam and Robert who were my other long-term lovers have both been this repetitive endless hump-hump-hump kind of thing, and I just don't get any pleasure out of that at all. I couldn't *bear* it with Sam, he would be sort of three-quarters of an hour bouncing around, and I'd be watching the clock thinking: Aw, shit, when's he going to come? I can't stand it! And he'd be sweating. Ugh!'

There is still a common male belief that women like their partners to go on for a long time, a belief that is bolstered by misinformation about female sexual response acquired from the fantasy land of male pornography. So the kind of premature ejaculation where the man manages to penetrate but comes very quickly is defined as a sexual disorder, yet Sam's sexual functioning would never be defined as a problem, though it might cause his partner real distress. The preoccupation with the time that intercourse takes has everything to do with the male culture of 'more is better', and nothing to do with women's pleasure.

LESBIAN SEX: THE ANSWER, OR JUST A DIFFERENT QUESTION?

Anne suggested that one way of fulfilling her need to go on 'talking, touching, fantasizing' after sex would be to make love with a woman. Since the early days of second wave feminism, lesbianism has been seen as 'right-on' sex because you weren't having your body colonized by the enemy. I found that for some women who saw themselves as heterosexual a romantic notion of lesbian sex became a repository for some of the things that they felt were missing from their sex lives. (See also Chapter 10.)

Women in lesbian relationships did bear out Anne's hypothesis that lesbian sex would have a different rhythm – lesbian sex is 'never-ending,' 'it has no natural finish,' 'it can go on and on' – because of women's continuing arousal after orgasm. And some lesbian relationships did fit with the fantasy of sensuous, imaginative sex with a lot of touching and physical closeness.

Fran said, 'We tend to be very tired in the week, so we tend not to have sex. We do a lot of massage, she'll get between my legs and do my feet, and I'll do her back. She always cuddles me in bed: when I was lighter I used to sleep on top of her, but now I'd just squash her! It's not heavily sexual, it's just soothing and relaxing. A lot's dictated by the children really. But if we go away, we would tend to have sex during the day rather than when we want to sleep, and we often centre it around eating as well – we have a fromage frais, some cheeses, creamy things, soft fruits. And if it's a celebration – any celebration! – we always have champagne and smoked salmon, and Ginny likes to put strips of smoked salmon over my body, so she eats her smoked salmon off me.'

Sheila found, however, that the kind of relationship Fran describes is not the only pattern for lesbian sex. 'I'd always assumed that because women were the gentler sex and they were the more loving, that love-making with a woman would be absolutely out of this world, it would be so gentle and tender and long and loving. And it ain't necessarily so – because in some cases women are no different from men – they're just as rough, they're just as greedy. One girlfriend I had, the moment she got me in her arms, her hand was in my knickers. I said to her one day, "I've had men doing this to me all my life and I've had to fight them off – now I find a bloody woman's doing it!"'

VARIETY AND PLEASURE

Since the 1960s, one of our dominant sexual ideas has been the equation of sexual variety with sexual fulfilment. As Sheila Jeffreys says, 'We have been encouraged to see sex as a range of practices, so that according to this analysis, the wider the range of practices, the more liberated the sex.'[27] Sexual liberation means variety of practices; it also, at least until the AIDS pandemic, meant variety of partners.

The emphasis on variety reflects how we think about pleasure in general. We live in a culture in which diversity and novelty are the essence of pleasure. Chinese, Italian and Moroccan cuisine jostle on the High Street, and there's a choice of five different channels on Sky TV. The way the science of sexology developed may also be a factor in our emphasis on sexual variety, for much of sexology, from Krafft-Ebing on, has been about the categorization of the perversions: the study of sex has been the study of various sexual practices. And most of us are undeniably intrigued by accounts of unfamiliar sexual practices. Stories of sex that involve defaecation, dogs or piercing for most of us have the quality of tall tales. We respond with a mixture of suspicion and fascination, much as the villagers in *One Hundred Years of Solitude* greeted the strange inventions from far countries brought by the travelling gypsies – the magnet and telescope and mercury with a 'smell of the devil'.[28]

The major evangelist of sexual variety over the past few decades has been Alex Comfort, whose *The Joy of Sex* was first published in 1972: it has recently been reissued to accommodate AIDS, but the text remains largely unchanged. In his own life during the sixties, Alex Comfort was an enthusiastic exemplar of swinging and group sex, but in his book he plays down the pleasures of having lots of partners. Instead, he urges us to 'enrich' our sex lives by adding a lot of different practices to 'the good old face-to-face matrimonial.'[29] Sex is equated with food: we are encouraged to choose from a menu of 'Starters', 'Main Courses', and 'Sauces and Pickles'. Despite all the detailed description of sexual practices, the book says virtually nothing about the woman's orgasm: it's just assumed to be there. There is only one kind of female orgasm that is so totally reliable and requires so little clitoral stimulation: that woman in the 'tasteful' line drawings with her perfectly-timed, taken-for-granted orgasm – she had to be faking.

I found women generally sceptical about this kind of variety. There was a sense that sexual variety was a substitute for the real thing – fulfilling sex, a passionate relationship. Sophie said, 'We tried all the things that were going on in the sixties, short of tying ourselves up on beams, we were deeply into all those things. But it wasn't until my affair that I was really able to talk about love, and that I began to really despise all the things I'd allowed myself to do before and think, How stupid, it's all in place of the real thing – really being part of someone else, and total overwhelming voluptuousness with a gorgeous person.'

But there is one kind of sexual variety that women in a female sexual Utopia might well introduce into their lives. Women talk about the powerful shower-jets on French campsites with gleeful lasciviousness, and a continental shower-room is a not uncommon setting for a first orgasm. Such easy stimulation can be obtained, of course, without the air fare. Vibrators have revolutionized sex therapy for pre-orgasmic women, and the rare women who had used vibrators were extremely enthusiastic about them. Jacqueline said, 'In my late twenties when my marriage split up, I was terribly driven in a sexual way, and I bought a vibrator. Then after this man moved in, I threw it away. My friend's got this story of me saying, "Farewell fond friend," as I put it in the rubbish bin, heavily disguised in lots of wrappings in case it should fall out en route to the dustbin lorry. I thought, Oh I won't be needing this anymore – worst mistake I've ever made! And I don't dare walk into Ann Summers, and *Spare Rib* don't do them anymore because they're phallic-shaped . . .'

Jacqueline disposes of her vibrator with care. Vibrators are embarrassing. They can only be obtained from sex shops or mail-order suppliers and they have a seedy image. Sex aids for men don't have the same image and are much more easily obtained. He can buy a soft porn magazine at his local newsagent, and his partner can buy a black basque, so she turns him on by looking like the pictures in the magazine, from her local department store. Men's use of alternative sources of stimulation is regarded as normal and indicative of a healthy sexual appetite, but vibrators suggest that dreadful sexual sin – female sexual greed. It is because the use of vibrators undermines the foundations of phallocentric sexual ideology, according to which the most overwhelming orgasm is experienced in intercourse with the phallic hero, that they are so unacceptable. The fear that men might become expendable underlies the notion that the woman who experiments with a vibrator risks becoming addicted. This common belief is quite unfounded – though it does provide the basis for a delicious piece of satire in Lisa Alther's novel *Kinflicks*: '. . . we took up hobbies. One dark snowy afternoon Laverne had shut herself into her room with her vibrator. Squeals of ecstasy filled the cabin. The electric lights in the kitchen where Eddie and I sat were dimming and brightening rhythmically . . . our electric bill had jumped five percent since Laverne had moved in.'[30]

So we come to the other kind of sexual variety, the kind that Alex Comfort kept quiet about in *The Joy of Sex* – variety of partners. Just as we tend to over-estimate the numbers of people who have extra-marital affairs,[31] we may also imagine the promiscuous lifestyle to be far more prevalent than it is in reality. For most people, sleeping around, if they do it at all, is a practice that is confined to a short period of their lives, before they settle into monogamy, whether of the permanent or serial kind. Yet the belief persists that the sexual good life means having lots of partners.

For some women, promiscuity is a straightforward moral issue. Other women do talk enthusiastically about this kind of sexual variety, but sometimes the reasons for their enthusiasm have little or nothing to do with sexual pleasure.

Ruth, whose marriage was sexually unhappy, and who is now in her seventies, remembers enjoying swinging parties in middle age – but look at the reason for her enthusiasm. 'Quite a few of us had rave-ups, with wife-swapping and so on, in middle age. It must have been a common urge – our boredom was pretty deep by then probably. My forte was to dance in the nude – mind you, it was practically pitch dark! We were all drunk, of course, and all in the same flat; we didn't run off with each other. I do remember saying to Will that he looked ten years younger when we were doing that. He looked bright as a button, it suited him.' Ruth liked swinging, but for the most nurturing and altruistic of reasons – because it was good for her husband.

Jacqueline also mused on a period in her life when she'd had a succession of partners. 'I think the sexual myth of our generation is that you need sex at least every day, if not more, preferably with as many people as you can lay hands on. I had a very promiscuous couple of years after my marriage broke up, which was very reassuring really, that men fancied me at all. I think I was very much driven by the myth of sexual fulfilment, and it's slowly dawned on me that the reality of what happened to me wasn't about fulfilment – and then I got herpes. And I thought, Well, I've got herpes – and I haven't had any orgasms for it.'

As we seek for new patterns in our post-AIDS world, pleasure in having lots of sex partners is something we would do well to give up. Perhaps this is not such a great loss. It remains true that the most ecstatic accounts of sex – in literature or in life – are not about sex with a stranger: they are about making love in a familiar and wonderful way to a familiar and loved person. It is a feminist commonplace today that 'sexual liberation' failed to deliver to women, and that the ideals of the sixties merely made women more sexually available to men. Jacqueline's experience seems to bear this out, and her final verdict on her lifestyle – herpes and no orgasms – makes a depressing epitaph for Cosmopolitan Woman.

In the public imagination, young childless women are the 'Women on Top' of Nancy Friday's recent collection of women's sexual fantasies.[32] Yet Cosmopolitan Woman's experience falls far short of the dream. There is little evidence for those abundant orgasms that she is supposed to be having: among the women I talked to, it was the norm to fake some or all of the time at twenty-five. There is little evidence that Cosmopolitan Woman is managing to ask for what she wants: she fakes because she cannot ask for the kind of stimulation she needs, and few couples seem to recognize in their love-making the different patterns that would suit women better, with less emphasis on penetration, and more time before and after.

But the most startling aspect of Cosmopolitan Woman's experience is the degree to which the most basic act of sexual self-assertion is still denied her. Cosmopolitan Woman still has sex when *he* wants it. Her right to choose is still constrained, whether by the brutality of date rape, or simply by the unquestioned assumptions about the primacy of male sexual pleasure that govern the sexual experiences of even the most assertive women.

CHAPTER SEVEN

Women with Babies:

The Sensuousness of Mothering

Here is Ruth looking back fifty years to the birth of her first child: 'There is one thing I·do remember – and I clung to the memory afterwards when things went wrong. As we walked down the hill to the hospital, I remember saying to Will that the one thing I was worried about was that there wasn't going to be any sex for a fortnight – which was perfectly true. I thought: How will I cope? So obviously our sex life was fine before, even though we weren't very experienced. Then after our son was born, I had to really work at it, I think for ever afterwards.

'I might have preferred it if Will had been one of those "wham-bam thank you ma'am" people. He'd say, "It's no bloody good to me unless you enjoy it and want it as much as I do." What the hell are you expected to do then when you don't? I went to a doctor – I absolutely hated it, but I did have a go. He just said, "Have you had an orgasm since?" and "Was there any damage?" and then he said, "Well I'm awfully sorry, but it's extremely common. We have no idea what we can do about it . . ."'

For Christine, whose children are five and seven, the experience is much more recent. 'It takes a long time for me to be interested again – definitely months, and I'm wondering perhaps whether it might be years. After my first baby I felt I would fall in half, I remember thinking: I have no idea what's happened to me down there, I can't possibly . . . If I didn't have a permanent man who was waiting for me to be interested again, I think I would quite happily have had nothing to do with sex for years after having children because I just felt all my energies were taken up with them.'

Tracy's daughter is four. 'I'm always thinking: God, when is it going to end? And I get comments like, "Well, if you tried a bit harder it would be a bit nicer." I was very, very sore after Amy and very tired, and she didn't sleep through the night – and also

Amy became more important to me than Keith was. And Keith let me down badly over Amy's birth – during my very difficult labour with Amy, Keith's only interests were when he could go home and when he could get something to eat. That was the first time I'd really needed him, because I'm quite strong, I'm the stronger one of the partnership in many ways, but I did need support then and I didn't get it, so that's flavoured our relationship ever since. I used to fantasize sometimes about having intercourse with someone else. That used to buoy me up: I used to think, I really fancy so-and-so. I didn't go into it in great detail, so perhaps it was only a momentary sort of fancy. And now I don't, now I think, I don't actually think I'd want to have intercourse with him either.'

In the months after childbirth, many women enter a sexual waste-land. They have no interest in sex, no sexual thoughts or fantasies, and no erotic dreams. Orgasms take longer and are less overwhelming if achieved. This state is not invariable, but, as Ruth's doctor said, it does seem to be extremely common. Women's loss of interest in sex is certainly a major reason for the striking reduction in frequency of sexual activity after childbirth. A recent survey in *She* magazine, for instance, found that nearly one in four of the women with children under two who responded were only having sex once or twice a month.[1]

Sometimes the wasteland stretches as far as the eye can see. In Ruth's case, her lack of sexual interest in her husband went on being an issue in their relationship till her husband's death.

There is now some recognition that childbirth affects libido. At antenatal classes you may be tentatively warned that you may get rather tired when the baby comes, and it's important to make time for your husband so he doesn't feel left out. Advice columns in mother and baby magazines also sometimes feature this issue. The woman is invariably advised to take some kind of action – to go out to dinner with her husband, perhaps, or to pamper herself in a nice hot bath with lots of scented bath oil. Two messages underlie this kind of advice. Loss of sexual interest on the woman's part is conceptualized as a problem that she must seek to solve, and the suggestions made imply that this problem is amenable to simple solutions. So if the hot bath and the candlelit dinner don't work, you're obviously in real trouble.

Women are starting to talk together about the effects of childbirth on their libido. Some of the women I interviewed had raised the subject with their friends. 'I've taken a straw poll round here: people just stop once they've got children. It's a standing joke – "Sex? What's sex?" – or, if someone gets pregnant – "Don't you have to have *sex* to get pregnant?" My friend said to me, "When you look in magazine surveys and they ask how often you have sex, there's never a category for me – I'm off the chart!"' The sardonic tone belies the potential pain in this situation, and the havoc that the woman's lack of sexual enthusiasm may wreak in relationships. Some partners may have affairs, some may become violent, and even the most loving and faithful husband may fear that his wife no longer loves him. On the woman's part, the loss of her libido will lower her self-esteem, and make her think, 'There must be something wrong with me.' There may be rows, there will certainly be resentment, and partners may begin to drift apart.

THE MUD-SEALED HOLE

When they go through the possible reasons for their loss of sexual interest, women invariably put tiredness at the top of the list – the totally spent feeling that follows the well-named 'labour' of childbirth, the dragging tiredness of the early months of parenting, the exhaustion you feel when you spend all day responding to the demands of a rampaging toddler. Tiredness seems such an obvious explanation, yet perhaps it isn't as straightforward as it might seem. If we say we go off sex because we're tired, this raises the question of why so many of us see sex, not as replenishment or refreshment, but as just one more demand. And in fact women rarely accept tiredness as a total explanation.

Then there is the physical and emotional aftermath of the birth itself. For weeks afterwards, and for months if the delivery was difficult, intercourse will hurt. A woman may worry, as Christine did, that she will split open. Often the physical pain has a psychological corollary, a woman's feeling that she doesn't want to be invaded again. Her body boundary has been breached by the birth itself, and by all those medical intrusions – internal examinations, breaking the waters, caesarean or forceps deliveries, being stitched up. In a more subtle sense, her boundaries are still being breached in the days after the birth; she continues to bleed, if she is breast-feeding she will be leaking milk, and she may feel so intensely physically and emotionally tied to the baby that she isn't clear where the baby stops and she begins. When a woman says, 'I want to keep myself to myself for a bit,' she is recognizing the essential psychological work involved in re-establishing her separateness and redefining the boundary round her body. In intercourse that boundary is crossed again: she may feel too fragile to take the risk.

Physical self-esteem may also be an issue. In our society, which is so ambivalent about fertility, the lactating woman with a bulging stomach is the antithesis of female attractiveness: this is why nursing bras are never flowery or lacy, and never made in sexy colours like red or black. Breast-feeding women often liken themselves to cows, tame and unattractive animals with limited sex appeal: lactation is not conceptualized as a sexual or powerful thing to do – though tigers also suckle their young.[2] Lack of time to spend on self-presentation is also a problem. Elegance, as Simone de Beauvoir observed, is like housework, and the woman with young children rarely has time for this particular kind of housework – she has too much else to do. The reactions of others may confirm the new mother's sense that she is no longer a sexual being: 'You never get any looks when you're out with a buggy,' said Penny, a little nostalgic, like many new mothers, for the whistles and crude remarks of her Cosmopolitan Woman days.

The hormonal changes that follow childbirth offer another kind of explanation. The effects of hormones on female sex drive are still not fully understood, but it is known that the hormone prolactin, which is released into the bloodstream during breast-feeding, inhibits oestrogen production, and lack of oestrogen may make the vagina feel dry, which will affect the woman's enjoyment of intercourse.[3] Oestrogen does not seem to have any direct effect on libido, but it has been suggested that prolactin itself, which has such a powerful tranquillizing effect, may also have a dampening effect on the woman's libido.[4]

Then there are the nutritional demands of pregnancy and early motherhood. As a society we are so preoccupied with 'slim is sexy' that the effects of nutritional deficiencies on female sexuality are little explored, yet it is possible that such effects may go some way to account for women's loss of libido after childbirth. The Women's Nutritional Advisory Service, who use a combined dietary and nutritional supplement programme to treat premenstrual tension, have found that many of the women who come to them for help have experienced a marked loss of libido around the time that the PMT became a problem. When they looked at the effect of their three-month nutritional programme on these women, they found that half the women said their libido had returned to normal, and that most of the remaining women reported an improvement.[5] It is possible that such a programme might also help women in the months after childbirth. Yet far from being given nutritional advice, women are often advised to go on slimming diets after childbirth, and baby magazines sometimes even feature slimming diets for breast-feeding mothers, though breast-feeding uses up 1,000 calories a day.[6] Good food, and enough of it, possibly combined with vitamin and mineral supplements, can make the difference between coping and exhaustion in the months after childbirth. Might good nutrition also make the difference between taking pleasure in sex and feeling you can't be bothered?

The risk of being disturbed is another factor to which women refer when they seek to explain what has happened to their sex lives. Just as you start to feel aroused, the baby cries, or you hear the familiar pattern of toddler noises – the door opening, the cheery approaching footsteps. Women as the main care-givers are more sensitized to these cues than their partners, and their arousal is consequently more inhibited by the sounds of infant activity. Since families stopped sleeping several to a bed, sex in the presence of children, even sleeping ones, has been tabooed. The knowledge that children might interrupt at any moment acts as a powerful aversive fantasy for women.

The social restrictions of the mothering role may also affect the woman's libido. When the female Wrinkled Hornbill is ready to lay her eggs, she is holed up in a nest sealed with mud by the male, who feeds her through a tiny aperture: she only leaves once her young are partially grown. The conditions in which women are expected to bring up small children can feel remarkably like the Wrinkled Hornbill's mud-sealed hole. A new mother may seldom see other men apart from her partner: she may feel cut off from the world of money, status and important work. Michelle linked this directly to her loss of libido after childbirth: 'Mothers are undervalued by society, and it does make you feel bad about yourself, because you earn no money. It's difficult to feel you're an important person, and if you don't feel you're important or significant, then it's difficult to feel that somebody might want you in a sexual way.'

Here then is an abundance of explanations for loss of sexual interest after childbirth. And all these different explanations share an underlying theme, for they all explain the phenomenon in terms of deficits. It is because of what she lacks or has lost – oestrogen, energy, sense of self, essential minerals, self-esteem – that the woman has gone off sex.

But there is another way of looking at what happens to a woman's sexuality after childbirth. Instead of looking at what has been lost, we could look at what has been gained.

LOVE AND RAGE AND FEAR

The new mother is caught in a vortex of powerful feelings – feelings about the birth, and feelings about the baby.

Childbirth is a rite of passage like no other. Ask a woman how she felt about menstruation, and you will very likely be told it didn't really change anything. Ask her about loss of virginity and she will probably say she was disappointed. But ask her about childbirth and you will be told it was completely mind-blowing. Whether childbirth is wonderful or appalling or a bit of both, it is one of the most overwhelming of human experiences. No wonder men in some tribal societies claim it for themselves with ritual enactments of pregnancy and birth.

Often women recall the moment of birth with romantic feelings, reliving it all as you might relive a love affair. They talk lyrically, singing the birth song: 'I think back and try to recapture the wonderful feeling of first seeing this baby – longing, before the baby's born, *longing* to see this baby and feel this baby feeding – particularly after the first one, I knew what breast-feeding was like, and really enjoyed it – wanting to hold the baby to me and have the baby feed, and when the baby's actually born, how wonderful this feeling is . . . It's very difficult to describe the feeling that you have when you first hold your child . . .' Or a woman may think back with anger, raging that somehow the romance was spoilt for her: the thinking back then may be more akin to the way we relive a trauma, trying to make sense of it. But whatever the content, we do think back. There is a ritual that mothers of new babies invariably go through when they meet for the first time – the exchange of birth stories.

Then there are feelings about the baby. Eve cried as she relived the feelings she'd had after the birth of her first son, now twelve. 'I was very wrapped up in the emotions of it all. I couldn't stop looking at him, I just couldn't take my eyes off him. I was terrified that he was going to die. I can remember crying when we came out of hospital. In hospital everything's germ-free and everything's safe, and I brought him home and thought . . . I'm going to cry now, it's strange after all these years . . . I just thought, I want him to die now and get it over with, because I know he's going to die . . . I can remember waking up one night, and I was crawling around the floor trying to pull him out of the water, I'd dreamt that he'd fallen into deep water, and I was trying to pull him out, I was actually on the floor crying – so it was very powerful.'

Kate said, 'When Alice was a baby she went into Special Care, and I was convinced she was going to die. I was absolutely determined to breast-feed her. They wheeled her incubator off and I thought if they gave her a bottle that would be it. I'd had an epidural in for fifteen hours, and I literally crawled along the corridor dripping blood, till the sister came along saying, "What on earth are you doing?" I was dragging myself along like some sea animal on land, dragging this huge weight, "They're taking my baby away, they're going to give her a bottle!"' For Kate the feelings after childbirth are so intense that she crawls along a public corridor, in defiance both of normal conventions of behaviour and her own physical weakness: for Eve the emotion is still so real twelve years later that she relives it even as she tells me about it.

These feelings after birth are a potent mix of love and rage and fear. The rage is directed at anyone who might harm the baby, and at the baby too, sometimes involving acts of violence that the vast majority of women carefully direct away from the baby. Eve recalled sometimes biting her baby's dummy so hard she left toothmarks in it: Claudia once kicked her crying baby's cot so hard that she broke her own toe. The fear for the baby that Eve describes so vividly can widen out to affect the way we think about many things. After childbirth we have a heightened sense of the dangers of the world. We rage at the arms trade, the industrialists who pollute the atmosphere, the young men who drive their cars like weapons. The parents of small children join environmental groups and campaign against unsafe food – like Pamela Stephenson with her campaign against Alar – not just because babies and small children are more vulnerable to all kinds of dangers, and not just because we are aware that our children will face the consequences of the damage we are doing to the earth now, but also because the vulnerability of small children reminds us of the vulnerability of all human life. After the birth of a first child, we think about death a lot more. These preoccupations may well have implications for a woman's libido. When we are pierced by emotions like those that Kate and Eve describe, sex may seem incidental, ephemeral, even trivial. Sex is a distraction from what we should be doing, our more important, more central concerns.

As the baby grows, the fear generally recedes. But for most mothers there is a residue of more or less permanent anxiety. Anxiety is a maternal attribute that in the bravado of our Cosmopolitan Woman days we may despise. We may see our own mothers as a repository of fears. Mothers are full of worries and admonitions about the dangers of the world – 'Always wear a vest', 'Don't let him put his long thing in you . . .' When we have children ourselves, we come to understand their fearfulness better. But this persistent anxiety is anathema to the risk-taking that is part of sex. Safety is opposed to daring: afraid, we become cautious, we retreat. The sex'n'drugs'n'rock'n'roll part of life comes to feel out of bounds. Sara said, 'When I'd had Tony I felt, "I'm a mother, I'm responsible for this child, I mustn't get into dangerous situations that might threaten this . . ." I was only eighteen, and I'd watched the television; I knew what happened to young girls that had babies, that it goes badly wrong – so I was very aware of keeping myself on the straight and narrow. I avoided dangerous people and drugs, because I knew I had to keep that security at home.'

Emily remembers how when her baby was tiny she made a bargain with herself about the place of sexual pleasure in her life. 'It sounds ludicrous,' she said, 'but I do remember that when I was having sex and starting to really enjoy it again, I used to have to keep checking out with myself that this wasn't more important to me than the baby – that I wouldn't choose this rather than the baby.' A woman may have a sense that sexual excitement is a potential threat to her child, and that this is one sensuous imperative that could tug her away from her bond with the baby. If you become too wrapped up in your own arousal, you may not stop when the baby cries: if you become wrapped up in a new love affair, you may put your own needs before your child's.

Some women described how being a mother restricted and shaped their sexual choices, especially if they were considering looking outside the marriage for sex. In such adventures, there would now be too much to lose: 'I wouldn't do anything that might endanger her, that might mean she could be taken away.' The belief that a sexual mother is a bad mother is still prevalent in our culture – and a bad mother might lose her baby. Women know that prostitutes did, until recently, run the risk of having their children taken into care: there is a cruel irony in this, given that it has so often been the need to provide for their children that has driven women into prostitution. Women know too that if a marriage breaks down and custody is contested, a woman's sexual conduct may be used against her.

THE CLOSENESS OF A LITTLE WARM BODY

The experience of caring for a baby is full of fear, physical discomfort and exhaustion, but it is also for most women a source of abundant physical pleasures. As they describe the smells and textures of new babies, women often use food metaphors to convey a sense of their child's deliciousness – they talk about the baby's 'honey-scented breath', or 'soft marshmallowy feel' – and they stress the sensuousness of the experience of mothering. 'I can remember really special times, just the closeness of a little warm body next to your body: I think it's just the warmth and closeness of them being next to you – and because you love them so much it's such an intense feeling.' 'I love the feel of their skin, their smell, their little heads. They're like little kittens tucking into you, they relax into their cuddles so much when they're tiny, they're just little bundles, and they trust you so much.' As these women talked, they both made a characteristic gesture, as though cradling a baby against their shoulder: the feelings are remembered with the body.

To hear about these feelings, and to witness the intensity of the mother-baby relationship, can be a disturbing experience. The mother cuddling her baby reminds us of the lost Nirvana of our own experience of being mothered, she reminds us of our own infant helplessness and dependency, and for men in particular there may be a painful sense of exclusion, especially if the mother is breast-feeding the baby. In our culture, we distance ourselves from these feelings by sentimentalizing the mother-baby relationship, and then being repelled by the sentiment. Both men and women participate in this process. It is nowhere more apparent than in our attitude to little girls' play with dolls and cuddly toys. 'Non-sexist child-rearing' means giving your daughter a dumper truck: no one gives their son a set of My Little Ponies. Traditional boys' toys have higher status than traditional girls' toys, and it is the girls' toys that most suggest nurturance, vulnerability and cuddliness –

the furry Brush-a-Love or Care Bear – that evoke the most repelled response from adults.

Because of the sentimentality, and in the absence of an alternative discourse about mother-baby sensuousness such as existed for the writers of the exquisite medieval Christian lullabies, the only language we have to describe these feelings is the language of the down-market greeting card. Yet the sentiment sits uneasily with reality. The sensuousness of the mother-baby relationship is not a sentimental extra: without all that cuddling and snuggling, babies die, as was proved by James I's grisly attempt to see what language babies would talk if denied human contact. Society's sentimental fantasy about motherhood clashes with the reality of the fierce emotional connection that a mother feels with her baby, the feeling that had Kate dragging her bleeding body along the hospital corridor. And the sentimental frame also fails to encompass the intensity of the physical experience. Shirley said, 'My first son was born when I was thirty-six, and to me this was an absolute miracle because I didn't think I'd ever have children, because before I met my husband I'd only been attracted to women. I was so over the moon with joy at this miracle before me that the day after he was born I took him into bed with me and I tucked him under the bedclothes and I was just lying with him on top of me, and I had an orgasm. Now, there was no sexual contact, none whatever, I didn't feel any kind of build-up to it, it just came out of the blue. I see that now as an overpowering expression of the love that I felt for this 7lb tot.'

As our children grow up, our sense of connection with them remains something that is powerfully experienced with the body. Separation from your children may be felt as a physical loss, as though part of your body is missing. When she was imprisoned in 1976 for a crime she hadn't committed, Annie McGuire was forcibly separated from her four children, then aged between nine and seventeen. She told a *Guardian* reporter, 'As a mother who had never left her children, not even with baby-minders, it was pure hell. Between 3.30 and 4 was difficult, when they would all have been coming home from school. I would get echoes of their voices in my head. I had real physical cravings – my whole body ached for them.'

Memories of breast-feeding seem to inspire particularly sensuous language. The early days of breast-feeding can be a physical agony of sore nipples and engorgement, but all the women I talked to who had breast-fed said they found it a pleasurable experience once the initial problems were overcome. For most women it was a source of gentle pleasures: they had enjoyed the extended cuddle, the closeness, the sense of doing something useful and right. But some women talked about the experience in absolutes: it was 'the most peaceful experience', 'the most wonderful thing anyone can do'. Jacqueline said, 'I really really loved it – just the whole closeness of it. It always made me feel incredibly magical, to be able to calm this child with my own body.' Anne said, 'I have never felt so ecstatic and yet so peaceful as when I was feeding them. Josh used to put his hand very lightly just there on my breast, just little light touches, and he used to look up at me with these big blue eyes and smile, without coming off the nipple. All my most ecstatically peaceful physical experiences have been when I was feeding.' And, as Masters and Johnson established, there are women who find breast-feeding physically arousing.[7] Penny said, 'I did used to get quite turned-on, when he started to wiggle his tongue.' Jacqueline said, 'I would describe it as sensual rather than sexual, although certainly there were times in the early days when I was so engorged with milk that there were sort of rippling effects, rather like an orgasm.' Women who enjoyed breast-feeding tell how they grieved when they fed what they intended should be their last baby for the last time.

For most women, then, mothering a baby or small child is an experience which incorporates many physical pleasures, occasionally even of orgasmic intensity. How does all this sensuousness affect sex?

Melissa said, 'I went off sex as soon as Ben was born ... oh, as soon as Ben was born. But I know the stage where it changed from being tired and not wanting to be touched. Now I want to start having sex with Gordon again, but I think, No, what's the point? Before, I used to go to bed and make sure it was good for him, because I got pleasure from that. But your priorities change. Ben has become more important than Gordon. You've got this baby – they depend on you for life itself, and they're all pink and hairless and clean and cuddly and milky, and you turn round to this great big hairy man, who's perhaps not had a bath and is farting in bed. He's what he was before but you never saw it in that light, and you think, No, not today – and then it's "Not today" again, and it just goes on and then you realize it's six months ...'

Linda was feeding her baby as she told me, 'I think it's probably one of the reasons why I don't feel like sex with a man at the moment, because I'm having this physical thing with Danny right now. My breasts are for Danny, they're not for fondling or for a turn-on, they're for milking. And everything's nice and small and clean – and you suddenly get this big hairy man, I find that off-putting. Once, before Danny was born, when my husband and the other two boys were in the bath, I was going along the line washing their hair, and I came to Alan, and I said, "My God" – and when I'm washing their hair I always put my fingers in their ears, and when I put my fingers in his ears, they were lost in these big holes, and I thought, Ugh, these nice little holes and then suddenly these great big holes – and, that's just it, men seem so *big*.'

For Linda and Melissa, the sensuousness of the baby outweighs the attractiveness of the adult sex partner. This is not how we were meant to feel. Your baby is not meant to be more attractive to you than your husband. Like failing to 'get your figure back', finding your baby more physically rewarding than your partner is, in our society, one of the cardinal sins of the new mother. This is what we were warned about in the antenatal classes and the baby magazines, when we were told that though we might feel a little tired it was terribly important to make time for our husbands. Alex Comfort seems to have been quite right in *The Joy of Sex* to have listed 'Children' under 'Problems'.

Implicit in Melissa's account, too, is that familiar conceptualization of sex as work. For Melissa, sex is not a source of refreshment or relaxation. Especially where sex was only a limited source of pleasure before childbirth, because the woman didn't have reliable orgasms, she may decide after childbirth that it simply isn't worth the effort. Underlying so many of the things women say about sex after childbirth is a deep conviction that sex – as refreshment, as relaxation, or simply as uncomplicated pleasure – is really for men. Marianne said, 'The child thing seems so much more straightforward, somehow. It seems so right, whereas sex doesn't really quite seem right. There's a lot of guilt and paradox about actual sex, and there's just none of that in the sensuousness with which you treat your children, it seems totally open and above board, it feels you have a right to it somehow, whereas you don't really have a right to the other thing.' Olive, now in her seventies, remembers her pleasure in breast-feeding. 'Yes, it's sensuous, and the fact that the baby's obviously getting so much pleasure from it, and it's a

completeness, a complete feeling, there's a wholeness about it. Oh
I think it's lovely!'

Sensuousness with babies, say these women, is complete and
whole: is there then something incomplete, something missing from
sex for women? Sensuousness with children feels right: mothering,
we still feel, is what we are meant to be doing, and sex still isn't
somehow. What women say about their easy relationship to the
sensuousness of mothering underlines their uneasy relationship to
the sensuousness of sex.

MY BODY'S MY OWN

There is, as every mother knows, a downside to this physical
relationship, in its sheer relentlessness: and given that sex is 'work'
for many women, this relentlessness also gets in the way of sex.
Tina said, 'Elisabeth was a very clingy baby and I remember feeling,
"Just leave my body alone!" I mean, it wasn't just sex, it was
everything, I felt like they'd been grabbing things off me all day,
physically as well as emotionally, and even if my husband just put
his arm around me, I felt that it was an invasion. After seven p.m.
my body's my own and just you leave it alone.'

Tina feels eaten up; she feels she is all bits to be given or grabbed
or taken. Much of the giving is with her body – hugs, comfort,
milk. In all our systems of imagery, a woman's body is a container
of good things for the use of other people. In psychoanalytic
imagery, for instance, the mother's body might be represented as
a larder or food shop. Sex is just something more to be given or
grabbed or stolen from the shelves, rather than something the
woman takes for herself, to replenish her own supplies.

Jennifer said, 'I enjoyed breast-feeding very very much, but in
a way I felt violated by it. I'd always previously liked my breasts to
be sucked as a form of sexual arousal, and I don't like it now, it's
just all too mixed up now. And it's a handicap because it's an easy
form of sexual arousal. Before I had my first baby, my mother said
to me, "You have to remember that you're a wife first, before you're
a mother," and I have since wanted to scream at her, "You have
to remember you are *yourself* first, before you're a wife, before
you're a mother." I feel it very strongly at the moment, and certainly
breasts are part of that. Those are mine, hands off everybody.'

Jennifer focuses on a specific way in which the image of the
body as a source of good things for others may stand in the way

of sexual arousal. When she is still feeding, a woman may dislike having her breasts touched during sex because they belong to the baby: now that Jennifer has stopped, she still wants to avoid this form of stimulation because her breasts belong to *her*. What had formerly been an easy form of sexual arousal for her remains unacceptable.

Eventually, of course, the children grow, and the whole thing becomes less exhausting. The woman stops thinking of herself as a container of good things to be freely given or greedily grabbed, and feels the boundaries of her body and psyche to be redrawn. But as this happens she also loses something, that intense physical intimacy of the early months and years.

These changes of course are right and necessary, and many of them are instigated by the mother. To discuss the sensuousness of mothering with women is also to uncover the host of subtle ways in which women control expressions of mother-child sensuality that are felt to be no longer appropriate. A woman may lightly move her six-year-old son's hand from her breast, or explain to her daughter that children don't kiss their mothers on the lips with an open mouth.

But there may be sadness too. In ten years' time, even when everything has gone beautifully and none of the fears of those disturbing early days of motherhood have been realized, it will be a different relationship with a different child. Anne said, 'Sometimes you think of those little children you bathed and made meals for and read stories to, and you wonder where they've gone. Sometimes I grieve for those children. Today my friend at work said she'd been woken at night, her little boy had a nightmare, and I said, "How old is he?" and she said, "Nine," and I thought of Susie and Josh at nine. They're so lovely at nine, I could see them at nine, and for a moment I wanted to cry. You think, Where have those little children gone?'

LOOKING FOR WOMEN'S MEANINGS: SEX AFTER CHILDBIRTH

The Yoruba people of Nigeria traditionally abstain from sex for three years after childbirth. The Dani people of Indonesia are claimed to have had a four to six year period of postpartum abstinence.[8] In our own society, a medical school joke runs like this: 'Question: When is it safe to resume intercourse after delivery?

Answer: Gentlemen wait till the placenta has been delivered . . .'

Societies in which sexuality is organized around fertility rather than around male pleasure may be less oppressive than our own to women after childbirth. If women often do, for an abundance of reasons, go off sex after childbirth, it is clearly better that this should be recognized. In our own society, the only vestige of such customs is the ritual of waiting till the six week check-up, at which the woman will be told that she can safely resume her sex life. But this permission may well be heard as an injunction, and if she doesn't want sex then – and especially if she still isn't enjoying it six months or a year later – her reluctance is conceptualized as a problem, an inappropriate response that she should struggle to overcome.

Common assumptions about the relationship between child-bearing and sexual pleasure clash with many women's experience. Pregnancy is for many of us a time of heightened sexual interest, possibly because of the increased blood flow to the pelvis. But in society's obsession with 'slim equals sexy', pregnancy is seen as anything but erotic. In the iconography of fashion, it's a virginal time, a time for regression to prepubescence, a time to wear sprigged cotton and little white collars. Because our ideas about sexual attractiveness are rooted in our culture's opposition to fertil-ity, the conspicuously pregnant woman is not seen as sexually attrac-tive or sexual. It is then scarcely surprising that women who maintain their heightened sexual interest throughout pregnancy are often upset to find that as their stomachs swell their partners' sexual interest declines. Because our society makes male sexual pleasure paramount, this common sexual incompatibility is never perceived as a problem; men are never urged to do all they can to satisfy their partners during pregnancy. But when after childbirth the tables are turned and it is the woman who has no interest, it's time to write to the advice columns and consult the therapists and sex manuals. Yet again we see how when male sexual pleasure is made paramount, our expectations about how our lives should be clash with the norms of women's sexual responses.

There is another way of looking at the whole issue of female loss of libido after childbirth. It could also be seen as one possible and perfectly normal response pattern which makes complete bio-logical sense. The human infant is extremely vulnerable for a long period of time. Given the dependence of the infant and the intensity of his or her need for mothering, it is highly adaptive that the mother should find her baby preoccupying to the exclusion of all else. The fierce sense of physical and emotional connection with her baby which for some women makes sex seem peripheral is good for the baby. If her reluctance to have intercourse is respected by her partner, that is also good for the species, because it will maximize the chances of the couple's offspring surviving: a wider interval between births means heavier and healthier babies.[9] This is one obvious reason why so many cultures have institutionalized a period of postpartum abstinence, often lasting until the baby is weaned. Viewed in a multi-cultural context, going off sex after childbirth appears the norm rather than an anomaly. And viewed from a biological perspective, it is an adaptive behaviour rather than an aberration.

To suggest that a behavioural pattern makes biological sense is not to say that it necessarily makes life easy or pleasant. Today we have a naive notion of the 'natural' as essentially benign, yet things that happen naturally do not serve everybody's interests. Even if we recognized that it was appropriate and adaptive for women to go off sex after childbirth, some men would still have affairs after the births of their children, and some couples would still be unhappy. But many couples might be helped by a wider recognition that it is perfectly normal for the woman's sexual interest to be reduced for some months, and even for two or three years after childbirth.

This theory is borne out by the experiences of Ruth and Christine and Tracy, the three women whose stories we heard at the start of this chapter, women for whom the sexual wasteland stretched for years. From what these women say, it seems likely that in each case after childbirth a couple dynamic was set up around sex that persisted into the time when the woman's sexual interest might have been expected to return. The interaction goes like this. She doesn't want or doesn't enjoy sex. He thinks this means she no longer loves him. He is hurt and confused and becomes more demanding. She resents the demands and becomes still more reluctant. He gets angry, she feels pressured, and sex becomes a battleground.

Christine said, 'I think we each argued our own side for a very long time. We did read some books and we did try things they suggested, like each having your own nights when you were the one who decided. Of course, what happens is that the person who wants sex most chooses it on their nights and you don't have it on the other nights. It didn't work because I used to feel worse if I felt I was being forced into it, and of course by that set-up I did feel I was being forced into it. Pete used to say, "But if you love me, you ought to want to," and "Well, *why* don't you want to?" – which is an impossible thing to answer, because there were times when emotionally I wanted to be turned on, but physically just wasn't, so that was something impossible to overcome. I've really had to force home the resentment that builds up when somebody is constantly making demands, and not accepting your point of view. And he would say things like, "I think you miss sex more than you realize, because you're more bad-tempered when we don't have sex very often," and that just used to make me angry because I used to think, I'm bad-tempered because you're making me angry because you're making all these demands . . .'

The dynamic that Christine describes arises because we continue to gloss over the fact that many new mothers go off sex, so the woman's lack of interest is seen as a personal, individual response, and a sign that something is wrong. This perception of the problem may have a lasting effect on the couple's relationship. Where the woman's loss of libido is read as a sign that something is wrong with the relationship, this belief may become a self-fulfilling prophecy. In her book, *Motherhood, What It Does to Your Mind,*[10] psychotherapist Jane Price describes the lifelong anger and bitterness which women may feel where husbands have sought to re-establish sexual 'ownership' of their wives as rapidly as possible after a new birth in the family, and suggests that women return to sex with more enthusiasm if they are allowed as long as they need to recover physically and emotionally from the birth. Here is one area where an assertion of women's meanings might make for greater sexual happiness in the long term for both men and women.

LOOKING FOR WOMEN'S MEANINGS: BREAST-FEEDING

The woman who is breast-feeding her baby rapidly learns to read between the lines of public effusions on the subject. Breast-feeding, she learns, is a beautiful thing, a wonderful expression of motherly nurturance, a magical way of shoring up her baby's resistance with all those lovely antibodies – and if she needs to do it outside the privacy of her own home, she'd better go and do it in the loo.

Double standards about breasts are a particularly stark reminder of the supremacy of male meanings in attitudes to female bodies and physical sensuality. The public display of female breasts for male delectation is everywhere acceptable: the woman with a hungry baby discreetly tucked up her jumper is not. There are many accounts of women who have fed their babies in public – in Harrod's tearoom, for instance – being told to leave.[11] The primary function of the breasts gives quiet or intense pleasure to mother and baby and excludes men: where male sexual values rule, it is unacceptable for men to be reminded that this is what breasts are intended for.

It is interesting to examine the reasons women give for their decisions on how to feed their babies. Because women's bodies are for men, women frequently cite reasons that are at root about male sexual pleasure, and have nothing to do with their own needs or those of their babies. They talk about the effects of their decision on their figures, the shape of their breasts, their physical attractiveness. The bait held out to women by health professionals who believe that women 'should' breast-feed is that the woman will 'get her figure back' more quickly. Women who choose to bottle-feed often say that they might have liked to breast-feed, but they feared what breast-feeding might do to the shape of their breasts.

A leaflet from Wyeth intended for distribution in antenatal clinics goes one step further in its advocacy of breast-feeding for male reasons. 'It's Your Baby Too' informs us that fathers 'do not take kindly to a little infant coming in on the act – and who can blame them. Fathers who feel this way may be cheered by some research that has shown that women who breast-feed their babies are more likely to resume sexual activity quickly than their bottle-feeding sisters! Also, many women find that they are more sexually active during the time they are breast-feeding than at any other time in their lives.'[12]

Perhaps the special pleading is justified, however specious the arguments, given the opposition to breast-feeding that so many men express. Some women are actually forbidden to breast-feed by their partners, and many men who wouldn't go that far make no attempt to hide their dislike of the process. Fran said, 'I really enjoyed breast-feeding, but I felt very conflicted. I was getting stretchmarks, and Tom wasn't very pleased about that. It didn't stop me doing it but it certainly crossed my mind to stop, and I found that irritating, that someone else should make me feel like that. I felt that in a fairer society people would say "Oh, how nice, you've had a baby, how wonderful, you must have fed for a long time!" I felt it should be a really positive thing.'

Fran suggests there might be different meanings for breasts that point down and for silvery stretchmarks: these marks on our bodies might be admired and valued as signs of maturity and experience. As Fran's comments suggest, there could be quite another approach to baby care, a woman-centred approach that ignores both the stern injunctions in the childcare books, and the male wish that we should continue to look like teenagers. Perhaps it is because Fran is now in a lesbian relationship and no longer dependent on male sexual approval that she can see these alternative meanings so clearly.

Fran's enjoyment of breast-feeding is typical of many of the women I talked to. Some women had desperately wanted to breast-feed but couldn't, and some had known that breast-feeding wasn't for them, but, as we have seen, many women had found breast-feeding physically pleasurable, and for virtually all the women who'd breast-fed, it was a special memory, something they were happy to have experienced. But the physical pleasures of breast-feeding, which are so apparent in women's accounts, are rarely part of a woman's original decision. Far from being seen as a sensuous activity, breast-feeding is perceived as messy, painful, hard to do, and something that is only achieved with a struggle. We learn this in hospital when we first try to feed. Ward regimes do little to encourage the idea that breast-feeding can be a relaxed and sensuous experience. However well-meaning the nursing staff may be, the rules on most maternity wards – no babies in bed with mothers, and feeding only at fixed intervals and for five minutes each side – make breast-feeding extremely difficult to establish. To feed successfully, most women have to suckle very frequently for a day or two. An experienced mother may decide not to say how much she's been feeding her baby, to avoid a reprimand from the nursing staff.

In the 'feeding by the clock' hospital ward attitudes to breast-feeding we can see the remnants of the barbarous childcare regimes of the fifties which caused such distress to mothers and babies, when fear and envy of mother-baby sensuousness deprived mothers and babies of the experiences they most needed. Mary remembered, 'You were only allowed to cuddle them for an hour, they had a playtime from 5 to 6, and then you bathed and fed them. You couldn't pick them up when they cried. That was being an over-conscientious mother – and I shall always, always regret it. I used to go downstairs with the baby screaming upstairs, and I *longed* to go and pick the baby up, but no, you've got to wait till

ten o'clock even if the child is screaming. Now I think it's unforgiv-
able. You do your best, you know nothing about bringing up children, you buy the books and read them. I think it damaged both
my children, but there's nothing I can do about it. It was all "Thou
Must Not" then, and I'm very much a law-abiding person, so I do
what I'm told.'

Childcare ideology has fortunately changed a lot. Nowadays, to
oppose to the rules of the maternity ward, we have the National
Childbirth Trust and the La Leche League, organizations which
promulgate a more rewarding approach to baby care, and in particular offer support and advice to women who wish to breast-feed.
But the older ideas linger on, especially perhaps for less privileged
women: breast-feeding is now overwhelmingly a middle-class practice, and the NCT is largely a middle-class organization. And for
women of all classes, mothering remains something of a ghetto:
mother-baby sensuousness may no longer be rationed, as it was in
the Truby King era, but it is still kept separate. Mothers and small
children are still excluded from public life, an exclusion that is
particularly marked in the countries of Northern Europe. It is this
exclusion that makes possible the sentimentalizing of mother-baby
sensuousness that we have already noted. When an image from the
real world of mothers and babies – rather than from the sanitized
soft-focus world of life insurance commercials and greetings cards
– intrudes into the High Street, it is met with shock. In August
1991, a Benetton poster showed a perfectly normal baby just after
birth, an image that even Mrs Mary Whitehouse described as 'really
rather wonderful'. There were 800 complaints in the first week the
poster was displayed.[13]

LOOKING FOR WOMEN'S MEANINGS: NATURAL CHILDBIRTH

A baby at the moment of birth. Isn't that a reminder of one area
at least in which women have successfully asserted new meanings
and intervened in male suppression of the physical relationship
between mother and baby? Isn't 'natural childbirth' a triumphant
assertion of female sensuousness, even of female sexuality? Sheila
Kitzinger for instance claims that childbirth 'can be the most
intensely sexual feeling a woman ever experiences, as strong as
orgasm, even more compelling than orgasm.'[14]

The advocates of natural childbirth have brought about certain

changes in the medical management of childbirth which have indu-
bitably benefited women. But I find some current thinking on natural childbirth deeply troubling. Much discussion of natural
childbirth seems to merge two ideas which are not necessarily
complementary and may even conflict with one another: the belief
that it is good to have choice and control during childbirth, and
the belief that it is good to do without pain relief. In the context
of the 'good birth', it is by refusing pain relief that you make your
choice and exercise your control.

The natural childbirth movement has its origins in women's
anger at the way their own wishes were routinely discounted, the
kind of anger felt by Joy in Chapter 3, for whom a rough internal
from a domineering consultant was the trigger that brought back
the repressed memories of her sexual abuse by her father. Taking
control and being able to choose are both vital if women are not
to feel violated by the experience of childbirth. We need to feel in
charge of what happens, to be given full information, to choose
what interventions we will have. But choice must also include the
possibility of effective pain relief. For most women, giving birth
hurts like hell. The Romans called childbirth 'poena magna' – the
great pain – and the experience hasn't magically changed just
because Grantly Dick-Read thought up some breathing exercises.
When women describe the pain of childbirth, they often talk about
death: 'I didn't know you could feel that much pain and not die';
'I thought, If this goes on, just let me die, I want to die.' But
because of our concept of the 'good birth', the woman who copes
with feeling near to death by accepting drugs will believe that she
has failed.

A few women – perhaps 3 or 4 per cent[15] – give birth with little
pain, just as a few women have orgasms on first intercourse, or
never get PMT. This is delightful for them, and their anomalous
experiences are interesting to read about. Unfortunately these
women also tend to teach the childbirth classes and write the books
on the rather nebulous advantages of doing it 'naturally'. Where
books by such authors are the main sources of information about
childbirth, women giving birth for the first time are quite unprepared for the actual experience of labour. A woman who attempts
to oppose her own experience to the ideology may not be listened
to. Jennifer recalled, 'After Jonathan was born, when I was still in
hospital, I was asked if I'd show him to the antenatal class that was
looking round, and if I would talk a bit about the birth. But I

was shut up when I started to talk about how painful it was, I was actually stopped – "Don't tell them that," you know.'

Why does the ideology of natural childbirth persist in the face of most women's experience? I would suggest that the notion that a 'good birth' is a birth without pain relief seems right because it actually perpetuates very old ideas about women's bodies – that women are born to suffer and that female pain is good. The apparently woman-centred ideology of natural childbirth is totally in line with the old Christian teaching that it was a sin to accept pain relief during childbirth because labour pain was caused by the working out of the curse on Eve for giving Adam the apple. When in 1847 James Simpson experimented with the use of chloroform to relieve labour pain, there was much opposition from the clergy, who attacked anaesthesia as 'a decay of Satan, apparently offering itself to bless women; but in the end it will harden society and rob God of the deep earnest cries which arise in time of trouble for help.'[16] It was only when Queen Victoria set a precedent by accepting chloroform that anaesthesia in childbirth became acceptable. Today, rather than patriarchal clergymen, it is pro-women women who extol the virtues of birth without pain relief. But women should be wary when anyone at all, even an enthusiastic earth-mother teaching an active birth class, tries to tell us that pain is pleasure.

To focus on the process of birth, and to seek to do it 'right', is to put our energy in the wrong place. The emotional high that we cherish in memory comes at the moment of delivery itself and in the moments which follow – when we hold the baby for the first time, study all the details of the perfect little body, and perhaps put the baby to the breast. There could be another kind of 'good · birth' – a birth in which the woman aims to give birth with as little pain as possible, so she still has the energy at the end of it all to relish those minutes or hours when she marvels over her baby. These intense pleasures may be denied us by the after-effects of natural childbirth because the woman who has given birth 'naturally' is often too weak and shaky to hold her baby. June said, 'It was a very short labour, I didn't really start having proper contractions till an hour before she was born, and I still think they probably weren't as painful as they are for many women. It was too late for me to have any drugs by the time I got into hospital. I coped with it, but at the end of it all I did feel in a state of shock. I just remember vomiting violently at the end of it, and Martin held Georgina, I was so grateful that he was there to love that baby

properly because I was just too much in a state of shock to cope
with it at all, and there was my beautiful baby and I loved her but
I couldn't do very much about her because I was in this weird
state.'

What are childbirth and mothering like now for the woman who
gets them right?

Today's good mother gives birth without pain relief, just as the
Victorian clergy advocated. She breast-feeds her baby because
'breast is best', and it will help her to 'get her figure back'. She
starts having intercourse again as soon as it's physically possible.
She goes on a diet so she is just as attractive a sex partner as
before. She enjoys cuddling her baby, but not nearly as much as
she enjoys having sex with her husband.

It is clear that our ideas about what constitutes a good mother
are shaped to a large extent by male sexual values and the belief
in the supreme importance of male sexual gratification.

There could be a different set of priorities. To choose a relatively
pain-free birth that leaves you strong enough to enjoy that part
that women enjoy most – welcoming your baby. To base your
decision about how to feed your baby on what you think you will
enjoy, rather than what will be best for your figure. To eat well to
keep your strength up to cope with the demands of mothering. To
recognize that many women don't feel like sex for months after
childbirth, and if this happens, to know that it is a normal pattern
with sound biological roots. To celebrate and indulge in the strong
physical connection between mother and child as a potent source
of sensuous pleasure in women's lives.

To assert the pleasures of mothering is always a risky enterprise,
because the assertion may seem to undermine women's strivings
for autonomy. Some feminist writers have played these pleasures
down, most notoriously Shulamith Firestone, who suggested that
looking after a baby is 'like spending all day, every day, in the
exclusive company of an incontinent mental defective.' To suggest
that a woman can be genuinely distressed by not seeing enough of
her children is to provoke an outcry from many of those who see
themselves as having women's interests at heart. In Maeve Haran's
book, *Having It All*, her heroine, Liz Ward, gives up a high-powered
job in order to spend more time with her children.[17] Critical
responses to the book included the statement that it was 'worse
than pornography'.

These responses are understandable. Women's achievements in entering the male world of work and reaping its rewards for themselves seem so fragile, and so easily overturned and likely to be snatched away. And none of the problems about motherhood that feminist writers have articulated have gone away. The conditions in which women are expected to bring up children are still appalling: the tendency to define women primarily in terms of their nurturing capacity persists. But surely there is no necessary contradiction between fighting to change these things, and recognizing and owning the sensuousness of mothering.

CHAPTER EIGHT

Women in Mid-Life:
Holy and Godly Matrons

'Look mercifully upon these thy servants . . . that this woman may be loving and amiable, faithful and obedient to her husband: and in all quietness, sobriety and peace, be a follower of holy and godly matrons.' This prayer in the old Anglican marriage service always intrigued me. Who exactly were these matrons, these exemplary women who would show the young bride how to live?

According to the dictionary definition, the matron is a woman who manages domestic affairs, or a married woman with expert knowledge of pregnancy. The matron is a woman who is older than the bride, a woman who has already had her children. More specifically, the word suggests the woman in mid-life, with daughters of marriageable age. In every society it is this woman who is expected to control and police the sexuality of younger women, and to ensure that they remain chaste according to the definitions of female chastity laid down by the patriarchal establishment.

It is the matron who tells the young woman that her virginity is precious and that she mustn't lose it before marriage. In parts of Africa, it is the matron who holds her daughter down while her clitoris is excised, because she believes that only then will her daughter be clean. And in pre-revolutionary China, it was the matron who guaranteed her daughter's desirability by arranging for her feet to be bound. The matron's concerns are the honour of the family and the fitness for marriage of her daughters. Though her actions may often seem cruel, the matron colludes with the barbarous patriarchal practices for protective maternal reasons, because she knows that under patriarchy there are grave penalties exacted from young women who don't live by the rules.

By ensuring that the old traditions are followed and the patriarchal values are acted on, the matron ensures the perpetuation of patriarchy. But her relationship to patriarchy is not a simple one. In her concern with the control of sex she often actually clashes with male sexual interests. In Victorian society, there was a flourishing crop of holy and godly matrons, women like Josephine Butler or J. Ellice Hopkins. These Victorian reformers sought to stamp out prostitution and rescue 'fallen women', and to protect women from unwanted sexual demands: they campaigned in favour of the Contagious Diseases Acts, or founded the Ladies Association for Friendless Girls, or were active in the Temperance movement, believing that it was mainly under the influence of alcohol that men forced their sexual attentions on their wives.[1] As prostitution was the great sexual theme of the Victorian era, so pornography is the preoccupation of our own: in our intensely visual culture, anxiety about the control of sex hinges not on what may or may not be done, but on what may or may not be seen. And in our own time, an outstanding example of a holy and godly matron can be found in MP Clare Short, who has campaigned to ban 'Page 3 girls' from newspapers. Like Josephine Butler, she embodies the central sexual preoccupation of the times.

The crusading Victorians are now variously seen by feminists as anti-sex, anti-life harridans, or as splendid activists with women's interests at heart. And Clare Short also inspires opposing views from feminists. She has a tremendous amount of support from ordinary women: virtually all the women I spoke to supported her campaigns. But some feminists have taken issue with her – for instance, Lynne Segal, reviewing Clare Short's book, *Dear Clare*,[2] wrote that she found the campaign deeply troubling, and pleaded, 'Don't, for pity's sake, add to the mythology that men like sex and women do not.'[3] The lack of feminist consensus on the work of such women reflects the long-standing ambivalence within feminism about sexuality. Since Victorian times, feminist theorizing about sex has been torn between the conflicting themes of pleasure and danger. Feminists have focused either on the horrors of male sexual oppression of women, or on the rights of women to open sexual expression, and have never quite managed to integrate the two.

In wider society, as in feminist theory, there is much ambivalence about the holy and godly matron. On the one hand, she is seen as disapproving and a killjoy. In the cartoon stereotype, she is associated with certain physical attributes which are seen as the antithesis of sexuality: she is tight-lipped, blue-rinsed, dressed in twinsets and pearls. She is there at the Conservative Party Conference or the Women's Institute, in an asexual hat, disapproving of things. She is 'Disgusted, Tunbridge Wells'. She is part of the demonology of the tabloid newspaper, 'sex is fun (but mainly for men)' culture: Clare Short, in particular, because she made a direct attack on that culture, has been vilified in the tabloid press as 'Killjoy Clare' and 'Ms Misery'. But the woman in mid-life is also seen in popular culture as a good influence, a woman of sound judgement with years of experience. Whenever child protection workers are being criticized in the media, as they were, for instance, after the Cleveland child sex abuse affair in the 1980s, government spokespersons and newspaper editorial writers alike invariably express the view that this work should be done by 'middle-aged women with children'. What is being yearned for here is the prayer book matron, the woman of maturity and wise judgement. The fantasy overlooks the inconvenient fact that many of the workers being vilified fall neatly into this category themselves – for instance, paediatrician Marietta Higgs and social worker Sue Richardson, who were at the centre of the Cleveland controversy, are both middle-aged women with children.

Even formerly outspoken advocates of 'sexual liberation' for women may become holy and godly matrons in mid-life. In her novel *Fear of Flying*, written when she was about thirty, Erica Jong extolled the no-strings-attached sex act, the 'zipless fuck'.[4] Today, in her late forties, she has a different perspective. She has become a devoted follower of the Twelve Steps spiritual growth programme, and when interviewed in *New Statesman*, she commented, 'We've just been through a decade of absolute obsession with material things – BMWs, money, drugs, sex, obsessive love affairs. Sooner or later, though, you have to cultivate your own garden. Those who find sanity have to find it on their own. It's not given by a relationship, however good.'[5] In *The Female Eunuch*, published when she was thirty-one, Germaine Greer wrote, 'Masters and Johnson supplied the blueprint for standard, low-agitation, cool-out monogamy. If women are to avoid this last reduction of their humanity, they must hold out not just for orgasm but for ecstasy.'[6] Today, in her early fifties, Germaine Greer takes a different view about the place of sexuality in human life. In an article in *Marie Claire* she questions what she sees as the current enthusiasm for masturbation: she calls it 'an exercise in futility' and asks, 'Whatever became of dignity?'[7] And on ITV's 'Sex Now' programme in July 1991 she said, 'There are some young women now who cherish a dream of being able to behave the way men do, or did, that they can have many lovers one after the other and that they won't suffer by doing that, that it doesn't deplete them or demean them in any way. That was more or less my own view, I may say. And I don't think they can, I think they do take a bit of a pounding, they are depleted in a spiritual way by these meaningless encounters.'

The expression of sexuality and the control of it are of course both essential aspects of human life and culture. What is worthy of note is the time of life when these women felt moved to gravitate from one concern to the other.

This then is the public voice of the holy and godly matron. She talks of the need to control soft porn imagery. She questions society's preoccupation with sex. She hints at spiritual values that might replace sexual concerns. But what of women's private lives? How does the holy and godly matron express herself in ordinary women's everyday relationships?

MOTHER, MAY I GO OUT TO SWIM?

As we see our daughters grow up and embark on relationships that may become sexual, there are so many reasons to be afraid. We know that sex carries real dangers. Teenage pregnancy is less of a stigma than it once was, but it still carries health risks to mother and baby, and is a major interruption to a girl's career plans when she has scarcely started out. Sexually transmitted diseases have always been a risk, but with AIDS the risks have become terrifying. Then there is sexual violence: we are constantly reminded by the newspapers that there is no haven from the murderous violence of strangers or lovers, not even for the most successful and competent women, the career woman like Suzy Lamplugh, or the brilliant student like Rachel McLean. Pornography, too, is full of reminders of the death-like aspects of male sexuality, the hatred of women that wears only the flimsiest mask of eroticism. There is every reason to be tight-lipped, disapproving, judgemental, full of admonitions.

Paula's daughter is six. Paula said, 'Tess has recently become aware of her body as provocative. She'll wiggle her body, flaunt it. I find it really difficult. There's a lot of my mother comes up in me. She was a total prude, the whole thing was disgusting and vulgar. I try to bite my tongue and ignore it, I don't want Tess to have that sort of hang-up. What worries me – and what my mother was worried about – is that men will be provoked.' Paula knows all about sexual violence: her sister was raped at thirteen, and Paula had herself fended off two sexual attacks as a child. When one in three women have experienced sexual abuse in childhood, and many others like Paula have been threatened with it, or heard how it happened to a sister or mother or friend, most women have enough personal experience to fuel their anxieties. While we may know on a conscious level that such attacks are never the victim's fault, our fears for our daughters come from a more primitive place. Seeing how actively sexual our little girls are, we may fear they will catch the eye and provoke attack, and that later, in seeking out sexual pleasure, they will be putting themselves terribly at risk.

Paula said, 'There's a lot of my mother comes up in me.' When we talk to our daughters about sex, the words that spring to mind are our mothers' words, and the advice that seems to come naturally is based on our mothers' admonitions. The voice of the holy and godly matron echoes down the generations. All women recognize this. When mothers of little girls talk about the advice they will give their daughters about sexuality in adolescence, they say they hope they will be open and accepting, but they know it will be difficult.

Monica said, 'Sharon had quite a concern about sexual identity from when she was about eleven. I used to talk to her about this, and I used to *pray* for her to find some boy attractive, and she did have several boyfriends. But then eventually she settled on the idea that she probably was lesbian, and in fact she now lives with a girlfriend. She gets very angry when I say, "It makes me sad that you will miss out on all the excitement and fulfilment you could get from a heterosexual relationship." She says, "What right have you to say that? How do you know that I don't have just the same sort of feelings?" I can't help feeling it must be a second-best. You think you're open-minded until you actually have to face it, and then you realize you've got some pretty deep in-built feelings about it.' When a woman considers her daughter's lifestyle or sexual orientation she may find she has a sense of how sexual relationships should be ordered which goes back further and is less clearly articulated or examined than her expressed political or feminist beliefs. In what Monica says, we hear the refrain of the holy and godly matron: 'Real sex is sex between men and women, sex that makes babies . . .'

In public, the matron speaks about the control of sexuality in society at large. But her private voice is directed specifically at daughters. Laura left her husband after many years of marriage.

She reflected, 'Had I had a daughter, I think my behaviour would have been quite different. Because I've had two sons I've not been ... well, obviously I *have* been an example to them, they've had to get used to a very wild mother, a very unusual mother, and I feel quite a conscience about their ladies, because they've both got very stable relationships. It worries me, because I would fight to the death that my sons aren't hurt, I would hate them to marry women who feel that, well, if it's not working out we can just leave each other because Laura did ... I would hate to pass that on to another generation, because I don't admire myself, but it was just the way I had to do things.'

When Laura worries about the example she may have set, she thinks, not about her sons, but about her potential daughters-in-law. And when she thinks of the daughter she might have had, she wonders whether she would have made different decisions. Laura has a clear image of how women in mid-life should be in relation to their daughters' sexuality – a source of good advice and an example of sexual continence and control, an image in fact of 'quietness, sobriety and peace', like the matron in the Marriage Service. It might be argued that in seeking sexual fulfilment for herself, Laura would actually have been setting any daughter a wonderful example, and one that is rarely given to women. But this is not what the holy and godly matron means by a good example.

What is it like to listen to the voice of the matron? Though her advice is rooted in fear and love, what her daughter hears is littered with words like Don't and Never. The matron says that sex is dangerous, marriage is important, and having babies is important. She used to say 'Nice girls are virgins when they get married.' Nowadays she might favour the revised version of that precept: 'When you first have sex, make it mean something.'

The communication of this advice is a two-way affair. And sometimes daughters hear these matronly prohibitions even when they aren't consciously intended. Perhaps the daughter hears the subtext, the worried words that don't get spoken, or perhaps she seems to hear her mother telling her to be a 'good girl' because that is what she expects mothers to do. When a mother talks to a teenage daughter about sex, between them and round about there are all the other mothers and daughters that they have been: the totally protective mother caring for the defenceless infant, the no-saying mother clearing up after the messy toddler, the anxious mother warning the schoolchild walking home alone for the first time about the dangers of the world. And between this mother and daughter too stand the mother and the daughter of public fantasy – the highly sexual teenager and the disapproving matron – images that further obscure their view of one another.

Alex said, 'I've had mixed messages off my Mum. Right through my teens I thought she was very disapproving about sex before marriage, because she said how she and Dad were virgins when they were married. So there was me sleeping with these boyfriends, thinking, Oh, a nightmare! In the end I had to tell her that I was on the pill, and she said, "I'm really glad that you're having a healthy sex life," and I said, "I thought you'd just be like so disapproving because of how you hadn't had sex before you got married," and she said "No, no!" So I said, "Why didn't you tell me that when I was little because I've been *suffering*!"'

Alex discovers that the message 'You should be a virgin when you get married' was not intended, yet throughout childhood and adolescence that was what she heard. There is no way of knowing what was actually said, and perhaps there were indeed mixed messages, for how can a woman who has grown up in our society not be ambivalent about sexual expression and sexual freedom? Because of the push-pull between old and new ideas about sex, our advice to our daughters must sometimes have the ambivalence of the mother's admonition in the nursery rhyme:

> Mother may I go out to swim?
> Yes, my darling daughter,
> Hang your clothes on the hickory limb,
> And don't go near the water.

But from what Alex says, it seems most likely that when her mother talked about how things were, Alex heard this as a prescription for how things should be. Daughters hear the holy and godly matron message even when it isn't intended – because this is how mothers are, and this is what mothers say.

The woman in mid-life, it seems, is expected to embody and to express a particular set of sexual values. The corollary of these expectations is that women are not very sexual in middle age. The woman in mid-life can set an example of sexual continence to the younger woman because her sex drive is well under control, she is no longer wildly sexually impulsive, she is not going to get carried away. The ranks of middle-aged women at the Conservative Party

Women's Conference or in the Church of England pews, those women in the tweed skirts and the polyester blouses with floppy bows – those women are the very antithesis of what we think of as sexual. Aren't they?

IN THE DARK WOOD

Over the past twenty years there has been a great deal of theorizing about mid-life, most of it about men. It has been suggested that the characteristic mid-life preoccupation with mortality may usher in a period of anxiety, depression and change. In middle age, you recognize that life is at least half over, that everything can't be mended, and that time, opportunity and hope are all limited.

In a celebrated essay on this theme, psychoanalyst Elliot Jaques looked at the work of artists like Shakespeare and Dante in mid-life, and suggested that the content of their work changes as they mourn the loss of youth, and face up to ageing and death. It was in this essay that Jaques coined the now widely-used term 'mid-life crisis'.[8] But the part of the essay that lingers in the mind is the opening, where he quotes from Dante's *Divine Comedy*: 'In the middle of the journey of our life, I came to myself within a dark wood where the straight way was lost. Ah, how hard it is to tell of that wood, savage and harsh and dense, the thought of which renews my fear. So bitter is it that death is hardly more.' Dante's poem tells of a visit to Hell, Purgatory and Heaven: it was written when Dante was thirty-seven, and it shows in its subject matter the preoccupation with death that is characteristic of middle age. In Jaques' essay, Dante's Dark Wood becomes a symbol for the uncertainties and fears of the mid-life passage.

Psychologist Daniel Levinson has looked at what happens to men in the Dark Wood, and in particular how mid-life fears affect the lifestyles of white middle-class North American males. He found that in mid-life these men, often regretting that they have invested so much of themselves in their work, tend to become more nurturing, and seek to direct more of their energies into their families: their change of direction comes a little too late, as their children are about to leave home.[9] Another typical male pattern is the disconcerting career change, as a man seeks to express some previously hidden side of himself: the policeman becomes a social worker, the minister a long-distance lorry driver.

But to the popular mind, the most fascinating aspect of the 'male

menopause' has been its sexual aspect, especially in the case of the
many men who in their forties or fifties leave their wives for women
twenty years younger. The belief in the magical redemptive effect
of sex with a very young woman or virgin is a recurrent theme in
human culture; one of its more distressing manifestations was the
Victorian belief that sex with a virgin was a cure for syphilis. When
men in mid-life turn to very young women as sexual partners, we
can perhaps see a similar underlying belief at work: the belief that
the embrace of the young woman will restore the man's waning
sexual powers. Barbara Gordon has called this phenomenon 'Jennifer Fever'[10] and explored its manifestations in the United States
today. In her book of the same name, middle-aged men who have
left their middle-aged wives for much younger women enthuse
about the delights of sex with their new young lovers.

But what about female sexuality? What happens to women in the
dark wood?

FOUR LOVE STORIES

Ruth is now seventy-six. When I asked her about her experience
of menopause, she said, 'It was absolutely wonderful, I was bloody
lucky.' Then she looked across at me thoughtfully and went on,
'Well, you know what I did in the menopause . . . now that's interesting. What I did, you know, I kept falling in love . . .

'The first time was just after my eldest son left home. He got
married – and I fell in love with his best man. Most extraordinary.
I do think that was absolutely extraordinary because it was a purely
physical thing that came over me. Jack, this man, he was incredibly
attractive. My son used to say that if Jack went into town to buy
toothpaste, when he came home there'd be a trail of women all the
way back. He came to stay with us over the wedding, and then he
stayed on a few more nights, and I used to take him a cup of tea
in the morning, he was usually snoring, I would just leave it beside
him, and on about the fifth morning I came out of the room and
I stood on the landing outside and thought: God Almighty! because
I'd felt sexually attracted to him. It was an absolute bolt from the
blue, certainly not expected, I hadn't felt it for anybody for quite
a while. I'm sure I blushed. Absurd. Normally for me, I would fall
in love with people's minds, whereas this was the physical thing.
After that we talked half the night many nights, my husband got
jealous as hell, and I don't blame him. Jack knew too, you know –

I could tell by the look in his eyes when he was giving me kindly smiles – talk about the melting moments bit!

'I was in a very emotional state, I was more than ready to fall in love – which of course is partly from not having had a good sex life for a long time . . . That was when I started having an affair with Philip. I was still pretty high on my romantic feelings, so I think I was just open to it. I was really in love with Philip, adored him, and I often thought: What would I do if he said, "Let's run away"? Awful thought really, I'm bloody glad he didn't. But I had all the agonies of being kept apart, it was total obsession. It was only any good if I could see Philip. It was misery in millions of ways. I just wanted to be with him. Absolute obsession.'

Laura is now in her late fifties. She said, 'I feel that I've almost behaved like a man over the past ten years, I've assumed roles that traditionally the man assumes. You know, the man has a mistress and the poor old wife stays at home and slogs on, keeps the house together – fragrant Mrs Archer and all the rest of it – and I've played an opposite role.

'I'd been married for twenty-five years before I actually split, so there were all those years of having babies and bringing babies up – and I changed, became a different person, and had to go out and find out a lot of things, which really I should have found out a lot earlier. I had to know more about life than I did know at that point. I couldn't go to my grave without knowing about wonderful relationships and ultimate wonderful passionate love. And then, in my middle forties, I had this most marvellous relationship with this extremely young guy. It was loving in a really sexual way, marvellous, terrific, absolutely wonderful. With him I discovered what it was like to be with a body in which every cell mattered, every bit of his flesh. We were just so totally whole.

'Menopause was brilliant. I had a thrombosis in my forties, because I was on the pill too late, so I came off the pill and I had to have Warfarin for six months – and then slowly I began to think I must have menopaused, and I've never had a period since. So all that time was when I was having the best sex in all my life, and it was just wonderful. I thought, What is this fuss about menopause? It was really rather marvellous never to have a period. Because the relationship continued a long time after that, you know, and I thought, This is just marvellous.'

*

Sheila is fifty-six. She said, 'All my life I fought my lesbianism, I wouldn't accept it, I was ashamed and guilty about feeling the way I did, but in the last five or six years I've come to accept it – and along with that has come acceptance of my body. At puberty I often used to feel like mutilating myself – I've known the time when I undressed in front of the dressing-table and covered my breasts with a scarf because I couldn't bear the sight of myself, but I now accept my body. And I've always loathed my hair – I think that's something to do with femininity – but now I've got it short and I'm quite happy with it, and I've never been interested in clothes, but over the last few years they've become an expression of me.

'For twenty-five years I'd been in the closet, I'd buried myself in my husband and my children. But then six years ago I met a couple of women and it was pretty obvious they were lesbians, and I was curious and fascinated by them, and I found myself more and more drawn to one of them, and I knew she was feeling that way about me, until eventually we started an affair. It upset me terribly that I hadn't got rid of those feelings, and I was crying all the time, in a dreadful state. One night my husband made me ring Lesbian Line – and then with his help and encouragement I started meeting other women and going round with lesbians.

'This all happened the year after I first became aware that I was in the menopause. To begin with, I approached the menopause with the attitude that it wasn't going to affect me. But when the relationship I was in went wrong, and the break-up of that relationship exacerbated the effects I was getting from the menopause, I went downhill very fast, I was losing a pound a day in weight, I was suicidal. I went to the doctor's and I got put on HRT, and I just went uphill from then on, and I've been on it for three years and I feel great.

'I do think that around this time of life there's a great desire to be in love, a great desire. Now, I don't know whether that's fear of old age, thinking: Uh-oh, my sell-by date's nearly here, and if I don't cram a bit more love into my life I'm not going to get any at all. There's a great desire to love and be loved. I do feel as if I've got a helluva lot to give to a woman who is prepared to accept it and give me some back. She would have to be at least twenty years younger than me, I'm afraid.

'I don't think I've ever been a very sexual person – I think it's very difficult to get me sexually turned on. At fifty-three, for the first time in my life, another person made me so excited in the genital area without being touched in that area that I thought I was going to pass out. She took me in her arms, and I thought I had a great big fat elastic band twanging away between my legs, it was hurting, it was so . . . bang, bang, bang . . . and I've never had that before, it was really really frightening, it was so intense. And that's not to say the feelings I had for her were that intense up here, in my heart: it was good, it was alright. But the physical thing was overwhelming.'

Anne is in her mid-forties: unlike the other three women, she is probably still several years away from the menopause. She said, 'My husband died two years ago. He was forty-three. And really the first thought that came home to me was, "My God, what am I going to do for sex?" I never thought it would be that important to me. I think when you're just used to having it, as part of the ground of your life, you just don't realize how fundamental and important it is. I can remember a couple of friends coming to see me about a week after he died, and I just sat on the floor and said, "What's it like, going to bed with another man?" Because I had never been to bed with anybody but John. I said, "I can't imagine it. Am I going to be capable of doing it? Will I ever get another partner?" That was my first thought, I must get another man, I didn't care who the hell he was.

'Within about two weeks my teenage daughter brought home her teacher. He was fifteen years younger than me, very attractive physically. I know now he was an absolute rat, but he gave me all sorts of signals and I threw myself unashamedly at this man. This is within three weeks of being widowed, I was that desperate. It was almost like, when you fall off a horse you've got to get back in the saddle, and it was extremely interesting having sex with somebody completely different, but it was very painful too because he was absolutely useless as a lover, and really didn't want a committed relationship, and I was just totally devastated, because he gave me lots of signals and then as soon as we did have sex he wanted to withdraw immediately, which was very hurtful for me, so I was bereaved more or less twice in the space of six months. I had to put myself together somehow, and in fact I went through an incredible voyage of self-discovery, and I bought a lot of those books like *Women Who Love Too Much*[11] – and I came to see myself as a woman who had been brought up to please men, and I was only validated as a human being if I had a man.

'Now I've got this bloke who is married, which is stupid. It's not a very satisfactory affair for all sorts of reasons, but I'm almost using him like I think men use women, for sex once a week – till somebody comes along who's really something. But until that time I will not compromise myself. I really miss the sex I had with John, the comfort of it, the knowledge that he was there, because to me sex isn't just sex, it's part and parcel of the loving relationship, the cuddles while you're watching telly. Just having someone to talk to and share your feelings with and do things with, the companionship of it. To me the best sex comes out of that.

'I like my body and I look after it. Now and then I have doubts about it, I spend a long time looking in the mirror and thinking, God! When John died I went through a period of enormous self-doubt and worry about my image and whether I would ever be attractive to anybody. I spend a lot of time and money on my appearance – that was my instant reaction to his death – and I think I'm more glamorous now than when I was married. And I think that's part of me saying, I'm OK basically, I will carry on.'

In mid-life, these four women find themselves in widely differing life situations. But the stories that they tell have strikingly similar underlying themes.

In all the stories the focus is on sex as a physical experience. There is little here of the soft-focus sexuality of the feminine stereotype. Ruth is used to 'falling in love with people's minds', but what she feels in the room where Jack is sleeping is a sudden startling impulse, a stirring of the body. Laura remembers her young lover with physical passion, lyrically expressed: 'Every cell mattered, you know, every bit of his flesh.' Sheila's lover simply takes her in her arms, and Sheila experiences genital sensations of such intensity that they frighten her. Anne's first reaction to her husband's death is urgent physical need: 'What am I going to do for sex?' In these accounts there is much romantic love as well, but the romance seems to follow from the physical feelings rather than to pre-empt them: the body rules.

As we have already seen, both Kinsey and Masters and Johnson[12] suggest that men typically reach their peak of sexual responsiveness at around seventeen, and women at around forty. Kinsey also found that the late thirties and early forties was the time when married women were most likely to have affairs,[13] and that as they get older women have more orgasmic dreams: for men, the peak age for such dreams is in their teens, but for women it comes between ages forty and fifty-five – only 2 per cent of women had had dreams to orgasm in adolescence, but one in three women were having such dreams in mid-life.[14] Sex therapist Helen Kaplan remarks that, though female sexual functioning around the menopause is extremely variable, 'many women actually feel an increase in erotic appetite during the menopausal years.'[15]

These suggestions were confirmed by many of the women I talked to. Women frequently told me that their sex drive had become stronger in their late thirties and on into their forties and fifties. Their orgasms were quicker, more reliable, and more likely to be multiple, than when they were younger; and they often said they felt 'tense', 'awful', or 'left in the air' if they didn't have an orgasm. Women in their teens and twenties occasionally said, as much older men might say, that sex can be enjoyed without an orgasm, but for most women in mid-life, orgasms are obligatory.

What of the people who inspire such sexual longing in these women? All four women are attracted to people much younger than themselves. The three male love objects in these stories are in their twenties, and Sheila says, somewhat regretfully, that the women she is most likely to want are twenty years younger. When André Previn left her for young Mia Farrow, Dory Previn sang poignantly of the lure of 'those lemon-haired ladies' for the man in mid-life. Much attention has been given to this tendency of middle-aged men to be attracted to much younger women. But it is rarely observed that women's sexual urges in mid-life may also draw them to much younger partners. Nor is it ever remarked on that the older woman/younger man relationship is potentially the most ecstatic of any heterosexual pairing, as both partners will be at the peak of their sexual powers.

What is more, when the women describe these people who attract them sexually, it is their physical beauty which is stressed. Their accounts resonate with active female sexual desire. This is a voice which has not often been publicly heard, with rare exceptions like the Hebrew Song of Solomon – 'As an apple tree among the trees of the wood, so is my beloved among young men.' Under patriarchy, women's active desire for men's bodies has only ever been given unofficial expression, as when women in kitchens and wine-bars and around the coffee machine in offices talk together about the shapely backs, slim hips and eloquent eyes of the men they lust after. Such conversations are the private female counterpoint to our public sexual themes, which are largely about men's lust for the bodies of women. Among the women who talked to me, it was most often women in their late thirties and forties who talked in this way. A woman in her late thirties listed the attributes of the men she found attractive – their beautiful eyes, slenderness, trendy clothes and appealingly androgynous appearance: 'Intelligence,' she said with a rather rueful smile, '*used* to be very important . . .' When younger women talk about what attracts them to men, looks matter – but only as one item in a list. Younger women have other concerns, they may be looking not just for sex but for a committed companion and a father for their children. But for Ruth when she takes Jack his tea, or for Laura when she goes to bed with her lover, the body is the focus of attention.

More like a man, you might say. Laura and Anne both make this connection. Laura feels she's 'almost behaved like a man' over the past ten years. Anne wonders if she is using her man friend for sex 'like I think men use women'. Theorists of mid-life have suggested that in middle age both sexes become more androgynous: men become more nurturing and women more assertive. But this hypothesis has never been carried through to its logical conclusion, which is that for many women, sexuality in mid-life approximates more closely than at any other time to the stereotype of male sexuality, with its focus on genital feelings, on the physical attributes of the person who is desired, and on the act of sex itself.

At forty-six, Anne is probably some years away from the menopause, but for Ruth, Laura and Sheila there is a striking synchronicity between the timing of their love stories and the onset of the menopause. Ruth keeps falling in love during the menopause. Sheila falls in love and rediscovers her lesbianism the year after her menopause starts. Laura has to come off the pill because of a thrombosis, and her periods stop – and during this time, she reflects, 'I was having the best sex in all my life.'

There may be physiological reasons for this synchronicity. Helen Kaplan comments, 'From a purely physiologic standpoint, libido should theoretically *increase* at menopause, because the action of the woman's androgens, which is not materially affected by menopause, is now unopposed by estrogen.'[16] It is the androgens that control sexual arousal in women. Oestrogen and progesterone, though they are often called the 'female sex hormones', do not contribute to our arousal. This is also a time when contraceptive precautions can be abandoned – and most forms of contraception interfere with female sexual pleasure.

But there are psychological changes too which may contribute to the peculiarly passionate flavour of women's mid-life stories. Mid-life has a different structure for men and for women. For women there is a distinct mid-life point, a discrete physical event – the last period. For both sexes, mid-life is about the fear of death and the recognition that possibilities are limited, but it is about death in a special way for women. A woman may have decided that her reproductive life has ended ten years before the menopause, for women generally don't go on trying for children into their late forties. But the menopause supplies unequivocal evidence that it is all over. Whether a woman has decided to have no children, has decided to have no more children, or has struggled to accept the fact that for whatever reason she will never have children, the menopause puts the final stamp on her contented decision or her painful acceptance.

Even when the end of reproductive life is welcomed, it is still a little death in itself. And when these women talk about sex, they also talk about death. Sheila muses on ageing, and her sense that time is running out: 'My sell-by date's nearly here.' Laura's need to feel what she's never yet felt is fuelled by the fear of death: 'I couldn't go to my grave without knowing about wonderful relationships and ultimate wonderful passionate love ...' And Anne is touched not just by the fear of death, but by the thing itself.

Fear of death is a powerful motivator, hence the intensity of the emotions the women describe – Ruth's 'complete obsession' with her lover, Laura's 'ultimate passionate love', and the suicidal depression that Sheila experiences when her relationship goes wrong. Anne in her bereavement puts a lot of energy into caring for her body, and seeking out new relationships. It's a way of saying 'I will carry on', and affirming her own aliveness in the face of death.

In Dante's Dark Wood, the straight way was lost. And these stories also show how the certainties by which the women have lived their lives either melt away or are snatched from them in mid-life. Sheila had struggled with her lesbianism in her twenties, a struggle which had caused her distress to the point of depressive illness. She had then been thrilled when the thing she had always wanted so badly had finally happened, and she was sexually aroused by a man. But in life stories, unlike children's tales, happy endings usually come in the middle: later we may see things differently. Sheila married the man who'd aroused her and lived as a wife and mother for twenty years, and there were real rewards for her, as she was able to have children, something she'd wanted and always feared would be impossible for her. But in her fifties she found she couldn't carry on: the happy ending looked more like a move in the wrong direction, and the suppressed lesbian feelings reasserted themselves and threatened to overwhelm her. Ruth had been a devotedly faithful if sexually unhappy wife, someone who only fell in love with people's minds. She herself is fascinated by her choice of love object, the best man at her eldest child's wedding. It is a choice rich in significance: she falls for a man who is both sex object and son. As her first child leaves home, there is a new freedom for Ruth, a rediscovery of herself as a sexual being, someone who is not only a mother of sons, but there is also a sense of loss, a need to replace the son who has gone. Laura, too, had lived as a good wife and mother – 'fragrant Mrs Archer and all the rest of it' – until, around the time of the menopause, in the shadow of death, the compromises that she had made to achieve a contented married life were no longer possible for her. And for Anne the certainties by which she had lived were suddenly snatched from her by the death of her husband. For all these women, the compromises on which they have based their lives, as everybody must, no longer work at the mid-life point.

If the straight way has gone, you have to find another way or be lost. Our post-Freud, post-Carl Rogers culture has a metaphor for this – the voyage of psychological self-discovery. So Laura discovers herself as a very sexual person, Sheila discovers herself as a lesbian and learns to accept the female body that in adolescence she had wanted to mutilate, and Anne wonders, 'Why do I need a man so much?' and after much reading and thinking comes to understand the origins of her behaviour better. Laura and Sheila and Anne all seem to say that it is in mid-life that you find out who you really are.

In Ruth's story, however, there is less of a sense of mid-life achievement. The other women are still close to the events they describe, but Ruth looks back from twenty years on. She does not view her mid-life loves with a mid-life sensibility. There is no sense in her story that these events told her something definitive about herself. Her mid-life narrative is presented rather as another step on the way, or another chapter, now closed, in the story of her life.

For Ruth in her seventies, musing on human sexuality, there is a fundamental mystery about the body's startling imperatives and the irrationality of passion. Human behaviour, her own and other people's, remains at root an enigma.

A VERY ODD SORT OF ANIMAL

Younger women dread the menopause. We dread its physical manifestations, without being very clear what those are likely to be. And we also dread its impact on our sexuality and sexual self-esteem. In a survey carried out in the United States in 1989 for the Kinsey Institute, 30 per cent of the people questioned thought that most women lose interest in sex after the menopause, though significantly women of thirty and older were more likely than younger women and men of all ages to get the answer right.[17]

There may be some justification for our anxieties about the physical manifestations of the menopause. Though most women I talked to had had an uneventful menopause, and were largely glad to be free of menstrual pain and PMT, some women suffer considerably physically and they may get little help for their symptoms. In *The Change*, Germaine Greer comments that very little is actually known about the process of menopause. She writes, 'We do not know what is happening. We do not know why it happens. We cannot tell in a particular case if it is about to happen, happening, or over ... We do not know what a hot flush is, beyond the fact that it is the one symptom that everyone associates with menopause ...'[18] While so little is known, and while the only major treatment for menopausal symptoms – HRT – remains controversial, there is some justification for our fears that the menopause will be a physically troubling time.

The common fear that the menopause also means loss of sexual pleasure, however, is quite another matter. The love stories we have already heard illustrate the active sexuality of some women in mid-life. Most other women I talked to felt there had been an increase in sexual pleasure around the menopause. Mostly they said it was quite slight, but distinct.

Three women recalled no increase. One was suffering from serious chronic illness. Of the other two, one had her marriage end with much bitterness mid-life, and the other had always found sex painful and was glad to give it up after the menopause. In addition, both these women had had hysterectomies, a fact that may in itself

explain why their experiences did not follow the pattern that was
the norm among my interviewees. If the ovaries are removed as
well as the womb, the operation will affect hormone function in a
way that may influence libido.

As we have already seen, there are a number of reasons why
sexual interest might increase in mid-life – the hormonal changes
of menopause, for instance, and the freedom from the fear of
pregnancy. For many women there are social reasons, too. Children
will be growing up or already adult, and will no longer demand the
enormous emotional and physical investments of their earlier years.
Mary said, 'For me the fifties were the most sexually joyful time
of my life, which sounds extraordinary. When I was obviously not
going to be at risk of having children, and we no longer had to
take precautions – then I think we developed more together sexually
than at any other time. We used to go away for what we called
"dirty weekends". Just occasionally – but it was fun. We'd make
love on the floor or do something we wouldn't do at home. We
were having a very difficult time, I had to nurse my mother-in-law
with terminal cancer, and the children were often ill, so home
wasn't a very safe place. I've often thought about that, in that we
got most of our enjoyment when we weren't in our home, or else
we were in the home on our own, but if there was mother-in-law
there, or the children, then that was it, for me anyway.'

The frequent increase in pleasure after the menopause takes
women completely by surprise. They think, like Mary, that they
are unique. The trend toward greater sexual interest and enjoyment
as the woman reaches the menopause seems to be accepted as
axiomatic in sexology books for professionals, yet it has had no
impact at all on lay thinking about sex. What woman, sexually
frustrated at thirty, comforts herself with the thought that she's
only just started and things will probably get better? Three hundred
years ago there were at least some misogynistic clues, warnings, for
instance, about sexual rapaciousness as one of the more alarming
side-effects of the menopause. 'There is a kind of latter spring
which gets into the Blood of an Old Woman, and turns her into a
very odd sort of animal,' wrote Joseph Addison.[19] But today the
equation of youth with sex is so pervasive that there aren't even
any misogynistic jokes about the disconcerting sexual enthusiasms
of the middle-aged matron.

There is of course permission in our culture to enjoy sex as you
get older: sex is meant to be fun, and people of all ages are urged

to find it so. But there is often a subtext of doubt about such urgings. A self-help book by Christine Sandford is called *Enjoy Sex in the Middle Years*:[20] a question mark seems to hang in the air, the very title has an aura of disbelief about it.

Why does the widespread assumption that the menopause signals the fading of female sexuality persist? There are two obvious explanations for the fact that what actually happens remains unacknowledged. Both follow from the dominance of male sexual values.

The first explanation concerns the typical male sexual life cycle. Male libido does not increase in mid-life: male sexual interest and capacity show a gradual decline from age seventeen onwards. In men there are two interconnected aspects of sexual functioning that are particularly vulnerable to the effects of ageing: the frequency of ejaculation, and the length of the refractory period – the time interval that has to elapse between one ejaculation and the next. By the time a man is fifty, he will probably be having significantly fewer ejaculations, and the refractory period will have lengthened considerably. At fifty, a man will also be rather less preoccupied with sex than he was in his youth: Kaplan remarks that, in his fifties, 'a man may be absorbed in his career for weeks without thought of sex and without having an erection.'[21] It seems likely that the typical shape of the female sexual life cycle is overlooked because it is so different from the male pattern. Under patriarchy, the male is the norm, and the female pattern is aberrant, especially when it doesn't neatly coincide with male needs – when women, for instance, feel sexy when heavily pregnant, or have a marked cycle of desire, or view penetration as a reasonably pleasant but essentially secondary part of sexual activity. Sexuality is defined by men and our definitions of sex are shaped by male needs. What doesn't fit simply isn't seen.

A second explanation hinges on the equation of female sexuality with attractiveness to men. The increase in libido around the menopause goes hand in hand with the loss of the attributes that in our society are equated so strongly with female sexual attractiveness. As the perfect sex object gets to be younger and younger, and the slim pubescent figure and luminous flesh of the teenager are increasingly valued above any other female attributes, so the menopausal woman seems more and more remote from any ideal of physical attractiveness. Under the sexual economy which declares that the children she has taught to read, the pictures she has painted, or the understanding of human nature that she has acquired, are worth nothing compared with the silky skin and firm breasts of the teenager, even the most creative and successful woman is severely sexually impoverished in mid-life.

Women in mid-life tell two different kinds of sexual story. The homily of the holy and godly matron contrasts with and seems to contradict the lyrical passion of the love story. The contradiction arises from the contrast between the patriarchal expectations of women in mid-life, which are rooted in male sexual values, and the sexual and biological realities for women around the menopause. There is a grim irony here for women. A woman's libido may be at its most intense, and her potential pleasure in sex at its greatest, at the very point at which she is dismissed as no longer sexual because she no longer fits current male definitions of sexual attractiveness. She may feel sexual, but because her experience of sexuality does not fall within the male definitions of sexiness, that sexuality is surprising or, as Mary said, 'extraordinary'. Because female sexuality is suppressed, we do not see that the holy and godly matron is also the woman in love.

CHAPTER NINE

Older Women:
Enough's Enough

'If I didn't have a child,' said Frances, 'I don't know when I'd have realized that I was no longer young. But just after Harriet was born, I was looking at her skin and it was so smooth compared to mine; mine's all wrinkled, with all these marks and things, and there was this curious moment when I suddenly thought: You're not young any more, you're getting old. Then I thought: Of course you are, you can't be a mother unless you're older than your child. And I thought: Does it matter? and I decided well, no – because I've got her, and I wouldn't be a mother, I wouldn't be experiencing all the pleasure I get from being a mother, unless I was old and she was young.'

Just as there are moments when we recognize that we are not immortal, as we may have once supposed, and that death will come to us too, so there are moments when we know we will not stay young forever. Frances has one of these moments of insight as she studies her baby in all her delicious newness. What are they like for women, these moments when we see that we too are growing old?

It is usually when we, like Frances, are in our late thirties that we become forcibly aware of the ageing of the body. But the words that ageing writes on our bodies then are more like poetry than fact; they are open to interpretation. It is up to us how we read these grey hairs and wrinkles. We could read them as welcome marks of experience and maturity: we do not have to see them as signs that we are heading down a long and depressing decline.

Some women do read them positively. A mother like Frances, for instance, can recognize that her pleasure in her child depends on her own maturity, and that her ageing is part of a continuity, part of the flow and ebb of life. Women with successful and enjoyable careers may also value aspects of ageing. They may find that as they get older they acquire more status and are taken more seriously: 'I think people imagine that if you're older you must have some authority and some previous knowledge base – I think in a professional world you get a lot of kudos just for being older, so I'm looking forward to that.'

I found that lesbians too could see things to appreciate in the ageing process. Lesbians seemed more at ease with ageing than heterosexual women, and more likely to view the early signs of ageing with interest or fascination – like Fran, who told me, eyes gleaming, 'I love it – I'm really quite excited because I'm going grey!' Perhaps the lesbian equanimity about ageing is connected with the way lesbians seem to see much more clearly than hetero-sexual women that the young do not have a monopoly on sexual pleasure. For Eve, another lesbian, the legitimacy of the older woman's sexuality is unquestioned: 'There are older women who I look up to and I really admire their sparkle and think: Yeah, it doesn't matter whether you're 45, 50 or whatever. I met a 75-year-old a couple of months ago – a lesbian – who was absolutely full of life and so attractive – and she'd just fallen in love as well!'

Fran recalled that her own mother had said she had considered becoming a lesbian in her fifties. 'My father left her for a much younger woman, and she wondered if being a lesbian was perhaps a much easier, less demanding way of getting the companionship and warmth that she wanted – without putting on a show. It's like that for me with Ginny – I don't have to put on a show.' Fran's mother felt that her own sexuality, just as it was, without pretence or fakery, might be acceptable to another woman, and that the charade of acceptable femininity which becomes increasingly diffi-cult to sustain as a woman gets older, would not be obligatory in such a relationship. There is support for her theory from some of the women in Shere Hite's book, *Women and Love*. Shere Hite comments, 'One of the surprising things in this study is the number of divorced women in their forties and fifties who are having love relationships with women and finding this a comfortable, in fact, excellent, way of life.'[1] She was intrigued to find that one in four of the lesbian women who responded had been over forty when they first made love to another woman.

Lesbians, mothers, working women. If there are things to enjoy about the early signs of ageing, it is clear that they are to be found in other parts of our lives than our relationships with men. It is when we look through the eyes of men that the doubts set in. Many women, whether gay or straight, might find Eve's sparkling

75-year-old attractive. Many of us, I suspect, can see the beauty in older women's faces. We may delight in studying the exquisitely patterned face of the woman in her seventies, and find in it a richness and complexity that makes the younger face, however lovely, seem rather bland. But what Eve saw that a straight woman may be unable to see is the older woman's continuing sexual attractiveness.

It follows that it is young heterosexual women who fear ageing most. As Pippa at twenty said, 'I think if I suddenly found myself boyfriend-less or husband-less I'd worry about losing my looks then more. Which is awful really, to say I'd want to make sure my looks were maintained just in case I suddenly had to catch a man when I was older – that's terrible isn't it really!' Pippa knows that her good looks are a commodity – what is given in exchange for a sexual relationship. And she knows that to catch a man she has first to catch the eye. The fear of ageing for heterosexual women is the fear of invisibility. We are afraid that as we age we will disappear from men's view, and become just another cipher among the masses of anonymous older women. We fear this sexual disappearing act of the older woman because we've seen it happen to others: sooner or later we start to realize that we will not be exempt. So we smooth in the creams with the mystical names – Regenium Night Renewal Cream, Intercell Anti-Time Principle – though we don't really believe their preposterous promises. We have known for as long as we can remember that women's sexual attractiveness to men is a fragile thing, and, like Cinderella's, essentially time-limited.

But if the general ageing of women's bodies is feared because it will make us sexually uninteresting, the ageing of the specifically sexual parts of the body is a focus for stronger feelings and deeper fears. In his best seller of 1970, *Everything You Always Wanted to Know about Sex but Were Afraid to Ask*, Dr David Reuben wrote: 'As the oestrogen is shut off, a woman comes as close as she can to being a man. Increased facial hair, deepened voice, obesity and the decline of the breasts and female genitalia all contribute to a masculine appearance. Coarsened features, enlargement of the clitoris and gradual baldness complete the picture. Not being a man, but no longer a functional woman, these individuals live in a world of intersex . . .' Robert A. Wilson, the American advocate of HRT, wrote that after menopause a chemical imbalance results in 'menopausal castration' and 'a mutilation of the whole body . . .

No woman can be sure of escaping the horror of this living decay.'[2]
There is a sense of revulsion here that is reminiscent of attitudes
to the body in the Middle Ages. In these gynaecologists' horror at
the degeneration of female bodies, there are echoes of the writings
of those medieval poets who tried to conquer their lust for pellucid
young flesh by reminding themselves that even the most exquisite
body ages and decays and ends in the grave:

> When the turf is thy tower,
> And thy pit is thy bower,
> Thy skin and thy white throat,
> Shall worms gnaw up.
> What use to thee then,
> All the world's profit?[3]

In patriarchal attitudes to women's bodies there is a push-pull of
desire and revulsion. The dark side of men's fascination with the
bodies of women is the revulsion which women inspire when they
no longer fit the template of physical perfection. The old dichot-
omies still govern our thinking: just as young women's bodies are
'the flesh' that lures and delights, so the body of the ageing woman
is the focus for all our fear of the decay of the flesh. The ageing
woman's body symbolizes degeneration for both sexes. The Greeks
believed that during conception the vital spirit of the man impreg-
nated the formless matter of the woman: today woman is still seen
as base matter and man as spirit.

One aspect of this horror at the decay of female flesh is the idea
that the female sex organs are particularly prone to disease. The
female body has always been feared as a cesspool of infection,
though in reality women are more likely to catch sexually transmitted diseases from men than the other way round: as we've
already seen, for women the risk of catching HIV from an infected
partner is double the risk for men, and in the case of gonorrhoea,
women are nearly three times as likely to become infected. In some
medical pronouncements there is a preoccupation with the ageing
female body as a potential site for cancer that seems to come from
the same cultural and psychological roots as the distorted fear of
sexual infection. Some doctors have actually advocated the mutilation of the older woman's body by the removal of healthy sexual
organs as a prophylactic procedure. Mary Daly has described how
American gynaecologists have justified the hysterectomy epidemic

in the United States by calling the uterus of the woman who is past child-bearing age a 'potentially lethal organ' and 'a possible breeding ground for cancer',[4] and British gynaecology professor James Drife recently wrote a provocative piece in the *British Medical Journal* proposing prophylactic double mastectomy 'either at the completion of her family or at the menopause', for women with a family history of breast cancer.[5]

A public health announcement in 1991 hinted at the same preoccupations. The Chief Medical Officer, Sir Donald Acheson, had advised women that a monthly breast examination was a waste of time because there was no evidence that it reduced mortality from breast cancer. A day or two later, the Department of Health hastily backtracked, concerned that the wrong advice had been given: but rather than suggest women carry on with monthly breast examination until further notice, women were now advised to look at their breasts *every day* for signs of disease. This bizarre injunction turns the sexual parts of the female body into a *memento mori*: every time you look at your breasts, think of cancer.

When the ageing female body is viewed entirely in terms of what can go wrong with it, there will be little understanding of the normal changes associated with ageing. These changes could at least be accepted, if not exactly welcomed. But at present there are real difficulties for women who want to understand their bodies as they age. Even for a sexually self-confident woman like Laura, a woman's ageing body can feel like a foreign country.

'I'm fifty-six – and I loathe my body now. The other day I went to my doctor, because I was thinking I must have something wrong with my vagina. I tried to stand on my head with a small mirror, and it looked horrible, I thought: There's bits there that I don't normally see. I rushed off and had to be reassured by my doctor. She said, "What you've got is called a post-menopausal vagina" – I don't know if she made the term up on the spot! It's amazing to think I was ever able to insert diaphragms and tampons and all the rest of it. You become less familiar with yourself, if you're older and don't have regular sex. And you get a lot tenderer as well, you're just not as resilient because you're not being pounded away at all the time, and you feel more like tissue paper and it's absolutely essential you use your KY jelly because otherwise it jolly well hurts. You go round feeling sore for days afterwards when you have sex if you don't make sure everything's properly lubricated.'

Changes in the body are aspects of ageing that will affect our sexuality – but they aren't the whole story. There is also the question of how ageing affects sexual response, the pattern of arousal and orgasm. And this is a quite separate issue, though because a woman's appearance is so often equated with her sexuality, the two are frequently confused: loss of sexual appeal to men is read as loss of sexual response, and loss of desirability in men's eyes is read as loss of desire.

For men there are clear physiological sexual losses in old age. Older men have a longer refractory period, need much more genital stimulation to achieve erection, and have a diminished sex drive with far fewer sexual thoughts and fantasies than in their youth. For men, the loss of the sexual urgency and orgastic potency of youth is probably the most fundamental of the losses of ageing. There are many elegiac poems by men that mourn these losses, like Yeats' 'After Long Silence', in which the poet finds intellectual conversation a poor substitute for the passion of his youth:

> Bodily decrepitude is wisdom; young
> We loved each other and were ignorant.[6]

There are no comparable losses for women. While there does seem to be some reduction in sexual interest for most women from the late fifties on, older women still have great potential for sexual pleasure. Women can have multiple orgasms into their eighties and nineties, and, according to Helen Kaplan, 25 per cent of seventy-year-old women masturbate – a striking statistic, given the inhibitions women of all ages have about self-pleasuring, and given that these inhibitions will be stronger for older women who were brought up in a more sexually repressive society.[7]

There is then nothing 'natural' about what happens to women's sexuality as we age. It is to culture, not biology, that we must turn to account for the sexual losses that women suffer as they grow older.

THE INAPPROPRIATE TURN-ON

Pippa, the twenty-year-old who was worried about ageing, was very apologetic. She felt it was 'terrible really' to see her youthful good looks so clearly as a commodity. Yet her fear is fully justified.

In her study of families that had been through divorce, *Second*

Chances, Judith Wallerstein came across many marriage break-ups in which men left their wives for much younger women. She writes:

> *I must admit – and here I show my prejudice – that the final pulling away was shockingly complete in many cases ... Many of these husbands who pull away after fifteen or twenty years of marriage talk about their wife's age as an important factor in the decision to divorce. They admit that they are repelled by the changes in her face and body, by the inevitable sags and wrinkles. I have the sense, as they speak, that they are frightened by an indirect vision of their own mortality. In seeking a younger woman, as many do, they seem to be trying to delay their own ageing and eventual death.*[8]

Women whose husbands turn away from them as they age are unlikely to find other partners. From the age of thirty-five, a woman's chances of remarrying after divorce begin to go down. A US Census Bureau study in 1985 found that of those divorced women who married again, 48 per cent remarried in their twenties, 33 per cent in their thirties and 11 per cent in their forties. Only 3 per cent of divorced women remarried in their fifties.[9] In Judith Wallerstein's own study of sixty families, 'Every woman who was forty or older at marital separation remained unmarried ten years later ... By contrast, half of their former husbands were remarried at the ten-year mark.'[10]

Of course, not all divorced women want another partner. There are plenty of women who treasure their independence after divorce. According to our sex-is-fun culture, the state of celibacy is an arid place, a desert – but for some women, like Josephine, it turns out to be a garden of delights. 'I love it, I just love it. Terrible, isn't it! I just love not having my father or Sam shouting at me, nagging me, abusing me, humiliating me, criticizing me. I love shutting the door in the evening, putting the light out in the porch and knowing that neither my father nor Sam is going to come up the drive and start making my life a misery. I've got all the things I want, I eat what I want when I want to, I don't have to do any housework unless I want to, I can spend my money on what I want, I can lie on the floor and listen to music if I want to, and go to bed when I want to go to bed, I can live in a tip or not, I can do anything. Sometimes I feel so ecstatically happy I can't believe it, and then I sometimes think: It would be nice to have a man to share this ecstatic happiness with. And then I think, No, because I wouldn't be ecstatically happy then.'

But there are many women left alone in their forties, fifties and sixties who do still yearn for the sexual fulfilment, love and companionship that marriage at its best can provide. The remarriage statistics hint at the quiet tragedy of these women's lives. A woman in later mid-life may be capable of enjoying sex much more than the nubile 22-year-old. There is a stark contrast between the sexual capacities of women in their forties, fifties and sixties and the sexual deprivations that are likely to be their lot.

A man may also come up against ageist attitudes to sexuality, but not until he is in his seventies and eighties. For the older man who retains an interest in sex, there are at least certain stereotypes, albeit not very flattering ones – the 'dirty old man', the 'Sugar Daddy'. The man who is sexually active in his seventies may be disapproved of by his children or his friends, but no one is really surprised by his continuing interest in sex. But sexual activity in older women is very differently viewed. The expression of sexual feeling by older women meets with such disapprobation that they may hide their feelings even from themselves. Doris said, 'You're aware that though you can still be turned-on, it's very inappropriate. I suppose I'm rather stuck with the old image that older women wouldn't follow through any sort of sexual attraction appropriately – and that makes the turn-on seem inappropriate.' If acting on your desire is inappropriate for older women, then even to feel desire may cause embarrassment or shame. So Doris tries to hide her feelings, even from herself. Younger women may fake sexual interest, because it's expected of them. How often do older women fake *lack* of sexual interest?

Doris is in her late fifties. Roger Moore was still playing love scenes at this age. Not only is the expression of the older man's sexual feelings in his private life acceptable, but the spectacle of the older man expressing his sexuality is considered so appealing that people will pay to watch it.

HELLO, YOUNG LOVERS

There are of course some rare examples of older women who do express their sexuality openly. What happens to the older woman who allows herself fully to experience and act on her desires?

Laura not only acted out her sexual feelings, but went still further in defying the norms by choosing a much younger man as her lover. We heard part of her story in the last chapter, when she described the physical joy of the relationship. Here we will look at the down-side, for Laura's doubts and fears exemplify the problems facing older women who remain sexual.

'He was twenty-three years younger than me, and it always worried me that it wouldn't stand up long-term, and I really destroyed it in a sense, I picked away at it. He wanted to marry me. I felt, I can't, this relationship won't go on for ever. So I went off to South America and got a job there, to see what would happen really, and to give my young lover some space to create a career for himself as well. I thought: I'll just get out of his life. But at the back of my mind I thought he would follow me, because he always did follow me everywhere, and he did, once, and it was quite difficult, and then he ran out of money and went back to make some more and never came back again. When I came home I told me he'd got engaged to someone two years younger than he was. I still find that terribly difficult. Physical beauty's quite impor-tant, you know, looking young enough is quite important. It's dread-ful, but it is. I was forty-six and he was twenty-three when we first met, and that's fine. But when I'm sixty-six and he's thirty-three or whatever it is, he would still be extremely young, and my life would have been lived in a way.'

The age gap between the older woman and the younger man can feel huge: in a slip of the tongue, Laura adds ten years to the difference between them. And in a culture in which there are few models for such a relationship, the lovers will feel those fears and anxieties that always beset us when we break with convention. It is because of such fears that Laura decides she must test out the relationship. In a post-feminist version of the tale of Patient Gris-elda, who was put to the test by her husband to see if she was indeed as constant as she seemed, Laura goes to the other side of the world, to see if her lover will follow. No woman in a more orthodox relationship which offered her such rewards would dream of putting it to the test as Laura does.

When Laura looked into the future and worried about what might go wrong with the relationship, it was the loss of her looks that she feared above all. Laura is a successful professional woman – but however successful we may be, our belief in our sexual attractiveness still depends on our conformity to the youthful stereotype. A woman may fear that her status, power and maturity actually detract from rather than enhance her sexual appeal, and all the evidence suggests that such fears are justified. Yet think of the attributes that can be eroticized in the successful older man. The silver-haired hospital consultant, kindly and paternal, the chairman of the board with his easy air of command, the fat and balding but infinitely powerful army general: all these figures are a potent source of erotic fantasy in our culture, and the trappings of their success – the glamorous car, the huge desk, the medals and the money – are routinely eroticized too.

The older woman/younger man love affair then may be undermined by the woman's own doubts. But not all the difficulties will come from inside the woman's own head; there may be disapprobation and even persecution from the outside world – cutting remarks from a woman's children, disapproval from office colleagues, even obscene graffiti at her place of work. A woman who has a relationship with a much younger man is clearly not motivated by any of the acceptable patriarchal reasons for pursuing a relationship. She is not after his protection, money, or status: she plainly has only 'one thing' in mind. Such an overt pursuit of sexual pleasure is still largely unacceptable in women. A relationship between an older man and a much younger woman, of course, is given startlingly different public treatment. There will be general public tolerance of the relationship, even admiration for the older man's evident virility. Revelations about Burton Group chairman Ralph Halpern's relationship with a teenage model actually enhanced his reputation as a dynamic businessman.

Here is one aspect of sexual relationships that must surely change as the balance of power shifts between the sexes. While women continue to have access to contraception and education, and so become both more powerful and more sexually assertive, we will see more heterosexual teacher/student, boss/employee and doctor/nurse pairings, where the higher status one of the pair is the woman. Women in increasing numbers will oppose themselves to the dominance/submission norm of heterosexual relationships by offering their status, creativity, achievements and sexual knowledge as part of an erotic exchange – and increasingly the offer will be accepted. As a consequence we will see more pairings where the woman is much older than the man.

Here is another area where greater mutuality in sexual relationships would benefit both men and women. Greater public tolerance for different patterns of relationship can only increase the opportunities for fulfilment available to both sexes. And the older woman/ younger man pattern, in particular, can plainly bring much joy and sexual fulfilment to women who do not look to men to make up for what they lack, who do not look up to men as sources of strength, protectiveness or worldly wisdom, and who, in so far as we reinvent family relationships in our erotic partnerships, are looking not for a father but for a brother or a son.

ENOUGH'S ENOUGH: WOMEN IN THEIR SEVENTIES

It is a reflection of our ageist attitudes that we tend to lump all post-menopausal women together. Yet thirty years of living and learning and changing may elapse between the menopause and the ending of life. And the woman in her seventies or eighties may have a quite different perspective on sex from the woman in her fifties.

Ruth, Mary and Olive were among the women in their seventies whom I interviewed. All three women had been widowed. I went to see them thinking that the taboo on sexual expression for older women would be the most obvious restraint on their sexuality. And I imagined that the difficulties older women might face if they wanted to find new partners would be the most obvious sign of this suppression. But what they gave me was something rather different.

Ruth said, 'Since being widowed and getting into old age, I've found it's still the same old thing. All these bloody men, they still want a woman to go to bed with, and that's the main reason they're interested. It's mucked up a couple of relationships I might have had, with two men I knew. I was buggered if I was going to pretend, I'm sick of pretending, I'm not going to do it anymore. When I was married I faked and I faked – and now there's an immediate revulsion, I'm not going to go and fake anymore, just bloody well not going to. There's something about it you don't like doing, it cheats everybody.

'With both these men, where something might have developed, I felt they were in too much of a hurry. I would be quite prepared to believe that if we could have gone around together, gone off on holiday – I've no idea what might have come out of it. But it had to be their way, and I wasn't going to promise, "Yes, I'll sleep with you every night for the rest of my life." Terrible thought. So I think it has to be a much more subtle thing for me. I don't think many men are very subtle about it . . .

'My sexual feelings are dead as a doornail now. But I have no doubt at all that the right man could turn them on again. If the man I had an affair with in my fifties was around now he could wake them up again.'

Mary said, 'Ted was very very ill for years before he died. We enjoyed loving each other and caressing each other, and we would get an orgasm – but simply by manipulation – we had to, because he couldn't do anything else. It wasn't really enough. I sometimes felt resentful, I knew he couldn't help it.

'I've been alone for the past four years. There are difficult things about living alone. Coming home to an empty house. Not having anybody to share the small things with – because we did do that, whatever happened I was always wanting to get home to tell Ted about it. And I miss having somebody special, because he was such a companion, and we were such a well-known couple, always together – always Mary and Ted, Ted and Mary. But yes, there are good things. Oh yes, I love it! Shameless, I am! I can do just what I like, eat what I like, go to bed when I like, I can be utterly selfish, I haven't got to consider him. Of course he was a very unselfish person, so in a way he was easy to live with, but in a way he wasn't because he'd always say, "Whatever you like, dear," so that put the onus onto me, I'd got to make sure he was happy, and I had to look after him physically, I kept him alive really. He was worth keeping alive – but that's gone, I now haven't got to bother about anybody else.

'I think I'm too old now to look for a new partner. I think perhaps if he'd died ten or fifteen years younger I might have done. You see, I was seventy, wasn't I, when he died. Shall I be truthful? It's completely selfish – but I do not ever want to have to look after anybody else ever again. I looked after my mother-in-law, my two children, my husband. That's enough. I'm looking after me now. If I married again, well, you never know – they might suddenly have a stroke and there you are, looking after another old man, aren't you? I loved Ted and I didn't mind looking after him, but enough's enough. That's it. I'll stick with being alone.'

Olive said, 'I haven't had sexual relations for twenty-three years. It is a miss, very definitely a miss – but it isn't just the intercourse.

it's the holding and loving and warmth, that's an awful miss. I've had a lot of intense feelings since I've been starved of it. Now I would like that to go into a book because, you know, people tend to feel the older you get, your sexual feelings lessen. Well, maybe they do if you're being satisfied, but if you're not satisfied, then they most certainly do not. I mean, I'm amazed by the strength of the feeling – you know, to watch something that really moves me on the television, I start to think: Golly, it really does . . . how can I explain it? You know what I mean? The feeling's very strong.

'This idea that older women don't have sexual feelings – it annoys me, because I'd like it to be known that it's not always so. I look at all the old women – there are millions of them, aren't there, walking around, and I think: I wonder if they still feel that they'd like sex? In fact, I get aroused far more easily and quickly than I did when I was married. I get enormous pleasure and sometimes to orgasm in my dreams – and I'm really pleased about that! The funny thing is, it's always my husband. Some image of him. It doesn't happen a lot, mind you, but every now and then it most certainly does.

'I spent a great many years not knowing who I was because my husband was a very powerful personality, and I look back sometimes and think: Why on earth did I not assert myself? I was always known as Arnold's wife, and I must have felt put-down by that, but I didn't do anything about it, because I was one of his worshippers like everybody else. But when after he'd died I was introduced as Michael's mother, I was livid, I said, "Hey, come off it, I'm *me*," and that sort of feeling now is very strong within me, and I am so happy with it. In my fifties I went on a counselling course and I learned to feel a darn sight better about my body, a lot better in accepting my sexuality, if you like. That training changed my mind about all sorts of things, and through the clients that came I learnt what life's all about, and I'm much more accepting and open to anything that comes along now.

'There have been times when I've thought: Now, what can I do? Shall I go on a singles holiday? But I never actually did anything. My Michael said to me years ago, "Mum, it's no good you looking for a man, you know, because you're too darn independent!" On my course we used to say people go round holding boards up, it's either "Come hither" or "Keep off" and I guess I've had a "Keep off" board up all this time. And now I've reached this great age, I think: No way do I want to get a man my age or older. The last thing I want to do – now this is where one has got selfish – the last thing I want to do is to be an old man's nurse, and lose my freedom.

'And you know if I had met someone I think I would also have had a certain sense of ... it's too strong to say disloyalty. But I think a lot about this actually. How can love go on year after year after year for someone who's been dead all that time? But it does. It's most extraordinary.'

Mary has been widowed for four years, Olive and Ruth for over twenty. All three women have at some level taken a decision not to seek out another partner.

We are told in Ecclesiastes that there is 'a time to embrace, and a time to refrain from embracing', and most of us accept that there are certain activities that are appropriate to certain stages of the life cycle. There are many stories, from the adventures of Dr Who to *The Picture of Dorian Grey*, in which the quest for eternal youthfulness is depicted as sinful or evil, and most of us are alienated by the Joan Collins, forever-young approach to the ageing of the body. Some such sense of what is appropriate may shape the decisions of older people of either sex whose partners die. Widows or widowers may simply feel that the part of their life that was about marriage is over: now they are doing something else. But when Mary and Olive and Ruth explain why they have decided not to seek out another partner, it is clear that there is more to that decision than a sense of what may be appropriate in your sixties and seventies. Their expressed reasons for their decision touch on the sexual experiences of women of all ages.

For Ruth, the reasons are explicitly sexual. Ruth locates her reluctance in the conflict between her own sexual needs and those of any potential partner.

Ruth has a clear sexual agenda. She doesn't want to have to fake, she doesn't want to have sex at times dictated entirely by the man's needs, and she wants the sex to grow out of a relationship. But when she imagines what sex with either of her two male friends would have been like, she fears that none of her conditions would have been met. She thinks of sex entirely at times of the man's choosing, sex to a male pattern, sex with necessary pretence on her part.

This sounds familiar. These are precisely the dissatisfactions that Cosmopolitan Woman also expressed, and now, with fifty years of sexual experience behind her, Ruth has had enough. So she makes her decision. If she can't have sex on her own terms, she isn't going to bother with it at all.

For Mary, too, a new sexual relationship would have come at a cost. For her the cost is not specifically sexual. Sex was always important to her, more important than it was to her husband, but she chooses not to express her sexual feelings in a new relationship because there is a price she is not willing to pay. Mary doesn't want to look after anyone else ever again.

Under patriarchy, nurturing is for women an integral part of sexual relationships. It is part of our courtship rituals – she cooks him a special dinner, washes his rugger shirt, straightens his tie. It is there in our fairy tales – *Beauty and the Beast*, for instance – and in male porn in the eroticization of the nurse. And it is at the heart of the unspoken marriage contract in the implicit agreement that the man will provide for the woman, and the woman will look after the man – and their children, both sets of parents, and various assorted friends and neighbours.

Mary and most of the other women of her age whom I talked to had lived by that contract. They had taken on the woman's traditional role and lived it out lovingly. For perhaps fifty years they had been mashing banana for babies or filling lunch boxes for schoolchildren or making up trays of food for elderly relatives to eat by the fire; they had washed and ironed everyone's clothes and wiped up everyone's mess; they had sat up all night with feverish babies and dying husbands. When you're looking after small children, as you wade through the endless overlapping tasks, you may fantasize about a moment without demands, a moment when you can finally put up your feet in a quiet house and look out of the window and do nothing in particular. If, as your children grow up, your parents or in-laws fall ill, and then in turn your partner, that moment is further postponed. Mary at seventy-six has finally reached that moment. In what she says, there is deep sadness at the loss of her husband: but there is also real pleasure in putting herself first for the only time since she married in her twenties.

Olive has been alone much longer than Mary. Even though widowed at a life stage when many women might long for another partner, Olive has at some level made a decision to stay on her own: 'I guess I've had a "Keep off" board up,' she says. When she thinks about what a new relationship might mean, Olive has the same aversive fantasy as Mary – the fear of becoming an old man's nurse – and for Olive too, there is much to celebrate about living alone. Widowed, mourning the loss of a deeply loved partner, she still values her independence, and enjoys being recognized in her own uniqueness, rather than as somebody's mother or somebody's wife.

For Olive there is also a big part of her decision that is about still feeling married. Olive's loyalty to the husband who died nearly twenty years ago is so moving because there is nothing cerebral about it, it is not willed or chosen, it is simply that at some deep level of herself she is still in love with her husband. She remains faithful to him even in her dreams, and when those dreams become orgasmic they centre on some image of him.

Here there are many reasons not to look too strenuously for another partner, but a lack of sexual interest is not cited as a reason by any of the women. These women express varying degrees of sexual interest – but none of them sees her sexuality as finished. Ruth sees her sexual feelings as dormant; they are part of herself that is still there, part that could be woken up again. Mary says that the sexual part of the relationship was still important to her right up to her husband's death four years ago. Olive's sexual feelings in her mid-seventies are more intense than they have ever been, and she muses on this with some surprise. It is very acceptable for a widow in her seventies to say she misses the cuddles, warmth and affection of a happy married life: Olive does miss these things, but she also misses the sex. Olive is a striking example of the female trend towards greater arousal and responsiveness as we get older. And in her account, we see how an older woman may be more aware than she has been since childhood that her sexuality is part of her, something that she owns, not something that only exists in the context of a relationship, in the space or closeness between two people.

The decision these three women have made is not grounded in a lack of interest in sex, nor in a sense that sexual pleasure is no longer one of life's possibilities. It is grounded rather in the women's perceptions of the costs of sexual relationships: having sex to a male agenda, having to be the nurturing one, and losing your independence – both in matters of daily decision-making, and in a more subtle sense, the sense in which a woman in a sexual relationship loses something of herself. Ruth, Mary and Olive remind us that for women sexual pleasure often comes with a price-tag attached. Because men have most of the power, so long as we remain emotionally involved with men we will make compromises to be liked and desired, compromises that involve subtly or not so subtly belittling ourselves. The compromises may be made in bitterness, or they may be made joyfully and willingly with a loved partner. But women who are no longer emotionally involved with or dependent on men don't make these compromises anymore. Olive recognizes this, as she muses on the implications of loving somebody as much as she loved her husband, and in the way that she loved him – 'I was one of his worshippers like everybody else.' That kind of loving can take something away from a woman – in Olive's case, the capacity for self-assertion and sense of her own individuality that were given back to her by her counselling course. In their pleasure in their independence, women like Olive tell us what feminist writers have also told us, and what perhaps many of us who love men have always doubted, deep down – that women do not need men to make them complete.

Sexuality does not end. The woman in her seventies may have a more vivid sexuality than when she was in her twenties. But in her clear-sighted appraisal of the meaning of sexual relationships for women, the older woman may simply decide that the price is one she will not pay again.

LOOKING BACK

As older women shared their sexual histories with me, they inevitably also reflected on the impact of the very different sexual mores that held sway when they were younger. Those sexual mores are now viewed in certain quarters with some nostalgia. When conservative social theorists talk about the degeneration of family life in Britain today, the focus of their nostalgia is the stereotypical family of the fifties, living in harmony in a cosy semi behind a privet hedge, with a traditional division of labour, a recognition of the rights of parents over children and husbands over wives, and a degree of sexual innocence in childhood and adolescence.

But when women in their sixties and seventies reflected on their lives, I found their looking back to be completely without nostalgia. Of the women over sixty-five that I interviewed, five had been married once – the others had either never married or had married more than once. Here is what the once-married women said about their sex lives.

*

'I just knew where I wanted to be touched, by feel you know, but he was very loath to satisfy me there, and of course it never occurred to me that I could do it. That's amazing to me now, I mean why? But there was this sort of guilt thing about touching yourself. In the end I suppose it just happened with the friction of the penis. It took a long time – I did have orgasms in the end, but I mean we'd been married years. If I remember rightly, it was certainly within the last five years that we had. I'd have been forty-six, forty-seven. That's ridiculous, isn't it? Absolutely crazy.'

'I was married when I was twenty-five, but I was a virgin for nine months after I was married because my husband couldn't consummate the marriage. And that was really through absolute fear on his part that he would let me down. We've talked about it since and I know now what it was, he found me very attractive, and he was scared of not coming up to the mark. I had no idea that an erection depended on the man's state of mind, I thought it was something you just switched on like a light, so I was quite unprepared for any necessity for foreplay. I was very confused and there was nobody I could talk to. After nine months I was so desperate, I said, "If you don't go to the doctor, I'm leaving," although it would have been a terrible sense of failure for me because I would have felt the whole world was laughing at me for being so unattractive. Anyway, the doctor reassured him and said he thought it was because of the sheath. It was wartime and we hadn't got a house of our own and we thought it was wrong to have a baby in wartime. When this doctor said, "Oh forget that, just go ahead and don't use any precautions," well, immediately I lost my virginity with no trouble at all. But I had my first child without ever experiencing any pleasure at all. I just felt thankful that we'd achieved it and that I wasn't all that terribly unattractive.'

'I think we were too ignorant – Will certainly wasn't experienced at all, and he loved me far too bloody much, put me on a pedestal. I don't think I ever got sex sorted out, it's rather a shame, perhaps next time round ... I think it all started because Will was away soon after our son was born, and he'd come back with such expectations, and there was me, still not feeling like it. I should never have married him. I can remember going "Ugh!" to myself. Yes, I hated sex really.'

*

'My sex life with my husband was ghastly. First of all he was impotent – and I was so convinced that I could do something about that. He actually went to the doctor after two or three years with me; it was a young doctor, I don't think he knew anything much about it. It made me angry, I think. It built up over all the years, because our marriage lasted for twenty-four years. I should have praised him and so on, but as the years went on I got more and more annoyed. He never really got an erection but he managed to ejaculate ... Oh dear, I hate talking about it, I don't want to remember all those nasty times.'

'I never really knew what an orgasm was till I finally looked it up in the dictionary. You think: Where did I go wrong? Perhaps I wasn't doing something I should have done. And it's not easy at times. Sometimes it's very hard staying married. There was nowhere for us to go then of course, you couldn't go off down the DHSS. You either stayed or were out on the street. It was either grin and bear it or out on your neck.'

The stability of those marriages contracted in the 1940s and 1950s had its price. As Gwen, the last speaker, points out, the cement that held many marriages together was not moral rectitude but financial necessity. These five marriages mostly endured: only one ended in divorce, that of Stella, the woman whose husband was impotent. But there is a lot of sexual pain here. The women's accounts are a reminder that sexual repression is especially bad for women. For men, sexual ignorance may mean a higher incidence of problems like impotence. But for women sexual ignorance often means getting no pleasure at all from sex.

Another reflective thread also ran through older women's accounts – their commentary on contemporary attitudes to sex. Older women, just like many younger ones, were irritated by certain aspects of contemporary sexual culture, in particular by the constant visual stimulation of men – the ubiquitous naked female bodies, the orgasmic girl in the chocolate flake commercial, the 'heaving buttocks' in television drama. But all the older women I spoke to opposed themselves decisively to the sexual ignorance and repress-ive attitudes of their childhoods and much of their adult lives, and suspected that their lives would have been enriched by more sexual knowledge.

'I'd have liked to have learned a bit more about it all. You hear about people shouting out and making lots of noise, I was still a bit quiet about it all I think, I didn't really want the kids to know or the neighbours – but it sounds as if it could be quite fun.'

'I didn't tell my daughter anything about sex, and I feel very badly about it – but I got no sex education from my mother and I had no idea how to do it. I gave her a book which was advertised as being very useful for daughters at school, but I could not have talked to her about it, there were words which we never used such as "penis", we just did not speak about sex at all. I am deeply sorry about that, but I didn't know how to.'

'My mother was dead against sex, she hated it, it was something you had to put up with. I've held it against her ever since, you know.'

'I think if I could say something, to stress it, it is the abysmal ignorance which we suffered from, which really did affect all our lives. I don't know what it would be like to grow up in the present day.'

Older women then were clearly very much in favour of sexual knowledge. But on the subject of sexual variety – the freedom to sleep with a number of different partners – they were more ambivalent. They tended to feel that there were gains as well as losses in limiting yourself to one partner. Mary said, 'I saw my daughter's sexuality as being much more pronounced than mine – well, more obvious, let's say – and I was quite envious of that, because she had so much freedom and I hadn't had it, and I knew that sexually I was just as aware as she was really, but it had all been bottled up. When she went to university, I was really envious of her. I know she slept around – and part of me thought that was wrong, and part of me wished I'd done it, and Ted and I used to say, "Oh golly, we wish we could have had some fun when we were young!" We talked about it, we laughed, but deep down we were very envious of that freedom. But now I'm not so sure, I'm not sure that we didn't have the most wonderful marriage – although it was full of difficulties, sexual difficulties and others, I'm not sure that after forty-six years we didn't have a closeness and a . . . something that perhaps you miss. But we both of us used to say, "Oh, I wish we'd known somebody else sexually besides each other!"'

Ending is a time for summing-up, and the last word on a subject is given special weight. In many societies wisdom has been regarded as the prerogative of the old, and old people's reflections on human affairs have been listened to with respectful attention. Today, we no longer believe that old age brings guaranteed wisdom, merely that it lends a rather different perspective. Yet when an older woman looks back on her sexual history, it is inevitable that we will sometimes hear what she says as a judgement or verdict.

Winifred was the oldest woman I talked to. If a woman's statement in old age can be taken as a verdict on the place of sexuality in her life, here is Winifred's.

'I've been divorced four times. I couldn't stay married – it was nothing to do with sexuality – at least, I don't think it had anything to do with sexuality – sexuality never seemed terribly important to me, and yet I suppose it was. I never thought sex meant very much to me, I never had the feeling it was something I longed for. Sometimes people have said to me, "I wish I had a boyfriend." I haven't felt that – what I would want was a man friend that I could go out with, but hoping he wouldn't want sex – I couldn't be bothered. Just occasionally I am interested by something on the television – mostly romantic – I don't think strongly about it, just a flicker of interest.

'The last relationship I had was when I was fifty-six. When I was fifty-four, I went to the Mission Hospital, and there I met a different kind of person. I suppose the men I met prior to that were commercial men, but at the Mission Hospital I met totally different people, and I realized I would have been much happier, or I would have lived differently, if I'd gone there earlier. I had a lover there when I was fifty-six. I had no worries about AIDS then, of course, I just knew I couldn't become pregnant, so that was alright. If I've thought of a man at all since, it's nothing to do with sex, it's been because I wanted friendship.

'I've lived on my own a lot, between marriages. Sometimes I see an elderly couple walking down the street, holding each other's hands or arm-in-arm, and they stop to look in a shop window, and I envy that, I think: God, they're very lucky – but at the same time I knew it wouldn't happen to me because I kept choosing the wrong kind of man.

'Living alone is hard at times. I've had no thought of being married, but sometimes I've wanted a man friend with a car, so we could perhaps go out to the countryside together. But over the past four years I don't think about that anymore. I am lonely. My friends are scattered all over the place, and because they're getting older they don't like driving through the town now. And because I've had a stroke I don't talk as well as I did, and that's a difficulty.

'I can become tearful very easily. I see the world full of people – they do this, they do that, they make mistakes, they do the wrong thing. More and more I see them as a lot of imperfect people in an imperfect world. I wouldn't blame them as I would have years ago.

'I suppose I married so often because I was looking for someone. I thought some man would have it but he didn't have it. I think I was looking for God: I didn't find him.'

Part Two

CHAPTER TEN

Fantasy

As they muse on the subject of female sexual fantasies, certain writers have been inspired with images of fecundity and lush plant life, of fruiting trees and rainforests. Nancy Friday called her pioneering collection of women's fantasies *My Secret Garden*: Jill Tweedie wrote that the collection made her think of 'a livid jungle sliced by the screams of the Monkey God: a dark forest lit by burning tigers . . .'[1] But when I talked to women, I had no sense of female sexual fantasy as an area of women's lives that is particularly lush or fecund. I wonder how much is actually growing in the average secret garden.

When a prostitute 'of the thigh-booted, whip-wielding variety' wrote in the *Guardian* about her work, she described how she sometimes asks her clients if they are interested in acting out their wives' fantasies, or if they even know what their wives' fantasies are. 'I am usually met,' she wrote, 'with a puzzled silence'.[2] To ask women themselves about their fantasies is also to be met with silence, a silence which is full of discomfort. Women are very reluctant to tell their fantasies.

Some of this reluctance is easily explained. By definition a sexual fantasy is something that arouses simply by being told. You may be able to describe a sexual act in a cool detached manner, but to describe the fantasy that accompanied the act will probably arouse you again, something a woman might want to avoid in an interview situation. There is also a common belief that sexual fantasies reveal a lot about our most secret selves: again, this is something not to be lightly done, whether to a sex partner or to a stranger with a tape-recorder. But even with these provisos, the sense of shame and the reluctance remain remarkable. We seem to feel so much more guilty and ashamed about what we *think* than what we do.

Sometimes the sense of shame doesn't just stop the woman from telling the fantasy, it even stops her from thinking it. I learned from talking to women just how often we shy away from erotic material.

Feeling ourselves becoming aroused, we turn off the television, close the book. Heather said, 'I often do inhibit feelings from watching films or whatever. I get extremely angry even though I might be feeling quite aroused by it – I just don't handle these things very well . . . I might feel something physically and I would blush and I would either think – I don't know – whatever cuts it out, or I would get cross. If it was something that was very erotic, I would turn the TV off or actually physically bring it to an end.' Heather switches off the television: other women told how and why they switched off the screen in their heads as well. Emily said, 'I used fantasies a lot when I first started having orgasms. I couldn't have come without them. But since I've started to come much more quickly, I've made a deliberate decision not to use fantasy. I just don't like what turns me on. Why does sex have to be associated with all these whips and things? But I suppose it is a restriction in a way, because I did find the fantasies very arousing.' Ruth would never have thought of using fantasy to increase her arousal with the husband who didn't turn her on any more: 'Think of someone else?' she said. 'That would have been just the worst insult.'

Remarkably, some women recall having a richer sexual fantasy life as children than as adults. Jacqueline said she'd had no sexual fantasies in adult life. As a child of six or seven, she'd had arousing fantasies with a masochistic content: 'Maybe that's why I never have fantasies,' she said, 'because it would always be masochistic.' Teresa said, 'I do remember having very vivid fantasies at about four – weird fantasies all about women and body parts, quite sadistic really. I think I felt a bit guilty about them even then, but I remember enjoying them too.'

Teresa may have felt guilty as a child, but there is also a sense that at least as a child she owned her sexual arousal to fantasy. She felt it was her secret, in the way that girls often feel that masturbation is their secret: it may make them feel guilty, but it is theirs, their very own secret source of pleasure. This sense of ownership or entitlement is notably absent from many women's accounts of their arousal to fantasy in adult life. The women I have quoted all have a sense of alienation from their fantasy lives. Sexual fantasy is experienced as something external, something that intrudes into the mind. It is almost as though the sexual fantasy itself were an abuser forcing himself on the woman, or an unwanted visitant from the darkness outside, tapping on the windowpane of consciousness. When television images turn her on, Heather is angry: she feels something has been done to her. Jacqueline envisions her fantasies as something out there waiting to come in: if she lets any fantasies in, she suspects she wouldn't like them. For Emily, the images that come into her head when she has sex are things that she feels she has to fight or deny, to push away again.

Marianne reflected, 'Somehow there's still a feeling that we don't have a right to sex or any sexual identity, and any ones that we're getting we're stealing from somewhere. It's so difficult to know what female sexuality is meant to be – I suppose because it's defined by men. It doesn't feel like it's ours. We're borrowing images to excite ourselves that aren't ours.' Some of us, like Marianne, borrow or steal things – but other women prefer the blank screen or the empty page to borrowed imagery.

'Sex', wrote Helen Kaplan, 'is composed of friction and fantasies.'[3] Fantasy is a fundamental part of arousal. Many women describe how they first reached orgasm by using arousing fantasies during sex or masturbation, and learning to fantasize is an important component of successful therapy programmes for pre-orgasmic women. Yet here we see women profoundly uneasy about sexual fantasy, uneasy to the point of anger when one of the 'borrowed images' is arousing, or to the point of not fantasizing at all. The image of the dark continent or the undiscovered territory seemed merely to mystify what was straightforward though hidden in women's physical sexual functioning. But it's an image that can very appropriately be applied to the subject of women's sexual fantasies.

FANTASY: ITS FORMS AND ITS FUNCTIONS

To find our way through this territory, we need a map. But there is no readily available model of sexual fantasy to serve as our guide. Freud of course was preoccupied with sexual fantasy, but not specifically with the fantasies that turn us on, rather with what he saw as the sexual roots of all our thinking and feeling. If you want to categorize the kinds of fantasies that turn us on, you necessarily have to improvise.

Marianne mused, 'I have one kind of romantic narrative that's gone on since I was twelve, which was my escape in boarding school. It's all to do with this bad man theme, this wild womanizing hard-bitten man, who'd done terrible things and then fell in love with you and you saved him. It's still effective now, and it has

various scenes I can replay. But there's a difference between running erotic and enjoyable stories in one's head, and trying to achieve
an orgasm – and you'd select different kinds of material for each.
The one is daydreaming, and generally boosting yourself up with
a daydream, and the other is actually mechanistically trying to
achieve an orgasm, and that's more like just coming into the room
and seeing an erotic scene on television. They're actually narrative
too, but much shorter.'

Marianne distinguishes between the long elaborate story that
helps her achieve a pleasant state of arousal, and the more nar-
rowed-down, focused and strongly visual forms of orgasmic fantasy.
Different forms of fantasy, she hints, have different functions. So
what are the different forms that fantasy can take?

If we imagine a stair going down into darkness, leading down
from the most accessible and conscious form of fantasy to the least,
we would first come to the use of the word that indicates that we
would like to have sex with someone: 'I have fantasies about him,'
we say, or 'I fancy her.' 'Fancy' is a sixteenth century version of
'fantasy'.

On the next step of the stair, we would find sexual daydreams,
like Marianne's daydream about the wild man. These are often
elaborate narratives that we consciously script and control. Sometimes they merge with the 'I fancy' kind of fantasy, as when the
narrative tells how you most unexpectedly bump into the man or
woman you currently lust after.

A little further down the stairway are orgasmic fantasies. Often
much less developed than sexual daydreams, these may be images
or remembered sensations rather than stories. If the sexual daydream is like an erotic novel in form, these are pages from a pornographic magazine. The degree to which we feel in control of
orgasmic fantasies will vary. We may deliberately switch on these
images to reach orgasm, or the sensation of heightened arousal may
seem to bring them into our minds without a conscious decision. Or
they can be compulsive: we may feel that they control us.

Daydream fantasies or orgasmic fantasies may occasionally be
described to a partner during love-making, though I suspect that
the sharing of fantasies advocated in the advice pages of women's
magazines as an enrichment of one's sex life is strictly a minority
interest. Sometimes one partner's fantasy will be acted out during
love-making. For the fetishist, the acting-out has a terrible urgency,
but for people less cruelly driven by their fantasies, acting-out will

be more like the sexual role-playing of children, where sex comes closest to play.

In the shadows at the bottom of the stairway are the least accessible and least conscious forms of sexual fantasy – erotic dreams. It is widely known that men have erections during dream sleep, and especially in adolescence may have frequent 'wet dreams'. It is less widely known that women have a similar pattern of arousal during sleep. Women lubricate during dreams, and many women too have orgasms during sleep. It is yet another sign of the lack of recognition of women's active sexuality that for women there is no label like 'wet dream', no term to distinguish an erotic dream that simply melts into another dream from an erotic dream that erupts into orgasm. It is only in medieval demonology that we find female orgasmic dreams acknowledged – though admittedly in a pejorative light: as well as the succubus, the female demon who came to men in the night, there was the incubus, the male demon who invaded the beds of women.[4] As you would expect from the typical pattern of sexual development in women's lives, orgasmic dreams become more common as women get older,[5] and we saw in Chapter 9 how Olive at seventy-six derived rich enjoyment from her orgasmic dreams. Erotic dream imagery may later be fed back into the woman's more conscious fantasy life.

To ask what forms fantasy can take is also to ask what functions it can serve. The fantasies we have around sex object choice will shape our choice of sex partner. Sexual daydreams will define how we see our sexuality even as they serve as a source of pleasure and escape. Orgasmic fantasies may be necessary to orgasm. And erotic dreams may point to hidden aspects of our sexuality, as when the heterosexual woman has dreams of ravishing eroticism about other women, or the woman who is turned on by degradation fantasies has dreams in which the tenderest caress is erotically charged.

This is one kind of categorization – by form and function. What about the content of sexual fantasy?

In *The Interpretation of Dreams*, Freud suggests there are three sources for the content of dreams.[6] The most obvious source is the physical: you have a full bladder, and you dream of hunting for a lavatory on a busy street. Another source is childhood experience: so in your dream you relive a childhood trauma, or you wander through the rooms of your childhood home. The third source, Freud suggests, is the here-and-now: something that happened at work, perhaps, the day before the dream.

Waking sexual fantasies have much in common with dreams. Like dreams, they are spontaneous productions of the mind over which we may feel we have little conscious control. Freud's dream model can perhaps be adapted to account for the content of sexual fantasies. In Freud's dream scheme there is a commingling of the body and the mind, the banal and the significant, and the deep past and the present. In sexual fantasies we can trace out a similar intermingling of elements.

The physical part of sexual fantasies is obvious, and the process is most like dreams when a physical sensation triggers the sexual fantasy – when a little girl rubbing herself on her pillows finds herself thinking about boys in her class whom she likes. The here-and-now element in sexual fantasies is also easy to trace out, as in the simplest kind of daydream or orgasmic sexual fantasy, where the man or woman you are making love to in the fantasy is somebody in your life now. The childhood element in sexual fantasies is the most elusive and problematic part. Yet the psychoanalytic belief that some adult sexual behaviours have their roots in childhood experience is now widely accepted and we are not surprised when we read of abused children who become abusers in adult life, or of people beaten in childhood who are turned on by sado-masochism in adult life. So we do have a frame for the idea that childhood experiences may resurface in adult sexual life.

Thus Freud's dream scheme, with its mingling of childhood, physical and here-and-now elements, does seem to be applicable to sexual fantasy. But there is one crucial difference between the content of waking sexual fantasies and dreams. Dream material largely comes from the person's own past and present, but sexual fantasies borrow much of their material from the public domain. Our culture abounds in sexual stimulation of all sorts – films, books, sexy commercials, sexualized clothing, pornographic videos. Today more than ever, our private sexual worlds are crowded out with public images.

We now have a rough grid to enable us to take our bearings in this dark continent. Fantasies may take the form of 'fancying' somebody, erotic daydreams, orgasmic fantasies, and erotic dreams during sleep. In the content of all these forms of fantasy, there will be a mixture of physical, childhood and here-and-now elements. And many sexual fantasies will also include images and ideas that are taken from shared public definitions of the erotic.

Now we can turn to women's own accounts, and ask what their
fantasies tell us about female sexuality and its suppression.

TRAUMA INTO TRIUMPH: ORGASMIC FANTASY AND
CHILDHOOD EXPERIENCE

Maureen said, 'I was emotionally and physically abused by my
father, in a horrific way. I don't think I was sexually abused – but
it's not the only form of abuse.

'It's affected my sexuality through and through. Me and my older
sister sat at the kitchen table for the first twelve years of my life
witnessing such a horrific relationship between my father and my
mother, and without ever saying it, we both formulated all these
plans about how it would never happen to us, and it never has.
She's been through three husbands, I've been through one, God
knows how many other men that we just can't let get close to us,
we can't be that vulnerable, because my mother was a hundred per
cent doormat to a violent horrible man, and she just made his tea
while he threw hot kettles at her.

'I remember with my first lover, in Richmond Park – I had
enormous struggles in losing my virginity to him, but we did sort
of manage the act, but with great difficulty – I can remember lying
under a tree in a hidden place having sex. It was discreet, there
was no fear of discovery, but I couldn't get turned on, I couldn't
get into it. It was happening, but I couldn't get excited – and I
started fantasizing about my father, and that turned me on. I wasn't
thinking – was I? – perhaps I *was* thinking that my father was
screwing me, I don't know what I was thinking – but that made
me sort of turn on to this chap.

'I often find that I can become more orgasmic by thinking about
certain subjects. They're all weird things, they're all things I want
to escape from, things I hate. If I was having sex with my husband
and I wasn't coming – there's that moment, isn't there, when you're
in it and you're not in it – then I would find coming into my
mind ideas which in some odd way turned me on, and I feel quite
frightened by what those ideas are. I suppose the desire to have
an orgasm and to enjoy the sexual feeling was so strong it overcame
my feelings of dislike of the particular fantasies that were coming
into my mind – but I don't like them and I don't understand them
and they do worry me. I've got a real hang-up about food and
being fat – and I used to see my body apart from myself, see this

fat fatness, rolls of flesh – it was something I hated so much, I hated it. And I have quite a difficult relationship with my daughter, and I used to find flashing into my mind those aspects of her which I find unacceptable, like her squint – it sounds ridiculous, but it upsets me somehow – and I would see her face with this disgusting awful squint, vastly exaggerated, and it would do something to me that would help sex. It was as though my mind was pulling in the aspects of life which I find most intolerable, pulling them into the consciousness of sex and kind of linking them up with sex somehow. It worries me that it should be such horrid nasty things which should be linked with achieving pleasure. It's certain things which are closest to my heart, which I wish weren't there, by thinking about them turn me on.'

Pam said, 'My father was very distant, cold and rejecting. I was desperate to be cuddled by him, I used to make overtures to him which he was very embarrassed about, he'd take me on his knee momentarily, then put me down again. But I had a lot of touching and cuddling from the women in my family. It was a matriarchal home. There was this absent father, who was actually despised and disliked by all these women. Men were referred to really as bastards: the word was never used, it was a very correct home, but that was the meaning.

'I'm really turned on by sado-masochistic fantasies, and when I masturbate I think about men being humiliated. When I was making love to Jake that was the only way I could reach orgasm, by silently fantasizing these things. I rarely reached orgasm because of things he was doing to me. It was lovely if it did happen, I was really happy that it would be that way, which I suppose is part of the guilt thing. When I first started having orgasms it was because I suddenly realized that this wonderful sudden surge of feeling could happen if I fantasized silently while we were making love. It started off by being fantasies about Jake dressing me in certain clothes and holding me prisoner. That lasted about a month, then I suddenly found I got even more success at having orgasms by imagining men doing things to men, and turning them into women, by a long drawn out process of conditioning them and dressing them, and that's really how I get an orgasm, I have various themes that I follow through. Then I start being guilty about why I should be turned on by this particular thing. Is it something to do with the fact that my father never loved me like I wanted him to and it's almost a revenge thing against my father?'

Fran said, 'When I was twelve we had a PE teacher who used to make us parade around the showers with nothing on, and you had to get your towels from this pile, so if you were the first one in you couldn't actually get your towel 'cos it was at the bottom of the pile, you were all the wrong way round, so there was this horrendous crush for the towels. And she one day very specifically said to us before we went into the shower, "I want you to listen very carefully to this because you must do exactly as I say, I want you to put on your skirts and your shirts, put on all your tops and your skirts and nothing else." I thought very carefully and I watched the other girls, and some put their knickers on and some didn't, but I was a very obedient child so I obediently did as she said, and then we sat on the bench and she came along and she was apparently looking for verrucas so she made you lift your leg and she looked between your toes, and she said to me, "You're a *good* girl . . ."

'I think I knew I was attracted to women for a long time. With my husband I used to think about women and he knew that, we had talked about that, and he thought that was fine, as long as I came quickly he couldn't care what I thought about. I used to think about the gym teacher, to be honest.'

One of the more troubling aspects of human sexuality is our capacity for deriving pleasure from pain, suffering and oppression – our own and other people's. These three sexual fantasies take us to a dark place where there is sexual intimacy with someone who is hated and feared but also a part of you, where things you hate to think of also turn you on, where abuse or the idea of abuse is arousing, and where revenge is taken for wrongs done to you in childhood. This is disturbing territory because it is when such stories are actually acted out that bad things happen – when girls get orgasms from cutting their wrists,[7] or a judge ejaculates when sentencing young men to death.[8] This is a place in oneself that one visits with trepidation but also with tremendous fascination.

Psychotherapist Robert Stoller describes a boy who as a small child was dressed in women's clothes by his female relatives, and who in adolescence came to derive sexual pleasure from cross-dressing. 'Now what had been traumatic was mastered, becoming his greatest pleasure,' writes Stoller. 'In this way the victim has his

own sort of triumph.'⁹ In Maureen, Fran and Pam's accounts, we
see how trauma can also be mastered in sexual fantasy, the kind
of fantasy that is not acted out. All three women experienced abuse
in childhood, physical, sexual or emotional, and for all three, trauma
becomes triumph in the sexual fantasies of adult life. So Maureen
fantasizes that the lover penetrating her is her abusive hated father,
Fran relives the incident of voyeuristic abuse by the gym teacher,
and Pam takes revenge on the remote unloving father of childhood
by turning men into women.

Each of these fantasies has a different formal relationship to the
troubling childhood experience. For Fran, the fantasy is a page
from a diary: the incident of voyeuristic abuse by the gym teacher
is simply lifted from life. Maureen's fantasies are more fragmentary,
images rather than narratives, pictures from a personal scrapbook
– though one she wouldn't choose to open. Pam's fantasy is a fully
developed narrative with alternative endings like an experimental
novel, a story that she gradually constructs for herself as she learns
to have orgasms. She is the author and creator of the fantasy,
though as it develops, like all the best novels as you write them, it
takes on a life of its own.

There is no apparent borrowing from the public world of shared
erotic imagery in these fantasies. All three women relate the fantasy
directly back to part of their personal history, and root it clearly
in childhood events, or in childhood feelings of fear, rage and
deprivation. And yet their fantasies are strongly reminiscent of
certain shared public fantasies. The eroticization of the dominant
hated father in Maureen's fantasy fits with many public sexual
themes that concern the erotic appeal of the feared and dominant
man: we shall look at some of these in the next chapter. The gym
mistress is a common figure in lesbian erotica, though Fran simply
takes her from life. The degradation of men by dressing them in
women's clothes is a not uncommon theme in homosexual pornography.

These three stories raise one of the most fascinating questions
about the relationship between the public and the private in fantasy.
The role of public images in the here-and-now part of our fantasy
lives is obvious – when, for instance, a woman reruns a sexy scene
from a film to turn herself on. But these three stories suggest that
public elements also impinge on the most private component of
fantasy – the part that is rooted in childhood experience. How does
this work? Is what becomes erotic for us from our own past histories

decided by society's current definitions of what is and is not sexy? For instance, might a woman eroticize an abusive experience from childhood because our culture eroticizes violence? Or are themes like domination and punishment recurrent public sexual stories because they relate to universal human experience – the mix of love and rage we feel towards parents and parental figures like teachers, or the envy, anger and fear that may be aroused in us by the bodies of the opposite sex?

Some of Maureen's fantasies, however, do not seem to relate to the public world at all, as when she describes how she can be aroused by a sense of revulsion at the fatness of her body, or by the image of her daughter's squint. Maureen experiences these sexual fantasies as unwanted and intrusive and they trouble her deeply.

They trouble her in part because they have no apparent connection with anything society defines as sexual. There is a sense in which pornography has put a straitjacket on sexual fantasy. Porn is highly stylized and conventional, and everyone is familiar with its style and conventions, even those who never use it. Because of the influence of porn, we now tend to think of 'a sexual fantasy' as a neat piece of narrative that has certain predictable themes.

But it is clear from Maureen's account that sexual fantasy can be quite different from pornography. The fantasies that accompany intense arousal may be fleeting images or sensations rather than a piece of narrative, and their content may bear no relationship to the conventional subject matter of pornography. The things that turn us on are many and varied – 'certain tenor voices – the high notes', 'dogs copulating – especially the way sometimes they can't separate for ages afterwards', 'the dentist probing gently but insistently in your mouth'. When images that have little relationship to conventional sexual imagery accompany intense arousal we may, like Maureen, be perplexed and wonder what peculiar branching network of associations joins these things up to sex.

But their idiosyncratic nature is not what most troubles Maureen about her fantasies. These images and sensations worry her so much because they are all things she hates. It is as though the sensation of arousal dredges up certain things from the sediment of experience and memory – 'things which are closest to my heart, which I wish weren't there.'

It is one of the precepts of our 'sex is fun' culture that in fantasy anything goes. As sex therapist Patricia Gillan says, 'The more things there are that turn a person on, the luckier they are!'[10] This is the line that is reiterated in that familiar kind of magazine article, in which women's fantasies are quoted and then interpreted by a 'psychosexual analyst' who explains that it's fine to have fantasies and we should all just lie back and enjoy them. It's a proposition that makes little sense to women like Maureen, who find themselves in the extremity of physical pleasure confronted by things that they hate.

The fact that these are all the kinds of fantasy used to achieve orgasm has relevance for the content. As Maureen sees so clearly, we are most likely to allow unacceptable material into the mind where the pay-off is greatest. So what might be rejected in a sexual daydream – material that might make us close a book, turn off a film, or force ourselves to think about something else – may be accepted where it will lead to orgasm. But some women will still find their fantasies unacceptable, even with such a pay-off. Such a woman may limit arousal by not fantasizing, or may even avoid sexual situations that bring unacceptable thoughts into her head.

In these accounts we see how fantasy matters. For Pam, Maureen and Fran, fantasy has been necessary for orgasm for most or all of their sexual histories. Their stories also remind us just how uneasy women are about fantasy. Even in the accounts of these highly sophisticated women, who have sought to understand the roots of their fantasies in an attempt to make peace with them, we keep hearing words like 'worry' and 'hate' and 'guilt'. And for Maureen the fantasy material is an intruder, and there is a constant struggle over what can be allowed into the mind during sexual activity.

THE FATHER OF MY CHILD: SEX OBJECT CHOICE AND THE HERE-AND-NOW

Marianne said, 'There was a man at work whom I really fancied. Then we were having lunch together one day and he told me he'd had a vasectomy. It was weird – I went off him, just like that. He just didn't turn me on anymore.'

A number of women said they enjoyed sex most when trying for a baby. In particular, penetration, often described in rather lukewarm language, became much more enjoyable. There may be practical reasons for this increased enjoyment: most contraception interferes with female pleasure. But penetration also feels better when a woman is trying for a child because it has a different meaning. The

aversive fantasy – How terrible if I got pregnant – is replaced by
the fantasy of the beautiful baby that will result from this union.
The fantasy enriches the physical experience and penetration feels
more erotic.

Marianne's account shows how this fantasy can affect sex object
choice. Marianne is happily married and has no intention of sleeping with the man whom she fancies at work: his vasectomy is of
no practical interest to her. But when he is no longer perceived in
fantasy as capable of giving her the gift of a dream baby, the sexual
attraction melts away. It's a striking instance of the way the 'father
of my child' fantasy can affect sex object choice.

Marianne is not unusual. In the magazine *Alaska Men*, men are
displayed as sex objects and women write in to the magazine in
the hope of pursuing relationships with the men they fancy. Susie
Carter, the magazine's founder, has remarked in a television interview that by far the most popular photographs, the ones that provoke floods of letters, show men with children or small animals.

The eroticism of fertility is a common theme in women's fantasy
life. But it is a sexual fantasy that men don't share. Where fertility
is not valued, and where male definitions of sexual pleasure predominate, babies are the antithesis of eroticism. Researchers have
found that most women's pupils dilate when they are presented
with photos of attractive babies, as do those of men who've had
children, but men who haven't had children signal no interest. For
young men in our culture, there is nothing libidinous about their
response to babies, and a woman's perceived capacity to produce
them is largely irrelevant to her sexual appeal.

Because the eroticism of fertility is an exclusively female preoccupation, it is largely absent from our public definitions of the sexual.
A man's potential for fathering is admittedly one element in the
closing pages of the Mills and Boon romance, but the emergence
of this theme coincides with a lowering rather than a heightening
in the erotic tension. A commercial for Calvin Klein's perfume
'Eternity' that showed the passionate couple dreaming of the child
who would result from their union, is an almost unique example
of an erotic use of this theme in contemporary public fantasy.

Yet the 'father of my child' fantasy can have great significance
for a couple's sexual happiness. Look at what can happen when
the fantasy has died.

Janet said, 'A lot of the time – this sounds awful – but I feel sex
is a bit of a chore. Graham had a vasectomy when he was married

before, and I thought it wouldn't matter, but eventually it did, so
he had a reversal done. We tried for two years and nothing happened, then they told me the only thing left to try was AID.* That
really seemed to turn me off, the fact that you were having sex but
to no avail, sort of thing. There didn't seem to be a lot of point in
it anymore. It's never really been as good since then, and I think
probably at the back of my mind a lot of it's to do with the fact
that I know we can't have children together. I've had two children
by AID – so I suppose I've been quite lucky. I do try hard not to
let it show for Graham's sake, but even now I think I would feel
much more interested if I thought we could have children together.'

Gwen said, 'I went into marriage thinking, This is marvellous,
now I can have a baby – and it didn't happen, which was an
enormous disappointment. We started off on this dreadful rigma-
role of why we couldn't. It was a most traumatic time in my life.
We're Catholics, and my husband had very high moral principles
– should we do this? Should we do that? He felt it was against his
beliefs – which could make life quite difficult. I think I tended to
go off sex – I thought, Well, what's the point? It seemed a pointless
exercise. I was so eaten up with the idea of having a baby that the
actual process seemed secondary to the end product. It was about
putting up with it.'

Neither Janet nor Gwen derives much pleasure from her sex
life: both feel it is because they can no longer see their sex partner
as the 'father of my child'. Sex makes them both ask the same
question: 'What's the point?' In reality sex is pointless from the
reproductive point of view for most of the monthly cycle, but in
fantasy having a partner who is or could be the father of your child
will shape the meaning of every act of penetration. In reality, both
these couples have children – Janet by AID, and Gwen by adoption
– and the husbands are devoted fathers to these children, but in
fantasy, the special magic of having sex with this man who is or
could be the physical and genetic father of your child is missing.
Because the biological purpose of sex was never realized, all sex
becomes 'pointless'.

No fantasy is a turn-on for all women, and that includes the
'father of my child'. And, needless to say, many couples who are
childless, whether by choice or circumstance, have fulfilling sex

* AID – Artificial Insemination by Donor.

lives, and many couples who have completed their families find their sex lives improve when the man has a vasectomy. We have also seen how the reality as opposed to the fantasy of child-bearing may actually have a deleterious effect on a couple's sex life. The fact remains that for many women the 'father of my child' fantasy will be one significant element that shapes their pleasure in sex and their choice of sex partner.

The idea that women may find fertility a turn-on is in direct opposition to our received wisdom on sex. There is no place for this notion in the sexual universe of sex gurus like Alex Comfort, who writes in *The Joy of Sex*, '... the sort of sex we are talking about here, almost excludes fertility.'[11] It is because our definitions of the erotic are circumscribed by male sexual values that this fantasy, which may have such a profound effect on women's sexual histories, simply isn't seen.

THE STRAIGHT WOMAN'S LESBIAN DREAM: EROTIC DREAMS AND THE HERE-AND-NOW

Jessica said, 'The first time I ever came during a dream, it was about me and another woman, and we were together in this public toilet. I was taller than her and had cropped hair like a man and was dressed in white, and she was dark with curly hair and very curvy and feminine, and we were just touching one another's breasts, and then I woke up with the orgasm. I never have lesbian fantasies when I'm awake – all my usual sexual fantasies are of the standard boss/secretary type.'

A great many women who see themselves as heterosexual have lesbian fantasies. A sex survey carried out for London Weekend Television's 'Sex Now' programme and the *Mail on Sunday* found that two out of three women fantasized about lesbian sex. The newspaper write-up describes this as 'the single most astonishing finding' of the survey.[12] Lesbianism is a common theme in male pornography, but always as a decorative margin to the main action. The journalist who reported on the 'Sex Now' survey was astonished because there is nothing in mainstream culture that reflects the erotic charge of lesbian themes in the fantasy life of many women who have adopted a heterosexual lifestyle.

The lesbian fantasies that women told me about came in all the fantasy forms. Sometimes they were of the simplest kind, on the top rung of the fantasy hierarchy – 'I have fantasies about so-

and-so'. Freud pointed to the unconscious sexual roots of all love relationships, and feminism has suggested that you are more highly evolved if you love women. In this context, the question 'Is this really about sex?' is one that many women will ask about their close emotional attachments to female friends. For Fran it certainly was really about sex: Fran's friendship with Ginny started as any close female friendship starts – 'I wanted to talk to her and be with her, I wanted to have my coffee with her, I wanted to share my Polo mints with her' – and developed into a lasting sexual love. Another time, a woman may love her friend without sensing any conscious sexual elements in her attraction. In between these two poles are those cases where a woman feels her sexual orientation to be primarily heterosexual but still wonders what it would be like to have sex with her friend.

Then there are the daydreams and orgasmic fantasies that may be exclusively lesbian, or, like Bernadette's, have lesbian elements: 'My fantasies always involve group sex, and there's always got to be women there, so there's always got to be a lesbian bit, but then there's always got to be a man who comes in and does the penetrating. It's very much group, but it's about being taken – that somebody, not aggressively, takes somebody, comes on to them and cajoles them into it and then eventually it happens.'

The form at the deepest level of our fantasy hierarchy was the erotic dream. The lesbian fantasies that women described to me most often came in this form. This is intriguing, because it seems likely that dreams are the part of our sexual fantasy life that is least shaped by culture. Women like Jessica who said they had no conscious fantasies with lesbian elements, would describe these dreams with an air of puzzlement, wondering what the dreams said about them, for it is a common belief that aspects of our personalities that are hidden or forbidden may be expressed in dreams.

It might be argued that these lesbian fantasies and dreams don't require any explication. Freud's conclusion that we all have a bisexual potential is widely accepted today, and, as we have seen, many women have already enjoyed sexual games or 'practised' sexual activities with other girls in childhood or adolescence. Many of those women who muse on the possible advantages of lesbian relationships would probably enjoy them if they acted out their fantasies. But it seems to me that there are certain elements in these fantasies that do warrant exploration – in particular, the very romantic flavour of the straight woman's lesbian fantasy.

Amanda said, 'Vanessa, who I was really really close to at school, wrote me a letter a year ago telling me she was a lesbian. I had a lot of dreams when she told me that, worried sexual dreams. I don't know if it's an awful thing to say, but we almost might have done it. It never crossed my mind, but now I think I was stupid and blind – like, I asked her to meet my boyfriend and she burst into tears and ran down the road when I wanted her to meet this guy. The girl she's going out with told me she'd never met two people so similar as me and Vanessa, and I do feel very similar to Vanessa, we were very psychic, I'd be at home and I'd go to the door even if I didn't know she was coming . . .'

Amanda, like a number of women I talked to, remarks on the magical, intuitive quality of the relationship with a female friend that might have become sexual. An intuitive level of understanding does sometimes develop between close female friends. But perhaps this theme also hints at certain childhood fantasy elements in the lesbian dream. In *The Rocking of the Cradle, the Ruling of the World*, Dorothy Dinnerstein suggests that, because children are brought up by women, there is for both sexes a special magic about the woman's body.[13] The heterosexual man finds this magic in the body of his lover in adult life, but for the woman, according to Dinnerstein, this magic resides in her own body when she feels desired and needed. Perhaps we also look for this magic in the arms of another woman. The lesbian fantasy is about oneness. This woman will be the missing part of yourself, like the mother who was also part of you when you were a baby. In this love there will be a oneness that you never knew in your relationships with men.

This dream of oneness then may have childhood elements. But there is also an overriding here-and-now element to these fantasies, for the dream of oneness is also a powerful critique of heterosexual relationships. The fantasized lesbian relationship becomes a dream of perfect sex, a repository for all those bits that are missing from sex with men. When women who wonder if they might enjoy sex with women talk about what it would be like, they sketch out a relationship that is tender, caring, reliably orgasmic, and doesn't stop when your partner has come. The other woman would understand your body, take plenty of time, talk to you, be gentle.

The reality may not be quite like that. Lesbian lovers are not repositories of unlimited tenderness and unconditional love, any more than mothers are. As women get more power in the world, and we see them operate as fallible and sometimes wicked human

beings, much like men, the notion of caring sharing women is laid
bare for what it always was – a reflection of women's powerlessness
rather than their moral superiority. And lesbian relationships are
just as troubling, contradictory and potentially rewarding as heterosexual relationships, with the important proviso that a woman will
understand another woman's body better than a man ever could.
The lesbian relationships that women have described to me have
run the gamut from the magically tender and erotic to the abusive
and violent. But the fantasy of the perfect lesbian relationship tells
us a lot about what is missing from the here-and-now of women's
relationships with men. The fantasy has tenderness in place of
violence or domination, and oneness rather than difference as the
source of its erotic charge. The fantasy, like Jessica's orgasmic
dream, tells us that oneness and tenderness can be overwhelmingly
erotic.

Both the prevalence and the invisibility of women's lesbian fantasies connect with the suppression of female sexuality. The straight
woman's lesbian fantasy is not only notably absent from the public
sexual world, it actually exists in opposition to that world, as a
critique of public heterosexual values. It is a telling comment on
those values that this fantasy of oneness can sometimes feel so
forbidden that it can only be expressed in dreams.

MASOCHISM AND GLAMOUR:
SEXUAL DAYDREAMS AND PUBLIC FANTASIES

A man in modern urban society who wants to purchase a sexual
fantasy can choose from a cornucopia of possibilities. There are
pornography magazines of all kinds, pornographic videos, role-play
with prostitutes, peep shows, strip shows ... For the woman who
wants to purchase a sexual fantasy, the choice is somewhat more
restricted. She will almost certainly buy a book.

The books that women use as a source of arousing daydreams
or orgasmic fantasies can be roughly divided into two parallel categories, the romance and the blockbuster. The names of publishers
like Harlequin and Mills and Boon have come to be synonymous
with the romance; in the case of the blockbuster it is the authors'
names – Judith Krantz, Jackie Collins, Shirley Conran, for instance
– that are familiar to the public. The romance is concerned with
the development of one relationship: the blockbuster, by contrast,
usually has a number of main characters involved in a number of

relationships as the story unfolds. The blockbuster is also more concerned than the romance with material goods, hence the trade label for some examples of the genre, 'Shopping and Fucking'.

Women buy a lot of these books. Mills and Boon have 1,500 titles on their list and sell between 80,000 and 100,000 copies of each title, and the sales of some blockbusters exceed one million copies.

Why do women use books almost exclusively as a source of erotic enjoyment? One obvious reason is the absence of anything else. Women hunt along the bookshelves for their fantasies because there's nowhere else to look. The lack of any erotic visual stimulation for women is a large issue in itself and one I shall explore in Chapter 13.

There is also the well-established fact that women anyway read far more fiction than men. A teacher who had observed that girls borrowed three times as much fiction as boys from the school library asked the children at his school to talk about their attitudes to reading: he found that boys saw reading as a 'girlie' or 'sissy' activity, and made comments like 'Girls just sew and read', whereas girls described how they enjoyed becoming absorbed in a story.[14] Women's extensive buying of sexual fantasies in book form is part of a wider pattern of female consumption. Here is one reason for women's enjoyment of erotic fiction that tells us nothing about female sexuality, and a lot about reading habits acquired in childhood.

Some writers however have argued that the use of books as an exclusive source of sexual daydreams for women is a reflection, not of the suppression of female sexuality, but of some essence of female sexual functioning. Ann Barr Snitow called the romance 'the true pornography of women',[15] Beatrice Faust called it 'the genuine pornography of women'.[16] The argument rests on the idea that women's preference for stories reflects something essential in female sexuality: we like stories because for us sex is only arousing, even in fantasy, if it is in the context of a relationship. Men, runs the argument, see you, fancy you, fuck you, and off they go: the transience of the impulse is epitomized by the single sexual image – perhaps the soft porn centrefold which is used primarily as a masturbation aid. But the woman wants a sense of emotional connection; her turn-on is a story of a developing relationship between two people. The story may be used, like the centrefold, to fuel an orgasmic fantasy, but is far more likely to be the source of an erotic daydream, a way of achieving a pleasant state of mild arousal rather than orgasm.

So does the main form in which public sexual fantasies are available to women indeed tell us something about female sexual fantasy? Is this apparent preference for stories an expression of an abiding sex difference which has its roots in the greater importance of relationship to women?

Women do stress the importance of a sense of emotional connectedness during sex. 'I've been straight into bed with someone I'd never seen before and knew I wouldn't see again, and it was wonderful. But there was still a relationship, and it was a very special experience.' 'I don't like making love from the back, I hate facing a wall. It has to be part of an embrace, I love the whole contact thing.' But the problem with using assertions like these as an explanation for the fact that only one form of sexual fantasy is publicly available for women is that the relationship aspect of sex is clearly also very important to *men*. According to the stereotype, men are inherently promiscuous, have sex without feeling connected, and move on. Yet to look around, one is compelled to conclude that romantic monogamy is actually of greater emotional importance to men than to women. One sign of men's emotional dependence on sexual relationships is the way many men can confide only in their sex partners. Another is the way, after divorce, it is so often the man who either collapses emotionally or rushes straight into another relationship, whereas divorced women often flourish, like some of the women we have heard from in this book. Even when male sexual activity seems most clearly divorced from relationship – when men use prostitutes – things may not be quite what they seem. Those men – a fairly small number – who pay for sex on a regular basis will often return again and again to the *same* prostitute.

Yet there is undoubtedly a sense in which relationship – 'getting to know you' – has to be part of women's sex lives in a way that it doesn't have to be for men. For heterosexual women, a potential sex partner who simply looks wonderful won't do. When we consider the possibility of a relationship, we don't just ask, Do I fancy him? We also ask: Will he beat me up? rape me? kill me? make me pregnant and then abandon me? abuse my children? For women, the elements of romance – the candlelit dinner, the long country walk – are opportunities for disclosure. Before we commit ourselves to sex – or very soon after – we need to know what we are letting ourselves in for. At the start of a relationship the paraphernalia of romance may indeed be more important to the woman than the man, but this says more about our powerlessness and vulnerability and financial dependency in sexual relationships than about our sexuality.

Here again something that is commonly taken to be a sex difference is revealed to have more to do with power than with sexual needs. We don't need romance to turn us on any more than men do – but we may need romance in order to survive. Women's apparently greater preoccupation with relationship may reflect, not some essence of female sexuality, but rather the social preconditions that must be fulfilled if women are to feel safe to enjoy sex.

So much for the form of these books. What about the content? Does the subject matter of the stories itself reflect some essence of female eroticism? In an attempt to answer this question, I shall look at two typical works, a romance and a blockbuster, and I shall draw out the two themes that I believe are the essential elements of the public sexual fantasies on offer explicitly to women.

A DURABLE FIRE: THE EROTICISM OF POWER DIFFERENCE

In their audio-cassette of advice for aspiring romance writers, *And Then He Kissed Her . . .*, Mills and Boon list the essential attributes of the romantic hero and the heroine: 'He is tall, handsome and powerful: she is young, spirited, and inwardly vulnerable.'[17] The attributes are not precise opposites – but they do suggest that an essential element of the characterization should be the difference between the hero and the heroine.

Sheila Jeffreys has defined 'heterosexual desire' as 'sexual desire that eroticizes power difference'. She goes on to suggest that heterosexual desire 'originates in the power relationships between the sexes and normally takes the form of eroticising the subordination of women. In heterosexual desire our subordination becomes sexy for us and for men.'[18]

Girls learn very early that power difference is an essential theme of romance. The eroticism of difference pervades the fairy tales that are the little girl's introduction to the story of sexual relationships. In *Cinderella*, he is a prince, she is a menial. In *Sleeping Beauty*, he is active and awake, she is passive and asleep. In *Snow White*, he is alive and she is dead.

In *A Durable Fire*, a Mills and Boon romance by Robyn Donald,[19] the most obvious difference between the hero and the heroine is the Cinderella difference – status. Kyle owns a sheep station: Arminel had a job once, but gave it up to be with her current boyfriend. The analogue of the relationship between the rich, clever, high-status male and the vulnerable woman is father/daughter. As Rosalind Coward wrote of the romances, 'In the adoration of the powerful male, we have the adoration of the father by the small child . . . before disillusionment and the struggle for autonomy set in.'[20]

Difference in sexual experience is also an essential element of the romance formula. Mills and Boon advise aspirant writers, 'Your heroine may or may not be a virgin, but she is unlikely to be sympathetic if she is promiscuous.'[21] Arminel is 'nice, like an apple, sweet and clean and crisp', but Kyle has had lots of women. The contrast between the hero's sexual experience and the heroine's virginal innocence is the source of the erotic charge in the first love-making scene in the romance, that typically uses rape imagery. When Arminel tries to push Kyle away, he stops her 'by the simple expedient of crushing her lips beneath his in a kiss that forced them apart.'

The contrast between the hero's strength and the heroine's vulnerability is also eroticized by acting as a metaphor for intercourse, which is conceptualized as the penetration of a soft quivering yielding organ by a hard forceful one. The equation of the male body with the phallus and the female body with the vagina is explicit. The male body has the 'hardness' of the erect penis: Kyle was 'like a statue carved by a master, beautiful, forceful, and stone to the core.' And Arminel had 'felt the urgency of his desire, his blind need to lose himself in the silken sheath of her body': vagina comes from the Latin word for sheath. As the narrative foreplay is extended and penetration is postponed to build the erotic tension, the hero's desire is suggested by his penetrating stare. With his 'eyes of the clearest, coldest grey she had ever seen, cloud grey, ice grey,' Kyle gives Arminel piercing looks which she feels on the surface of her body, or deep inside. 'She managed to avoid watching him, but her skin acted as her eyes, telling her exactly where he was in the room.' The penetrating looks and phallic physique hint at the never-mentioned penis. The imagery was of course not invented by the romance writers. The use of hard/soft imagery is very much in the tradition of D. H. Lawrence, whose Lady Chatterley 'yielded with a quiver that was like death, she went all open to him . . . open and helpless', and who felt the penis as the 'thrust of a sword in her softly opened body.'[22]

The hero's hardness has a psychological corollary – his total control over his emotions. The romantic hero is remote and inaccessible: the romantic heroine is in touch with her feelings, and cries and confides. She is certainly kind, but he may be cruel. Mills and Boon tell aspirant writers, 'He may be cynical, mocking, or even ruthless.'[23] Kyle has a hint of the satanic about him, the 'countenance of a dark angel'. When he is in the grip of desire, he becomes almost evil, a beautiful rapist: 'Something ugly flickered in his eyes.'

It is at moments like this that we see most clearly that the eroticization of power difference is in essence sado-masochistic, and leads inexorably to the eroticization of sexual violence. Where there is power difference, violence won't be far behind. But in the romance, the violence is never explicit, and even the fantasy of violence is carefully contained within the story. At the end of the romance, the hero's sexual bullying is retrospectively excused: he only did it because he loved her so much. 'He is mine, she thought, amazed and afraid, and he knows it, and that, that is why he hates me.' As Louise Kaplan writes, the heroine 'patiently peels away each of the many shells of phallic hardness until at last she arrives at the soft custard of domestic desire at the center of the man's being – the caring, protective, loving, *husband.*'[24]

The moment when the 'soft custard of domestic desire' is revealed is the narrative climax of the story. But it isn't sexy. The turn-on lies in the dominance/submission theme.

In *A Durable Fire*, the theory that it is power difference which is the essence of eroticism is at times stated baldly: 'The virility and effortless authority which were so basic a part of Kyle's character would overwhelm any other man – and appeal to that primitive core deep in all women which yearned to be protected and dominated . . .' Submission/dominance then is what heterosexual love is really about, deep down. This is why in the romance there is often a 'wimp', another actual or potential lover, who is rejected. In the woman's inner world, the wimp is friend or brother rather than father. He is the one she *likes*. Whereas for Arminel thinking of Kyle, 'What she had taken to be dislike was now revealed as the pull of desire, deep-seated, the simple call of woman to man signalling submission and availability . . . until those explosive minutes in Kyle's arms she had always thought that attraction and liking went together.' Sex, we are told, has nothing to do with friendship. Real sex, the overwhelming, ecstatic, wonderful sort, is more akin to hate.

LACE: THE EROTICISM OF GLAMOUR

Shirley Conran's highly successful novel, *Lace*, is preoccupied with clothes.[25] Women are rarely described without their clothes being detailed. The usual formula is to state fabric, colour and designer: 'her Chloe brown velvet suit', 'her pink wool Jean Muir suit'. Material success and sex are the two conventional themes of the blockbuster, and clothes play a part in both. Glamorous clothes are both the symbol and the reward of success; once Judy becomes successful, her clothes become mouth-wateringly lush, like the ingredients of a dessert – 'the creamy raw-silk safari suit, worn with vanilla suede pumps'. But it is the part that clothes play in the sexual stories that is of particular concern here.

At the start of the book, three of the main characters, Kate, Maxine and Pagan, are shown in adolescence at finishing school in Switzerland. For these girls growing up, the initiation into adult sexuality is primarily an initiation into adult glamour: their exploration of their own sexuality seems largely confined to an exploration of the sexual possibilities of adult clothes. Sexual concerns may be expressed, either by showing more flesh, as when Maxine cuts a daringly low neckline on Kate's 'dull Debenham's cream moire dress', or by enjoying the sophisticated meanings of restrictive underwear. 'Some of the continental girls wore an entrancing garment called a "Merry Widow", which encased the wearer from armpit to suspendered thigh in black satin and lace. It was backed with steel strips and as uncomfortable as the whalebone stays worn by Victorian women, but it was sexy. All over the school girls without one wrote home by airmail, begging money for extra violin lessons . . .'

But it is in the depiction of Lili, another central character, that clothes are most clearly equated with sexuality. Lili is a film star who starts out as an exploited actress in pornography, enabling the writer to use the titillating conventions of porn writing without alienating female readers, who are encouraged to empathize with Lili's exploitation even while they enjoy the arousing descriptions of the making of porn films. Lili is the most overtly sexual character, and this is shown by the fact that she wears the most overtly sexual clothes, whether on or off the film set: 'Her wet hair was dripping over her shoulders and what remained of her pink dress concealed very little of her nubile seventeen-year-old body.' There is an alternative version of glamour as an expression of sexuality in the depiction of one of the minor characters, Pagan's mother, who is a child abuser. Her misuse of cosmetics hints at her corrupt sexuality: 'the daily masterpiece, a scarlet glistening mouth, was painted over her real mouth, which was much thinner; red traces of Pagan's mother could be found on glasses, cups, towels and innumerable cigarette butts.'

In the blockbuster, sexual desire itself may be manifested, not by daydreaming or walking into doors as in pre-existing romantic convention, but by a preoccupation with clothes. When Maxine falls in love, 'she always changed her mind at least three times and left her bedroom untidily strewn with clothes. Her mother cheered up wonderfully at these unusual signs. Indecision in one's wardrobe usually meant a man.' For Kate, desire is expressed in a change of wardrobe. 'Suddenly Kate's neat navy suits were seen no more; instead she appeared in an amethyst linen suit from Yves Saint Laurent that she wore with no blouse underneath. This went down so well that she went back and bought another version in shocking pink. Shortly afterwards she turned up at the office wearing a Spanish orange jersey jumpsuit. Nobody in the office needed to be told that Kate was in love.' When Lili is about to embark on a new relationship, she expresses her interest by what she chooses not to wear: 'She wore a white silk blazer and a finely pleated skirt that matched; besides that she wore nothing, no blouse, underwear or jewellery, except for the glowing aquamarine that settled at the base of her throat.' If men show desire by their actions – which in this materialistic world usually means showering their object of desire with gifts – women show it by what they choose to wear or not to wear.

Women's clothing is also a central part of sex itself. Shirley Conran deliberately uses lace as a recurrent motif in scenes of sexual activity, and the lace is usually there in order to be torn off or torn up, for instance in the sexual games instigated by Charles during his marriage to Maxine. 'There on the grass verge of the country road he made her wriggle out of her panties, then he threw the flimsy scrap of peach chiffon over the hedge, pulled Maxine into the back seat, put her over his knee and spanked her.' 'Later

that night he would tear off her frail nightgown – he rather liked
to tear fragile lace-covered garments off his wife – and say, "That
was what the General wanted to do to you, wasn't it?" . . . Maxine
had never dreamed that married life would be so laced with hazard
and surprise or that her lingerie bill would be so large. She loved
every dangerous moment of it.'

In *Lace*, glamorous clothes are the mark of initiation into adult
sexuality, they signify a woman's sexual hopes, they show what her
sexuality is like, and they are a major focus of attention during
sexual activity. Glamour means sex, and sex means glamour.

Women are reluctant to fantasize, embarrassed to tell their fantasies, reluctant to let their imaginations run free. But when women
do describe their personal fantasies and sexual dreams, they lift
the curtain a little on an inner world of female sexuality which, like
the sexual world that little girls inhabit, is varied and anarchic, a
world in which a woman may be turned on by sadistically dressing
men in women's clothes, or tenderly caressing a woman who feels
like part of herself, or fucking a hated father, or urgently seeking
out the father of her child. There is sadism as well as masochism,
and tenderness as well as cruelty, and in plenty of the fantasies
men are absent or only a means to an end.

In the public fantasies sold to women, however, two themes alone
are taken to epitomize women's sexuality. Books like *A Durable Fire*
or *Lace* are sometimes called 'bodice rippers'. The label is a neat
encapsulation of the two themes, glamour and masochism, which
I have suggested are the pervasive themes of the public story of
sex for women.

These stories are read almost exclusively by women, and have
been called 'the genuine pornography of women'. They purport
then to convey something quintessentially female. Yet to look at
the content of these stories in search of that essence of female
sexuality is to conclude that women must fit very neatly with men's
specifications. For glamour and masochism are also precisely the
attributes that are presented as the essence of female sexuality, in
the much larger volume of erotic materials that are used almost
exclusively by men. This is what men are told about women by
the images in pornography: the ever-available woman in white silk
stockings in the soft porn magazine, the beautiful woman who thrills
at being penetrated by the white-hot steel penis in the Harold
Robbins novel, the mutilated woman in shreds of clothing in hard

porn. Women are sold a gentler version, a version in which the explicit violence that would turn most women off is suggested in imagery only, or retrospectively excused. But the themes are disconcertingly similar.

The fantasies about female sexuality in both male porn and female sexy stories complement our definition of male sexuality. Under patriarchy, male sexuality is about power, control, and the act of penetration. Men find domination sexy, men maximize their sexual enjoyment by initiating and controlling sex, and 'real sex' is the act that gives most pleasure to men – intercourse. In the public fantasies, the definition of female sexuality fits with the definition of male sexuality as the scabbard fits the sword, or the holster fits the gun. If men get their turn-on from power, women have to get theirs from submission and vulnerability. If men do the choosing, women have to do the attracting. If sex is entirely about intercourse, conceptualized as aggressive penetration, women have to be turned on by submission, by being, like Lady Chatterley, 'all open to him . . . open and helpless.' The expectations of women's eroticism are a mirror image of the patriarchal definition of male sexuality.

Fantasy matters. Our fantasies shape our arousal, influence our choice of sex partner, affect our capacity for orgasm. What does it mean for women's chances of sexual pleasure that female sexuality is publicly sold as masochism and as glamour?

CHAPTER ELEVEN

Masochism

In 1987, New York lawyer Joel Steinberg and his cohabitee Hedda Nussbaum were charged with the attempted murder of their adopted daughter, Lisa, who had been found at their apartment in a coma from which she never recovered. The televised trial that followed attracted great public interest, and public attention focused in particular on the personality of Hedda Nussbaum, as the extraordinary details of their relationship emerged in court. Steinberg had subjected Nussbaum to extreme physical abuse and psychological torture, yet she still insisted that she loved him. Though she was a successful career woman and could have walked out, she had clearly chosen to stay. Many women were both fascinated and repelled by this appalling acting-out of the common fantasy theme of female masochism.

It was Leopold von Sacher-Masoch, an Austrian academic and writer, who gave his name to masochism. In 1870, he began publishing novels about men who were aroused by women inflicting pain on them. His best-known work, *Venus in Furs*, has all the ingredients of what was to become the stereotypical sadomasochistic scenario. Wanda, the cruel fur-clad beauty, has her lover tied up; after a deft change of outfit into a 'splendid loose coat of red satin' she proceeds to beat him. ' "You want it," she said. "Then I will whip you." . . . "Whip me," cried her lover, "I implore you!" '[1]

In *Venus in Furs*, masochism means male masochism. And sex research has established that masochism as a sexual practice is a predominantly male preference. Women rarely initiate sadomasochistic sex, whether as dominant or submissive partners: when a couple enact a sado-masochistic scenario, she is far more likely to be participating in his fantasy, than he in hers. Yet in our public sexual fantasies, masochism is seen as a quintessentially female attribute.

Before we consider what implications the equation of masochism with female sexuality has for women's sexual pleasure, there are some more general questions that beg to be addressed. Why does our culture make so much of sado-masochism in its public imagery? Why do so many people in our society apparently find pain, violence and cruelty – in reality or fantasy – sexually arousing? There are a number of places that we could turn to in search of answers: we could look, for instance, at our child-rearing practices, at our religious iconography, and even at the very words we use to describe sexual acts and sexual feelings.

Our culture has a long tradition of punishing children's bodies with deprivations and beatings. Significantly, these punishments seem to have been particularly cruel in the Austro-Prussian empire at the end of the last century. This was the culture in which Sacher-Masoch was writing: it was also the culture out of which Nazism grew.[2] The regimes advocated by writers of the time, which included the use of mechanical devices to straighten children's bodies, would today be classified as child abuse. Yet even today there is still a vocal lobby in favour of modifying children's behaviour by the infliction of pain. My GP's surgery sells paperbacks about the benefits of hitting your children with titles like *Dare To Discipline*. The psychoanalytic understanding of sado-masochism is that such physical punishments become eroticized for the child: where loving care-givers inflict physical pain, love and pain get muddled up for the child, and certain kinds of physical pain will lead to sexual arousal. The meaning of 'discipline' in the brothel derives from its meaning in the nursery.

The iconography of Christianity has surely also influenced our society's attitude to the body. Despite the rapid secularization of the past thirty years, the Christian preoccupation with the sufferings of the body remains a profound influence. In Christian art and literature, the belief that physical suffering brings spiritual rewards is illustrated with an abundance of images and descriptions of the tortured bodies of both men and women: for instance, the martyrdoms of the Virgins, with their graphic descriptions of the mutilation of young women's bodies, read rather like modern pornography. Famous works of art that explore these themes have regularly been interpreted in an explicitly sexual way. Donatello's statue of St Teresa pierced by the angel's arrow is treated as an analogue of sexual ecstasy, and the martyrdom of St Sebastian, celebrated in numerous paintings in which Sebastian's pellucid flesh is sensuously pierced by arrows, has become a favourite homo-erotic theme, explored for instance by Derek Jarman in his film *Sebastiane*. In numerous powerful images, ecstasy is linked with physical pain.

In our whole way of thinking and talking about sex, we can also discern a sado-masochistic pattern. The penis is a weapon, a sword, a stick: intercourse is penetration, screwing, rooting: the penis is readily equated with violence. We clearly don't have to think this way; we saw in Chapter 2 how survivors of child sex abuse can be helped to enjoy intercourse by learning to envisage it as containment or embrace. But there are sado-masochistic elements too in the very words we use to describe desire, arousal and orgasm, as they are experienced by both men and women, regardless of sexual orientation. To be sexually attracted to someone is to be 'pierced by Cupid's dart'. In Elizabethan madrigals, to come is to 'die'. Sexual passion is often experienced as fear. Thousands of years ago, Sappho wrote that when she was near her lesbian love:

> trembling shakes my body
> and I turn paler than
> dry grass. At such times
> death isn't far from me.[3]

In *The Passion*, contemporary novelist Jeanette Winterson describes her heroine's love for another woman like this: 'We who were fluent find life is a foreign language. Somewhere between the swamp and the mountains. Somewhere between fear and sex. Somewhere between God and the Devil passion is and the way there is sudden and the way back is worse.'[4]

There is food for thought in the prevalence of such imagery, across cultures and regardless of sexual orientation. Is there a sado-masochist dimension that is intrinsic to sex, some irreducible essence of feeling without which sex cannot be sexy? As two lesbian writers wrote in the *Feminist Review*: 'Is SM a clearly delineated physical practice which only a certain percentage of lesbians will ever be into? Or is SM the crystallization of the most vital components of *all* erotic tension: teasing, titillation, compulsion and denial, control and struggle, pleasure and pain?'[5]

Sado-masochistic urges, then, may be encouraged by some of our child-rearing practices, and sado-masochistic imagery may echo some of the themes in our religious iconography. This is part of the background to the eroticization of domination and violence in our culture. Sado-masochism may even be 'the crystallization of the most vital components of all erotic tension.' But even if we accept that shades of sado-masochistic feeling are indeed an intrinsic part of sexuality, the theme is still capable of numerous variations. What is striking about the use of the theme in most of our public sexual fantasy is that the sado-masochism takes one form, and one only. To demonstrate this, we don't need to turn to *Blue Velvet* or *The Story of O*. The eroticization of power difference that is at the very heart of sexual masochism is there in Mills and Boon romances, even in Perrault's fairy tales. In fairy stories and feature films, in romances and hard pornography, we see that domination by men is sexy, and submission by women is sexy, and the logical extension of male domination of women – male violence to women – is sexy too.

How do these ideas impinge on women's sex lives? I shall look at their effects on three aspects of our sexuality: our choice of sex partner, our sexual practices, and our sexual fantasies.

WEREWOLVES, VAMPIRES, BEASTS AND HEROES

Some of the relationships that women described to me hinted at underlying fantasies that involved a degree of masochism on the woman's part. I've identified four archetypal kinds of male lover in these masochistic relationships. I've called them the werewolf, the romantic hero, the vampire, and the sick beast.

Bernadette said, 'My relationship with Rick ended two months ago. He beat me to a pulp and I ended up in hospital, so there was lots of violence about. It was a really strange relationship because he was actually very caring in bed, but I think looking back I was very much attracted to this kind of animal power that he had – it was ultra ultra power – he was tall, this guy, very tall, and he was very powerful and very big, and looking back I cued into that, I actually liked the sense of danger and power that he had. I'm really interested in looking at myself in that relationship, because there was violence and I stayed, it was only when he put me in hospital that I realized it had to end. He'd roughed me up, he'd thrown me around, he'd never hit me but he'd marked me, he'd picked me up and thrown me and threatened me with knives and things, and even after that, the sense of being attracted to him was enormous – and even now I still think about him very sexually, I'd just like to see him and touch him, he was pure beef, you know.'

When she seeks to understand what drew her to Rick, Bernadette says she was excited by his 'animal power' and the 'sense of danger' about him. If there is a sexual archetype informing Bernadette's attraction, it is the werewolf, the man who is half-animal, and whose sexuality is expressed as an animal attribute. He's dangerous but attractive: he's attractive because he's dangerous.

There are plenty of werewolves in public life and public sexual fantasy. Mike Tyson, the heavyweight boxer found guilty of rape in Indianapolis in 1992, is a classic example, a man who exudes a sense of physical dangerousness, and who also has a huge female following: during his trial, women would gather outside the court and try to touch him as he went in.[6] David Lynch's television soap opera, 'Twin Peaks', made a very literal use of the werewolf theme, showing the transformation of an ordinary man into a murderer of attractive young women. At the end we were reminded that the wolf can get inside any man, even Dale Cooper, the spotless FBI agent.

Bernadette remarks on Rick's sudden changes of mood. And the hope to which the werewolf's mood changes gives rise, the hope that keeps the woman hanging on in there, is that just as he switched from affection to brutality, so he will switch back to heart-stopping tenderness again. Bernadette stresses that Rick was very caring in bed. It is worth noting that it is the change back from wolf to man that is the source of the sexual charge. It is sexual caring in the midst of brutality that is the turn-on, not the other way round. This is beautifully realized in the final lines of Angela Carter's version of Little Red Riding Hood for grown-ups, *The Company of Wolves*: 'See! sweet and sound she sleeps in granny's bed, between the paws of the tender wolf.'[7] In the fantasy, tenderness is the consummation: the tale ends with an ending of the fear. But that's never how it ends in real life for women who love men like Rick.

When the violence that has been such a turn-on in fantasy becomes irrefutably real, Bernadette gets out. In real life, violence from male sex partners causes tremendous suffering. Such are the misconceptions around, that this still needs spelling out every time a woman acknowledges the hold of a violent man on her sexual imagination. Intimate violence causes so much distress that it is a major cause of suicide and attempted suicide in women. A study of one hundred women with violent husbands found that half the women had attempted suicide at least once,[8] and some research on people admitted to hospital after attempting suicide found that

one in four of the women had taken the overdose shortly after
being attacked by their sex partner.[9]

Men like Rick are strictly a minority interest. In most violent
relationships, the woman doesn't find out about the violence until
she has committed herself: often her partner doesn't start hitting
her until she is pregnant or has had children. But there are undeniably some women who, like Bernadette, have learned to feel the
lure of the werewolf. In imagination, the werewolf can be tremendously attractive: but the consequences of sharing your bed with
one can be devastating.

Marianne said, 'Definitely I'd be attracted to what I would see
as power in a man. I've had two relationships which were terribly
sexually charged, and they were just about sex really, and I suppose
one of the exciting things about these men was their total inaccessibility, they were both totally arrogant and inaccessible men, they
were seducers, and were enormously attractive. And part of their
appeal was that they were both men who were soon going to go
away and hurt you. With Jeff, the first time we touched, when
suddenly we realized we were going to fall on the bed together,
we fell over and I came instantly – the only time that's happened,
purely psychically, in the head, coming in the head without any
physical contact at all.'

Looking back over her sexual past, Marianne recalls how she
has been drawn to men who were arrogant, inaccessible and
womanizing. For Marianne there is tremendous sexual excitement
generated by her attraction to such men. With Jeff, she comes
when they first touch. This is a rare physical event, an orgasm
without any genital stimulation.

The men who attract Marianne are in the tradition of the long
line of romantic heroes. Darcy in *Pride and Prejudice*, Rochester in
Jane Eyre, Heathcliff in *Wuthering Heights*, Maxim de Winter in
Rebecca, and Rhett Butler in *Gone with the Wind*: all these men
share those attributes that Marianne finds so alluring. Today's
Mills and Boon heroes with their extreme emotional control are
cast in the same mould. In the romantic novel, the hero's uncaring
air is an illusion or aberration. As the story develops, his remote
persona is peeled off like a mask, to reveal his true face, the face
of the faithful and passionate lover. But in real life it is the sexual
caring that is the aberration, and in the final chapter of the real-life
relationship he has 'gone away and hurt her'.

When I asked Polly if she was ever drawn to men like this, men

who were domineering, cold or distant, she laughed ruefully. 'Yes,'
she said, 'I married one. The man I married is very distant emotionally, very difficult to get in touch with. I think I've always found it
a challenge. My problems with it are to do with having the children.
When you're just a couple it can be a very attractive relationship,
you can be very independent within it – but once children arrive
the whole dynamics change. It makes a very difficult environment
to bring children up in.'

Where a woman chooses a romantic hero as her marriage partner, the prospects are not good. On first acquaintance, emotional
inaccessibility may be one aspect of an appealing sexual persona –
on a level, perhaps, with a mean jaw-line, an attractive growth of
stubble, or a penchant for leather jackets. But emotional distance
is experienced very differently when lived with on a daily basis.
Relationships with men who are cold and distant and refuse to
share or confide cause a lot of distress to women. In her study of
women's experience of long-term relationships, Shere Hite found
that emotional unavailability in all its manifestations was the quality
that women complained about *most* in their sexual partners.[10]

The next sexual archetype, the vampire, is not exclusive to
heterosexual fantasy, but has also been widely used by homosexual writers. Vampire stories have a number of obvious erotic
elements. Vampirism like sex takes place at night in a private
space, usually a bedroom, and like sex it involves an exchange of
bodily fluids. The bite itself is often called a kiss, and is described
in voluptuous language, in scenes that are full of the glamour
of the forbidden: 'I could feel the soft, shivering touch of the lips
on the supersensitive skin of my throat, and the hard dents of
two sharp teeth, just touching and pausing there. I closed my
eyes in a languorous ecstasy and waited – waited with beating
heart . . .'[11]

Count Dracula has a continuing hold on our sexual imaginations,
particularly as gesture and iconography. There is an image that
constantly crops up on the covers of sexually explicit books or films.
It's there on the dustjacket of a recent sex manual, Dorothy Einon
and Mike Potegal's *Sex Life*,[12] and on the case of Andrew Stanway's
sex education video, *The Lover's Guide*. The image isn't sexy
because of how it feels: it is rather the extreme vulnerability of the
position for the woman that is the source of the erotic charge. In
the picture, the woman has her head thrown back, a cascade of
wonderful hair falls down her back, and her white throat is exposed,

lips parted in ecstasy, while the man tenderly kisses her jugular vein.

The relationship between the male vampire and his female victim is the archetype of a particular kind of heterosexual relationship. The vampire is the seducer who feeds on the young girl's innocence and vulnerability, who uses, abuses and abandons her. He is elegant, rapacious, experienced and smooth, and has decidedly ulterior motives. He is Lara's seducer in the opening scenes of *Dr Zhivago*; he is Lovelace, the rake in *Clarissa*.

Doris was fortunate. Her encounter with a rather vampirish man was thoroughly delightful, though had she got pregnant it might not have worked out that way.

'I lost my virginity in my twenties. He was older than me, and highly sexually experienced, a man who was totally not my type or anything that my parents would have approved of. He was extremely smooth with a small black moustache and he was a perfect seducer; he had a most amazing capacity for going slowly and found me a glorious curiosity. I imagine he couldn't believe his luck, finding somebody of that age who hadn't yet been dragged into bed by somebody. I do have to admire his patience, looking back, because he spent at least a year in a very slow patient seduction, so I barely noticed my virginity disappearing. I can actually remember saying to him one night, "Am I still a virgin?" when it was perfectly clear that I couldn't possibly have been for at least the past three or four months. I shall always remember the swine saying, "Of course, darling, of course." I enjoyed it enormously, but I think I must have been doing a very fine blanking off. It's interesting that I chose someone like him, because the other part of me couldn't possibly have entertained him in any permanent relationship.'

Doris is looking back many years. In some ways the vampire archetype now seems a bit out of date. Where young women are no longer 'innocent', and the valuation of chastity and the stigma attached to pregnancy outside wedlock are both fading fast, there is less scope for the eroticization of the difference between sexual innocence and sexual experience, though that difference is still one of the essential ingredients of the Mills and Boon romance. Doris' story suggests that if power difference is your turn-on, you could do worse than choose a vampire.

The sick beast, however, is quite another matter. I've taken his name from *Beauty and the Beast*, the fairy tale which tells how a repellent beast is transformed into a handsome prince by the magical power of a woman's love. The lure of the sick beast is highly dangerous to women. Robin Norwood's book, *Women Who Love Too Much*, is an exploration of the devastating effect of this archetype on women's lives.[13] Her book contains many case histories of women who are only attracted to men who are disturbed or addicted, women who believe that if only a woman loves a man enough she can change him for the better. Under patriarchy, there is approbation for the woman who obeys the injunction to 'Stand by your man'. Because male needs are paramount, women are urged to tolerate intolerable behaviour in men, and even to experience the most unlovely attributes as part of the man's sexual allure. Robin Norwood suggests that whenever a woman says, 'I thought I could save him', this is a sign that this archetype is informing her relationship.

I met Celia on a casualty ward, where she'd been admitted after attempting suicide. 'I really loved my husband,' she said, 'I tried to understand. You see, he was born with a big red mark on his face, they used to laugh at him at school, maybe he feels he can't be loved, I thought I'd change all that. When it came to sex he was like an animal, you'd just lie there and it would be something he did to you. I tried to teach him with my affection. He had some love from his mother, but it's not like a woman's love. He was an alcoholic when I met him, he used to wet the bed, I thought I could save him.'

The relationship that Stella described in Chapter 9 had a similar dynamic. She knew her husband-to-be was impotent: 'But I was so convinced,' she said, 'that I could do something about that.' Her belief that she could 'do something' to help him proved groundless: the hope that she could help led to years of sexual unhappiness for her. Women who fall for a sick beast may commit many years of their lives to attempts to salvage what is beyond salvaging.

For the woman who is drawn to the werewolf, the romantic hero, the vampire or the sick beast, the turn-on is at root masochistic. The essence of the man's attractiveness is his animal power, his emotional distance, his sexual experience and ulterior motives, or his psychological or sexual inadequacy. Where masochistic fantasy informs sex object choice there can be devastating consequences for women. The fantasy can lead women into life-threatening danger. At its most extreme, the fantasy becomes the organizing principle of a life, as it did for Hedda Nussbaum – a principle to which everything, even the life of a child, could be sacrificed.

There are indisputably moments of great passion in women's stories of their relationships with these men: Marianne's orgasm from a first touch: Bernadette's sexual obsession with Rick: Doris' long slow seduction. The fantasy can have great erotic power. But the long term prospects for sexual satisfaction are not good. As the relationship develops, the reality begins to conflict with the fantasy. In the fantasy all was well in the end: the wolf took the girl in his tender embrace, the romantic hero came close and told of his love, the sick beast was miraculously transformed. In reality, we see Polly unhappily married to her romantic hero and finding his emotional distance unacceptable: Stella sexually miserable, enraged by the impotence of the man she was going to save: Marianne abandoned: Bernadette badly injured on the casualty ward.

SOME OTHER KINDS OF DIFFERENCE

The werewolf, the romantic hero, the vampire and the sick beast are archetypes that recur in women's sexual histories, but they are by no means universal: one woman's hero is another woman's villain. There are other markers of power difference, though, which are so routine as to be banal, and which hint at fantasies that are much less clearly delineated and particular than those we have looked at so far, and which seem to be almost universal in their influence on women's choice of sex object.

Height is one of these markers. The Mills and Boon hero has to be tall[14] – but so do the partners of women who are not ostensibly looking for romantic heroes in their lovers. Difference in size is the most concrete outward and visible sign of power difference: it is also proving to be the most persistent. How many women, apart from Woody Allen's various partners, get off with men who are seriously shorter than themselves? The extraordinary persistence of this pattern signals the persistence of fantasies of protectiveness and domination in heterosexual attraction. It also has the obvious and sexually limiting effect of restricting the range of possible partners for tall women and short men.

Age is another very basic marker of difference. Sally said, 'When I was younger I always had this thing that I never had any interest in boys, I always had this great interest in men. They had to be forty at least, when I was eighteen. That was definitely to do with them being superior in every way. Someone whom I couldn't compete with, it had to be out of the realms of possibility that I was in competition with him, and he would control what we did and what I did and everything.'

What are the sexual implications of a wide difference in age? One fantasy that may underlie the attraction is the notion of the older man as a sexual teacher, the one who will 'unlock' the woman's sexuality, her guide to the land of sexual plenty. This is a frequent theme in soft porn, in all those books and films about a young girl's sexual awakening at the hands of an older man. Occasionally it happens, but in most sexual histories, a woman's sexuality is 'unlocked' by her own hands. If you wait for a wise and experienced sexual teacher to give you your first orgasm, you could be in for a long wait.

The psychoanalyst would hold that in our sexual attachments we relive or reinvent our earliest love relationships. The older man, then, may stand for the woman's father. This meaning of the relationship may be the source of its erotic charge – but it may also have an inhibiting effect on the woman's sexual expression. Robin Norwood says of relationships between father and daughter that are exceptionally close but not incestuous, 'The unusual emotional availability of her father may cause the daughter to focus her burgeoning sexual feelings on him more than she would under ordinary circumstances. In an effort to avoid violating, even in thought, the powerful incest taboo, she may numb herself to most or even all of her sexual feelings . . . The result is a young woman who may be uncomfortable with any sexual feelings, because of the unconscious taboo violations connected with them.'[15] It follows that a woman who seeks her father in her lovers may be very attracted to older men – bosses or mentors, for instance – only to find herself inhibited or uneasy when the couple actually make love, because of the taboo on sexual expression between father and daughter. The self-assertion that is necessary for happy sex may be impossible for her.

Even where there are no obvious markers of difference, like twenty years or ten inches, we may create a sense of our own inferiority as part of the game of sexual attraction. In a world where women and men are equally educated, equally opinionated and potentially equally influential, but are still turned on by power difference, women have to play along to keep the illusion going. For the title of the book in which they explore this issue, Sally Cline and Dale Spender borrowed a phrase of Virginia Woolf's – *Reflecting Men At Twice Their Natural Size*.[16] I suspect that every woman immediately understands that phrase. Here is Marianne reflecting men at twice their natural size: 'I think men do like to feel that you're rather delicate. They like you to let them push you around a bit, that sort of play on helplessness – like when you pretend you can't change a plug and go all Aaah! and end up on the floor having a fuck – that sort of thing.'

In every other sphere we assert ourselves, but faced with a man we want, we diminish ourselves. We play down our achievements, stress our helplessness, or find some area of vulnerability and expose it for his approval. Emotionally it's like Manet's *Déjeuner sur l'herbe*: she is naked, he is fully clothed.

Emily and Jacqueline both discovered that power difference, far from being necessary to sexual pleasure, can actually reduce it. If self-assertion is easier with a partner who feels equal, sexual pleasure will be maximized in more equal relationships. Emily said, 'For a long time I was only turned on by father figures – I always fell in love with the boss. Then I came to realize that all my ghastly sex had been with men like that. My best sex has been with men who feel equal, who I don't feel at all intimidated by and don't sort of look up to.' Jacqueline said, 'I'm always so self-conscious in bed. But it was alright with this young man, we had quite a bawdy sort of relationship anyway, we met at college and so we'd had a jokey friendship to start with before we got involved, and a lot of banter, so it didn't seem particularly awful to be using banter and lewd words in bed.'

When the loved partner is brother rather than father, colleague rather than boss, friend rather than teacher, sexual self-assertion is easier, and sexual pleasure becomes more accessible. But we have to find this out for ourselves. There aren't many brothers or friends among the archetypal male sex objects of public fantasy.

A final thought on the fantasies that may shape our choice of sex partner. There are some recent discoveries which hint that the whole romantic notion that difference is erotic may have serious limitations. Especially at the deepest and least conscious levels of sexual attraction, sameness can be sexy too. Marriage researchers have known for years about 'assortative mating' – the way people tend to choose sex partners who are similar to them in various obvious ways.[17] More recent research has found that happily married couples often have a number of more subtle similarities too: they may be alike, not just in their place in the class hierarchy or the shape of their faces, but in obscure physical attributes – their blood pressure readings, for instance, or the amount of nitrogen in their blood. These findings hint that some unconscious or pre-conscious recognition of similarity may govern our choice of mar-riage partner.

There is further evidence for the eroticism of similarity in the phenomenon of 'genetic attraction', the strong attraction that is often felt between genetically related people who are reunited after life-long separation. It has been found that when adopted sons trace lost mothers, or sisters meet brothers from whom they were separated as babies, the reunited pair not infrequently fall passion-ately in love. This intriguing phenomenon has been attributed to the couple's recognition of the genetic similarities between them.

These discoveries point to the tremendous erotic charge in simi-larity. When in Wagner's *Die Walküre*, Siegmund and Sieglinde, genetic siblings separated in infancy, meet and fall in love, they tell one another, 'You are the likeness that lay hidden in my heart.' This sense of recognition is for many people the essence of falling in love.

In our public heterosexual fantasies, desire is generated by the excitement of difference. But in the real world, is sexual attraction something that happens when I see in the other something of myself?

MASOCHISTIC SEXUAL PRACTICES

Louise Kaplan writes, 'Practitioners of S and M make a distinction between SM and BD – bondage-discipline. BD, they insist, is the *true essence* of sado-masochism. The giving and receiving of pain is merely a special sub-heading of the larger drama of dominance and submission . . .'[18] Today bondage appears to have become the most popular of all the deviant sexual practices; for instance, one in five of the women who responded to a recent sex survey in *Elle* magazine had experienced it.[19] This is a recent development. Sex researcher Robert Stoller, writing in the late 1960s, described bondage as 'an odd and dangerous perversion', and had only encountered a very small number of cases.[20]

Linda said, 'I was tied up once, and it was just immediate freeze and frigidness, but then I thought, If I freeze it might hurt, I must just relax, and once I did relax, I enjoyed it. You're so vulnerable.' Linda hints at the different ways in which bondage can be understood.

At one level, bondage is simply a technical device to heighten orgasm. Where the stimulation that the passive partner receives is totally under the active partner's control, the effect of the temporary postponement of satisfaction may be to enhance pleasure, because a longer period of arousal usually means a more intense orgasm. The intensification of sexual tension by restraint or prohibition is a big sexual theme in cultures which have a lot of prohibitions about sex. In the romantic narrative – in *Dr Zhivago*, or *The French Lieutenant's Woman* – the excitement generated by restraint intensifies the erotic charge when the lovers finally kiss or make love. In real life, restraint heightens sexual tension for every pair of parted lovers who leap into bed with renewed desire on being reunited. So in bondage the erotic pleasures of sexual restraint followed by fulfilment can be acted out by the lovers.

A further element in bondage is what one woman described as 'not being able to control having nice things done to you.' Passivity willingly chosen can be highly sensuous, and the partner who is tied up can abandon him or herself to the pleasures of sensation without any responsibility for anything that happens.

But there is also another way of seeing it. Bondage is a practice with a very obvious symbolism that is about sexual aggression. Before she forced herself to relax and enjoy it, Linda felt afraid.

Bondage was popularized by Alex Comfort in *The Joy of Sex*, published in 1972. The book puts bondage in a context of male dominance and female submission. This is rarely done explicitly, for Comfort pays lip-service to the idea of sexual equality between men and women, and when he sings the praises of 'healthy sexual aggression' he doesn't usually specify which partner should be the aggressor. But at certain points in the text his prejudices show through the mask of unjudgemental jolliness. When he writes about gagging, for instance, the distribution of sexual roles that he is envisaging is perfectly clear. 'Gagging and being gagged turns most men on – most women profess to hate it in prospect, but the expression of erotic astonishment on the face of a well-gagged woman when she finds she can only mew is irresistible to most men's rape instincts . . .'[21] The aggression he so enthusiastically promotes as a healthy part of sex is here clearly male aggression. The woman has to submit and take her pleasure as best she can in the slipstream of his – however much she professes 'to hate it in prospect'.

Angela had rueful memories of her encounter with this approach.

'When we were having an awful time sexually we went to see a clergyman at a church we attended who had a reputation for being good with sexual problems. He was very keen on "exploring your sexuality", which actually seemed to mean acting out sadistic fantasies, and he said how after his divorce he'd had this beautiful sexual experience with a woman where he'd tied her up and the next morning she'd said just what a beautiful experience it was. We had a go, but it didn't do anything for us. I didn't know how to have an orgasm anyway.' For the clergyman who talked to Angela, 'exploring your sexuality' meant what it usually means in *The Joy of Sex* – exploring your sadism if you're male and your masochism if you're female. It's a rather limited prescription.

Our sexual culture has moved on since the 1970s. Today, after three decades of 'sexual liberation', the hints of sexual sadism in *The Joy of Sex* look relatively innocent. Because of the influence of pornography, there is a widespread belief that sophisticated sex – sex for grown-ups – is inevitably sado-masochistic, and friendly affectionate sex may be denigrated as the bland, flavourless, Walt Disney version – 'bambi' or 'vanilla' sex. Reay Tannahill points out that the highly explicit sex manuals which were in use in Taoist China make no mention at all of SM practices, suggesting that it is possible for a sexual culture of considerable sophistication to flourish in the absence of sexual activities which involve the infliction of pain, actual or symbolic.[22] But today SM has become so integral a part of our public representations of sex that such a sexual culture seems unimaginable.

Because of the wide availability of violent pornography today, women's sexual needs and desires are being subordinated to men's in new ways. It is clear that women are being forced to participate in SM scenarios that their sex partners have lifted from videos and magazines, scenarios that fill the women with revulsion. Some of the women who wrote to Clare Short in the course of her campaign to ban 'Page 3' pictures described this new form of sexual oppression.[23] Here is a way in which the subordination of women to men in the sexual arena has actually become more marked over the last two decades.

Many women are unable to assert themselves in such situations because of their partners' violence. Joy however was not at risk of violence – and when she felt less than enthusiastic about the scenario her partner wished to act out, she found a very effective way of making her feelings known. 'Dave had this thing about bondage.

He tried it with me, and I thought, I'm not going for this, so he decided he'd have a go. He was stripped naked, spread-eagled on the bed, and I tied him to the legs of the bed. Then I opened the curtains and left the room. Someone had just come round to clean the windows, and he'd leant his ladder against the window, but I hadn't tied the knots very tight, and Dave managed to escape. It never happened again.'

Linda, Angela and Joy were all going along with someone else's scenario. This is the usual pattern. But what about those hetero-sexual women who do want to be dominated or hit during sex, and who are able to say so?

Many women I talked to were aroused by fantasies about being dominated in bed, but only two expressed an interest in the fantasy being acted out. One of them was Penny. 'A few years ago I quite liked the idea of – not being hurt really badly – but sort of treated a bit rough. I think I wanted to be a mystery woman, I wanted the man to think: *Why* does she want this? That's interesting. But now I'm myself, which is why I have orgasms now I'm sure. I know what I like, I ask for it, I relax, and have orgasms. I've always wanted to be of interest to men, sort of sexy and mysterious, and I've managed that in a lot of ways, but now . . . I'm just me now.'

Penny describes a shift in her sexual needs that takes place around the time that she becomes orgasmic. Before, she took plea-sure in giving pleasure, in fascinating her partner. She enjoyed sex, but she didn't have orgasms, and her pleasure in being the mystery woman seems to have been a substitute for orgasm, an alternative form of gratification. When she becomes orgasmic, her focus shifts. Her concern is no longer the fascinating persona she wants to project, but rather her everyday authentic self, getting the pleasure she wants: 'I'm just me now.' Her formula for how to enjoy sex is precisely the one I've used in this book – self-knowledge and self-assertion: 'I know what I like, I ask for it . . . I have orgasms.'

Penny had always enjoyed sex, but the very much greater enjoy-ment she derives from sex once she starts having orgasms coincides with a shift away from wanting rough treatment. I've wondered whether for some women there is an even more direct link between wanting to be hurt or dominated, and lack of sexual pleasure. If sex is tepid or boring, and even at its best is no more pleasant than scratching an itch, then if he's rough or dominant or hurts you, at least you do feel something. Wanting to be hurt can be an attempt to salvage some kind of intensity out of an experience which feels pointless or empty.

Mary made a direct link between enjoying the symbolic meanings of intercourse that are about dominance and submission, and not really feeling anything very much: 'The mere fact that the man is penetrating you and he is imposing himself on you, there's a glorious feeling of submission to that, which I can't see anything wrong with. I suppose initially that was what I got most pleasure from – the fact that I loved him and I was giving him pleasure and opening myself to him and submitting. For a long time that was really the only sort of pleasure I got from sex.'

This section, like most of this chapter, has been exclusively concerned with women who love men. I found that the tone of discussion about SM practices among lesbians was very different. Lesbian culture does have its own SM subculture, with spokespeople such as Gayle Rubin and Paula Webster, but in fact most of the lesbians I talked to were opposed to SM practices. Beth and her partner, however, had experimented a little: 'One time Shelley and I decided we would try hitting one another – and I hit her and I really enjoyed it, it was just trying it out, it was fun. But I certainly don't ever think of being dominated or anything like that. Mostly Shelley talks to me when we're having sex, she tells me little stories, and they're always very gentle stories of some kindly person, and it's usually very non-sexual in a way – "Let me look at your leg, I'll just move this hair . . ." It's all very gentle.'

Being hit by a man during sex is an act with a wider meaning. It cannot be detached from its context of male violence to women, and in particular the widespread violence of men towards their female sex partners. But if you hit or are hit by your lesbian partner, there is no such aversive context: you can simply focus on the immediate and sexual meanings of the act. For Beth, hitting Shelley was 'fun' – a word never used of SM scenarios by heterosexual women.

There is little sign then from women's accounts that for heterosexual women the adoption of submission/domination sexual practices enhances sexual pleasure. One woman may be made to participate in SM scenarios against her will: she is forced to take her pleasure as best she can, in the slipstream of his. Another woman may manage to enjoy certain sexual practices such as bondage, but only after making an effort to overcome the fear that the experience initially inspires. And in some women's accounts, experiences on the SM continuum are a kind of second-best, a substitute for orgasmic pleasure: Penny and Mary both locate their pleasure in rough treatment or in the dominance/submission meanings of intercourse in a time before they fully enjoyed sex. There is nothing in women's experiences of SM practice to justify the belief that is expressed in so many of our public fantasies – the belief that masochism is the essence of female sexuality.

MASOCHISTIC FANTASY

I asked women about films they'd seen that they had found erotic.

'*A Room with a View*, where eventually they go away together. It's all very beautiful and romantic, just their bodies in bed cuddling. It's that gentle caressing sort of thing that tends to turn me on, rather than anything explicit.'

'It's got to be in a romantic light, him treating her very nicely and gently, sort of light coming through the window.'

'*A Room with a View* – where he comes and snogs her in the poppy field.'

These comments were typical. Only one woman chose a scene with a masochistic theme.

But when women describe the images that enter the mind unbidden when they're highly aroused, or the kind of material that they use to reach orgasm, they describe very different scenes. There is a great difference between what women would choose to watch or read about, and what they think about during sex. Very many women have orgasmic fantasies about being degraded, dominated or hurt. A study of US women found that half had submissive fantasies.[24] Fantasies of rape and domination abound in Nancy Friday's collection, *My Secret Garden*.[25] A majority of the women I talked to said they were turned on by masochistic fantasies.

The fantasies that women use to reach orgasm are kept in the head and virtually never acted out in real life. Where masochistic fantasies influence your choice of sex partner, they may lead you into trouble. But does it matter if you reach orgasm by being degraded or dominated by the anonymous male strangers of masochistic sexual fantasy? Does it matter if a woman reaches orgasm by visiting a torture chamber in her head, though her favourite turn-on from the picture album of public images is an impetuous kiss in a sunlit field in Tuscany?

Nowadays the consensus on sexual fantasy is that anything goes.

Sex manuals, sex education videos and articles in women's magazines all reiterate the message. Just as the public voices mostly insist that sex is good for you, so they also insist that any and every sexual fantasy is acceptable.

Yet no matter how often we're told that it's fine to have such fantasies, women still feel uncomfortable about them. This discomfort is one reason why women stop fantasizing altogether. Emily had made use of a scene from the sado-masochistic novel *The Story of O*. She said, 'It made me feel bad to be turned on by those things, so I stopped using it. I hated myself for finding it such a turn-on.' This kind of discomfort is also a major reason why women shut out certain external sexual stimuli – switching off the television, closing the book. If a masochistic fantasy is a turn-on, a woman may choose to sacrifice the arousal rather than face the bad feelings that accompany or follow the arousal.

If the stimulus can't be switched off, we may even choose to switch off our awareness of our bodies. In laboratory experiments, women have been shown to be just as turned on by pornography as men, but unlike men, they may deny that they are feeling aroused and express disgust.[26] If the cost of the turn-on is to collude with the ideas in the pornography, many women will choose to ignore what their bodies are telling them.

Some women do make a temporary truce with their fantasies. But these women may still feel a need to control and limit the use of the fantasy. Hilary said, 'At the time I think it's lovely – but at other times I think, Why on earth am I thinking this? Some of the things in the real context of life are absolutely horrific. It's verging on people doing things to you against your will, torture chamber stuff. It's a really horrific thing to think because people experience that in real life, where it really is sick, where they're really hurt and damaged by it, and here I am, getting great pleasure out of imagining it.'

The cliché explanation for fantasies like Hilary's is that they free us from guilt. Women are frequently told that we use fantasies in which we are forced, taken or overpowered because they free us from responsibility. For instance, Nancy Friday writes, 'More than any other emotion, guilt determined the story lines of the fantasies in *My Secret Garden*. Here were hundreds of women inventing ploys to get past their fear that wanting to reach orgasm made them Bad Girls.'[27] This explanation is very widely accepted. Yet it has its limitations. There is the obvious complication that under patriarchy the fact that sex was forced on her has never absolved a woman from responsibility – the woman who conceived out of wedlock as a result of rape was thrown out of the family home, and even today women feel guilty about being abused or raped. There is also the fact that many women say, like Hilary, that they are appalled by their fantasies. These comments must at least cast some doubt on the sex-without-guilt theory. For Hilary, and for very many women, sex with masochistic fantasy is sex *with* guilt. And there is little evidence that we do find submissive fantasies liberating. Far from freeing us to indulge in imagination in all sorts of sexual acts, the masochistic frame inhibits women. We have seen how many women keep a tight rein on their sexual imaginations, or stop themselves from fantasizing at all, because they hate the masochistic pattern of their fantasies.

If the sex-without-guilt theory won't do, how then can we explain the almost ubiquitously arousing effect of these fantasies on women? I think we use them because they are there, and because they fit.

We do not construct our sexual fantasies from nothing: we eroticize what we know – images and scenes from our own life-histories, and from the public world of shared sexual fantasy. Like Emily with her scene from *The Story of O*, we may simply lift a scene from a book or film and replay it as a turn-on. It is only since the rise of pornography in the sixties that these SM images have been widely available in the public arena – and it is only since that time that women have been turned on by them. The intrusion of the torturers, rapists and sodomizers into women's private fantasy worlds is a recent event. In the early fifties, the Kinsey researchers found that only *4 per cent* of women interviewed said they had ever had a fantasy with any sado-masochistic content.[28]

We use these images because they are there. But of course there is more to it that that: the interplay between the public and private sexual worlds is a subtle and complex thing. Though we may be surrounded by SM imagery, we won't find it sexy unless it fits. And it is because they fit so neatly with the social relationships we see about us and have experienced, that these fantasies turn us on. This is also why they trouble us so much.

I was intrigued to find that among the women I talked to, those most turned on by submissive fantasies were in their thirties, forties and fifties. There is a story that fits many women in this age-group. It is the story of a woman who grew up believing herself to be vulnerable and powerless, and in need of a strong man's protection, status and money. Then, after a period when she discovers just how much these beliefs have limited her, often during an unhappy marriage, she begins to ask questions, she learns to assert herself, and perhaps achieves a bit of power in the world. But her sense of herself as an autonomous powerful person is quite fragile. She's moved so far, so fast, there must be a degree of self-doubt. She knows what she once was, she doesn't feel 'entitled', she doesn't feel she quite has a right to all this male stuff – which Louise Kaplan in a wonderful phrase calls the 'stolen phallic trophies'.[29] This woman knows how it feels to be weak: she can remember it well.

If in her sexual fantasies, this woman is turned on by submission, she may be deeply uneasy. The fantasy fits: it confirms her self-doubt. Deep down in her essential sexual nature, it seems, she really wants to be dominated. It is scarcely surprising that such a woman should feel uneasy about fantasies that seem to confirm her doubts about her own autonomy, and undermine her efforts to trust men as equals, and sabotage her struggles in the world.

Much younger women, women under twenty-five, did not seem to be turned on by these submissive fantasies. Women like Alex and Pippa, who had grown up in homes with explicitly feminist values, were particularly likely to say that they found the appeal of such fantasies incomprehensible. Nancy Friday, in her study of the sexual fantasies of young women today, *Women on Top*,[30] found that women now in their twenties described very different fantasies from those she had collected in the 1970s. The women who are now in their early twenties have grown up in a culture in which public SM imagery is more explicit than it has ever been, but it is also a culture in which some women have been seen to achieve power. Alex and Pippa don't believe deep down that men are really more powerful: how could they, with the image of Mrs Thatcher towering above their adolescence? If a fantasy tells you about male domination, and you believe deep down in men's greater strength or entitlement, it may arouse you. If deep down you know yourself to be equally strong and equally entitled, the same fantasy will probably make you laugh. Or if a woman does enjoy such a fantasy, it will be in the way that Beth enjoyed hitting Shelley, for 'fun'. She won't feel that her fantasy is, in Nancy Friday's phrase, 'a true X-ray of (her) sexual soul.'[31] She won't believe it is telling her how things really are.

It is clear that there are very valid reasons for women's uneasiness about submissive fantasies. We are uneasy because we feel that these fantasies undermine our struggle to assert ourselves in the world and take some power for ourselves. And it is impossible not to conclude that this is precisely why these fantasies are so very available at this moment in history. At a time when women look like they might make it out into the public world and grab some power for themselves, how very convenient if many of us are turned on by thoughts of the superior strength, assertiveness and danger-ousness of men. At a time when women are beginning to see themselves as having a right to sexual pleasure, how very convenient if a woman's fantasy tells her that her greatest pleasure lies in submitting to a man's sexual will. So today we see all around us the SM imagery that a few years ago was confined to hard pornogra-phy. Our television dramas and our films on general release are full of sexy female corpses, or beautiful women covered in sexy bruises, or women in torn clothing who submit to SM rituals with voluptuous moans. Submissive fantasies are a powerful force in maintaining the status quo. No wonder we are almost deafened by the chorus of voices – the sex therapists, the magazine columnists, the voice-over on the sex education video – telling us that it's absolutely fine to be turned on by such things. It's certainly fine for the patriarchal status quo.

Yet the voices that urge us to go on fantasizing are right in one sense. Where women avoid sexual fantasy altogether, or feel guilty about their fantasies, or limit their use of fantasy, there will be serious implications for their sexual functioning. Fantasy is an inte-gral part of arousal: so much human sexuality happens in the head. Therapists who work with sexual dysfunctions make extensive use of fantasy. Learning to fantasize is an important part of sex therapy programmes to help women who haven't yet achieved orgasm. Fan-tasy is also used as a therapeutic tool with people who have little interest in sex. Sex therapist Patricia Gillan seeks to help people with lack of desire by the use of 'stimulation therapy', which includes the use of erotica to 'teach clients how to fantasize effec-tively': she has established that this is the most helpful element in her work with disorders of desire.[32] Many women can't have orgasms without fantasizing, like Pam who learnt to come by work-ing out complex sexual fantasies in her head. So the woman who is repelled by her fantasies and keeps them under strict control may have difficulty getting aroused.

What is the answer? Can we change what turns us on? The
psychoanalyst and the behaviourist would, I imagine, be united in
answering no; we can't change the triggers for our arousal by an
act of will, any more than we can change what makes us salivate
by will-power. But the evidence of young women like Alex and
Pippa suggests that, as relationships between men and women
change, and as women acquire more power in the world, so our
fantasies will change too. There may be quite a time-lag – but in
the end the fantasies that belong under the old dispensation won't
work for us any more.

We use submissive fantasies because they fit, and because they
are there. If they no longer fit, they will eventually lose their erotic
charge. But perhaps we could accelerate the speed of change by
deliberately trying out new fantasies. This was the line that sex
therapist Betty Dodson took when approached by a friend who
was troubled by her 'passive and helpless' fantasies. Betty Dodson
writes, 'I told her that it was alright to have those fantasies. She
could simply experiment with new ones. She now has more assertive fantasies, yet, if she gets stuck or is in a hurry, she brings out
the Five Cops and the rape scene . . .'[33]

It would be easier to experiment with new themes if there were
a greater variety of public sexual fantasies on offer to women. We
desperately need alternatives. The typical Mills and Boon story is
about a woman's weakness which offers an erotic contrast to a
man's strength, and this remains the usual sexual story. Most sexy
books by writers with explicitly feminist sympathies have remarkably
similar themes to the most conservative romances. Such books may
feature women who are successful in their careers, but the sexual
story is so often about weakness-in-the-midst-of-strength, a new
variation on the same old theme. Erica Jong, describing her novel
Any Woman's Blues, puts it like this: 'My heroine, Leila, is like
many contemporary women. In many ways she's very successful,
yet here she is submitting to this snake-hipped cad. She rises in
the outside world and falls in the bedroom. I've seen this going on
all around me, I've done it myself. I've seen how, as women get
more successful in the boardroom, they need more and more domination in the bedroom. We win all this power and then find someone to dominate us in our personal lives.'[34] In Julie Burchill's
Ambition, the story is given a different twist: here the degradation is
externally imposed. As a condition of giving beautiful and ambitious
Susan Street the job that she craves, her boss makes her undergo

various sexual trials in exotic locations. However public or unpleasant the sex, Susan is invariably orgasmic.[35]

Rising in the outside world and falling in the bedroom, giving things up for love, sexual degradation as the cost of career success: these themes are all attempts to reconcile women's evident and increasing power in the world with the belief in women's need for sexual domination which is such an integral part of the patriarchal scheme of things. For men, of course, the sexual story is completely different. For men, sexual pleasure is the *reward* for success. Sex is one of the phallic trophies that the man is assumed to win in his moments of triumph, and his achievements in the killing fields, on the football pitch or at the ballot box greatly increase his sexual allure.

Our sexual fictions haven't kept up with life. The story of the high-status middle-aged woman enjoying a rapturous love affair with a beautiful man twenty years younger than her is a real-life story that we've heard in this book, but it's a plot you won't encounter in a work of erotic fiction. Laura's story in Chapter 8 might be many women's dream: it is not, however, as yet 'the stuff of fantasy'.

Some feminist writers and film-makers have deliberately set out to produce ideologically-sound erotica. The consensus seems to be that by and large these attempts have failed, and that the wholesome democratic 'good girl' sexual fantasy just isn't a turn-on. Perhaps the problem is simply lack of practice. There is no obvious reason why tender sexual fantasies shouldn't be sexy; tenderness can certainly be sexy in reality, and it is certainly sexy in some of those fantasies least susceptible to public influence – in the straight woman's lesbian dream, for instance.

Tenderness isn't obligatory though. Fantasies don't have to be gentle or democratic or ideologically sound to be different. What most matters for women is that there should be alternatives to the shame-inducing masochistic fantasies. Philippa Gregory's *Wideacre*,[36] for instance, uses all the conventions of the historical romance – the melodramatic plot, the aristocratic protagonists, the wonderful clothes – but has a thoroughly wicked heroine who explores all manner of sexual perversions before finally meeting a violent death at the hands of the childhood sweetheart whom she had previously attempted to murder. There's cruelty and perversion here, but the narrative movement is new, a refreshing change from the banal repetition of the undermining lesson that women really only want to be dominated. In *Wideacre*, we see woman as initiator and dominatrix, and sex as the reward for success, with each new ill-gotten gain bringing a new sexual excitement.

Wideacre was extremely successful. And it seems that the lascivious heroine with the wicked schemes in her head and the whip in her hand may be more of a turn-on for women than Erica Jong's Leila submitting to the snake-hipped cad. Sex researcher Julia Heiman found that women were more turned on by stories in which women were sexually active and took sexual initiatives than by stories in which they played a conventional passive role.[37] Here is yet another reason to question the notion that sexual pleasure for women is about a moment of surrender.

The women in this chapter have shown what dangers and distortions follow from the equation of masochism with female sexuality. Yet to point to the perils of masochism is not to argue that all sex and all sexual fantasy could be or should be tender and mutual. The sexual activities and sexual fantasies of little girls were at times violent and bizarre. Dogs and sticks and the thrill of illicit nakedness were part of the excitement, as well as the tenderest touching. And even if our social relationships were Utopian, there would probably still be elements of cruelty in sexual fantasy, for our fantasies will necessarily encompass aspects of our personalities which are anarchic or perverse. But greater equality between men and women might eventually free us from the banal and repetitive eroticization of power difference which is expressed in masochistic sex object choice, practice and fantasy. And if a wider variety of sexual fantasies were available to women we might be enabled to give our sexual imaginations free rein, without feeling that with every step towards the castle where 'O' is confined, we are compromising ourselves and sabotaging our aspirations to equality and social justice.

CHAPTER TWELVE

Glamour

People, both men and women, have always liked to dress up. Ornate clothing, jewellery, paints to decorate the surface of the body: these have been enjoyed in every culture. Prehistoric graves have been found to contain bracelets and necklaces, and both men and women in Sumer, the earliest civilization, are known to have painted their eyes.

For heterosexual men, dressing up has in all cultures been associated with status. The clothes a man wears show what class he belongs to and what power and wealth he possesses, and highly decorative clothes have usually been reserved for high status men. In medieval England, these rules were formalized in the sumptuary laws, which forbade certain clothes to people below a particular rank: only people of the rank of squire or above were permitted to wear cloth of gold, silver girdles or high quality wool. In Britain today, though our rules about dress are more flexible, we still distinguish between blue collar and white collar workers, and dressing in finery remains the prerogative of men who hold certain important positions – the general with his medals and braid, the bishop in his cape encrusted with embroidery and jewels, the professor in his flowing gown and fur-trimmed hood. Elaborate male clothing may acquire sexual meanings for men: many homosexual men say they find uniforms arousing,[1] and it seems at least possible that many heterosexual men feel the same, though no one has asked them if they do. But these meanings are secondary to the obvious meanings and remain largely covert in mainstream culture.

For women, the interplay between sex and power in dress is different. In much female clothing it is the sexual meanings that are primary and overt. The power dimension is there too, of course: dressing up for women as for men involves a display of affluence and status, though the status that is displayed is usually not the woman's own but her partner's. When Ferdinand Marcos was overthrown in the Philippines, it was Imelda Marcos's three thousand pairs of shoes that came to symbolize the wealth and corruption of the regime. But there is much female clothing in all cultures that is more about sex than about power. The virgin bride and the prostitute are both defined by the clothes they wear.

In our own time, the difference between the decorativeness considered appropriate for men and for women has been tremendously exaggerated, because of the rise and rise of the business suit. The current drabness of men's clothing is historically anomalous. Yet no matter how extravagantly decorative male clothing has been at certain epochs, women's clothing has invariably been more sexualized than men's, with an occasional exception such as the embroidered Tudor codpiece. The tendency for the part of self-decoration that is about sexual display to be reserved for women seems to persist across cultures. This is one way in which humans differ markedly from the rest of the animal kingdom. In the natural world, from the Argus Pheasant of Borneo to the Magnificent Bird of New Guinea, it is the males who display.

The equation of female sexuality with glamour is a major public theme in our own culture. It's there in our fairy stories, the little girl's first lessons in romance: a kitchen girl, she learns, can only win a prince if she has a comprehensive makeover and some glamorous new clothes. It's there in the blockbusters and romances, the major sources of erotic daydreams for women. And it's there in male pornography: on the covers of the magazines on the top shelves at the newsagents, the clothes – the flowery G-strings, fishnet stockings and silver sandals – are integral to the images, and between the covers the sexual interest is generated by the striptease. In such images, the clothes *are* the sexuality: the reader's arousal is controlled by the game of hiding and showing.

We can also see the equation between female sexuality and sexy female clothing in the choices made by transvestites. When men dress as women, they don't adopt the kind of clothing that women usually wear. No transvestite gets a kick out of jumpers and skirts, or button-up polyester blouses, or tracksuits and trainers. Instead, they choose stilettos, basques, feather boas, Lycra mini-skirts. It is the clothes that are labelled sexy, even though they are only worn by a minority of women, that are believed to contain some magic essence of womanhood.

But the equation of female sexuality with female clothing becomes most explicit in the fetish. The word 'fetish' derives from the French 'factice', meaning 'artificial': sexual fetishism, says the

psychoanalyst, is about the creation of fictitious or artificial genitals.[2] So the fetish – the piece of blue velvet, the stocking or shoe
– stands in for the body, and specifically for the woman's sexual
organs. This is a male use of female clothing which is totally dependent on the assumed equivalence between female sexuality and
clothes.

The idea that a woman's clothes give crucial information about
her sexuality is universally accepted by both men and women. When
women pass remarks about other women's clothes, they are usually
making judgements about the other woman's sexuality, and if they
feel she's got it wrong – too sexy, not sexy enough – they can be
scathing. 'When you see a woman in really high fashion clothes,
it's obvious what she's after. I saw a woman at a bus stop recently,
just like the kind of thing you see in a magazine. I thought, She
just looks such a tart.' 'When I've seen problems arising in people's
marriages, I've often thought, Well, I'm not surprised that your
husband doesn't look all that keen to see you when he comes home.
I just couldn't become a slut. My friend's husband was away as a
pilot, and when he came home, she made no effort at all. That
ended in divorce years later – but it alerted me there could be
trouble . . .' In her sex therapy manual, aimed at other professionals working in the field, sex therapist Patricia Gillan shows
how she uses her judgements about the clothing and self-
presentation of her female clients as a crucial part of her assessment
of their sexual functioning. The dress styles adopted by the women
when they first come to her are read as signs of their sexual dysfunction. 'Her clothes were strict and tailored and her grey hair was
scraped back into a chignon which made her look like a
spinster . . .'[3] 'Veronica . . . came for therapy wearing a most drab
grey dress with a brown jacket. She would not have looked out of
place as governor of a women's prison . . .'[4] Changes in self-
presentation towards a more 'sexy' appearance during the course
of therapy are taken as evidence that the therapy is going well.
'Ann dressed in rather a dull manner, usually wearing rather old-
fashioned blouses and skirts. Later on in therapy she surprised the
therapists by turning up in a very smart tracksuit that transformed
her . . .'[5]

All the women I talked to made the same sort of equation about
themselves. Every woman said she was more likely to feel sexy,
sexually aroused and attracted to someone if she felt she was looking attractive. The public message seems to be borne out by

women's private experience. It might be argued that glamorous clothes are simply a valuable adjunct to women's sexual pleasure and an enhancer of arousal.

In this chapter I want to look at the benefits and the costs for women of the assumption that glamour equals sexuality. I will look at the connections between glamour and sex that women made in their conversations with me, and ask what implications these connections have for our chances of sexual happiness.

THE SEXUAL USES OF GLAMOUR

Gwen shone with pleasure as she recalled her most special outfit. 'I went out with a very attractive RAF fellow during the war. He was coming home on leave, and I wanted to wear something nice. My sister was a dressmaker, and she scrounged enough coupons to make this superb suit – it was pink and I had powder-blue accessories. It was in the days of austerity, everything was grim. When I went to meet him on leave, I felt like a million dollars. I've still got the buttons from it.'

Wearing her sensuous pink suit was for Gwen a delightful act of self-affirmation amid the bleakness of wartime Britain, and the memory is something she seeks to hold on to – she's still got the buttons. In Gwen's story, as in the blockbusters and romances, a woman's feelings for her lover are expressed in her choice of clothing, and pleasure in attracting her partner merges with her own narcissistic delight in her appearance. When Gwen got married, she found little joy in sex, but in her memory of these sexually attractive clothes there is an unambiguous pleasure.

Mary too remembers certain clothes with great delight. 'Some of the frocks were absolutely stunning – nipped-in waists and low necks and long flowing skirts, they were beautiful. You feel you move differently . . . Rhythm and dancing are the things that turn me on, I realize now that the feelings I had when I went dancing were definitely sexual, it was the rhythm and rhythmic movements – a slow foxtrot or something like that – and probably the closeness too.'

For Mary, the beautiful clothes were part of a whole constellation of sensuous feelings. When she remembers the low necks and the long skirts, she also hints at a major source of pleasure in dress for women – the concealing and revealing of body parts. Legs seem particularly important. When I asked them to describe the outfit they had found most sensuous, women usually described a very long or a very short skirt. The pleasures of revealing and concealing are enhanced by the vagaries of fashion. The sensuous pleasure of wearing long skirts, and the exhibitionistic pleasure of wearing short ones, both depend on change. The long skirt feels lush rather than drab when the sensation of cloth swishing round your ankles is unfamiliar: the short skirt only feels naked and exciting rather than banal when legs have been covered up for the past few years. The alternate concealment and exposure of parts of women's bodies is one of fashion's preoccupations. Women's comments show that these changes are a potential source of sensuous pleasure.

Gwen's suit was about sex because she wore it to please her boyfriend, and in pleasing him to please herself; Mary's dance dresses were about sex because, like the slow foxtrot and the closeness, they were part of an ambience that she found arousing. But there is also a tradition of female clothing that is still more directly part of sex – clothing that is used specifically as an adjunct to the sex act. For instance, the pornographic novel, *The Story of O*, is full of descriptions of clothing, old-fashioned, romantic clothes that are arranged to allow instant access to the woman's body. For her sado-masochistic ordeal at the Castle of Roissy, O is dressed in period costume – a 'whalebone bodice which severely constricted the waist', a 'starched linen petticoat', 'cascading folds of green silk'. The clothes play a part in the sadistic rituals, emphasizing the vulnerability and instant availability of the woman. 'He took her by the waist with one hand and raised her skirts with the other, making her turn, displaying the costume's practical advantages, having O admire its design, and explaining that, simply by means of a belt, the skirts could be held at any desired height, thus, which meant that all that was exposed was very ready to hand, thus.'[6]

The pornographic conventions that associate sex with certain kinds of female clothing are also apparent in sex manuals. To judge from the illustrations in a recently published sex manual, Dorothy Einon and Mike Potegal's *Sex Life*, you would think a merely naked woman was incomplete.[7] When engaged in sexual activity, the women in the pictures wear fishnet stockings or little ruched Lycra mini-dresses or lacy French knickers, or even an ear-ring attached to a nipple: but the men are simply naked, unless they have been in too much of a hurry to take off their shirts. Alex Comfort is also very keen on women dressing for sexual activity. With some monotony of epithet, he advocates 'tiny tight G-strings . . . tight shiny black leather . . . black stockings . . . long tight black shiny boots . . .' He talks about men dressing up for sex too – but only in the context of transvestism. 'Some women are bothered that a man who occasionally likes them to dress him in their clothes is unvirile . . .'[8] Here, the man is dressing up to enhance his *own* arousal: again male pleasure is paramount. In a brief concession to mutuality, Alex Comfort suggests that men could dress in sexy clothes for their partners' pleasure too. But there are no clues as to what these male sexy clothes might be.

As is clear from the illustrations in these books, the genre of female clothing that has come to be identified most closely with sexual activity is underwear. Female underwear that was glamorous rather than utilitarian first appeared around the turn of the century, and over the past few decades it has become a major source of visual stimulation for men. Like the undressing games played by the little girls in Chapter 2 who had learnt at nudist camp that nakedness is ordinary, underwear serves as an enhancement of nakedness, a way of rediscovering the excitement of the naked body that might otherwise seem banal. Certain items of underwear focus the observer's attention on particular body parts; stocking tops and suspenders frame the vulva, just as the above-the-elbow gloves worn with the strapless evening gowns of the fifties drew the eye to the naked shoulders and cleavage. Underwear may also emphasize the sexual parts by distorting the shape of the body, as a tight basque for instance pushes up the breasts.

The point about the role of underwear in the visual stimulation of the late twentieth century male is nicely put by Nicola Six in Martin Amis' satirical novel, *London Fields*. 'Nicola was amazed – Nicola was consternated – by how few women really *understood* about underwear. It *was* a scandal. If the effortless enslavement of men was the idea, or one of the ideas (and who had a better idea?), why halve your chances by something as trivial as a poor shopping decision? . . . To ephemeral flatmates and sexual wallflowers at houseparties and to other under-equipped rivals Nicola had sometimes slipped the underwear knowledge. It took about ten seconds. Six months later the ones that got it right would be living in their own mews houses in Pimlico and looking fifteen years younger.'[9]

It seems likely that underwear becomes eroticized for many men because it is associated with the first forbidden glimpses of female nakedness. According to prostitutes, the underwear many men find most erotic is not the latest fashion, but the kind their mothers wore when they were little boys – and in London in the sixties prostitutes reported 'a sudden demand for gas masks and bath-robes, the very garments that mothers would have been wearing in the air raid shelters when the middle-aged fetishists were little boys of four or five.'[10]

The erotic associations that underwear or lingerie has acquired are enjoyed by many women. Dressing up for sex can be part of a sensuous ritual. Lily said, 'I like having satin pyjamas and night-dresses, because I feel sexy in things like that. I used to dress up for sex with Jim. If I'd suddenly feel it was about time we had a really good session, I'd have a bath and put perfume on, and I'd put make-up on to go to bed in, and then I'd put on a glamorous nightdress. He'd love that because it was a signal to him.' Women may also enjoy these meanings in an auto-erotic way. We may take pleasure in wearing clothes that have acquired sexual meanings not as part of a scene with a partner, but for ourselves. The enhance-ment of the secret body and the play of hiding and showing can still be erotic even if nobody knows. Janet said, 'I like to feel that I've got nice underwear on even though nobody knew anything about it, and I think stockings and suspenders always make you feel more feminine.'

In Lily's account, the pleasure she takes in being looked at by her partner could be loosely labelled exhibitionistic: in Janet's account the pleasure comes at root from an exhibitionistic fantasy. Exhibitionism is the one source of arousal that has been categorized as a perversion which is permitted to women. Little girls will try anything from sadism to bestiality, but when little girls become mature women, only exhibitionism is allowed. 'I'll show you mine', usually without the mutuality of 'if you'll show me yours', is the one sexual theme above all that is encouraged in women, just as it is largely forbidden to men.

Faith said, 'I do a lot of acting. Going onto the stage and dis-playing myself to audiences gives me a big sexual thrill. In the last part I played quite an attractive woman, and I got a lot of satisfaction out of having people say, "Gosh, you look absolutely beautiful." At one point everyone is in bed, in nightclothes, and I was wearing a glamorous nightdress, and after the first dress rehearsal the direc-tor said, "You can't wear anything under these nightclothes, we can see the line of everything." The other women all got very upset about this – "I'm not going on stage without knickers!" But it didn't bother me in the slightest, I was happy just to take it all off.'

Here Faith acts out the arousing fantasy of being looked at and desired by a mass of people. It's the same sexual pleasure as is afforded by wearing a short skirt or a revealing neckline, writ large in Faith's case as she enjoys the admiration of the whole audience.

For women who enjoy wearing sexy underwear or nightgowns, the eroticism comes from the meanings the clothes have acquired by association with sex. But for a minority of women, clothes may also feel sexy because they are physically stimulating. Psychotherapist Louise Kaplan tells the story of Sally, one of Robert Stoller's patients, who derived profound physical pleasure from slowly pulling on a pair of men's Levi's, and would have an orgasm as the seam hit her crotch.[11] A woman quoted in the Hite Report used jeans for her favourite masturbation method: 'I prefer to be wearing tight blue jeans and pulling so that the seam presses against the tip of my clitoris. I can even do it in public without being observed, I think, with the tight blue jeans method.'[12] In her book *Women and Pornography*, Beatrice Faust suggests that women can be turned on by wearing corsets and high heels: 'Walking in high heels makes the buttocks undulate about twice as much as walking in flat heels with correspondingly greater sensation transmitted to the vulva. Girdles can encourage pelvic tumescence and, if they are long enough, cause labial friction during movement.'[13]

Clothing as a direct form of sexual stimulation does seem to be a minority interest. The enthusiasm with which women have bought comfortable and unrestrictive styles – flat boots, tracksuits and leggings – suggests that for most women the discomforts of restrictive clothing outweigh any possible erotic frisson they may give us. The feel of silky fabrics, however, is one sensuous adjunct to sexual activity that many women do seem to enjoy. Kinsey maintained that women derived more pleasure than men from all-over touching and skin-to-skin contact,[14] and this may be linked to the pleasure many women take in the sensuousness of silk, with its affinity with the softest skin. Beth said, 'Shelley, my lover, really likes clothing – suspenders and all that – red! I wouldn't wear red! Black I sometimes do. But my favourite thing is a satiny nightie – it doesn't show anything, and it's got some embroidery in peach, and it's all in a pearly creamy colour. It's soft and gentle and I imagine it's very sophisticated and feminine, and I feel very confident wearing it. I couldn't actually wear a babydoll and frilly knickers!' Beth wears suspenders, a little reluctantly, for Shelley: the satiny nightdress, the silky second skin, is for herself.

Silk feels sexy because it is like skin: as Sylvia said, 'like babies' – and like mother's skin too, the soft skin that gave us such pleasure in infancy, in our most primitive sensuousness. This equation of clothes with the body is the source of their power and romance. Clothes remind us of bodies in general – but they also remind us of the body in particular, of the person who wears them. Because they mould to a person's body and acquire their shape and smell, something of a person's presence attaches to their clothes. This is why we are superstitious about clothes. In some cultures dead people's clothes are considered unlucky: in our own, there is much significance attached to the moment when the widow or widower finally clears out the lost partner's clothes. Where witchcraft is practised, a witch may acquire power over an enemy by stealing the clothes he or she wears. As a social worker, I once had to wait outside court with a group of tough, streetwise girls who were all facing burglary or robbery charges. They pointed out a girl whom they regarded as a pariah because she had stolen another girl's clothes. Disapproving, they turned to me for corroboration: 'You shouldn't do that, Miss, should you? Take somebody's *clothes*?'

Men's clothing in general is not eroticized like women's, but because clothes stand for or represent the body, an individual man's clothes may be eroticized for a particular woman. One of my favourite examples of this can be found in Daphne du Maurier's novel *Rebecca*, when the romantic hero, Maxim de Winter, puts his jacket round the shoulders of the child-like heroine, who is falling in love with him. The jacket symbolizes the man's arms around her, and the gesture is both erotic and fatherly, encompassing both the thrill of a lover's embrace, and the warmth, security and safe familiar smell a little girl enjoys in the arms of a loved father. 'I was young enough to win happiness in the wearing of his clothes ... this borrowing of his coat, wearing it around my shoulders for even a few minutes at a time, was a triumph in itself, and made a glow about my morning.'[15]

Though the process is much less universal than the sexualization of female clothing, some women do have favourite male garments – leather jackets, perhaps, or business suits – which they consider to enhance men's sexual attractiveness, and when women say what they find attractive about men, they sometimes include details of clothing: 'I might go for lines of power – like chest hair showing through an open shirt.' And in the mid 1980s, the popularity of BBC television presenter Michael Wood, who acquired a cult following among women, undoubtedly had as much to do with the eloquent fit of his jeans as his lyrical discourse on the Fall of Troy. But the most explicit erotic use of male clothing is of course made by lesbians.

For lesbians today there may be an element of play in the mixing of male and female signals. Sheila for instance enjoys the style that she has developed since coming out in her fifties, the mix of male and female meanings – cropped hair, tailored trousers and soft silky blouse. Some of the women photographed by lesbian photographer Della Grace play around with these meanings in an appealingly outrageous way, for example wearing a tutu with a silver leather jacket and brogues.[16] For other women, butch or fem styles may be carried through into every detail of self-presentation, as a statement of sexual identity and as a way of signalling the kind of sexual relationship they want. Sandy said, 'You see a lot of butch and fem couples, it'll be down to the suit and the tie and the men's shoes. And on a Saturday night, the partner'll have the short skirt on and the furs, the butch won't wear deodorant or perfume or anything. Personally I don't identify with it at all – I could never be attracted to anybody who looked butch. I just can't understand why a woman would want to dress up like a man and imitate a man.'

But there are in fact many reasons why a woman would want to dress up like a man. There is a long history of cross-dressing by women. It has sometimes been associated, as it is today, with sexual orientation. When it was a hanging offence to be a lesbian or 'tribad', a woman who loved women might have chosen male impersonation as a 'lifestyle' in a rather literal sense, as a matter of survival. But female cross-dressing has more often had nothing to do with sex. Again we see the almost exclusively sexual meanings of female clothing: male transvestism seems to be entirely about the sexual meanings of female clothing, but for women cross-dressing has usually been about something quite different. Male impersonation has been a way of gaining access to opportunities that women would otherwise have been denied – adventure, travel, a chance to use their talents. The exploits of one such cross-dresser are celebrated in the folksong 'The Female Drummer', which tells how Mary Ann Talbot dressed as a man in order to join the army, 'To rush into the battlefield with a broad sword in my hand, To hear the cannons rattle and the music play so grand.'

Dress as a man, and the world opens up. This is still true. In

January 1989, the American jazz musician Billy Tipton, who died leaving a wife and three adopted sons, was revealed after her death to be a woman.[17] She had lived as a man for fifty-five years. Her wife explained that Tipton thought that the only way to join a swing band in the 1930s was to become a man. In the UK in 1989, conjuror Sophie Lloyd joined the Magic Circle, a magicians' society from which women were then excluded, by impersonating a fifteen-year-old boy. Two years later, when women were finally admitted to the society, Sophie unmasked her illusion, to the great consternation of the six hundred male members who had failed to see through her trick.[18]

Eve is one woman who loves wearing male clothing. 'I like to look really butch – because I'm not actually; my girlfriend kind of jokes and says "Oh you're so *butch*!" I love it because I don't see myself like that at all. But I like that image very much. My clothes are a statement, they're a statement to my mother who thinks I ought to be wearing Marks and Spencers clothes, they're a statement about my position here – because in fact I'm the boss here, I'm the matron – and to be dressed like a dyke – I enjoy the rebelliousness of it! When I'm looking butch, I feel more everything, more powerful, I walk better and, yes, I suppose I feel more sexually aware. I feel as though I can walk as though I own the street . . . No, I don't mean that! I just feel as though I have a right to be there, and that I can get what I want in shops, 'cos I used to be so very very timid – and, yeah, I like the new assertive person I've created for myself.'

Listening to Eve, I felt tremendous envy. The nearest I've come in my own life to feeling such a surge of power from clothes was at graduation, wearing that unisex symbol of intellectual and class status, academic dress. In that billowing black gown, I felt like Eve that I could walk as though I owned the street – and like Eve when she says, 'No, I don't mean that,' I too felt guilty, because the sudden sense of power was so intoxicating.

Eve's telling comments underline a problem that is intrinsic to female clothing and implicit in the sexualization of dress for women. If dressing butch can make a woman feel this good, this powerful, how does dressing in a feminine way make us feel? What is the cost of glamour for women?

THE MORALITY OF APPEARANCE

There are moments of real pleasure in women's accounts of the place of glamour in their sexual histories – Faith on the stage naked under her satin nightdress; Gwen wearing her beautiful bright suit to please her dashing man friend; Janet in her stockings and suspenders, feeling sexier even though nobody knows. But these are not simple pleasures. The erotic pleasures of glamour for women are paradoxical and potentially fraught. There is a downside to the role of glamour in women's sexuality.

Firstly and most obviously there is the cost – the cost in time, preoccupation, effort, worry and money, of producing the perfect look. Mothers of young children so often look 'frumpy' because they are simply un-retouched women. They don't have the time, and anyway they are thinking about something else. A lot of work goes into the construction of the glamorous look. To do it right, first there is the body, which you must exfoliate, depile, tint, shampoo, condition, set, cleanse, tone, moisturise, make-up . . . Then there are the clothes themselves, which you must choose, vary, mix and match, accessorize, constantly replace, and care for.

All this activity takes a lot of thinking and planning. For most women, appearance is an arena for constant nagging thoughts and preoccupations when we could or should be thinking about something else. When she was in prison before going on trial for killing her lover, Ruth Ellis, the last woman in Britain to be hanged for murder, seemed unconcerned about her defence. Her only preoccupation was how to get some peroxide into the prison to touch up her roots so she would look her best for the trial.[19] A splendid affirmation of self and act of defiance, perhaps. Or is this more accurately seen as a terrible cautionary tale?

Why do we work so hard at appearance? Rarely, I suspect, because the rewards are so great that the pleasure makes it all worthwhile. Often we work at appearance because we feel we *should*. Naomi Wolf has identified the use of a religious language of guilt, contrition and absolution in the wording of cosmetics advertisements: 'Q. I am over forty-five. Is it too late to start using Niosôme Système Anti-age? A. It's never too late . . .'[20] There is so much morality about appearance for women. When I talked to women about clothes, 'ought' was a word I heard a lot, and a lack of interest in their appearance was something women felt they had to apologize for. Grace said, 'I wish I was more interested and therefore spent more time getting things together that look good. I tend to buy things which are comfortable rather than fashionable – which in my job isn't always a sensible thing – medicine's a very conservative profession. It's easier to look smart and therefore indistinguishable from all the rest than to look comfortable and distinguishable.' The fact that self-decoration is an area of moral imperatives for women perhaps explains that familiar feeling of weariness which overcomes some of us when we open yet another magazine full of pictures of exquisite anorexics in wonderful clothes. Even when she is contributing as much to society as Grace, who is a GP in an inner city practice, the woman who can't be bothered with self-decoration will still feel a residual guilt about not participating in this activity which is seen at one and the same time as frivolous and obligatory. The woman who 'lets herself go' is a target for moral censure. You have to reach the moral status of a Pauline Cutting before you can be excused from evaluation on the basis of your appearance.

These oughts and shoulds may have more to do with the man who passes us in the street than with our own sex partners. Plenty of women leave their legs unshaved in winter, when only their sex partners see, but shave them for the street in summer. Our sense that glamour is a moral issue and a duty is confirmed by the sense of affront that many men express at the sight of a woman who doesn't please – the overweight barmaid in tight bright Lycra, perhaps. The opprobrium such a woman inspires reminds us that it is our duty to be easy on the eye of every passing male. Fashion journalism is full of these oughts and shoulds, and littered with dire warnings about the many ways we can get it wrong.

As we have seen, virtually every woman I talked to said she felt sexier and was more easily aroused if she felt she was looking attractive. We might deduce that glamour can be an intensifier and enhancer of women's sexual pleasure – and in the first section of this chapter we saw how it can often be just that. But there is also another way of understanding this. If glamour is an 'ought', a moral duty, is it just one more item to add to the list of conditions that must be fulfilled before women can enjoy sex? Do we have to *look* sexy before we can let ourselves *feel* sexy? What woman, grabbed by her lover early in the morning before she has put on an acceptably glamorous persona for the outside world, has not pulled back just a little, with a quick apology: 'Oh, but I haven't shaved my legs, I'm so fat, my breath must smell, my hair's a mess . . .' Only once we have listed our shortcomings can we let ourselves be desired.

Since women have achieved more power, the morality of appearance has taken a new twist. In her paper 'Womanliness as a Masquerade' published in the 1920s,[21] psychoanalyst Joan Rivière pointed to the way 'some powerful and liberated women had taken to disguising themselves as women': their strivings in the male world were acceptable – to themselves and to society – only if they adopted a very feminine manner and appearance. Therapist Louise Kaplan describes the many similar women who come to her for therapy today – women who are highly successful, but who never feel quite entitled to the fruits of their success. Such women may experience their achievements in the male world of work as 'phallic trophies' they have stolen. After each new professional triumph, these women feel the need to behave in an ingratiating, submissive, feminine manner – to disguise themselves as women – as though to propitiate the malign fates who might snatch their achievements away. Cultivating a very feminine appearance and giving a lot of attention to all the things stereotypically feminine women are meant to care about – clothes and make-up and hairstyles – can be part of a deliberately cultivated though alien feminine persona, which the woman feels makes her less threatening. She may fear that if she doesn't abide by at least some of the rules about womanhood, the phallic trophies will be stolen back.[22]

In the person of rock star Madonna, we have an intriguing instance of a public figure who manages to place herself outside the morality of appearance. Women love her – but men are more ambivalent about her appeal. Why do male rock critics so frequently claim that this beautiful woman in these exciting clothes isn't sexy? The answer is, I suspect, that Madonna isn't 'sexy' because she isn't serious. Like Louise Kaplan's clients, Madonna is a female female impersonator, but Madonna's motive is different. For the troubled women whom Kaplan describes, dressing-up is a deadly serious device to avert punishment for their presumption in invading male territory: but for Madonna dressing-up is play. Madonna reminds us of the time before the oughts and shoulds. Her clothes may be full of outrageous sado-masochistic signifiers, but she remains the little girl trying on her mother's high heels and corsets in front of the mirror with delicious glee, taking us back to a time before dressing-up was hedged about with rules and prohibitions, a time before our clothes were intended to please or impress other people or to avert their disapproval. Abuse survivor Marilyn Monroe had a public persona which was totally other-directed, and therefore profoundly sexually attractive to men. Monroe's dressing-up was serious. But Madonna is somehow able to imply that the dressing-up is just for herself – for fun.

OPTING OUT

There are plenty of women who have little interest in glamour. 'All this stuff about clothes is a bit of a puzzle to me quite honestly.' 'I think perhaps I don't take as much interest in clothes as I should. I always feel I look dowdy and so what's the use? It doesn't matter that much to me as long as I look reasonably unobtrusive and reasonably clean and tidy.' 'I'm not at all interested in clothes: what I wear is what people leave behind when they come to stay ...'

Because glamour is equated with sexuality in women, the universal assumption is that the glamorous woman is more orgasmic and easily aroused and likely to have a wonderful sex life than her less glamorous sister. Yet in reality a woman's interest in glamour says nothing about her interest in sex. There are plenty of women who like to wear the 'sprayed-on Lycra' so dear to the blockbuster novelist, and who are happily celibate: there are plenty of women in anonymous jumpers and skirts who have urgent erotic concerns. The information that a woman's appearance gives about her sexuality is as likely as not to be misinformation. Yet the belief that clothes equal female sexuality is taken so seriously that in the early 1970s sex researcher Seymour Fisher actually set out to establish whether women in tight frocks had more orgasms. Women were asked to give true or false responses to such statements as 'I like close-fitting, figure-revealing dresses' and 'I approve of the Bikini bathing suit and wouldn't mind wearing one myself'. Seymour Fisher concluded: 'The clothing attitudes measured in this way proved to be unrelated to orgasm consistency ...'[23] Among my own interviewees, the women who were most interested in glamour might have placed themselves anywhere on the spectrum from sexual misery to sexual bliss. What did unite the most glamorous women was the fact that they were very visual people, sometimes artistically talented and trained, and always deriving much pleasure from their visual sense.

Yet for women who don't want to be bothered with glamour, it is extraordinarily hard to opt out. Feminists in the seventies may have succeeded in changing the styles, substituting dungarees and bovver boots, hennaed hair and ethnic earrings for more conventional dress, but the preoccupation with clothes remained. Those of us who were involved in women's groups then may remember to our shame the cold-shouldering of women who gave out the wrong visual signals – women who turned up for consciousness-raising wearing high heels and lipstick and little pearl studs in their ears. Because women's clothes are so loaded with sexual meaning, there is no option, as there is for men, of simply not joining in. It is impossible for a young woman to dress in such a way that no judgements about her sexuality will be made on the basis of her appearance. Cheryl said, 'Most of the time I don't want to be noticed as a female, I just want to be somebody you talk to. I don't like it when I think I'm being measured up.' But women who share Cheryl's sentiments are unlikely to succeed in their aims.

In an analysis of the illogicalities of the feminist party line on appearance in the 1970s, Janet Radcliffe Richards wrote, '. . . a feminist whose main motivation was to put as little time and money into [clothes] as possible should presumably go around in the first and cheapest thing she could find in a jumble sale, even if it happened to be a shapeless turquoise Crimplene dress with a pink cardigan. No feminist would be seen dead in any such thing . . .'[24] The Crimplene dress won't do because it signals too. 'Frumpy' clothes also have meanings that are to do with a woman's sexuality, and even women who don't want to attract men would not wish to have those meanings applied to them. For older women there may be certain successful alternative styles that sidestep the sexual meanings – the bobbed grey hair and grey cardigans of Senior Common Room or Quaker style, for instance – but these styles have different meanings on younger women. Whatever a premenopausal woman wears can be read as information about her sexuality. Except in a gay bar, a man's clothing will never be read in this way.

WEARING SOMETHING FAIRLY SENSUAL

What if you choose to opt in? What is it like to dress as the magazines tell you to, and conform to the sexy stereotype?

Amanda said, 'We went to a party the other evening and I wore a small black velvet thing, and I thought it would make me feel sexy. In fact it made me feel uncomfortable, I was pulling it down the whole time.' Bernadette said, 'I've got this denim skirt, which

I was wearing yesterday, and I decided I'm never going to wear it again because it's too restrictive, and I like to walk very confidently and quickly through town, and I was having to teeter, which I hate, plus it attracted people's attention to my legs, which I don't like. I like to get attention when I want it and not to have it forced upon me. I know that if I dress in something fairly sensual then I'm going to get lots of looks and it's not always what I want.' Hilary said, 'At Christmas we were going to this disco with Neil's football crowd. I thought, I want to look really nice tonight, and I went out and bought a whole new set of underwear, which wasn't M and S cotton knickers, but it was very lacy and flowery, and stockings, and a very slim-fitting short black dress, and I felt really good that night. But I haven't been near them since, and I feel quite peculiar about that. I actually feel quite cross that I wanted to look like that – I did feel good, but it was because I was fitting the image that those people there would expect me to fit in. I looked good but they weren't really me.'

In women's accounts of dressing as the perfect sex object, there was a lot of uneasiness, a lot of fiddling with buttons and tugging down of hems. Dressing to look sexy is full of risks. The exposing of flesh has to be perfectly attuned to the ambience of the occasion, or it becomes a source of the embarrassment we always feel if we give out too overtly sexual a signal for the context. When the skirt rides up higher than you intended, or the shirt gapes or the buttons come undone, your erotic dream quickly shades over into that nightmare that Freud believed to be universal, the one in which you find yourself in a public place with crucial items of clothing missing.

But there is more to the anxieties stirred up by wearing sexy clothes than this largely practical problem of getting the exposure right. When she dressed butch in her leather jacket and jeans and boots, Eve felt strong, and knew she had 'a right to be there'. The corollary is that feminine clothing takes our power away, and makes us both appear and feel more vulnerable. This is why very powerful women never look 'right' – why fashion journalists, for instance, constantly carped at and criticized Mrs Thatcher's appearance. There are many workshops that promise to show career women how to dress for the boardroom. We may be irritated by such enterprises, because by their very existence they seem to reiterate the message that what we look like is more important than what we do. But perhaps these workshops also represent an attempt to deal with a genuine problem: how to look powerful wearing women's clothes.

The more sexy clothing becomes, the more vulnerable we appear. Image consultant Mary Spillane has this warning for businesswomen attending corporate events held in the evening: 'If you show too much, you'll blow your chances ... the more skin you show the more power you lose.'[25] Because women are subordinate, and women's sexuality is seen as masochistic, female clothing that gives out overtly sexual signals becomes imbued with masochistic meanings. This is most apparent in the meanings that have accrued to female underwear. Sheila Jeffreys has pointed out how sexy women's underwear is used for its masochistic meanings in sado-masochistic scenarios in both gay and lesbian pornography. She comments, 'If the very same kind of garments can be used by both men and women in rituals of sexual humiliation it would suggest that these clothes represent not "women" but the crippling, restrictive and inferior role which has been assigned to woman in the gender role system.'[26] The masochism is also stressed in those scenes from romances or male pornography where glamorous female garments, like Maxine's wispy little knickers in *Lace*, are torn off the woman and ripped up by the man in the course of sexual activity. Some awareness of these meanings of sexy female clothing is, I would suggest, the reason for many women's ambivalence or unease when they wear it. This is why Hilary said, 'I feel quite cross that I wanted to look like that.'

There is one particular attribute of stereotypically sexy clothing which Sheila Jeffreys links to its masochistic meanings, the attribute that is most apparent to the wearer – the way it restricts the body. Even since the invention of Lycra, most sexy clothes remain uncomfortable to wear and prevent us from moving freely, like the tight skirt that made Bernadette 'teeter'. Throughout history, items of clothing have been used to restrict and control women: in the cases of foot-binding or Medieval chastity belts, we see these usages carried to horrific extremes. Today, the restrictive meanings of female clothing are most clearly demonstrated by certain items of underwear. Corsets much like those that women wear now as erotic accoutrements were worn by our mothers or grandmothers purely to flatten their stomachs, and not so long ago, wearing a corset was not just restrictive but actually painful. Betty Ryan, a Wimbledon tennis star before the First World War, remembers how the steel-boned corsets in which the women played were hung up to dry in the changing rooms: 'It was never a pretty sight,' she says, 'for most of them were blood-stained.'[27] It is because such garments restrict and control the body that they occupy such a central place in sado-masochistic ritual, whether in fantasy or practice. The appeal of restricting garments to the male voyeur perhaps links with the male feeling that women's bodies simply as they come are too much – that they need to be controlled. We could see the male penchant for looking at women in underwear as a manifestation of male fear of the excesses of female flesh. In the soft porn magazines which celebrate the acquired erotic meanings of underwear, the stockings and suspenders serve the same purpose as the neat little rectangle of wispy pubic hair: they frame and contain the genitals, making them neat and non-threatening. Such images seem to have nothing to do with the extravagance of ordinary women's bodies as they really are – the lavish menstrual flow, the swelling stomach of pregnancy, the hard full breasts of early lactation, the multiple orgasms.

The impulse to restrict and control the body until it has the shape that is currently deemed to be sexy – the impulse that is expressed in a penchant for tight basques or underwired bras – can today be taken one step further. The last few years have seen a cosmetic surgery boom, which has been given only the smallest setback by revelations about the potential dangers of silicone breast implants. Given the unsavoury details of the treatments themselves, and the pain that is always part of the deal, it is easy to see cosmetic surgery as a perversion, a deathly thing, an expression of hate for the body. Yet it is undoubtedly a distortion to see it as no more than that. There is also a life-affirming aspect to it. Submitting to the surgeon's knife is about making yourself beautiful in order to be loved. How does this connect to a woman's sexuality?

Cindy Jackson, interviewed in *Bella* magazine by Julie Fairhead, had spent £20,000 on cosmetic surgery, and the pain, she said, was 'excruciating'. She explained, 'Ever since I was a child, I'd wanted to look like my favourite doll . . . I thought I was truly ugly – especially when I compared myself with my Barbie doll.' Her current boyfriend, she says, is 'tall, dark and gorgeous, and we've been together for more than two years. Although he doesn't really like me having all these operations, he understands my reasons . . . I know no one would have looked twice at the pre-surgery me. Now I can knock 'em dead and have men yelling at me out of cars and other girls eyeing me jealously.'[28] Cindy Jackson seems to have had the surgery in spite of, rather than because of, her sex partner. It is not tall dark gorgeous Bill she wants to turn on with her new body, but the passing male, the stranger. For Cindy, being looked at and desired by the anonymous man in the street takes priority over her sexual relationship with her boyfriend.

Changing her body into the perfect shape does not seem, in Cindy's account at least, to have very much to do with the woman's own sexual pleasure. But sometimes the disjunction between sex and beauty is even more marked. Sometimes physical perfection and sexual pleasure may be in direct conflict. Controlling, restricting and cutting the body can have drastic effects on a woman's sexual potency. The woman who slims too strenuously will lose all sexual feeling. The woman who has her breasts perfected by surgery may lose all nipple sensation. When a woman damages her body and gives up on certain sexual pleasures in order to please the passing male, we have another striking instance of the subordination of women's pleasure to men's. The perfect sex object who can no longer enjoy sex or who has her capacity for sexual pleasure restricted is one of the most striking embodiments of the suppression of female sexuality. It is to such a woman that Germaine Greer's evocative label, 'the female eunuch', can most appropriately be applied.

We are told in so many ways that glamour is an intrinsic part of female sexuality. Sex manuals urge women to dress up for sex. In the blockbusters and romances, clothes are an expression of a woman's sexuality. In fashion journalism, wearing sexy clothes is called 'expressing your sexuality'. And a recurrent image in fashion advertising has the frock as orgasm, as a woman with tousled hair, parted lips, arching spine and dilated pupils displays the latest offering from some fashion house.

As we have seen, the pleasure that glamour gives to women may have some erotic components. Women may like to wear stockings because of their sexy associations, or may find the sensuous feel of silk a pleasant adjunct to sex, or may derive an exhibitionistic pleasure from raising their hemlines six inches. But the erotic elements of glamour can be problematic. The morality of appearance means that women won't let themselves feel sexy *unless* they are looking their best. Younger women can't opt out of the sexual meanings of clothes – we will always be either sexy or frumpy. And wearing 'something fairly sensual' is at best an ambiguous pleasure, for we are all aware, at some level or other, that sexy clothes have masochistic meanings, and that to wear them is to emphasize our vulnerability and to give away our power.

But even where women are not too troubled by these ambiguities and restrictions, the erotic component of glamour can surely only ever be a mild and tangential thing. It may be very pleasant to slip into a short black velvet dress: there may be a mild erotic frisson at the thought that someone you lust after will find you desirable in it. But no one could call such a feeling ecstatic. It is only the rare woman who masturbates with the crotch seam of her Levi's, who finds a profound eroticism in clothing.

Why then are we told that glamour is so central to our sexuality? The answer, of course, is that it is very important to *men*. The primary erotic purpose of sexy female clothing is to enhance male sexual arousal. Looking at women in sexy clothing is a major source of sexual stimulation for men. Yet sexy clothing is sold with the promise of sexual fulfilment for women. We are urged to wear it because it will give us erotic pleasure.

Emily believed the promise. 'When I was very sexually frustrated,' she said, 'and I'd never had an orgasm, I used to sort of go shopping for orgasms. I spent hours trying on jeans. I used to think, if only I could find the perfect jeans, the ones that fitted absolutely perfectly, then perhaps I'd attract the perfect lover, the man who could actually make me come. Since I've started having a good sex life, I just don't think about clothes in that way anymore.'

The promise that glamour holds out to women is a lie. If we believe the promise, we will look in the wrong place for sexual happiness. If we expect glamour to bring us sexual fulfilment, we will be disappointed. A frock is not an orgasm, in spite of what the iconography of advertising seems to be telling us, and you cannot find sexual fulfilment among the racks of alluring outfits in the clothes shops, however hard you try. For, as Jacqueline sees so clearly, there is a world of difference between being desired and desiring, between looking sexy and being sexual, between giving pleasure and feeling it for yourself.

'I think until recently I always used to dress to look sexy to some extent. Not the sexy look with high heels and big boobs because I was never the right shape, but I suppose I'd go for the wild look, it was the sort of "Come hither" and "look like you've just tumbled out of bed" look. And I did briefly go through a phase of wearing white cotton Indian blouses which had embroidery on, and then not wearing a bra – and I've always been flat-chested so the effect was rather boyish, a boyish femininity, I suspect.

'I think clothes are a mask – more a mask than a means of self-expression. Even the sexy bit – it was a mask rather than a statement, because I wasn't actually orgasmic. I might have been sexy, but I wasn't orgasmic.'

CHAPTER THIRTEEN

Looking

There is a male monopoly on erotic imagery in our culture. The public arena is crowded out with myriad images meant for the eyes of men. Most of these images are intended for heterosexual men, but there is a small subculture of images intended for homosexual men. There is almost nothing aimed at women.

The images are there, it is frequently said, because men are turned on by looking and women are not. It's a belief that fits neatly with the 'dark continent' theory of sexuality – the idea that male sexuality is simple and female sexuality is mysterious and complicated. 'Male sexual response,' writes Alex Comfort in *The Joy of Sex*, 'is far brisker and more automatic: it is triggered easily by things, like putting a quarter in a vending machine.'[1] The 'things' here are the woman's body and clothes.

The idea that male sexual response is more easily triggered by 'things' goes back to the Kinsey Report. The Kinsey Institute researchers asked women if they were never, seldom or often sexually aroused by sexual pictures, and found they usually answered 'never' or 'seldom'.[2] Kinsey's results may tell us more about the availability of erotic pictures to women in the 1950s than about the enduring characteristics of women's sexual response: a woman can't know what her response to sexual pictures might be if she's never seen any. Yet Kinsey's somewhat dubious conclusion is now taken as axiomatic. The belief that men are turned on by looking and women are not has become one of the most widely accepted beliefs about sex differences. Ask the man or woman in the street about differences between male and female sexuality, and this is what they will say.

ARE WOMEN TURNED ON BY LOOKING?

I asked women what they thought of images of naked men. Their answers would seem to support the Kinsey theory of gender differences in response to looking. Almost without exception, women stated emphatically that they weren't turned on by images of naked men. It was only then that most of them went on to reflect that, outside art galleries, they'd never seen any ... But they insisted that even if erotic images of men were available 'it would do nothing' for them, or that they simply found such images funny.

Yet though women are convinced they're not aroused by looking, most women do clearly prefer to sleep with men who are good to look at. Most women told me that looks were very important in their choice of sex partner. Sometimes this was an aspect of their sexuality that they felt guilty about or struggled to keep under control: 'Looks *are* important – too important really.' 'There's part of me that's a female version of what I don't like in men.'

There is no stereotype of male attractiveness, and men feel no compulsion to change the body with the aid of make-up, hair-dye, silicone implants or Lycra bodyshapers: it follows that there is tremendous variety in what women find attractive. Puny men, Italian-looking men with a bit of Greek and a bit of Lebanese, men who haven't shaved for a while, men with interesting, well-worn faces, ascetic types, weedy cerebral types, androgynous-looking men, Richard Gere, Michael Caine, Nelson Mandela ... There is great variety too in the parts of men's bodies that women most like to look at – backs of necks in T-shirts, clean hands with nice nails, slim hips, bum in tight jeans, bum – no jeans.

What rarely gets a mention is the kind of body that has to be steered sideways through doors. Muscles are usually assumed to be about sexual display, and men tend to believe that the powerful muscle-bound physique is the kind of body which women find most desirable. But muscles are not about sexual display – they are there primarily to impress other men. Writer Beatrice Faust distinguishes between this kind of man-to-man or epideictic display, and epigamic or man-to-woman display. She comments that men assume that there is no difference between the two, and that what impresses other men will also impress women, but that they are wrong in this assumption.[3] Epideictic display is the only kind of display of their bodies that has been permissible for heterosexual men to date: the title of Mr Universe is not given to the most beautiful in the line-up, but to the most muscle-bound.

Penis size is another aspect of epideictic display. To women's considerable amusement, penis size continues to be one of the most common male sexual concerns,[4] and is such a delicate issue that Masters and Johnson refused to tell *Playboy* what the average length was, for fear they might upset those readers who didn't measure up.[5] Women frequently assert that penis size is mostly irrelevant to their pleasure: though some women may prefer certain kinds of penises as they prefer certain dress styles, bigger isn't essentially better. It is presumably because penis size is about man-to-man display that men are never reassured by these assertions. Women can't reassure men about penis size because men aren't actually bothered what women think; at root it is the censure or mockery of other men that a man fears.

But however much the visual stimuli that turn us on may differ from male assumptions about what women want, appearance remains a crucial element in their choice of sex partner for most women. And there are plenty of other pieces of evidence too for the importance of looking in female sexuality. Little girls enjoy looking and show just as much sexual curiosity as little boys: as we have seen, the voyeurism in children's sex games is mutual. Where heterosexual women have the power to surround themselves with attractive men they do not hesitate to do so: there were always several 'matinee idols' in Mrs Thatcher's Cabinet, just as Elizabeth I was reputed to favour the more attractive young men among her courtiers. Laboratory experiments have established that women are physically aroused by pictures of naked men.[6] The looks of favourite male rock singers or film stars or tennis players matter a lot to women. And there is also support from sociobiology. Though those who wish to maintain the sexual status quo may argue that it is only natural for men to want to look at women and not vice versa, the evidence from the natural world points the other way. In the animal kingdom it is usually the male – the peacock or the bird of paradise – who puts on the sexual display, and the female who chooses.

But the most convincing evidence for the proposition that women are turned on by looking comes from lesbians. If lesbians can be aroused by looking this must be relevant to heterosexual women too. It is highly implausible that the mechanisms of arousal in heterosexual women would be any different, given that lesbian and heterosexual are in no way discrete categories; women may move from one to the other, or recognize a bit of both in their sexuality – as do the many women who have highly erotic lesbian dreams or fantasies, but choose to sleep with men. And the lesbians who talked to me said that looking turned them on. Fran said, 'We have had sexual magazines that were more for men. I do enjoy that imagery. It's something I'm not into in an amazingly big way, but there are certain pictures that I find attractive.' Eve said, 'Thinking about pornographic magazines, I find women's breasts usually very attractive. It's the kind of mild interest I might get by looking at a cookery book – "That looks like a nice quiche lorraine . . ." It does worry me because it's all about beauty and stereotypical nice figures and all that stuff. In fact my partner at the moment is very big, very powerful, not at all what you'd say is Page 3 stuff, but I think her body's absolutely wonderful, I absolutely love her, I love everything about her physically.'

It seems that we choose our sexual partners at least partly on the basis of looks, that our bodies show arousal when we look at naked men, and that little girls are just as interested in looking at little boys' genitals as boys are in looking at girls'. Yet only adult women who love other women say they are turned on by looking. Why this discrepancy?

THE FLASHER AND THE STRIPPER

Anne said, 'I can remember the first time I saw John naked, in the sense of seeing his penis – it was something that I almost had to steel myself up to do. I felt it a long while before I looked at it, to break myself in, as it were. Now it just doesn't bother me one bit.'

Penny said, 'Male nakedness turns me off rather than turning me on.'

Sylvia said, 'Naked men look better with boxer shorts on. I do think the nice shapes and symmetry of the male body are slightly spoiled.'

It seems that there is a problem for women about male genitals. The naked male body can be a turn-off, not a turn-on. As these comments make clear, when they are having sex with men they love and desire, many women are actually struggling with what they experience as the anaphrodisiac quality of male genitals. It is rare indeed to hear a heterosexual woman speak about the body of her lover with the kind of straightforward lust and delight that Eve expressed, 'I think her body's absolutely wonderful – I love everything about her physically.' Anne has to steel herself to look: Penny is turned off. The feelings generated by the sight of the naked male body are not an erotic stimulus but an obstacle to sexual pleasure that has to be overcome, and the sign that the obstacle is successfully overcome is not that the woman starts to find male genitals erotic and appealing, but that like Anne she finds that 'now it doesn't bother me one bit.'

What we like to look at depends on how we have learned to look. We see through the filter of past images and past experiences. When eighteenth century travellers crossed the Alps they pulled the blinds down; it was only once nineteenth century landscape painters like Ruskin had given the ordinary man or woman in the railway carriage a new way of seeing that mountains became beautiful. What is it about women's ways of seeing male genitals, even the genitals of men they love and find physically desirable, that makes them so troubling?

Gwen is now in her late sixties. When I asked her if she had had any experiences of sexual abuse in childhood, she said, 'I only once had a fright, I don't know whether that put me off men in a way. I was about eight, I was coming home from school, and I was aware of a man on a bike, he followed me home. We had a house with an entry, and I ran up the entry – and my mother had locked the garden gate. I banged and banged – and you know what he did at the bottom of the entry – he exposed himself. When I did get in, I couldn't speak, I was so frightened, I was absolutely terrified, I never did tell anyone about it, you're the first person I've told. I can see it quite clearly now, him sitting there on his bike. Oh, I hope I don't start thinking about it, I hate to think about it!'

Later I asked Gwen about her wedding night, when she had lost her virginity. 'In a way I was very frightened,' she said, 'it was all a bit unknown. The way they talk about it today it's like going to have your tea. I was horrified at the sight of a naked man to start with. I'd never seen that kind of thing before – it's off-putting.'

Here Gwen is wrong. She had, of course, 'seen that kind of thing before,' as a little girl. Her childhood experience has all the ingredients of nightmare. She runs up the narrow passageway, trying to get away from the threat behind her, only to find that the door is bolted. She turns and, filled with fear and disgust, sees her pursuer exposing himself. This is the only time before her wedding night that she sees male genitals. Then, when for the first time she sees the man she loves naked, she doesn't respond to the sight with curiosity, lust, or delicious anticipation of the delights to come. Instead she is horrified.

One of the most popular current theories about the mechanism involved in sexual arousal is the conditioning theory. Patricia Gillan says, 'Many people are conditioned to respond sexually to certain types of stimuli. The process starts early on and continues through a person's life. It is probably at its most powerful when the individual is sexually developing.'[7] According to the theory, we learn to respond to certain cues or images because we come to associate them with sexual arousal. But it follows that we can also learn to associate potentially sexual cues with feelings that are the very opposite of arousal. In Gwen's story, we see how this works. A powerful link is forged between the sight of male genitals and the very antithesis of arousal – feelings of fear and disgust. In the language of behaviourism, this is an aversive stimulus – and for Gwen it is a powerful one. The abusive incident casts a lifelong shadow over her sexuality.

One in three women are abused in childhood (see Chapter 3) and for the most part in these incidents the girl is forced to look at and touch the erect penis. There are many other women with experiences like Gwen's, which don't come within the narrow definition of child sex abuse that I used in Chapter 3, but which also involve having the sight of male genitals forced on them in situations of sexual threat. For at least one in three women, their first encounter with an erect adult penis will be in a context, not of love, lust and mutual exploration, but of repulsion and fear. For older women like Gwen, who grew up in a society in which there was less nakedness than today, the abusive situation will often have been the first time they saw male genitals *at all*.

Patricia Gillan suggested that the process of sexual learning is at its most powerful in childhood. It is likely that this is also true of the kind of lesson that teaches us to be repelled and afraid at the sight of male genitals. But in adult life, too, there will be reminders that the nakedness of a male stranger deliberately displayed is not intended to please. Linda got off a train and found herself the only person on the platform. 'The train pulled away,' she said, 'and I heard a whistle and I looked up and there was a man standing at the window with no clothes on. I felt awful, absolutely awful, really angry. It really shook me. I'm angry that I'm scared to go out after dark . . .'

Once again, we see how pleasure and danger are 'woven fine' in the making of women's sexuality. Here is another direct link between sexual violence and women's problems with sexual pleasure.

For the man it is different. For the man the nakedness of his lover is overlaid with very different images. Where men encounter the public nakedness of a woman with whom they have no relationship displayed in a sexual way, it is in a situation not of abuse but of pleasure – the soft pornography magazine, the stripshow. The massive inequity in the access of men and women to sexual pleasure is nowhere more apparent than in the contrast between the two most commonly encountered forms of male and female sexualized nakedness publicly displayed – the flasher and the stripper. The flasher is ugly, seeking to shock: the stripper is beautiful, tastefully lit, shown off to best effect, seeking to please. The flasher is doing it for himself: the stripper is doing it for her male audience. The flasher is aggressive, frightening: the stripper is vulnerable, seductive. His nakedness is a threat – the threat that he will rape the woman: her nakedness is a promise – a promise about what she might let him do to her. The man watching the stripper feels pleasure, desire, arousal. The woman on whom the flasher forces the sight of his genitals feels fear, and rage that he has made her afraid. And so it goes on.

For the man, then, the naked body of his female lover is overlaid with all those other images of naked bodies, desirable, beautiful, judiciously arranged, and some of those past desires accrue to any woman's body. But for so many women looking at their naked male lover, first there was the flasher, rapist or abuser. One of the captions that accompanied photographs of men's genitals in a recent show by photographer Robin Shaw was this: 'Through taking the photographs I am learning to look – not to be afraid.'[8]

To compare the flasher and the stripper is to see just how different the rules about looking are for women and for men. The situation is at the very least unfair. But does it matter for women's chances of sexual pleasure?

'Stimulation therapy', the method that sex therapist Patricia Gillan has devised to help women with low sexual desire, involves the use of erotic materials including slide shows in which both men and women feature as sexual objects.[9] She has found stimulation therapy a highly effective way of increasing women's interest in sex. Heterosexual men in our society exist in a permanent state of 'stimulation therapy', but for women there are few sources of such stimulation. Not only are there few public erotic images aimed at women, but in our private lives men rarely make concessions in their self-presentation to the pleasure that women could take in looking. As Rosalind Coward has written, 'One of the major consequences of men's refusal to be the desired sex ... is that sometimes even women have difficulty in finding them attractive. There is a sort of failure of the will at the heart of heterosexual desire.'[10] Patricia Gillan's experiences with women suffering 'disorders of desire' suggest that the lack of erotic visual stimuli for women denies us a potentially significant source of arousal. It is also possible that the availability of attractive erotic imagery intended for women would go some way towards counteracting the aversive effects of experiences of abuse.

There is a distinction to be made here between looking at a body you find attractive, and watching people having sex. The scenes of intercourse that are such a frequent feature of television drama appealed to very few of the women I talked to. Presumably such scenes are included because they always involve some display of the woman's naked body and therefore appeal to men, but there is nothing in them for most women. 'The actual scenes of humping – God, it's like a dog, let's face it.' 'I find nothing less of a turn-on than two people having sex on the telly. I'd actually go and make a cup of tea in the middle of a film that I might be enjoying, because I find it boring and it tends to put me off the film.' Watching people having sex is a minority interest, and one that is irrelevant to our enjoyment of sexual activity. But how we feel about looking at the bodies of our lovers is highly relevant to our pleasure in sex, and where women do like to look their pleasure will be enhanced. 'I like androgynous men, but I'm not interested in sex with women: my androgynous object definitely has to have a penis. I'm really turned on by penises. I don't know that I'm turned on by them unless they're attached to a man I fancy. But if there's an opportunity to look, I'd have to.' 'I'd love to see photographs of beautiful men, because the beauty aspect is quite important to me. I've never felt the need to see a stripper. Over the past ten years I've been involved with several very beautiful men, so I've had a stripper in my bedroom, which is wonderful ...'

Pleasure in looking could increase women's pleasure in sex, and there are certain changes in our sexual culture that would undoubtedly enhance our arousal – the availability of erotic imagery intended to please women, and a willingness on the part of men to be objects of desire. There are only the smallest signs that these changes are starting to happen. Why can't we look? Why is the patriarchal fiction that women aren't turned on by looking so stoutly maintained?

The feminist analysis has suggested that the answer can be found in the pattern of dominance and submission between the sexes. Looking is about power.

LOOKING AND POWER

There has been massive support among women for Clare Short's campaign to legislate against 'Page 3 girls'. Almost all the women I spoke to disliked 'Page 3' pictures; they found them irritating, exploitative, hateful, embarrassing.

Amanda was an exception. She had had an experience that made her change her perception of such images. 'I used to work in a night shelter, and the men there – we called them guests – tramps, you know – they always used to read the *Sun* and soft porn magazines. I used to be quite morally high-handed about that kind of thing, and I changed because somehow I felt their enjoyment wasn't going to make them more likely to rape someone or look at women from a certain angle. They were doing it purely as relaxation: "Ooh, she's nice." The reason I'd always criticized it was because it makes men look at women as objects, but somehow I couldn't see that link anymore.'

Amanda used to dislike 'that kind of thing'. But when it is completely powerless men, the men right at the bottom of the heap, who are doing the looking, it no longer upsets her. These men, she thinks, can do no harm. Looking at soft porn is simply a legitimate source of pleasure in an otherwise miserable existence. Amanda's change of attitude is a fascinating exemplification of the feminist axiom that under patriarchy looking with lust is about power, and that this is what worries women so much about men's use of porn. When the power dimension is removed, the looking and lusting no longer disturb.

In her book, *Against Our Will*, Susan Brownmiller argues that the fear of rape is one of the weapons that patriarchy uses to keep women in their place.[11] Her assertion raises the question of how this is done. How are women constantly reminded of the sexual threat? The answer, as every young woman knows, is that it is done by looking – by the looks of passing men, and their comments on what they see. Looking implies sexual dominance. This is why the artist who paints a naked model is always assumed to be having sex with her: visual intimacy implies physical intimacy.[12] Young women are reminded that looking means sexual dominance every time they walk down the street. He looks at you, you look away: the old rules still hold, and it feels dangerous to break them. The woman who does try breaking the rules quickly uncovers the hate that lurks beneath the sexual evaluation. To look back and respond to the remarks, however pleasantly and straightforwardly, is invariably to be told, 'Fuck off, you old cow.' There is great intensity in women's accounts of these exchanges. Which of us has never had fantasies of whipping out a gun, or grinding our heels into his groin? As Bernadette said, 'I despise men ogling. I do keep-fit, and I'm wanting to spit blood sometimes, the fact that blokes are standing there looking 'cos there's a heap of girls in leotards, that makes me physically ill.' It is because we understand the power meanings of these looks that we feel so enraged.

No wonder that men, knowing what sexual looking is about for them, so fear the looks of women. No wonder that men, who have for millennia been safe from the direct sexual evaluation that women face everywhere – in every street, every bus queue, every workplace – will fight to maintain the sexual status quo on looking. No wonder that even men who are employed as sex objects may seek to keep control of the looking and to establish themselves as sexually active rather than passive, to keep hold of the power. In a recent court case, a man who worked as a 'strip-a-gram' was found guilty of indecent assault on his clients: 'dressed as a policeman or Rambo', he had handcuffed the women and subjected them to 'outrageous indignities' with a vibrator.[13] Giving up the power doesn't come easily to men. Sarah Kent, in her essay, 'The Erotic Male Nude', has pointed out how the text accompanying the images in *Playgirl* served to remind women reading the magazine that in the real world men do the looking: 'Bartender Dennis Cadean says his favourite aspect of surfing is the scenery: "You get a great view of all the beautiful women on the beach." '[14] In *Penthouse*'s new magazine, *For Women*, the captions are less blatant, but we are still reminded of the persistence of the old rules governing relationships between women and men: 'Enzo does dream of finding a girl who cooks lasagne like his grandmother did. We were quite shocked. This is the modern world, Enzo, we said, Learn to cook your own lasagne. Then invite us round to share it.'[15]

There is one exception to the rule that women aren't allowed to look, but it's an exception that serves to prove the rule that looking is about power. For there is one group of females in our society who are permitted and even expected to use pin-ups, to discuss in detail the physical attributes of male rock singers, or to scream with delight when their favourite male soap star slinks onto the pantomime stage wearing luscious lurex tights. They are, of course, the least powerful group of sexually mature women in our society – adolescent girls. Note how, if there is a lot of female excitement at the appearance of a sexy tennis player at Wimbledon, the television commentator will always assume that the delighted shrieks come from 'his teen fanclub'. Just as Amanda could tolerate the 'tramps' looking at Page 3, so men can tolerate the lustful looks of the completely powerless.

THE PROOF OF MALE POWER

Sophie recalled, 'One of the things that got me really angry quite early on was *Last Tango in Paris*. There was a scene where the lovers were rolling around in this empty warehouse in Paris, beautiful Marlon Brando, beautiful Maria Schneider, and there was an early full-frontal pubic shot of her – but he seemed to do it with his trousers on.'

Things have changed a little since then: now we do occasionally see penises displayed in public. But there is still a great deal of visual protection extended to the penis. When Jo Mennell made his film *Dick*, showing shots of 1,000 penises accompanied by a commentary of one-liners from interviews with American and British women, he found it very difficult to get any media coverage. The *Los Angeles Times* and *San Francisco Chronicle* refused to carry their critics' reviews of the film, and in the UK Jonathan Ross managed to show the film to his studio audience – but all the television viewer saw was a blank screen.

All the penises in *Dick* were flaccid. The erect penis is still totally forbidden in public display. Images which many women find highly offensive are permitted in high-street porn, but it is still the erect penis which makes hard porn hard.[16]

As Phyllis Chesler says, 'Since the penis is the proof of male existence, the proof of male power, it is too important and too vulnerable an organ to be displayed publicly – especially to women.'[17] The phallus has tremendous symbolic value under patriarchy as the symbol of male dominance. Much male imagery hints at phallic power – guns, lasers, speedboats – whatever is penetrating, fast, dangerous. In the action film, the very presentation of the male body – Sylvester Stallone, for instance, all straight lines and

muscle – hints at the phallus, making an equation between the
hardness of the physique and the 'hardness' of the erect penis. But
it is only because the real penis is never displayed that the phallus
can have such power. Routinely viewed in its ordinariness, the
power of the phallus as a symbol would crumble.

There are accounts of tribal peoples who would not be photographed because they feared the camera would steal their souls,
and there are myths that tell how power and even life itself can be
stolen by the gaze of another. The stories and the beliefs both
point to the human experience that looking is power and that being
looked at takes away your power. In the archetypal story in which
looks can kill, the myth of Medusa, the one who looks is a woman.
The story hints at men's fear that the essence of phallic power can
be stolen by the looks of women. And when we note how women
react on those rare occasions when the penis is actually displayed,
the fear seems to be justified.

One reaction is disappointment. Women tell how they bought
Playgirl when it first came out in the seventies with a sense of eager
anticipation, only to feel let down by the images themselves. When
I was twelve, I was exploring the Victoria and Albert museum with
a girlfriend when we were accosted by a museum warden who told
us in urgent excited tones that we must absolutely not go into a
particular room: 'There's a six foot high statue of David – naked
– in there.' We managed to get away and rushed straight to the
room in question, but we viewed the illicit statue with deep disappointment. Where male nakedness gets such a build-up, disappointment in the image is inevitable, however magnificent its
execution.

Another reaction to the display of the penis is laughter. 'Did you
see all those pictures of naked men in *Marie Claire*?' said Jennifer,
referring to an edition of the magazine which illustrated an article
about men's feelings about their bodies with photos of front and
back views of naked men. 'We had a really good laugh at them.'
Arthur Koestler located humour in the 'clash of two mutually
incompatible codes.'[18] For women looking at pictures of naked men
there is just such a clash; the fantasy of the magic phallus – epitome
of power, strength, dominance – collides with the reality of man
caught with his trousers down.

Women laugh, or feel disappointment. But men who see the
penis displayed in its ordinariness, devoid of phallic power, sometimes seem appalled. In 1980, the art exhibition 'Women's Images

of Men' broke attendance records at the ICA and everywhere it was subsequently shown. The women who organized the exhibition have attributed at least some of the success of the exhibition to the comments of art critic Waldemar Januzczack, who asserted that 'an aura of sensationalism, of penises for penis' sake, undermines the savagery with which some of the exhibitors have entered the arena'[19] – a pronouncement which had the public pouring through the doors in their thousands. As the organizers have pointed out, there weren't in fact all that many penises in the art on show.[20] What critics like Januzczack were responding to was presumably the way these penises were displayed – in particular, the unfamiliar lack of reverence in the depictions.

As women artists like those who exhibited at the ICA create their own images of men, we will learn new ways of seeing. In women's representations, the penis is divorced from its patriarchal burden of significance. No longer overvalued as the powerful phallus, the symbol of male dominance, it can be seen simply as part of the body – as friendly, irritating, arousing or banal. If we learn to look as some of these artists have done, we will rediscover the visual curiosity we had as little girls, before the patriarchal prohibition on looking hit us between the eyes.

Women who have relearnt how to feel comfortable about looking can talk with pleasure, amusement, excitement or frustration about the vagaries of penises they have known:

Lindsey: I find the penis – well, it's a pretty odd thing to have hanging off the front of your body . . .

Cleo: I have flashes of seeing erect penises and thinking, How odd – but then I have other memories of seeing erect penises and feeling very turned on because I know that penis is erect for me.

Bridget: You've erected it!

Cleo: I've erected it, I'm so incredibly sexy . . .

Lindsey: Oh no, I don't feel like that, because it doesn't take much to erect a penis. I don't really flatter myself that it's me . . . I can remember seeing a film once, and some girl saying, 'Ooh if I had a penis I'd be playing with it all the time because I'd just find it so fascinating to have this thing hanging from me' and I can really relate to that. I find it a very odd thing, this penis.

Where the penis no longer symbolizes phallic power, 'penis envy' means no more than the kind of feeling that Lindsey describes – 'I'd just find it so fascinating . . .' This is the straightforward curiosity that both men and women may have about what can never be known – what it would be like to inhabit the body of the other.

A ROOM WITH A VIEW

The ICA exhibition was a landmark – at one and the same time a sign of a change in sensibility and an event that in itself served to change our perceptions further. And in the intervening decade there have been some signs that the monolithic male monopoly on looking, though not totally undermined, is at least crumbling away at the edges.

Mothercare may seem an unlikely place to start a search for images of men devised for women's eyes; but there he was on the cover of the Mothercare Spring 1987 catalogue – an attractive half-naked man, muscular but gentle, cuddling two naked babies, an appealing embodiment of the 'father of my child' fantasy, his contact with the babies' soft skin hinting at the touchableness of his own. Then there were those pleasing and surprising moments when for the first time on the television screen we saw a man taking his clothes off or easing them on in a deliberately sexual way, in the celebrated Levi's 501's campaign. The past few years have also seen the appearance of posters and calendars with black-and-white photographs of pensive 'tasteful' males – men who are only half undressed. 'Pin a different guy on your wall every month just where you want them,' says the advertisement, shrewdly hinting at the pleasure, a rare one for women, of taking charge of your own erotic scenario.

The calendar is advertised in the newspaper under 'Presents for her'. These products are aimed at women. But gay men will presumably also enjoy them, and the sensuous presentation of men's bodies in these images – as touchable, available, and there to be looked at – is in fact derived from the conventions of homosexual soft pornography. Historically, the acceptability of public representations of sexually attractive men has had nothing to do with women's needs or desires: it has depended on the status of love between men in the culture. Reay Tannahill suggests that the 'ambiguous adolescent nudes' of Verrocchio, Botticelli and Leonardo reflect the 'increasingly bisexual tastes of Italian men' during the

Renaissance.[21] In our own society, conventional male display styles serve as an assertion of stereotypically male qualities like invulnerability or physical strength, but they also have another function, one that is crucial in a homophobic society like our own; the hard bulging muscles, the square silhouette, and the exclusion of all sensuous or seductive curves or hollows or softness, also serve as a defence against sexual desire between men. To set out to look like a machine or a Cubist painting is to forbid other men, as well as women, to view you as an object of desire. The new availability of sensuous images of men may have more to do with the partial liberalization of attitudes to homosexuality in the last few years than with the demands or effects of the women's movement. But women as well as homosexual men are the beneficiaries.

In the new climate in which homosexuality has become more acceptable, androgyny has become sexy. There are elements of androgyny about certain heterosexual male figures currently very popular with women: so tennis player Andre Agassi, who has a large female following, combines in his self-presentation certain 'feminine' attributes – baby face, long blond curls, tender smile, and care about his clothes – with very macho signifiers – strong aggressive movements, and an abundance of dark chest hair showing at the neck of his carefully chosen sweatshirt. The new images also go hand in hand with a softening of the rigid emotional armour that prevents men from expressing their feelings, in order to keep tenderness between men at bay. During the Gulf War, we saw the new vulnerability that has become acceptable for man even at his most macho, when Coalition pilots cried and said how afraid they were and how deeply distressed when their comrades were killed. It was against this background that the *Guardian* printed on its women's page a sensuous photograph of a naked serviceman alone in a desert landscape, washing himself after combat.[22] As macho man shows his feelings and lets down some of his defences against expressing his affection for other men, so he also becomes more accessible to the female gaze.

When I asked women whether they could single out any films on general release which had turned them on, I found an intriguing continuation of this theme. The choice of *A Room with a View* was repeated by a number of women, and the television series 'Brideshead Revisited' was also a favourite. These two films have an interesting common denominator. The novels on which both films were based were written by authors with homoerotic interests, and in both cases the homosexual fantasies hidden in the stories shape the female viewers' perceptions of the male hero. In 'Brideshead Revisited', Charles falls in love with his friend Sebastian, and we understand the relationship to be sexually expressed. Because he is first presented in a homosexual relationship, the viewer is enabled to see Charles as someone who can be desired, who is not just desiring. When later he falls for Sebastian's sister, our awareness of him as an object of desire heightens the eroticism of their encounter. *A Room with a View* has an overtly heterosexual boy-meets-girl plot, but the film picks up the hidden homosexual pre-occupations of the author in an extended scene of naked men playing in a woodland pool which draws on the conventions of homosexual soft porn. As she watches the play of light and shade on male flesh, the female viewer comes to see the hero's body in a more sensual light; he too becomes an object of gaze. The covert homosexual fantasies in these films serve to heighten their appeal to women because they change the way we view the hero.

So there are clearly some visual presentations of men derived in feeling or form from the tradition of homosexual soft porn which do appeal to women. But more explicit images intended specifically for female eyes – the pictures in *Playgirl* or *Viva*, for instance – have been less successful. The commercial failure of magazines like these has been exacerbated for reasons that have nothing to do with women's sexual interests: the reluctance of advertisers to have advertisements placed opposite photos of naked men has been a major commercial problem for such magazines. But by and large women do describe a feeling of disappointment on looking at such images. The conventions of pornography present their own limitations. The woman in high-street porn is made to look aroused, with the aid of Sellotape or buckets of ice. But in comparable porn intended for women's eyes, the man cannot legally be shown in a state of excitement. The message is clear enough. The woman looking at the picture cannot fantasize that the man is interested in her. This is not a situation of sexual tension: there is no promise here of fantasy sexual satisfaction. He is not there for her, sexually, in the way that the woman in soft porn is there for the man. There is a rather literal sense of let-down about these images.

But there are also problems about the presentation of such images which could surely be circumvented by canvassing women's opinions. The passivity of the images, for instance, is universally disliked by women. 'Men find it attractive to see a woman lying on a couch with nothing on – so they think to arouse women they just change the sex of the person on the couch. But a half-clad man on a horse or chopping wood – a powerful active symbol – might be more attractive.' And we don't like to see men deliberately posed. 'The few I've seen, they tend to be rather oiled and sleek, which doesn't do a lot for me really. I'm more likely to be aroused by someone stripped to the waist and hewing wood – or washing up, even bathing the children – than deliberately presented.' There is a striking contrast between images like those in *Playgirl* – the ill-at-ease, rather ineffectual man with excessively groomed hair – and the male nudes photographed by Robert Mapplethorpe. Mapplethorpe's photographs are firmly and explicitly placed within homosexual culture, but his beautiful, shocking and powerful photographs are of great sexual interest to many women even though intended primarily for the male gaze. Yet in so many erotic images created explicitly for women there is evidence of that 'failure of the will' that Rosalind Coward identified at the heart of heterosexual desire. Somehow it is never done quite seriously.

The sense of disappointment felt by women who have seen these images is echoed by women who have been to stripshows aimed at a female audience. The characteristic audience reaction at such events is to shout and scream with a total lack of inhibition, but, given that women who had been to stripshows said that they weren't in the least erotic, it seems likely that much of the shrieking has more to do with revenge than sexual excitement. Such group situations give women a chance to yell out a lot of disgust or irreverence, to express more fully feelings like those Jennifer had when she sat and laughed with her friend over the pictures of naked men in *Marie Claire*, or that Melissa had as she joked with her friends about her lover's penis, complaining not because it was too small but because it was too big: 'Really, I think he's anaesthetized me down there.' Some of this behaviour is reminiscent of stories anthropologists tell of women-only group activities that express aggression against men, activities that often have erotic or obscene elements. 'In medieval Ukraine,' writes Rosalind Miles, 'village women at weddings united to overthrow all normal canons of modest wifely behaviour: in a ceremony of female flashing known as "burning the bride's hair" they would hold their skirts waist high and jump over a roaring fire. Men who intruded on these activities did so at their own risk. In Schleswig at the same period any man who met the women of his village in their ceremonial procession to celebrate the birth of a child would have his hat filled with horse-dung and rammed back on his head . . .'[23] Women who yell at a stripper may be taking a kind of revenge for all the injustices men have inflicted on them, like the women in Schleswig with the hat filled with horse dung.

Recently, however, as part of the shift in sensibility towards a more sensuous presentation of male bodies, we have seen the emergence of a kind of floor show which women do seem to find genuinely erotic. For instance, the US erotic male dance troupe, the Chippendales, have enjoyed tremendous commercial success. For the entrepreneur who asks if women are turned on by looking, there is clearly considerable advantage in deciding that yes, they are. When the Chippendales came to my town, a male psychology lecturer asked by the local paper to comment favoured the hat-filled-with-horse-dung theory: 'For women it's the equivalent of a good rude joke, but when men go to see a female stripper, the motives are different . . .'[24] There is a subtext here of reassurance for men who fear they might be looked at and found wanting: women, it is implied, don't look to get turned on. Women from the packed audience who saw the show, however, had a quite different perspective. They did not have the air of having just enjoyed a 'good rude joke' as they enthused about the men's 'gorgeous bodies'.

Going to such a show affords women a rare opportunity to look with desire in a situation that is entirely risk-free. In a society like ours that is riddled with sexual violence, it is always risky for a woman to look in a sexual way at a male stranger. We fear to do anything that might hint at sexual interest or willingness, and our fear that our looks or actions might be interpreted in that way is encouraged by the patriarchal establishment – as in the notorious case of the woman who was raped while hitch-hiking, and who was accused of 'contributory negligence' by the judge. But women in a group can look without fear, freed from the aversive fantasy – 'If I dare to look, he will rape me.' As the Chippendales ease their black leather trousers down those perfectly moulded thighs, they offer women a unique chance to look with lust at a stranger, while staying safe. No wonder the formula has been such a success.

OBJECTS OF DESIRE

To show interest in the kind of male self-presentation that makes
male physicality more sensuous and accessible is not to demand
that men become preoccupied with appearance in the way that
women have been expected to be. It is to ask simply that men
should present themselves as people who might at times be looked
at in a sensuous way, and to challenge the common male belief
that a total inaccessibility to sexual evaluation is the epitome of
manhood.

Certain fairly small changes in male self-presentation might
make a lot of difference to women's sexual pleasure, and to the
sexual success of individual men. To ask women what they find
attractive about men is often to broaden the subject out, to include
taste and smell.

Bridget: If I think a man's dirty, that's it.
Andrea: It depends if it's clean dirt or dirty dirt. If it's smelly,
          days old, yuk!
Bridget: If it's cheesy foreskins, there's just no way. If you see
          this guy and he's gorgeous, got wonderful clothes, and
          you think, Bloody hell he's gorgeous – and then you think
          to yourself, I wonder what it's like pulled back . . . no
          way.

Sophie said, 'I do have one particular blockage and that's oral sex.
I had a very bad experience with a lover who turned out to be
impotent – so I was trying desperately to do everything to help this
poor impotent man, and it was just this awful taste. If men don't
wash, you know, the smell of urine on the penis is ghastly, and I
almost gagged. Now I really require that the man washes beautifully
first. If he's going to expect that in bed then he'd better have
showered.' Sophie's stipulation is repeated whenever women are
asked what they want in bed. A recent survey in *New Woman* magazine found that one of the top three sexual demands made by
women was that the man should 'be very clean.'[25]

Sex therapist Helen Kaplan suggests that there is a close relationship in the nervous system between olfactory and sexual functioning: she writes, 'An unpleasant odour emanating from a sexual
partner, even if not consciously recognized, may be a powerful
deterrent to enjoyable sexuality.'[26] Women are more aware of smells

than men: researchers have found that the lower the oestrogen level, the less acute the sense of smell. Women may love the smell of fresh sweat on their lovers – the 'clean dirt' that Andrea described – but the stereotype of masculinity that equates dirt with machismo may cause real sexual problems for women. In her survey of women's experiences of sex, Sheila Kitzinger found that many women complained about their partners' unpleasant habits – farting, burping, scratching. She remarks that it is striking how little effort many men seem to make to please.[27]

The lack of concern about self-presentation evinced by so many heterosexual men certainly contributes to the lack of interest in looking that many women profess. Yet a beautiful male body will compel a woman's attention, just as surely as a woman's beauty will compel a man's.

'One time I was on an escalator and I ran my hands down this man's back. My friend was mortified. I never saw his face, I think he was too embarrassed to turn round. But I just had to touch him, he had this leather jacket on, and his back was so wonderful.'

Melissa in Chapter 2 told a story she remembered from childhood. A little girl of four had been made to undress by the boys. 'When I said, "Let's look at one of the boys," Melissa recalled, 'it was "Ooh, we're not going to show what we've got – huh!"'

The debate about whether there is too much explicit sexual imagery in our society rages on. Yet what does seem to be beyond contention is that the present situation, in which the typical male attitude is the attitude of the boys in Melissa's story, is grossly unfair. If there is to be any pretence of equality of sexual opportunity for men and women, then there must be equal exposure. Women must be able to look at men as men look at women.

And sometimes of course this happens now, in spite of all the prohibitions. Jacqueline said, 'The biggest turn-on for me – and I'm always caught out by it and feel it shouldn't happen – is a man asleep. A quite macho man completely asleep, completely oblivious to me – and it's the arousing of him in order to do something to me. It's incredibly rare that that's actually happened, but the times when I have plucked up courage and woken him, it's been quite nice . . .'

Jacqueline's looking is very tentative: she feels she doesn't quite have a right to it. But as she describes the interchange of roles, the play of passive and active, of subject and object, in the sexual scenario which she has enjoyed on 'incredibly rare' occasions, she sketches out the shape of a different kind of sexual relating – a way of loving that is more mutual and richly pleasurable than so many relationships today. She looks at him, she wakes him, he looks at her. It's a good place to start from.

CHAPTER FOURTEEN

Epilogue

So much of this book has been about sad and painful sex – sex in which women fake orgasms, or are reminded of childhood experiences of abuse, or are turned off by looking, or have the orgasm when their partner goes to the bathroom, or are troubled by fantasies of anonymous male torturers, or are forced to act out sadistic male fantasies, or watch the clock and long for it to end.

Josephine told me about a different kind of sex. Josephine has had her share of sexual unhappiness: she reflected, 'I haven't by and large found sex to be a very pleasurable thing, to be honest,' and she is now living a celibate life. But she also told this story.

'There was a man I went out with in my twenties, and the sex with him remains in my life like some sort of holiday in another country which I've never been back to. With him, for some reason, everything was different. With him, unlike with my first boyfriend or with my husband, I was turned on, I was ready for it – which I never was with the other two, I always had to go out and buy creams and bits of jelly. But with this man I used to be dying for it, I don't know why, and he used to kind of slide in, and it wasn't this mad crazy humping that the other two go in for through the night, with him it was this really beautiful wave-like experience, we would have gentle sex, and then we would reach this simultaneous orgasm, and as it happened I used to really feel transported into a peaceful wonderful level of colour and light, it was colours and lights and swimming and no pain, and he used to say the same, that it was like an explosion of light, it was really lovely, really really nice. It was incredible, my relationship with him. I don't know why that should be. I don't know why it was that it just seemed different.

'Afterwards I often wondered about it and remembered it, and wondered I suppose if every other woman has that all the time, if that's the norm, and would I ever meet anyone again who would be that kind of lover. I've never tasted anything like that with anyone before or after. All the years with my husband I used to have an orgasm, but it was something I used to get by physically and emotionally and mentally working on it. I never ever touched that swimming, beautiful, colourful pool that I used to get every time with this man, without any effort or fantasy at all, I don't know why.

'It wasn't for long in my life – six months, nine months, I suppose. But I've always remembered it, filed away as a possibility of human life which I've never had again.'

Josephine talks about sex as a physical experience that transcends physicality, that seems to take her somewhere else, beyond the body. In this book I've concentrated on those aspects of sex that are within our control – our self-knowledge and our self-assertions. But Josephine reminds us of the part of sex that can't be prescribed for, the mystery which makes our sexual relationships so perennially fascinating.

The transcendent sex that Josephine describes doesn't often happen to anyone, male or female. But implicit in the discussion in this book there is a more attainable vision of what sex could be like for women – a vision of sex that is reliably orgasmic and freely chosen, and of sexual relationships in which we are less preoccupied with self-presentation and our own desirability because we take more initiatives, and in which the typical patterns of the sexual life cycle are recognized. There are many women for whom that kind of sex seems just as impossible a dream as the transcendent sex that Josephine describes. But there are also increasing numbers of women whose sex lives do approximate to this new ideal of orgasmic fulfilment and mutuality.

The sex that Josephine describes will remain something apart – a holiday in another country, not a place where one lives. But perhaps in a sexual culture that was friendlier to women, more of us might visit that place.

Acknowledgements

I would like to thank the following people.

Madeleine Fullerton read the typescript for me. Roy Umney at Bookstall Services of Derby hunted out all the books I needed with his usual efficiency. Janet Perry, Joan Rudderham, Margaret Speke, The Women's Nutritional Advisory Service, and Pat Garratt and Clare Shaw at *She* magazine, all helped at the research stage. At HarperCollins, Michael Fishwick's enthusiasm sustained me in the process of writing, and Juliet Van Oss has been a source of sensitive encouragement. I'd especially like to thank Sara Menguc at Murray Pollinger for all her work on my behalf.

I'd also like to thank my husband Mick and our daughters Becky and Isabel for coping good-humouredly with my preoccupied air and frequent absences during the writing of the book.

The people to whom I am most indebted, though, cannot be thanked by name. They are, of course, the fifty women who told me about their own experiences and feelings, and whose anonymity must be preserved. Talking to them was a marvellous experience: what they told me was always fascinating, often very funny, sometimes terribly sad. I am deeply grateful to them, and I trust they will be reasonably content with the use I have made of what they so generously shared with me.

References

CHAPTER ONE

1. Dorothy Einon and Mike Potegal, *Sex Life*, Bloomsbury, London, (1990), p. 5.
2. Andrew Stanway, *The Lovers' Guide*, Pickwick Video.
3. Wilhelm Reich, *The Mass Psychology of Fascism*, Penguin, Harmondsworth, (1978).
4. William H. Masters and Virginia E. Johnson, *Human Sexual Response*, Bantam, Boston, (1986; first published 1966).
5. Alex Comfort, *The Joy of Sex*, Quartet, London, (1974), p. 11.
6. Nancy Friday, *My Secret Garden*, Quartet, London, (1975).
7. *Mail on Sunday*, 21 July 1991.
8. Shere Hite, *The Hite Report on Male Sexuality*, Macdonald, London, (1981), p. 1103.
9. John Bancroft, *Human Sexuality and Its Problems*, Churchill Livingstone, Edinburgh, (1983), p. 368.
10. Deirdre Sanders, *The WOMAN Book of Love and Sex*, Sphere, London, (1985).
11. J. Bancroft and I. Coles, 'Three years' experience in a sexual problem clinic', *Journal of Family Planning Doctors*, 2, (1976), pp. 41–8.
12. K. Garde and I. Lunde, 'Female Sexual Behaviour: a Study of a Random Sample of Forty-year-old Women, *Maturita*, 2, (1980), pp. 225–40.
13. Shere Hite, *The Hite Report*, Corgi, London, (1981).
14. Hite, *The Hite Report*, p. 257.
15. Vanessa Feltz, 'If You Can't Make It, Fake It!', *SHE*, February 1992, p. 98.
16. Reay Tannahill, *Sex In History*, Sphere, London, (1990).
17. Gloria Steinem, 'The Real Linda Lovelace' in *Outrageous Acts and Everyday Rebellions*, Fontana, London, (1984).
18. Quoted in Louise Kaplan, *Female Perversions*, Doubleday, New York, (1991), p. 335.
19. Germaine Greer, *Sex and Destiny*, Pan, London, (1985).
20. Anne Dickson, *The Mirror Within*, Quartet, London, (1985).

21. Nancy Friday, *Women On Top*, Hutchinson, London, (1991).
22. Rosalind Miles, *The Women's History of the World*, Grafton, (1989).
23. Alfred C. Kinsey, Wardell B. Pomeroy, Clyde E. Martin and Paul H. Gebhard, *Sexual Behaviour in the Human Female*, Saunders, London, (1953), p. 371.
24. Stanway.
25. Quoted in Beatrix Campbell, 'A Feminist Sexual Politics', in Feminist Review (eds.), *Sexuality: A Reader*, Virago, London, (1987), p. 24.
26. Comfort, p. 34.
27. Susan Crain Bakkos, 'The best sex tips ever – honest!', *Cosmopolitan*, March 1992.
28. Comfort, p. 21.
29. Lucy Goodison, *Moving Heaven and Earth*, The Women's Press, London, (1990), p. 12.
30. Gunter Schmidt and Volkmar Sigusch, 'Women's Sexual Arousal', in J. Zubin and J. Money (eds.), *Contemporary Sexual Behaviour: Critical Issues in the 1970s*, John Hopkins University Press, Baltimore, (1973).
31. Hite, *The Hite Report*, p. 208.
32. See Maryon Tysoe, *Love Isn't Quite Enough*, Fontana, London, (1992), for a summary of the research.
33. Helen Singer Kaplan, *The New Sex Therapy*, Penguin, Harmondsworth, (1981).
34. Sheila Jeffreys, *Anticlimax*, The Women's Press, London, (1990), p. 19.
35. Sigmund Freud, *On Sexuality*, Penguin, Harmondsworth, (1977), p. 141.
36. Quoted in Jeffreys, p. 101.
37. Jeffreys, p. 274.
38. William Masters and Virginia Johnson, *Human Sexual Inadequacy*, Bantam, Boston, (1980), p. 305.
39. Einon and Potegal, p. 5.
40. Comfort, p. 4.

CHAPTER TWO

1. Philippe Ariès, *Centuries of Childhood*, Penguin, Harmondsworth, (1973).

2. Blake, 'The Little Girl Lost', *Songs of Innocence*.
3. Wordsworth, from *Intimations of Immortality*.
4. Kinsey, p. 105.
5. Kee MacFarlane and Jill Waterman, *Sexual Abuse of Young Children*, Holt, Rinehart and Winston, London, (1986), p. 20.
6. Tannahill.
7. Betty Dodson, *Liberating Masturbation*, published and distributed by Betty Dodson, New York, (1974).
8. Alice Miller, *For Your Own Good; The Roots of Violence in Child-rearing*, Virago, London, (1987).
9. Freud, p. 109 and pp. 143–4.
10. Patricia Gillan, *Sex Therapy Manual*, Blackwell, Oxford, (1987), p. 225.
11. Jane Cousins-Mills, *Make It Happy, Make It Safe*, Penguin, Harmondsworth, (1988), p. 45.
12. Nancy Friday, *My Mother Myself*, Fontana, London, (1979).
13. J. S. Victor, 1980: cited in MacFarlane and Waterman.
14. Clare Shaw, 'Privates in Public', *SHE*, May 1991, and personal communication.
15. Claire Rayner, *The Body Book*, Pan, London, (1979), pp. 37 and 38.
16. Joani Blank and Marcia Quackenbush, *The Playbook for Kids about Sex*, Sheba, London, (1982).
17. Louise Kaplan, p. 82.

CHAPTER THREE

1. Angela Carter, *Sleeping Beauty and Other Favourite Fairy Tales*, Gollancz, London, (1991).
2. J. M. Masson, *The Assault on Truth*, Penguin, Harmondsworth, (1985).
3. Kinsey, p. 121.
4. Judith Lewis Herman, *Father-Daughter Incest*, Harvard University Press, London, (1981), p. 11.
5. Herman, p. 50.
6. For summaries of recent research findings, see Derek Jehu, *Beyond Sexual Abuse*, Wiley, Chichester, (1989), pp. 3–7, and MacFarlane and Waterman, pp. 3–12.
7. June M. Reinisch with Ruth Beasley, *The Kinsey Institute New Report On Sex*, Penguin, Harmondsworth, (1991), p. 157.
8. Reinisch, p. 7.

9. Jehu, p. 219.
10. Quoted in Bernard Zilbergeld, *Men and Sex*, Collins, London, (1980).
11. Jehu, p. 259.
12. Dorothy Rowe, *The Experience of Depression*, Wiley, Chichester, (1978).
13. Steve Humphries, *A Secret World of Sex*, Sidgwick and Jackson, London, (1988).
14. Maya Angelou, *I Know Why The Caged Bird Sings*, Virago, London, (1984), p. 73.
15. Elizabeth M. Ellis, Beverly M. Atkeson, and Karen S. Calhoun, 'An Examination of Differences Between Multiple and Single Incident Victims of Sexual Assault', *Journal of Abnormal Psychology*, vol. 91, no. 3, (1982), pp. 221–4.
16. Jehu, p. 235.
17. Ray Wyre and Anthony Swift, *Women, Men and Rape*, Hodder and Stoughton, Sevenoaks, (1990), p. 38.

CHAPTER FOUR

1. Fay Weldon, *The Life and Loves of a She Devil*, Hodder and Stoughton, Sevenoaks, (1983), p. 5, p. 9.
2. Wendy Chapkis, *Beauty Secrets*, The Women's Press, London, (1988).
3. Roberta Pollack Seid, *Never Too Thin*, Prentice Hall, New York, (1989).
4. Wayne Woolley and Susan Woolley, 'Glamour' survey, University of Cincinnati College of Medicine, 1984.
5. Seid, p. 21.
6. Naomi Wolf, *The Beauty Myth*, Chatto and Windus, London, (1990), p. 149.
7. Prestage, Michael, 'Narrow Minded', *Times Educational Supplement*, 20 September 1991.
8. Quoted in Tannahill, p. 24.
9. Comfort, p. 20.
10. See Seid, pp. 279–87, for a summary of the studies.
11. Shahihul Alam, 'The control of girls', *New Internationalist*, November 1991.
12. Elizabeth Wilson, *Adorned in Dreams*, Virago, London, (1985).
13. Chapkis, p. 11.
14. Seid, p. 266.

15. Seid, pp. 290–1.
16. Claire Clifton, 'Sour Tastes of Solitude', *Guardian*, 18 January 1992.
17. *Guardian*, 28 June 1991.
18. Wolf, p. 152.
19. Hermione Lovel, 'Wasted Pregnancies: The Hidden Sorrow', in *People: The International Planned Parenthood Federation Review*, vol. 15, no 1, (1988), p. 5.
20. Gail Sforza Brewer with Tom Brewer, *What Every Pregnant Woman Should Know*, Penguin, Harmondsworth, (1979).
21. Lawrence et al, 'Double-blind randomised controlled trial of folate treatment before conception to prevent recurrence of neural-tube defects', *British Medical Journal*, vol. 282, (1981), pp. 1509–11.
22. Gordon Bourne, *Pregnancy*, Pan, London, (1975).
23. *Clothes Show Magazine*, December 1991.
24. Melanie Klein, 'The Effects of Early Anxiety-Situations on the Sexual Development of the Girl', in *The Psycho-Analysis of Children*, Hogarth Press, London, (1932).
25. Friday, *My Mother Myself*.
26. Quoted in The Bristol Women's Studies Group, *Half the Sky*, Virago, London, (1979), p. 86.
27. *Times Educational Supplement*, 2 August 1991.
28. Paula Weideger, *Female Cycles*, The Women's Press, London, (1978), p. 174.
29. Ann Treneman, 'Cashing in on the Curse', in Lorraine Gamman and Margaret Marshment (eds.), *The Female Gaze*, The Women's Press, (1988).
30. *Guardian*, 18 June 1991.
31. *Times Educational Supplement*, 17 April 1992.
32. Weideger.
33. Steinem, p. 338.

CHAPTER FIVE

1. 'The New Super Beauties', *Cosmopolitan*, September 1991, p. 174.
2. Sappho, translated by Mary Barnard from *The Penguin Book of Women Poets*, Penguin, Harmondsworth, (1979), p. 42.
3. Tannahill, p. 254.
4. Sharon Thompson, 'Search for Tomorrow: On Feminism

and the Reconstruction of Teen Romance', in Carole S. Vance (ed.), *Pleasure and Danger*, Routledge and Kegan Paul, London, (1984).

5. Celia Cowrie and Sue Lees, 'Slags or Drags', in Feminist Review (ed.), *Sexuality: A Reader*, Virago, London, (1987).

6. Linda Gordon and Ellen DuBois, 'Seeking Ecstasy in the Battlefield; Danger and Pleasure in Nineteenth Century Feminist Sexual Thought', in Feminist Review (ed.), *Sexuality: A Reader*.

7. Cowrie and Lees.

8. Angela Carter, *A Company of Wolves*, 'The Bloody Chamber', Penguin, Harmondsworth, (1981), p. 114.

9. Tannahill, p. 371.

10. Judy Blume, *Forever*, Pan, London, (1984).

11. Thompson in Carole S. Vance (ed.), *Pleasure and Danger*.

12. Kinsey, p. 139.

13. Kinsey, p. 125.

14. I. D. Rotkin, 'A comparison review of key epidemiological studies in cervical cancer related to current searches for transmissible agents', *Cancer Research*, vol. 33, (1973), pp. 1353–67.

15. Debbie Taylor (ed.), *Women: A World Report*, Methuen, London, (1985), p. 59.

16. Kinsey.

CHAPTER SIX

1. Erica Jong, *How To Save Your Own Life*, Grafton, London, (1978), p. 243.

2. Hite, *The Hite Report*, p. 257.

3. Masters and Johnson, *Human Sexual Inadequacy*.

4. Helen Kaplan, p. 44.

5. Kinsey, p. 263.

6. Seymour Fisher, *Understanding the Female Orgasm*, Penguin, Harmondsworth, (1973).

7. Kinsey, p. 172.

8. Gillan, pp. 38–9.

9. *Marie Claire*, September 1991.

10. Gillan, pp. 38–9

11. There are a number of useful self-help books for pre-orgasmic women on the market. See for instance: Julia Heiman and

Joseph LoPiccolo, *Becoming Orgasmic*, Piatkus, London, (1988), and Anne Hooper, *The Body Electric*, Virago, London, (1980).
12. Anne Hooper, *Women and Sex*, Sheldon, (1986), p. 19.
13. Susan Brownmiller, *Against Our Will*, Bantam, New York, (1981).
14. AA Members' Newsletter, Spring/Summer 1991.
15. Hilary Burden, 'Date rape: it could happen to you', *Cosmopolitan*, March 1991.
16. Tannahill, p. 51.
17. Jeffreys, p. 244.
18. Jenny Campbell, 'The death of the housewife', *Guardian*, 18 September 1991.
19. Michèle Roberts, *The Visitation*, The Women's Press, London, (1983), p. 158.
20. Reinisch, p. 96.
21. H. J. Eysenck, *Sex and Personality*, Open Books, London, (1976), p. 224.
22. The Panos Institute, *Triple Jeopardy: Women and Aids*, Panos Publications, London, (1990), p. 4.
23. The European Study Group on Heterosexual Transmission of HIV, 'Comparison of female to male and male to female transmission of HIV in 563 stable couples', *British Medical Journal*, vol. 304, 28 March 1992.
24. Ceri Hutton, 'Bed Etiquette', *New Statesman*, 6 July 1990, p. 22.
25. Anne Koedt, 'The Myth of the Vaginal Orgasm', in The Radical Therapist Collective (eds.), *The Radical Therapist*, Penguin, Harmondsworth, (1974), p. 141.
26. Hite, *The Hite Report*, p. 168.
23. Jeffreys, p. 91.
28. Gabriel García Márquez, *One Hundred Years of Solitude*, Pan, London, (1978), p. 13.
29. Comfort, p. 10.
30. Lisa Alther, *Kinflicks*, Penguin, Harmondsworth, (1977), p. 348.
31. Reinisch, p. 7.
32. Friday, *Women On Top*.

CHAPTER SEVEN

1. *SHE*, March 1991, p. 50.
2. Geraldine Palmer, *The Politics of Breast-feeding*, Pandora, (1988), p. 18.
3. Heiman and LoPiccolo, p. 137.
4. Janet Balaskas and Yehudi Gordon, *The Encyclopedia of Pregnancy and Birth*, Macdonald, London, (1987).
5. 'Pre-menstrual Tension and Loss of Libido', leaflet, Women's Nutritional Advisory Service, Hove, East Sussex.
6. Weideger, p. 21.
7. Masters and Johnson, *Human Sexual Response*, p. 161.
8. Germaine Greer, *Sex and Destiny*.
9. Barbara Pickard, 'Preconception Care', *Journal of Obstetrics and Gynaecology*, 4 (suppl. 1), (1984), S34-S43. The World Health Organization has recommended that women leave an interval of at least 18 months between the beginnings of pregnancies. See World Health Organization, *Social and Biological Effects on Perinatal Mortality*, vol. 1, (1978).
10. Jane Price, *Motherhood, What It Does To Your Mind*, Pandora, London, (1988).
11. Angela Phillips, *Until They Are Five*, Pandora, London, (1989).
12. 'It's Your Baby Too', Wyeth Nutrition.
13. *Guardian*, 4 September 1991.
14. Sheila Kitzinger, *Woman's Experience of Sex*, Penguin, Harmondsworth, (1985), p. 210.
15. Aidan Macfarlane, *The Psychology of Childbirth*, Collins, London, (1977).
16. Quoted in Adrienne Rich, *Of Woman Born*, Virago, (1977), p. 168.
17. Maeve Haran, *Having It All*, Penguin, Harmondsworth, (1992).

CHAPTER EIGHT

1. Sheila Jeffreys, *The Spinster and Her Enemies*, Pandora, London, (1985).
2. Kiri Tunks and Diane Hutchinson (eds.), *Dear Clare . . .* , *This is What Women Feel about Page 3*, Random Century, London, (1991).
3. *New Statesman*, 31 May 1991.
4. Erica Jong, *Fear of Flying*, Panther, St Albans, (1974).

5. Ros Coward, 'Coming Down', *New Statesman*, 10 August 1990.
6. Germaine Greer, *The Female Eunuch*, Granada, London, (1971), p. 44.
7. Germaine Greer, 'Self-love or Self-abuse?', *Marie Claire*, October 1990.
8. Elliott Jaques, 'Death and the Mid-life Crisis', *International Journal of Psychoanalysis*, 46, (1965).
9. Daniel Levinson, *The Seasons of a Man's Life*, Knopf, New York, (1978).
10. Barbara Gordon, *Jennifer Fever*, Fontana, London, (1989).
11. Robin Norwood, *Women Who Love Too Much*, Arrow, London, (1986).
12. Masters and Johnson, *Human Sexual Response*, pp. 240–1.
13. Kinsey, p. 417.
14. Kinsey, p. 201.
15. Helen Kaplan, p. 138.
16. Helen Kaplan, p. 139.
17. Reinisch, p. 17.
18. Germaine Greer, *The Change*, Hamish Hamilton, London, (1991), p. 182.
19. Quoted in Greer, *The Change*, p. 321.
20. Christine Sandford, *Enjoy Sex in the Middle Years*, Martin Dunitz, London, (1983).
21. Helen Kaplan, p. 135.

CHAPTER NINE

1. Shere Hite, *Women and Love*, Penguin, Harmondsworth, (1989), p. 622.
2. Reuben and Wilson, quoted in Kitzinger, p. 231.
3. Taken from 'Wen The Turuf Is Thi Tuur' in Theodore Silverstein (ed.), *Medieval English Lyrics*, Edward Arnold, London, (1971).
4. Mary Daly, *Gyn/Ecology*, The Women's Press, London, (1979), p. 238.
5. James Owen Drife, 'Are breasts redundant organs?', *British Medical Journal*, vol. 304, 18 April 1992, p. 1060.
6. From W. B. Yeats, 'After Long Silence', in A. Norman Jeffares (ed.), *W. B. Yeats: Selected Poetry*, Macmillan, London, (1968).
7. Helen Kaplan, p. 139.

8. Judith Wallerstein and Sandra Blakeslee, *Second Chances*, Corgi, London, (1990), p. 71.
9. Wallerstein, p. 80.
10. Wallerstein, p. 80.

CHAPTER TEN

1. Friday, *My Secret Garden*, p. 6.
2. 'Ordinary People', *Guardian*, 16 August 1990.
3. Quoted in Kitzinger.
4. Tannahill, p. 266.
5. Kinsey, p. 200.
6. Sigmund Freud, *The Interpretation of Dreams*, Penguin, Harmondsworth, (1977), p. 247.
7. Dr Robert Hale, in a psychology workshop, London, 1981; personal communication.
8. John Mullin, 'Lord Chancellor's dress query hangs in air', *Guardian*, 20 August 1992.
9. Robert Stoller, *Sex and Gender*, Hogarth Press, London, (1968), p. 182.
10. Gillan, p. 89.
11. Comfort, p. 62.
12. Matthew Norman, 'Britain's Bedroom Secrets', *Mail on Sunday*, 21 July 1991.
13. Dorothy Dinnerstein, *The Rocking of the Cradle, the Ruling of the World*, Souvenir Press, London, (1976).
14. Mikael Davies, 'Worlds Apart', *Times Educational Supplement*, 19 July 1991.
15. Ann Barr Snitow, 'Mass Market Romance', in Ann Barr Snitow, Christine Stansell and Sharon Thompson (eds.), *Powers of Desire*, Monthly Review Press, New York, (1983).
16. Beatrice Faust, *Women, Sex and Pornography*, Penguin, Harmondsworth, (1980).
17. *And Then He Kissed Her . . .*, audiotape from Mills and Boon, Richmond, (1991).
18. Jeffreys, *Anticlimax*, p. 2.
19. Robyn Donald, *A Durable Fire*, Mills and Boon, Richmond, (1984).
20. Rosalind Coward, *Female Desire*, Granada, London, (1984).
21. *And Then He Kissed Her . . .*
22. Quoted in Jeffreys, p. 65.

23. *And Then He Kissed Her* . . .
24. Louise Kaplan, p. 325.
25. Shirley Conran, *Lace: The Complete Story*, Penguin, Harmondsworth, (1986).

CHAPTER ELEVEN

1. Quoted in Tannahill, p. 379.
2. Louise Kaplan, p. 420.
3. Sappho, from *The Penguin Book of Women Poets*.
4. Jeanette Winterson, *The Passion*, Penguin, Harmondsworth, (1988), p. 68.
5. Susan Ardill and Sue O'Sullivan, 'Upsetting an Applecart; Difference, Desire and Lesbian Sadomasochism', Feminist Review (ed.), *Sexuality: A Reader*, p. 287.
6. Playthell Benjamin, 'Beauties and the Beast', *Guardian*, 27 January 1992.
7. Carter, *The Company of Wolves*, p. 118.
8. J. J. Gayford, 'Wife Battering: A Preliminary Survey of 100 Cases', *British Medical Journal*, 1, (1975), pp. 194–7.
9. S. Platt, J. Foster and N. Kreitman, 'Parasuicide in Edinburgh 1984. A report on admissions to The Regional Poisoning Treatment Centre, Royal Edinburgh Hospital.'
10. Hite, *Women and Love*.
11. Quoted in Richard Dyer, 'Children of the Night', in Susannah Radstone (ed.), *Sweet Dreams*, Lawrence and Wishart, London, (1988), p. 55.
12. Einon and Potegal.
13. Norwood.
14. *And Then He Kissed Her* . . .
15. Norwood, p. 72.
16. Sally Cline and Dale Spender, *Reflecting Men At Twice Their Natural Size*, Collins, London, (1988).
17. See Tysoe, p. 47, for a summary of the research.
18. Louise Kaplan, p. 448.
19. *Elle*, April 1992, p. 32.
20. Stoller, p. 218.
21. Comfort, p. 126. See Jeffreys for a fuller analysis.
22. Tannahill, p. 169.
23. Tunks and Hutchinson.
24. Wolf, p. 111.

25. Friday, *My Secret Garden*.
26. Gillan, Introduction, p. vi.
27. Friday, *Women On Top*, p. 1.
28. Kinsey, p. 164.
29. Louise Kaplan, p. 282.
30. Friday, *Women On Top*.
31. Friday, *Women On Top*, p. 5.
32. Gillan, p. 144.
33. Dodson, p. 47.
34. Coward, *Coming Down*.
35. Julie Burchill, *Ambition*, Bodley Head, London, (1989).
36. Philippa Gregory, *Wideacre*, Penguin, Harmondsworth, (1987).
37. Gillan, p. 35.

CHAPTER TWELVE

1. James Spada, *The Spada Report*, Signet, New American Library, New York, (1979).
2. Louise Kaplan, p. 35.
3. Gillan, p. 69.
4. Gillan, p. 145.
5. Gillan, p. 78.
6. Pauline Reage, *The Story of O*, Corgi, London, (1976), p. 14.
7. Einon and Potegal.
8. Alex Comfort, *The New Joy of Sex*, Mitchell Beazley, London, (1991), pp. 161–9.
9. Martin Amis, *London Fields*, Penguin, Harmondsworth, (1989), p. 71.
10. Louise Kaplan, p. 65.
11. Louise Kaplan, p. 246.
12. Hite, *The Hite Report*, p. 91.
13. Faust, p. 49.
14. Kinsey, p. 468.
15. Daphne du Maurier, *Rebecca*, Pan, London, (1975), p. 39.
16. Della Grace, *Love Bites*, GMP/Editions Aubrey Walter, (1991).
17. Julie Wainwright, 'Girls Will Be Boys', *Guardian*, 24 September 1991.
18. *Guardian*, 27 September 1991.
19. Robert Hancock, *Ruth Ellis, The Last Woman to be Hanged*, Weidenfeld and Nicolson, London, (1963).

20. Wolf, p. 73.
21. Joan Rivière, 'Womanliness as a Masquerade', *International Journal of Psychoanalysis* 10: pp. 303–13.
22. Louise Kaplan, p. 268.
23. Fisher, p. 53.
24. Janet Radcliffe Richards, *The Sceptical Feminist*, Penguin, Harmondsworth, (1982), p. 225.
25. Mary Spillane, *The Complete Style Guide*, Piatkus, London, (1991), p. 139.
26. Jeffreys, p. 171.
27. Quoted in Wilson, p. 99.
28. Julie Fairhead, 'The pain is worth it', *Bella*, 14 September 1991.

CHAPTER THIRTEEN

1. Comfort, *The Joy of Sex*, p. 34.
2. Schmidt and Sigusch.
3. Faust.
4. Reinisch, p. 43.
5. Wolf, p. 113.
6. See Gillan, and Schmidt and Sigusch.
7. Gillan, p. 140.
8. Katie Campbell, 'Foreign Bodies', *Guardian*, 14 August 1990.
9. Gillan, p. 230.
10. Coward, *Female Desire*, p. 230.
11. Brownmiller.
12. Sarah Kent, 'Looking Back', in Sarah Kent and Jacqueline Morreau (eds.), *Women's Images of Men*, Pandora, London, (1990), p. 58.
13. *Guardian*, 8 June 1991.
14. Sarah Kent, 'The Erotic Male Nude', in Kent and Morreau, p. 88.
15. *For Women*, Spring Special, 1992.
16. Suzanne Moore, 'Here's looking at you, kid!' in Gamman and Marshment (eds.), *The Female Gaze*, The Women's Press, London, (1988).
17. Phyllis Chesler, *About Men*, The Women's Press, London, (1978), p. 218.
18. Arthur Koestler, *The Act of Creation*, Picador, London, (1975), p. 35.

19. *Guardian*, 3 October 1980.
20. Jacqueline Morreau and Catherine Elwes, 'Lighting a Candle', in Kent and Morreau (eds.).
21. Tannahill, p. 276.
22. *Guardian*, 31 January 1991.
23. Miles, p. 125.
24. *Leicester Mercury*, 27 July 1991.
25. 'Sex and Sexuality' supplement, *New Woman*, April 1992.
26. Helen Kaplan, p. 65.
27. Kitzinger, p. 138.

Select Bibliography

John Bancroft, *Human Sexuality and Its Problems*, Churchill Livingstone, Edinburgh, 1983.

Joani Blank and Marcia Quackenbush, *The Playbook for Kids about Sex*, Sheba, London, 1982.

Susan Brownmiller, *Against Our Will*, Bantam, New York, 1981.

Jane Cousins-Mills, *Make It Happy, Make It Safe*, Penguin, Harmondsworth, 1988.

Rosalind Coward, *Female Desire*, Granada, London, 1984.

Anne Dickson, *The Mirror Within*, Quartet, London, 1985.

Feminist Review (ed.), *Sexuality: A Reader*, Virago, London, 1987.

Sigmund Freud, *On Sexuality*, Penguin, Harmondsworth, 1977.

Nancy Friday, *My Mother My Self*, Fontana, London, 1979.

——, *My Secret Garden*, Quartet, London, 1975.

——, *Women On Top*, Hutchinson, London, 1991.

Lorraine Gamman and Margaret Marshment (ed.), *The Female Gaze*, The Women's Press, London, 1988.

Patricia Gillan, *Sex Therapy Manual*, Blackwell, Oxford, 1987.

Germaine Greer, *The Change*, Hamish Hamilton, London, 1991.

——, *The Female Eunuch*, Granada, London, 1971.

——, *Sex and Destiny*, Pan, London, 1984.

Julia Heiman and Joseph LoPiccolo, *Becoming Orgasmic*, Piatkus, London, 1988.

Judith Lewis Herman, *Father–Daughter Incest*, Harvard University Press, London, 1981.

Shere Hite, *The Hite Report*, Corgi, London, 1981.

——, *The Hite Report on Male Sexuality*, Macdonald, London, 1981.

——, *Women and Love*, Penguin, Harmondsworth, 1989.

Anne Hooper, *The Body Electric*, Virago, London, 1980.

Steve Humphries, *A Secret World of Sex*, Sidgwick and Jackson, London, 1988.

Derek Jehu, *Beyond Sexual Abuse*, Wiley, Chichester, 1989.

Helen Singer Kaplan, *The New Sex Therapy*, Penguin, Harmonds-worth, 1981.

Louise Kaplan, *Female Perversions*, Doubleday, New York, 1991.

Sarah Kent and Jacqueline Morreau (eds.), *Women's Images of Men*, Pandora, London, 1990.

Alfred C. Kinsey, Wardell B. Pomeroy, Clyde E. Martin and Paul H. Gebhard, *Sexual Behaviour in the Human Female*, Saunders, London, 1953.

Sheila Kitzinger, *Woman's Experience of Sex*, Penguin, Harmonds-worth, 1985.

Melanie Klein, *The Psycho-Analysis of Children*, Hogarth Press, London, 1932.

Aidan Macfarlane, *The Psychology of Childbirth*, Fontana, London, 1977.

Kee MacFarlane and Jill Waterman, *Sexual Abuse of Young Children*, Holt, Rinehart and Winston, London, 1986.

J. M. Masson, *The Assault on Truth*, Penguin, Harmondsworth, 1985.

William Masters and Virginia Johnson, *Human Sexual Inadequacy*, Bantam, Boston, 1980.

——, *Human Sexual Response*, Bantam, Boston, 1986.

Rosalind Miles, *The Women's History of the World*, Grafton, London, 1989.

Robin Norwood, *Women Who Love Too Much*, Arrow, London, 1986.

Gabrielle Palmer, *The Politics of Breast-feeding*, Pandora, London, 1988.

The Panos Institute, *Triple Jeopardy: Women and Aids*, Panos Publi-cations, London, 1990.

Jane Price, *Motherhood, What It Does To Your Mind*, Pandora, London, 1988.

Susannah Radstone (ed.), *Sweet Dreams*, Lawrence and Wishart, London, 1988.

June M. Reinisch with Ruth Beasley, *The Kinsey Institute New Report on Sex*, Penguin, Harmondsworth, 1991.

Roberta Pollack Seid, *Never Too Thin*, Prentice Hall, New York, 1989.

Gloria Steinem, *Outrageous Acts and Everyday Rebellions*, Fontana, London, 1984.

Robert Stoller, *Sex and Gender*, Hogarth Press, London, 1968.

Reay Tannahill, *Sex in History*, Sphere, London, 1990.

Debbie Taylor (ed.), *Women: A World Report*, Methuen, London, 1985.

Maryon Tysoe, *Love Isn't Quite Enough*, Fontana, London, 1992.

Carole S. Vance (ed.), *Pleasure and Danger*, Routledge and Kegan Paul, London, 1984.

Paula Weideger, *Female Cycles*, The Women's Press, London, 1978.

Elizabeth Wilson, *Adorned in Dreams*, Virago, London, 1985.

Naomi Wolf, *The Beauty Myth*, Chatto and Windus, London, 1990.

J. Zubin and J. Money (eds.), *Contemporary Sexual Behaviour: Critical Issues in the 1970s*, Johns Hopkins University Press, Baltimore, 1973.

Index